MONOLOGUES

FOR

WOMEN

BY

WOMEN

MONOLOGUES

FOR

WOMEN

BY

WOMEN

EDITED BY TORI HARING-SMITH

HEINEMANN
Portsmouth, NH

Heinemann
A division of Reed Elsevier Inc.
361 Hanover Street, Portsmouth, NH 03801-3912
Offices and agents throughout the world

Library of Congress Cataloging-in-Publication Data
More monologues for women, by women / edited by Tori Haring-Smith.
      p.   cm.
    Includes bibliographical references and index.
    ISBN 0-435-07022-3 (alk. paper)
     1. Monologues. 2. Acting. 3. American drama—20th century.
4. Women—Drama. I. Haring-Smith, Tori.
PN2080.M67 1996
812'.045089287—dc20   96-5549
                                              CIP

Editor: Lisa A. Barnett
Production: J.B. Tranchemontagne
Manufacturing: Louise Richardson
Design: Tom Allen, Pear Graphic Design

Printed in the United States of America on acid-free paper
99 98 97 96   DA   7 6 5 4 3 2 1

Contents

Subject Index

Aging

Body Image

The Feminist Movement and Individual Acts of Rebellion

Friendship

Appel, Friendship
DeFranco, Angel's Share
Halvorson, One Hundred Women
Galloway, Lardo Weeping
Presti, Tipped Uterus

Identity

Anderson, Barbed Wire Under Your Armpits
Baley, Signs of Life
Litwak, Rosie
Margraff, House
Maynard, The Handwriting, The Soup, and The Hats
Monroe, Other People's Ancestors
Romero, Glow in the Dark Woman
Rose, Based on a True Story

Lesbian Identity and Relationships

Gage, Babe
Gordon, Jigsaw
Wallace, The Bird

Marriage and Dating

Brabant, Gracie and Butch
Dixon, La Casa de las Mañanas
Dorsey, Gideon and Josephine
Eisenstein, A Cock. A Dream. A True Story.
Hansell, Affair on the Air
Harold, Eggs and Bones
Iizuka, What Mary Says After

Sex and Sexuality

de Lancie, F-64
Ensler, Vagina Monologues
Gordon, Jigsaw
Iizuka, What Mary Says After
Lennon, Grace, Honey
Medley, Waking Women
Shapiro, Making It (Part 1)

The Silenced Woman

Davis, asylum/holdin on
Gage, Babe
Galloway, Lardo Weeping
Hansell, Don't
Ross, Boxes
Wilson, Southern Utah: Another Tragedy

Violence and Rape

Galloway, Lardo Weeping
Hansell, Don't
Newman, When Our Daddies Come
Nibasa, A Line of Cutting Women
Obolensky, The Lion

Introduction

Why Another Collection of Monologues for Women, by Women?

In 1989 *The New York Times* ran a cover story in its Arts section chronicling the struggles that several major women playwrights faced in being produced. *Backstage* ran a similar cover story in 1993. Producing groups like The Women's Project and The Magic Theatre have showcased women's talents. These are only some examples of the growing attention paid to the need for women's voices in the theatre in the late eighties and early nineties. But what has happened in the two years since the first volume in this series, *Monologues for Women, by Women,* was published? A quick glance at the offerings at regional theatres and in New York shows that women's voices are still hushed. In a time of increasing financial strain in the arts, theatres are becoming understandably cautious about their seasons. They are afraid to "take risks"; every show must be a "hit." Unfortunately, this often translates into a reliance on the familiar (read "male") canon.

Despite all the attention drawn to women playwrights, they are less well-represented today than six years ago. In 1990–91 roughly 15 percent of the plays produced by theatres affiliated with Theatre Communications Group (TCG) were written at least in part by women. In 1995-96, less than 14 percent of TCG productions will have women writers, lyricists, or composers affiliated with them. And because many of the plays written by women are intended for children, only 12 percent of the plays presented in 1995-96 outside the context of "youth theatre" were written at least in part by women. (The statistics for both 1990-91 and 1995-96 are based on the preview of seasons announced in *American Theatre,* October

1990 and 1995, respectively). Things are not getting better—they're getting worse.

In December 1995, in an essay called "Why I Write for Television," playwright Theresa Rebeck submitted this report from the front: "There's not enough theatre out there for women. Every single time I have a play produced, anywhere, women hunt me down and *thank* me because they're so starved for theatre they can relate to. A lot of women I know won't go to the theatre anymore because, they tell me, they are finally tired of only being offered plays about men. There are many female artists out there, and a huge female audience, and the system is denying us access to each other. This is an absurd situation."

Why is it important for women to write and to be heard? When the theatre is so heavily dominated by men's writing, the story of human experience presented there is, well, incomplete. While all women experience the world as individuals, there is no question that women's experiences are different than men's. Being socialized as a female, being subjected to particular female strictures ("don't be so aggressive," "let the boys win," "act like a lady") that we embrace or resist, being told that we "asked for it" when we are beaten or raped, feeling trapped in the label "virgin" or "whore," knowing that we have the capacity to give birth and that to do so will be both excruciating and exhilarating, being told that we are not fit parents because we work or go to school—these are things men can appreciate only from a distance.

This is not to say that all women's experiences are the same. The experience of a black heterosexual is necessarily quite different from that of a white lesbian or an Asian bisexual. Privileged women lead very different lives from unprivileged ones. Our views of life change as we go from twenty to forty to sixty, and as we pass from daughter to mother, or from partner to loner. But women's stories are still different from men's, and they deserve to be told. Women are, after all, in the majority on this planet.

And, of course, actresses (who outnumber male actors in the professional unions, if not on the stage and screen) need an opportunity to present themselves through the words and visions of other women. Unfortunately, most actresses are asked to represent female characters who were born not from actual experience but from a man's fantasy of what it feels like to be a woman. And then, to top it off, these actresses are usually directed by men who may well "correct" their performance, telling them in effect, "A woman would never do that." Such women deserve to speak words written by other women and shaped by other women for the stage.

As I said in the introduction to the first volume in this series, *Monologues for Women, by Women,* "Until we recognize the centrality of female lives to our entire society, producers and artistic directors will continue to sideline our experiences, fearing to stage more than one 'women's play' (if that many) in a given season. The more we can demonstrate the importance of 'women's issues' to our entire society, the more likely that some day powerful people will worry about doing too many 'men's plays.'"

Each of the monologues in this collection represents a unique woman's voice expressing a moment of her experience—the anger of the female athlete, the surprise that an older woman finds in passing menopause, the guilt of a priest, the fears of a pregnant woman, the joy of a deep love. Some of the pieces were designed as one-woman shows. Others were written as audition pieces or excerpted from longer works. In the back of the book, you will find biographies and contact addresses for each of these writers so that you may write to them about their other work.

This collection is for those of us who are committed to celebrating women's experiences as captured in their own voices. It is a collection for those of us who have not given up hope, who still believe that theatre can be a place where women's voices can scream, shout, whisper, wail, and sing out in ecstasy. In reading pieces submitted for this book, I was struck by the anger and pain I felt between the lines of this prose. Is there any wonder? It takes strength to keep believing that women have a place in the theatre, especially when the statistics show that women playwrights are losing ground. But women keep writing anyway. And, as these monologues attest, their voices remain strong and clear.

Tips on Auditioning with a Monologue

Choosing a Monologue

In order to perform a monologue well, you should have some personal connection to it. You need to understand the character's emotion, and be passionate about her concerns. After all, you are going to have to explore this character in depth and then generate enough energy to make her live for your audience. In some cases, actors are drawn to monologue characters because they have undergone similar experiences. If the character is talking about death, and you have recently lost a loved one, you may be able to share something of yourself—your grief—in bringing the character to life. Remember, acting is about sharing yourself. That's one reason why actors must learn to be vulnerable, and yet relax. When you audition, your audience wants to know who you are, as well as who you can be. Your choice of a monologue often reveals you, so choose carefully.

It is common advice that monologues should talk about the present, not just recount the past. I think this advice, while well-intentioned, is artificially limiting. There is nothing wrong with a monologue that tells a story from the past as long as you, the actor, make it present and active. As long as the story is a vital part of the character you develop, it will stir emotions, shape interactions, and reveal layers within the character. Remember that all monologues have at least one silent stage partner, someone who is listening and responding to the character, perhaps driving the character to keep speaking. Sometimes the silent partner is another character, sometimes another facet of the speaker, and sometimes the theatre audience. As long as the monologue connects with your passions, you will be able to make it live for your silent stage partner, and for your audience.

Even though a monologue springs from the interaction of two characters, it must not be too dependent on the context of the play if it is going to stand on its own in an audition. That is, the monologue needs to make sense and be important in its own right—not just because of its function within the play. Many of the most exciting monologues in full-length plays simply cannot stand on their own, because in isolation they do not reveal the character fully enough. Most successful audition monologues do not refer to too many people other than the speaker. It's difficult to keep track of a woman's lover, husband, daughter, and business associate in the course of one two-minute monologue! The primary purpose of a monologue is to showcase you, not the play or the playwright. A monologue should require no more introduction or explanation than the title of the play.

It is important that a monologue (or pair of monologues, if you are performing two together) allow you to show a range of emotional, physical, and vocal qualities. While you can get some range by choosing a pair of contrasting monologues, each piece you do should have some variety within it. The emotional state of the character needs to be dynamic, so that you can show more than one side of your emotional, physical, and vocal life. If you are choosing a pair of monologues, you will probably want to find speeches of different subjects as well as with differing tones.

When choosing a monologue, try to find material that will be new to your audience. When I audition large numbers of people, I frequently hear the same monologues over and over again. I have to force myself to listen to painfully familiar pieces like the twirler from *In the Boom Boom Room*. When you choose a classical monologue, think about how many Juliets or Kates your auditioners will have heard on the professional stage and in auditions. Try to find some new material. Women playwrights from the Middle Ages, Renaissance, Restoration, and eighteenth century are just now being rediscovered and published. Look for collections of their work, and you may find wonderful new monologues. Although this collection will not help you find a classical monologue, it will provide you with fifty previously unpublished or hard-to-find contemporary pieces.

Finally, be sure the monologue is suitable for you, and for the theatre or film you are auditioning for. This does not mean the character has to match you identically in race, gender, age, or geographical location. Just be sure that you understand the character and how she responds to life. If you feel that you would respond as she does, you probably have a sympathetic relationship to the character. If you are playing someone much older or younger than yourself, do not "play age"—play yourself. Avoid pieces that require a strong accent unless you are told that you need to demonstrate particular dialect abilities.

Think about the suitability of the monologue for the medium in which you are auditioning. If you are being seen for television work, the monologue should be rated "PG." If you have been called for a particular role, try to find a monologue that is stylistically linked to that script or role (i.e., use a comic piece if you're auditioning for a comedy) but is not from the script itself. The auditioners will have all kinds of preconceived notions about the roles they are casting. If you pull a monologue from the play they have been dreaming about for several months, you may not seem right to them if your interpretation of the character does not match their ideal for it. If the auditioners want to see you in the part, they will ask for a cold reading.

Finally, think about the length of your monologues. Do not cram so much into your two or three minutes that you feel rushed while you are performing. Respect the time limits set by the auditioners. Some of the monologues in this book are obviously too long to be done in an audition. In those cases, you can easily extract a two- or three-minute audition piece from the longer selection. Having the entire monologue not only gives you context, but also gives you material for longer performances in showcases and workshops.

Preparing and Rehearsing

As you rehearse your monologue, either alone or with a coach, use the techniques that have been most successful for you in preparing full-length roles. If the piece is from a longer work, read the play. But do not rely on the longer work to "explain" the character—your auditioners may not know the piece. The monologue must stand on its own as a comprehensible piece, telling the auditioners all they need to know about your characters. Also, don't let the full play's context limit you. Don't assume that because the character in the play is insane, your interpretation of the monologue must also reveal insanity.

More important than any research in the library, more important even than reading the full script is careful examination of the specific text you are going to present. Think about the character drawn there, and ask yourself the usual character development questions, such as:

- Who is this person talking to? Does that shift at any point during the piece? What does the listener want from the speaker?
- What question or event is the speaker responding to? What happened just before she began to speak?
- What does the speaker need? Why does she keep on speaking? (Make this need as important as possible.)
- What are the conflicts within the speaker, and between the speaker and her listener(s)?
- What does the speaker's language reveal about her? What is the speaker's favorite word in this monologue?
- How is the speaker different after she has said her piece than before? What has she gained, lost, discovered?
- What line in the monologue is the most important? Where does the speech make emotional turns, and reach a climax?

As you explore the character, keep reassuring yourself: You are not looking for the "right" answers. You are looking for emotionally truthful answers that you can play. Be faithful to your own experience and your own sense of truth—not to what someone else thinks that character "should" be like. Do not be satisfied with quick, easy answers. Keep probing.

As you work on the character, consider her vocal and physical life. Would she sit down, or is she too overwrought? Does she try to hide her strong emotions behind civilized, controlled speech, or does she speak out? Experiment with different actions you might give the character as well. Is she knitting while she talks? Fidgeting with a button? Putting on make-up? Consider her stance. Does she stand tall? Hunch forward? Sit primly? Be sure you make choices that allow you to keep your head up and that do not force you to move so frenetically that the auditioners cannot "see" you for the movement. Know where your silent partner is. Do not make the auditioner a silent partner—no one wants to be forced to participate in an actor's piece. Does the silent partner move at any point? Where, when, and why?

As you rehearse, concentrate on your primary goal of making your character present and active. Command attention—think of what Linda Loman says about Willy: "Attention must be paid." If you know what the character wants, you will have no trouble bringing that need out for the audience.

Once you begin to put your performance together, consider how you will start. You are, in fact, "on" from the moment you walk onto the stage. Practice introducing yourself pleasantly and efficiently:

Hello. My name is _____, and today I'll be doing monologues from Joan Lipkin's *Making a Community*, and Mary Pix's *The Innocent Mistress*.

Then work on the transition into your first monologue. Take a moment to visualize your character's situation, to ground yourself in her needs, to place your silent partner, and to think about the question or event you are responding to.

Practice this kind of preparation, and you will not need more than five to ten seconds to accomplish it.

Work through the transitions between monologues in the same way. After you have chosen an order for your pieces, consider how you will move smoothly from one to the other. Be sure that you complete the first monologue, give it a beat to sink in, then alter your physical stance in some way and quickly launch into your second piece. As you rehearse, have someone time your work. When you are performing, you want to be able to think about the character, not the clock. Take your time to live the character fully but not self-indulgently. And, above all, don't be afraid of being boring. If you think you're boring, you're going to telegraph that to your auditioners, and your worst nightmare will come true.

Plan what you will wear to the audition. Think of something that complements your body type and doesn't distort your presentation of either of your characters. You do not want to look costumed during your audition; you want to look as much like yourself as you can. The goal of the audition is to reveal yourself and the range of your abilities. You may costume one character by adding or taking off a jacket or sweater, but do not plan elaborate costume changes. Most people do not change costume at all during their auditions. After all, you should be able to present the character without relying on a costume to support you. Similarly, you may need one small prop in one of your monologues—a pencil, a book. If you need more props than that, you have not chosen an appropriate audition piece. Remember that the only furniture you can count on having is a folding metal chair. Try to be as self-sufficient as possible, and not to rely on costumes, props, or furniture. Your acting, and not the technical aspects of your performance, must be the focus. Your auditioners should remember you, not your costume.

As you rehearse, keep exploring. Take risks—that's what rehearsals are for. If you find that you're afraid of looking foolish—playing either too big or too small—face your fears.

Do the monologue as you fear it might be seen at its very worst. Facing your fears will make them dissolve. But if you don't face them and enact them, they will inhibit your spontaneity, and make you censor yourself. Sometimes, you will discover that your worst nightmare may have been an excellent choice for the piece—you were just afraid of taking the chance. Don't be afraid to be quirky or bold.

Some people hire coaches to help them prepare monologue work. Whether you rehearse alone or with a coach, at some point you need to practice performing your work in front of different audiences. Don't always practice or perform in the same studio. Move around. Get used to performing anywhere so that the strangeness of the audition situation will not throw you. If you can perform with equal concentration and comfort in a living room, on a stage, in a classroom, and out of doors, you're probably well prepared for your auditions.

Presenting Yourself and Your Work

Before your audition, try not to establish expectations. You should be aware of any rules that have been set for the audition—number of pieces you should present, your time limit, requirements for the types of monologues—but go into the audition without any expectations about the process itself. Don't "picture" the room, because you may be surprised, and then you'll have to deal with that surprise when you should be acting. If you think, "Oh, I'll be up on a big stage in a 2000-seat auditorium," and you end up auditioning in a hotel conference room, you'll have trouble making immediate adjustments, and doing so will distract you from concentrating on your monologue.

Don't even make assumptions about the behavior or number of people who will be watching you. Sometimes you will be performing for one person, sometimes for fifty or sixty in combined auditions such as Straw Hat, or Midwest Theatre Auditions. Don't anticipate rapt attention from your auditors. They may look at you intently, they may eat while you perform (they often don't get lunch breaks), or they may pass papers around or talk about you. Don't be surprised, don't be thrown. Just do your work and let them do theirs. It is hard not to be offended if someone is talking while you perform, but keep your concentration on your work. Remember, they may be saying, "She's perfect for the part, isn't she?"

Get a good night's sleep before your audition and wear comfortable clothes. If you're going on a callback, wear the same or similar clothes that you wore to the first audition. If the auditioners liked that person, they will remember and like the same person during callbacks. Wearing a T-shirt and jeans to the first audition and then a suit to the callbacks only confuses the people who are trying to find the real you. Bring extra copies of your picture and résumé in case you need them.

Know where you are going and give yourself plenty of time to get there. You may have forms to fill out, and you will want to warm up before your audition. Find a quiet place to center yourself, warm up vocally and physically, and run over your piece to be sure you are comfortable with it. If you can't find a private place, just close your eyes, focus, and take yourself through the piece in your head. Follow the emotional track of the character and visualize your silent partner. In other words, perform in your head. This is the same practice that professional athletes engage in when they visualize themselves making a free-throw or kicking a goal before they act.

When it is time for you to audition, you will be admitted into the audition room by a monitor or the casting director. In most cases, you or the casting director will have sent your picture and résumé to the director. If not, hand them to the director as you enter the room and cross to the audition area. If the director initiates a conversation, respond politely and efficiently. Think of this as a cocktail conversation. Most directors, though, will not initiate conversation. They're rushed and they just want to see who you are.

As soon as you enter that room, seize the space. Walk confidently and know that for the next three minutes, you are in charge of what happens. It is all too easy to experience auditions as a kind of meat market, in which you are just a number. In fact, auditions are often like this, but you must never present yourself as "just one more actor." Take the stage. Know you're important.

If you need to move a chair or set up the space, do so quickly. Then pause to be sure that the director is ready for you to proceed. In some cases, a monitor will indicate when you should begin. Introduce yourself and your piece, making eye contact with the director or with as many of a large group of directors as possible. This is the only time during the formal part of the audition that you should make direct eye contact with the auditioners. Set up your space so that you are facing the auditioners, but put your silent partner to one side of them, or behind them. Once your introduction is over, take a few seconds (no more) to focus completely on your work, and then go.

At the end of the performance, wait a beat, break character, and then say, "Thank you." If, for some reason, the director wants to see more of you, you may be asked to do a cold reading or additional monologues. Always have some additional work in reserve. It is not uncommon, especially in graduate school auditions, for directors to request specific types of monologues. "Do you have something more upbeat?" "Do you have something in verse?" "Can you show us a more vulnerable character?" You can never be prepared for all requests, but have a supply of work at your beck and call. If you are not asked to do additional work, however, don't be depressed. You may not have suited the role, or you may have been so perfect that the auditioners know immediately that they want to see you at callbacks.

When you've finished, never comment on your own work. Especially do not apologize. The most important thing is to be confident and to look like you're having a good time throughout the ordeal. Don't even comment on your own work by scowling, frowning, or shrugging as you walk away.

Once you have left the audition, try not to second guess the director. Even if the director seemed to respond well to your work, don't begin to fantasize about what it will be like to work with that director or on that project. If you don't get the part, you'll just be doubly disappointed. Every actor needs a strong support system. You put yourself on the line daily—you are the product that you are selling—and although you know that not everyone wants or needs your product, it is never easy to take rejection. Remember that even famous actors face rejection every day. Keeping faith in yourself and in those around you who stay by you in your times of need will see you through and keep you sane.

Auditioning can be a nightmare, but it can also be fun. You meet lots of different people, get tips on upcoming projects, and have a chance, however brief, to perform. Just keep reminding yourself that you are in control of your performance. No matter how good you are, you will only be right for some roles. Can you imagine Roseanne Arnold as a sensitive figure-skater? Keep true to your own sense of self, keep polishing your acting skills, and be sure that you have other ways of measuring your self-worth aside from getting cast in any one given role.

MONOLOGUES

FOR

WOMEN

BY

WOMEN

Barbed Wire Under Your Armpits

ELLEN K. ANDERSON

(Chimera is in the middle of her adult ballet class, doing grande battements (big kicks). Her ballet teacher has asked her to think of her arm as the wing of an angel.)

CHIMERA: Don't talk to me about angels, goddammit. My sister hangs angels in her house. (*Her angel arm transforms, now holding the end of a noose. She gives it a yank.*) My sister with the Ph.D. and the Volvo has angels hanging everywhere in her house. And I have to say—well—never mind. (*Hands in prayer position.*) Outside her front door there's a praying angel. I happen to know that it hangs *outside* the house because *mom* gave it to her. When I look at it—which you have to do in order to get into my sister's house—I always fluff the top of my hair, hoping my nubby horns won't show. (*Fluffs her hair.*) My sister's husband sometimes calls her angel. Has he looked at her ass lately? I mean how could you get it off the ground? She'd need rocket boosters under her feathers. Angel. There are angels in her bathroom, in her kitchen, in the garage. The toilet paper rolls have wings. Her car has a bumper sticker that says, "Angels Arise." Sometimes he goes as far as to call her angelface. (*Makes an ugly face.*) My father said I slid out of my mother with a scowl on my face and a firecracker up my butt. They named me Chimera (*pronounced shimera*) after my great-grandmother. They told me my name meant shimmering. The shining one. Pretty nice, ha? (*Tilts her face to the light for a moment.*) I went to college. I, the shimmering freshman, Chimera floated off to Greek

I

Mythology class. The professor called Chimera *(pronounced kimera)* Mathews. I said, "No, it's Chimera *(shimera)*. Chimera, Chimera, like in 'shimmering.'" *(As her professor.)* "That's very interesting," he said. "In Greek Mythology there is a creature called Chimera *(kimera)*. Spelled exactly as your name is, Chimera *(shimera)*. A Chimera *(kimera)* is in fact a fire-breathing female monster resembling a lion with a goat grafted to its back, along with the tail and wings of a dragon. Not unlike a gargoyle." *(Her face contorts into a gargoyle.)* No wonder I always felt more like screaming than shimmering. My sister was the angel. Angel face, angel ass. Cherubs fly from her mouth when she talks. And I am, I am—the gargoyle. *(Her whole body becomes gargoylish as she does astonishingly strong grande battements.)* A beautiful dancing gargoyle.

Mamma

DOROTHY ANTON

(The high point of Mamma's week is Saturday afternoon, when her grown son comes for dinner. Mamma enters from the kitchen, carrying a large, hot apple pie, which she sets to cool on the table. She wipes her hands on her towel, then notices the audience.)

MAMMA: Whattya doin here? Hey!! Whattsa matter with you?? Do you know what time it is?? Frankie, every Sunday you come for dinner with your Mamma, every Sunday you are late. Today, you are so early, you're on time! Whattya trying to give me a heart attack or somethin'? I'm still cookin, it's not ready yet, I'm inna kitchen here, ahh Frankie, it is good to see you! How are you, my handsome son! You look terrible, so skinny. Ahh, your Mamma is so very proud of you, you good for nothin! So, come here, ain't you gonna give your Mamma a kiss, heh? . . . . DON'T come over here, I just waxed that floor! Sit, sit, so how are you, Frankie, heh? . . . . . .

You wanna talk? Okay, so talk. Fix your collar, Frankie. FIX YOUR COLLAR! . . . . . . There, that's better, is that the shirt your Mamma give you for Christmas? It looks very good on you, is your iron broken? . . . . No, it looks good, so you don't believe in Clorox neither . . . . No, you always look good, Francis, you are very nice looking . . . just wear a smile and you will be fine . . . fix your hair, Frankie. FIX YOUR HAIR! Cmon, we use the Magic Thumb . . . . that's better, that's it . . . . Now you look good. *(Sniffing.)* Frankie, what is that you are wearing? Calvin Klein or chewing tobacco? Why you gotta use that blow dryer on your hair . . . . Frankie, look

3

at you, *(making the Sign of the Cross)* some gray hairs and you not even married yet!

Okay, so you wanna talk, we gonna talk; you gonna talk, I'm gonna cook . . . . No, go ahead, . . . okay, so talk . . . . you know you can say anything you want in your Mamma's house . . . . . . okay, so talk! . . . . . Frankie, I am your Mamma, whatya think I'm GONNA YELL AT YA OR SOMETHIN?? (*Turns toward kitchen to exit, abruptly returns in response.*)

FRANCIS ALBERT, you don't talk like that to your Mamma!

FRANCIS ALBERT ROOSEVELT, you don't be making jokes like that . . .

(*Almost whispering*) Frankie, don't you know people are DYIN in this town?

FRANCIS ALBERT ROOSEVELT DiMAGGIO FOC-CACCIO ERNESTO JULIO!!! Your Mamma gonna wash your mouth out with soap! . . . . Whattya trying to do, give me a heart attack? . . . . . . Frankie, don't be silly, you don't got no disease! . . . . . You can't . . . You don't shoot up with the nee-dles . . . you don't do drugs . . . you don't like girls???. . . . . . NO, NO! You do not tell me that!!! NO, NO! Your Mamma knows what she don't wanna know! . . . . You don't tell me nothin, young man, all you gonna tell me is when my floor is dry there! Heh? you don't know nothin! You see a doctor, heh? They don't know nothin, what they give you?. . . . . . AZT??? Frankie, you HAD acting classes already! You had your First Holy Communion, you had your oatmeal every morning, you had your vitamins with the little dinosaurs on 'em . . . . . you never stayed in the bathroom too long! Frankie, you are a good boy, you never hurt nobody, you were altar boy even! Your Mamma was so proud of you, all through high school, I never worried about you because I knew you were there with your friends, celebrating the Holy Uterus! NO, NO! You don't know! You think you know, but you don't know!! Your Mamma knows that you don't know that you don't know!!!

Sure, you come in here and tell your Mamma you don't like

4

women, heh? Sure, why should you? You know what a woman is? She's a LOSER! You think about it! What is the very first thing a woman do: she lose her heart! And then, second thing, she lose her innocence, and then, she lose her figure, and all her sleep, and her patience, her good humor . . . in the end, you lose your husband, your home, . . . you lose your boobs, even! BUT YOU NEVER EVER LOSE YOUR BAB. . . . . . . Frankie, your Mamma is never gonna lose that moment when she sees you being born, fresh from the hand a God, looking so very beautiful, all wrinkled up and purple, just like the fruit rotting under your Grampa's tree out back, and you screaming and your face getting all jaundiced and yellow, just like the color of puked-up mustard, so beautiful, you don't know. . . . .

You don't know! Your Poppa, Frankie, 23 years he goes out every morning with the Fire Department, 23 years, and one afternoon he don't come back. And you know what the priest says to me? He says, "Mamma, it's the will a God." And my brother Vinnie, your Uncle Vinnie, he goes off to Vietnam, and he don't come back. And they all say, "It's the will a God." SO DON'T YOU COME IN HERE YOUNG MAN AND SAY 'MAMMA, IT'S THE WILL A GOD' . . . BECAUSE GOD DON'T KNOW! HE DON'T KNOW! Now your Mamma knows, that you don't take care of yourself! Look at you, so skinny!! . . . . . . NO, YOU SHUT UP, WE AIN'T GONNA TALK NO MORE . . . . . WE AIN'T GONNA TALK . . . WE GONNA EAT! Now you gonna sit, I gonna cook! You rest, and I gonna finish cooking, we gonna sit down to a nice dinner, you gonna eat, you gonna get strong again. Your Mamma knows, you'll see. We gonna eat, and your Mamma gonna give you garlic, you gonna take it three times a day, I don't care if it kills you! We ain't gonna talk no more about disease, your Mamma knows how to take care of you, you'll see, you are gonna be okay, my Frankie . . . . . You don't gotta worry no more . . . You gonna be okay . . . Your Mamma knows! *(Makes the Sign of the Cross while hurrying out to the kitchen.)*

5

Friendship

DORI APPEL

(Janie, a woman in her early twenties, is intense, slightly awkward, and appealing. She is leafing through her address book and counting. She looks up and addresses the audience.)

JANIE: Nineteen. According to the information in my address book, there are nineteen people in this world who I could legitimately claim as friends. If I died tomorrow, nineteen people besides my parents would be sure to come to the funeral. *(She considers.)*

Eleven would definitely come. Five are only very slight acquaintances, and three live far away, including Anne, who has always been my best friend, since the first grade. From the time we were six, it was Anne and Janie, Janie and Anne. But Anne has been in Nepal for the last two years, chanting and bathing lepers, and I have gradually learned that at that distance she is not to be counted on. *(She considers again.)*

Of the eleven, six are relatives, which leaves five. And two of those are sort of friends of friends—you might say friends by association. Three. I have three actual friends. That's a lie. One of them is Gretchen March, who's the reason I've been tallying up my friends in the first place.—Oh, don't tell me my problem, I know my problem. My problem is hyper-sensitivity. Over anything. Over nothing. It's just the way I am, but I don't expect you to understand this. Anne is the only one who ever did. Anyway, what's to tell? The whole thing's a non-event, right? Gretchen's one of the people at work who happened to be nice to me when I started there a few weeks ago. Undoubtedly, she's nice to everyone. I shouldn't have assumed friendship on the basis of nice.

"Want to have dinner together after work?" I said casually the other day, except that with my hyper-sensitivity to rejection—which amounts to something like a lethal allergy—it wasn't entirely casual.

"Oh I can't tonight." And she gave me one of those smiles that people use to try and cover their aversion. "But let's do it another time, okay?"

Another time. Not tomorrow, not next Wednesday or next Thursday. Got it.

It was probably her name that gave me hope. Before Gretchen, the only people I ever heard of before named March were the ones in *Little Women*. As a kid, that family constituted some of my best friends. Likewise, Sara Crewe, The Bobbsey Twins (both sets)—and Lassie. *(She reflects.)* Lassie was big. Flicka was also big.

I know, I sound like a misfit. But remember, there *was* Anne. Anne to walk to school and back home with, Anne to tell secrets to, Anne even to fight with, though that never lasted for more than a day or two. You don't stay mad at your best friend for long, you just don't. *(She peers at the audience.)*

You can tell just by looking at me, can't you? You know I made it up. In a matter of seconds you knew that there's no Anne, and I never did have a best friend, and if I died tomorrow maybe three or four people besides my relatives would come to the funeral if they didn't have something better to do!

Some animals have the same problem, did you know that? There are pariah dogs—perfectly nice, agreeable animals who other dogs will cross the street to get away from, or else murder rather than have to be dragged into conversation with. *(Beat)*

Growing up, I did occasionally connect with other outcasts. In the fourth grade there was Norman Beebe who weighed about twelve pounds and got in a lot of trouble when he was caught stealing carrot and celery sticks from other kids' lunch boxes. Not cookies or cake or candy bars, you understand, but *celery* and *carrots*. And in fifth grade

7

there was Lois Keppel who sat in the back of the room and wet her pants every day just before afternoon recess.

So why was I such an outcast? I didn't pee in my pants or steal people's celery sticks, and I wasn't out and out strange like that Mary Agnes Something-or-other who came for a few weeks and spent every day eating library paste and banging her head on her desk. But whatever it was, everyone could spot it instantly, just like with the pariah dogs.

The thing about pariah dogs is that they've never figured out the doggie code, so they don't give the right signals back. Like when the Alpha dog looks at you funny, you're supposed to fall to the ground on your back and expose your underbelly . . . *(She demonstrates, with lolling tongue and begging forepaws.)*

"Sorry, Boss, I'm just an asshole—don't tear my throat out, okay?"

(As herself) The signals aren't very complicated, but it seems some dogs are just stupid when it comes to reading them—like me with Gretchen March. Wrongly assuming friendship from small gestures of politeness.

"But you wagged your tail, didn't you? Doesn't that mean you wanna be friends? *(Beat)* You weren't wagging your tail, you were just getting a kink out of it? *(Sheepishly)* Sorry."

(She reaches inside her address book and withdraws several letters.) You want to know what this is? It's pariah mail. Never anything personal, which is why I'm never in a rush to open it. *(She glances at the envelopes.)* A bill, credit card offer, another bill, Save the Harp Seals. *(She stops and regards the next envelope with surprise, then slowly opens it and reads.)* "Sorry I couldn't do dinner. I'm having a few people over for my birthday on the twelfth. Can you come?" *(Astonished)* From Gretchen March. *(She looks at the letter again, then puts it down and gives a couple of pleased but puzzled barks.)* Woof! Woof! *(She shrugs.)* Okay.—I mean . . . Sure!

8

Signs of Life

DEBORAH B. BALEY

(Sal and Abe are in the desert, at the low point of their cross-country journey. Sal is digging a hole in the desert sand. Abe stands beside her. She stops suddenly and looks up.)

SAL: If I can find life here . . . I can find it in me. *(Sal starts digging again.)* That's what I'm lookin' for! I'm lookin' for a sign of life . . . *in me!* 'Cause I haven't been able to find one! I've seen it everywhere else . . . but not in me! I've seen it through the car-door windows when we're drivin', blowin' through the grass and trees . . . and I've seen it at night, when I walk past houses with all the lights turned on . . . and I've heard it, through open windows, when children are playin' in the street! And I've seen it in you, when you look at the stars and talk about your dreams. But I can't find it in me. *(Sal stops digging.)*

I wonder if it exists at all, if life is just a thing of our dreams . . . if it's something we only imagine. Maybe there's really no people in those houses at night, just shadows, movin' on the wall . . . maybe there's really no children, just sounds that disappear, the minute you look out the window. Maybe there's no life in you either . . . *(Sal starts to dig again.)*

But I have to know. I have to know if there's such a thing as life, or if I've only made it up! I have to have a sign. 'Cause there's no life in me, Abe. I can't find a sign of life anywhere. There's nothin' in me at all but a dry river of rocks, that's all there is, just a dry river of rocks runnin' right through me . . . no water runnin' over 'em, no grass growin' between 'em, no trees growin' beside 'em, no nothin'! No water, no rain, no soil, no dirt, no ground, no grass, no trees, no nothin'! Just

9

rocks, only rocks! *(Long pause. Sal has stopped digging. She looks out over the desert, then continues.)*

I thought the magic star was gonna give it to me. I thought it was gonna be the thing to fill me with life. That it would make me so full that I'd spill over, like that spring of water . . . runnin' all over the place. And I thought you would do that too . . . that all the life I saw bubbling over in you would spill into me and I would fill up and spill over into . . . someone else. *(Long pause. Sal looks out over the desert.)*

But the magic star is gone, and the water was bitter. The desert called my name and . . . *(Long pause. She looks into the hole.)* I think I know now what it was that I came here to see . . . There's no life in the desert . . . and there's no life in me . . . *(She runs sand through her fingers.)* That's why I came here . . . I came to the desert . . . because the desert . . . is *me*. *(Long pause. Sal looks out across the desert.)*

Gracie and Butch

SUSAN BRABANT

(We are at Gracie's bridal shower in a church basement in August of 1946. Gracie is 25 and, having experienced a profound sense of bonding with other women during the course of the afternoon, her certainty about her upcoming marriage wavers. Her tattooed fiance Butch suddenly crashes the shower.)

GRACE: Okay. Okay . . . so lemme get this straight. You're saying you . . . as a man . . . are my natural protector, and that you know things I don't.

This is a little confusing to me. I mean, don't get me wrong, Butch. It's poetic . . . It's very romantic, actually. I just can't figure it out. If men are my natural protectors, why can't I walk down Flatbush Avenue alone at night when I wanna? Who am I afraid of?

I trust God, but I am convinced he's a man, too. I mean, WHO ELSE woulda come up with cramps, or the monthly blues, or this horrible way to have babies? WHO ELSE woulda come up with menopause and hot flashes and stuff like that? *(Butch tries to interrupt.)* I agree with you, Butch. God's a guy, no question.

It's like when my dad says to me, he says: "Hey," he says, "Behind every great man there's a woman." Like that's supposed to be some kinda big deal compliment or something. All that means to me is: "In front o' every great woman there's gonna be a man." *(Butch is outraged. She shrinks a bit.)* Oh, hey . . . present company excluded o' course . . .

It's just that, now don't take this detrimental or anything . . . but . . . I don't get why I have to give up all my dreams

II

when we get married, and you don't. All my dreams, like . . . I wanna be an actress, Butch. Not for the money or fame. Just to do it. Yeah, because I want to. It's . . . what I do. Me, y'know? I wouldn't *be* me without it, ergo, I wouldn't be the person I am now, and since *this* is the person you're in love with . . . how could we get married and expect it to last? Who will I be in five years, anyway? Are you even gonna like her? Am I?

Why do I have to go live with you, and cook and fold your underwear an' stuff, just cause you were born with that which I was not? Or vice versa? (*Pause*) This is no longer making any sense to me, Butch. I know there must be something here I'm missing, some important piece o' the puzzle which will bring it all into place. Like adjusting the tuner on the radio juuust enough and suddenly the music's clear as a bell.

I guess what I'm saying is, I don't want to get married. (*Overlapping, again, a little frightened.*) Nothing personal, oh, please don't take it personal. I just realized that . . . this wife stuff is one heck of a deal . . . for one of us . . . (*With rage, almost tearfully.*) And just because I don't want to do things exact, according to the "plan," you call me a ballbuster. A BALLBUSTER! (*To audience.*) Ever notice when you match wits with a guy, and you win, he calls you a ballbuster? (*As a "guy."*) "Hey, she's a real ballbuster." Kinda makes you wonder just where they think their wits are. (*Butch tries again to interrupt.*)

I've been listening to you for ten thousand years . . . I'M speaking now! I'm telling you I don't want to get married, ever—unless I can find me a partner instead of a king. I'm sorry. G'bye, Butch. Take care, huh?

Lily

JENNIFER CORLEY

(The present. A bar. Lily (30's) holds a dark, stiff drink and talks to a man next to her on a bar stool. He is slumped over and passed out from drinking.)

LILY: Since my mother's death, I've tried to figure out exactly what my feelings for her were. I swear, it never gets any easier. You know, like when you're a kid and you think you'll have everything figured out by the time you're 30. Well, I'm— beyond 30, and I'm far from enlightenment. I thought once my mother died some epiphany would occur to me and I would understand that all the different feelings I had for her were a normal part of everyone's life, saving myself thousands of dollars in therapy. Well, I'm still waiting.

You know, when I was a kid I used to curse her up and down under my breath, using all those words I heard her use. It drove me crazy, the way she used to do my hair. You know, that "Sunday Best" hairdo. She'd fashion my bangs into that little turd-roll look. And each day, on my way to school, I would be sure to step on every single crack on the sidewalk.

When I was a teenager I got really apathetic. You know, six years of the cold shoulder and silent treatment. Of course I talked to her, but as little as possible. I was too cool for her. She couldn't accept that I had my own life—she wouldn't let go. She bought me suits for work and tried to set me up with "nice young men" from her Church. I stopped returning her calls, and when I did talk to her I tuned out her guilt trips. I would pretend I was smacking her face every time she uttered a phrase.

Then, one day I got a call. She was put in the hospital for cancer. Of course I flew home to see her, but do you know what my very first thought was? The first thing to enter my mind? "Put her out of her misery"! I mean my God, I didn't even know how serious it was! I seemed mighty quick to jump on that euthanasia band wagon! That really took me by surprise . . . and then it occurred to me that she hadn't even told me. My own mother hadn't told me she had cancer. So sitting by my mother's bed, I had to start on some serious evaluation of my emotions. Had I pushed her so far away that she felt she couldn't come to me? —*Of course* I had! And then I wondered why I really cared. Any more than I would for any other human being, I mean. Didn't I spend my whole life trying to get her away from me? Isn't this what I wanted? *Yes!!* I caught myself smiling—actually laughing! Sitting by my dying mother's bed! All these people came in and automatically attributed it to denial or some other Kubler-Ross reaction, of course. But guess what I attributed it to? *Freedom!!* For the first time in my life, freedom! I was actually happy that my mother was going to die! I know you think I'm some sort of monster, but I'm just telling you the truth—and hey, talking about it's healthy! I just saved another $200!

The only thing is, here's the strange part. My euphoria died along with my mother. 2:02 a.m. In fact, not only did my good mood fade, I found myself positively *upset!* Well, that's really putting it lightly. I was hysterical. I was crying— well, sobbing. I was crying to God—God?! Now talk about scraping barrels out of desperation! That was one route I had not gone in a long time! I was begging God to bring her back! Whoa, bring her back? What the hell was I *thinking?* After all these years? Bring her back? I was screaming and crying to get her back to me!

I had to step back and think. Of course I didn't start doing that until quite a while later. If I had gotten her back, what would I have done? Would I have been nice to her? Would I have *loved* her? Did I ever love her? That's why I'm so messed up now I guess. I've scrutinized and analyzed my feelings for her over and over again. I asked myself why I honestly can't think of one instance in which I felt love for her. And do you know what I've come up with?—I don't know.

Wax Joints

BRENDA CUMMINGS

(Icky's mom enters through a crowd of Greek spectators, dressed in a toga.)

MOM: Let me through! Make way for the boy's mother you bumbling bards. Did you think you could keep me in my place? You'll tell your story whether I'm here or not, but let me see my son one last time. *(She looks to the sky.)* Icky! Honey! Don't get too close to the sun. I don't know how that father of his talked him into this. Daddy is as bull-headed as the minotaur with these inventions of his. And this one hits home. That child has never flown before. Like a moth to the flame. Apollo! Turn down the heat! Apollo. I'm speaking to you. He can't hear me. They aren't so la dee da as they make themselves out to be, these Olympians. Of course, they never listen to nobodies—Wives—Mothers like me. Are *you* listening gentlemen? . . . Didn't think so . . . The Gods. Ha! Give me Mother Earth any day. She's there to catch you when you fall. These hotshots sit up there on Mount Olympus, sticking their immortal noses into everbody's business—and getting very little done, what with the wars, murders, incest, bestiality . . . I ask you—Is that any way for Gods to behave? Makes your skin crawl. *(She looks to the sky.)* Watch where you're going for the love of Gaea. There's a Pegasus right over . . . . *(She sits.)* When these new Gods took over, the whole thing fell to pieces. In the old days, a father would never get away with this. Can you believe the man sends his own child up into the air, wearing a pair of wings held together with nothing but wax at the joints? Was my opinion asked? Will I even be part of the story, oh wise bards? Noooooo. You go through

16

all the pain and agony of having the child, feeding the child, nurturing the child, and then—POOF! You don't even exist. Just what will your story be? *(No answer.)* There's thanks for you. There's appreciation. That's my child too! . . . But does that matter? No. They take them all away. Turn them into soldiers. Send them to their deaths. Daddy did not have to resort to this. He knows the way out of the maze—he built it for God's sake! . . . Thinks it's faster with a pair of wings. Technology. Ha! . . . . I'll never forgive that man. I'll never forget this. *(She looks to the sky and sees that Icky is falling.)* Not so soon. Not yet . . . . Icky!!!!! *(She falls to the floor overcome, then slowly recovers.)* Go on. Get out of here. You've got your story. The end. Turn it into a heroic tale. Tell your lies and perpetuate the myth.

asylum/holdin on

LIZZY DAVIS

(This piece is *not* an exercise in "playing" insanity (please, no twitches and tics). It is an exploration of the pressures, frustrations, and urgent needs that result from living out of a mind that subtly yet actively refuses to be what you know it should. The speaker has recently left a mental institution. She is responding to her lover's suggestion that she return. She is not a child. She is an adult with an adult struggle.)

I dont see anything but hands. And I'm scared.

Yeah, it's worse—I dont feel anything keepin me from the dangers of the kitchen/medicine cabinet/window sill/—Not sleep, not Oprah, not sex, not just lovin you, not the calming, soothing, so carefully chosen, womb-like color of our walls. Nuh-uh, they aint cuttin it anymore because all I see comin *in*, is hands. Hands cupped are askin, hands stretched are wantin, hands tight are screamin, hands clutched are hurtin, but hands holdin onnnnnn . . .
and hollllllldin onnnnn . . .
are holdin-me-here,
in this room.
  handswarmwannabewarmwanna beheldn'holdin
  mewarmn'tightn'warm andwannabe heldand

you can help me, Dennis! you *lovin* me! . . . not them.
(Beat)

OK look, here it was:

> Rosa—she always played the shit outta the piano—it was real—her everything;
>
> Alex—always made sure people could still laugh "you can laugh, right? aint nothin to it but to do it just do it and that'll be all—everything and all";
>
> Me—quiet and cautious—everything I let show was nothing—I saved up my all for self-inspection in private.

Everyone focused on one tiny thing or nothing—made it their all and then it got written down and filed. They didn't know anything about what I've got. And when they tried to take away my all—tried to put me up with someone else—and share my no-compromise my . . . *shit*, Dennis, I got out—because people pulling on my everything? clutching at my all?—

How is that safe? Im not goin back—even if it *is* all hands now.

youdontknowyou dont youdont dontknow yourself in there. you cant . . . have yourself. its written down, or its a symptom to look up, or its sick—and— im scared —

imscared your handstheyre scaring me. i cant see anything else. they
stretch with . . . *clutching* power. just hold on . . . just hold. because my hands
are . . . limpand . . . cold
and . . . I . . . dont . . . think . . . I . . . can . . .
tighten them.

19

Angel's Share

CASEY DEFRANCO

(Loretta is trying to come to terms with the death of Dixie, her friend of fifty years. Dixie's room is piled with boxes, half packed, things hanging out of boxes, piles of clothes on the floor, it is a mess. Loretta goes into the room, pours a glass of cognac, and takes a drink. She is not drunk, just fallen into a habit.)

LORETTA: Are you here? I can still smell you . . . not your perfume, but the scent of . . . do you know that it reminds me of those cognac caves in France. Remember? The cognac aged in the barrels and half of it would evaporate into the air and cling to the walls . . . they called it the Angel's Share? We . . . liked it that we could breathe what was meant for the angels. *(She looks around the room.)* So . . . nothing . . . well, I keep hoping, it's been what? A month, two months? So . . . how do you like your shrine? Nice huh? I keep waiting every night but you're not here . . . you know all sorts of people see ghosts . . . granted they're usually from Kansas . . . "And then I saw Uncle Chester rising from the corn crib . . . ." You know even people who don't want to . . . see ghosts . . . but me? No, I wait and wait . . . I think that if I want it bad enough . . . just one little visit . . . I feel like . . . Mrs. Houdini . . . Hey Dix . . . I didn't even get one of those good-bye dreams. One of those standing-at-the-end-of-my-bed-looking-peaceful things . . . I get nothing . . . not even a creepy feeling when I come into your room . . . Lilly says that I have to let you go or your spirit will wander around in torture or something . . . So good! I think I'll keep you wandering until I pay you back for this dirty, stupid, dumb, dumb, trick. *(She pours another glass and downs it.)*

I'm so mad at you Dixie because . . . because I'm scared . . . I hate that Dix . . . I've never been scared being alone . . . not after the husbands, not after the baby left . . . not even when you were living in Europe and I was pregnant. At least you were on the planet . . . but now . . . *(She has worked herself into a rage, she is flinging things around the room.)*

You left me too soon . . . you shouldn't have gone so easily . . . so quietly . . . you wanted to leave me. And for that I will never, never speak to you again . . . I could have saved you . . . *(Exhausted she sits on the bed and views the mess. She finds Virginia's rosary beads and fiddles with them.)*

You know what, Dix? Maybe Eve's right, maybe nothing is really different . . . I've been thinking about that . . . no . . . no . . . she's wrong . . . I remember you everyday . . . and you're still as dead as you were before. I want you to walk through that door . . . say anything you want . . . just one word even, I want you back just for one little moment . . . is that too much to ask? Are you so busy that you can't do something? Don't you have some special power now . . . Come on, Dix . . . come on . . . I'm counting on you . . . I really am . . . come on . . . one measly word . . . I'm waiting . . . *(She stops and closes her eyes and waits. Then opens her eyes. She throws the rosary beads across the room.)* Nothing . . . *(She gets up and walks to the door.)*

OK for you, that was your last chance. I'm not coming back in here again until someone gets rid of everything . . . Maybe I'll keep one thing . . . maybe . . . *(She looks around and sees Dixie's glasses on the bedstand. She goes over and picks them up and puts them in her bathrobe.)* I'll keep your glasses . . . and you know what Dixie? I hope that wherever you are you need them . . . real bad . . . because all you've left me is your Angel's Share . . . and that's not enough. *(She leaves the room and shuts the door.)*

F-64

CHRISTINA DE LANCIE

(Nicola is a photographer. She is talking to her husband, Michael.)

NICOLA: Late one afternoon, a while ago, I took a walk. *(Pause)* It was a long time ago. And I took a walk in a park. I like to take walks. Do you? Very soothing. Gives you time to think. I always take walks by myself. Have for years. But then, you know that about me, don't you. *(Pause)* And there's so many places to walk to. If you have the time. Which of course I don't anymore. *(Pause)* But this was a long time ago. And I was very young.

I suppose I'd walked for a long time. That particular afternoon. It had been raining lightly . . . more like little shivers of rain. The kind of rain that wouldn't prove an impediment to anyone or any activity. So I hardly noticed it and just kept walking. And I suppose I'd walked a very long time because I suddenly realized it was getting dark. The light was fading, as they say. And I didn't know where I was. How far deep into the park I'd gone. Should I retrace my steps? Should I keep going? Eventually I'd have to come out the other side. Of the park. *(Suddenly distraught)* I mean, it couldn't go on forever. This park. This park couldn't go on forever. *(Pause)* But I didn't do anything. There wasn't anything to do. *(Pause)* I was already there. *(Very far away)* In as deep as I could be . . . now.

The rain had stopped. Everything was drenched with water. The quality of the light, the stillness of the garden, so heavy with moisture . . . it all created an almost exquisite gloom. *(Pause)* Then something attracted my attention. Something seemed to move. Off the path. A ways off the path. In the shad-

22

ows. Deep inside the greenery. I stood very still . . . and, I knew. *(Pause)* Oh yes. I must have. All along. I must have always known. In my heart of hearts. You see, I was the intruder. It was *me*. I was intruding on *them*. I knew immediately.

It was late one rainy afternoon in the park and I saw two figures moving about in the bushes. I went closer to them. To see. *(Pause)* To watch. *(Pause)* There was a man . . . and a girl. And the man, the young man, was showering the girl with kisses. *(Pause)* That's what you say, isn't it . . . showering with kisses? When the trees are shaking water and the woman's eyes are closed and the man's hands are making love to her and his mouth is showering her with kisses. *(Dreamily)* And they looked so beautiful together. The man now undressing the girl. Showing her what to do with such tenderness. There was such tenderness in those shadows. Such tenderness . . . that I had never felt. *(She is suddenly bewildered.)* I couldn't turn away. I couldn't walk away. *(Pause)* I could only *(Speaking with difficulty.)* . . . stand very still and watch . . . something that I had . . . *never had . . . never felt.*

(She takes a long breath and speaks quite rationally now.) I had never felt that showering of love under the trees in the almost rain.

(Considering) Was I just imagining their closeness? The closeness between this man and this woman. It wasn't ordinary closeness. Something denser. *(Pause)* Was it true they were nearer than I could ever be . . . to someone? *(Devastated)* But I knew I wasn't there. That I was intruding. *(Pause)* And in this park, under those trees dripping water, was the first time I ever experienced jealousy. The first time I ever knew what it was like to be jealous. To be excluded. *(Pause)* It's a terrible thing to want what you can never have. To want to *be* what you can never be.

As I looked on . . . because the sex was not awkward, not difficult to watch, but graceful, even. Elegant. And the man's face grew in beauty to me. Opened up to me, you could even say. His sincerity . . . his murmured appeals . . . the concen-

23

tration. The woman was so sure, so certain of him. They were completely complete. The both of them. Impassable. Dense. So impenetrable. *(Pause)* It was their completeness, their connection . . . that finally pushed me away. The power of it *had* to push me away . . . Leaving me with such tears and envy. Leaving me . . . excluded.

I left them there. Lying in each other's arms. Not needing anyone else. Not needing me. I left them there and wandered back through the park the way I'd come. *(Pause)* I believe that's what I did. I wandered . . . And finally came to sit down on a bench. *(Pause)* It seemed as though many years passed by as I sat on the bench in the near darkness at the edge of the park. I remember I was so tired I barely moved on that bench. So tired and so confused that I even feared a bit for my . . . sanity. My clarity. And I devised a little game to play inside myself to keep myself together, as it were. To keep my clarity. *(Pause)* I watched the seasons go by. *(Pause)* Don't kid yourself. It's a subtle game, watching the seasons go by. Takes great skill and resource. Great inner resource. Not to mention a certain kind of forgiveness.

After a while, a man approached me. Very straight this man stood, his eyes shining, hardly noticing the rain that fell on his face . . . his mouth thick, wet . . . so beautiful. He approached the bench, my bench, and asked if I'd mind if he sat down. He said he didn't want to frighten me and wasn't it a lovely night. I replied it was a lovely night and I wasn't frightened. *(Pause)* Because it was him, of course. It was the same man. The man with the girl. *(Pause)* We spoke for a long time, sitting on my bench underneath my umbrella. He was sincere. I felt his concentration resting on *me* now. And he was kind. He opened up to me, you might even say.

And for those moments . . . for I never saw him again. He walked away a little while later and I never saw him again . . . but for those moments sitting on the bench on the edge of the park . . . he never knew what I knew. *(Pause)* And I pretended I had what I could never have.

La Casa de las Mañanas

LISA DIXON

(Maria, a Mexican woman in her mid-forties, enters the space—carrying shopping bags, wearing a coat; she is loaded down with things. She has just gotten off from a long shift at work. There is a table and chair at which she sits, and a table/mantlepiece in the background on which sits a framed photograph of a man. Everything else she takes out of her bags. Much of her monologue is seemingly delivered to a character offstage.)

MARIA: Helloooo!! I bought things for dinner . . . some nice tomatoes, a little rice, and some wine. I thought we should celebrate tonight, yes? O.K. Fine. *(She sits.)* I don't like these shoes. They call them work shoes, but I believe this is because it is so much work to wear them. These shoes are difficult. These are *obstreperous* shoes. *(Pause)* Some American words are very useful.

¡Ay! My poor feet, they ache all over. I know just the cure, some wine will do for you. *(She takes a bottle and glass out of bag, opens the bottle and pours herself some.)* DO YOU WANT SOME WINE? NO? All right then. More for me. Ah, Paolo, this is the anniversary of the seventeenth year of our marriage. SO YOU HAD BETTER BE GOOD TONIGHT! *(Laughs.)* HMMM. If the swelling in my feet doesn't go down, it may not be able to go up somewhere else, yes? *(Looks to audience.)* What, do you think that that is vulgar? Well you're right. I can never say I didn't learn anything from Americans! When I first came here, years ago, I was a shy, quiet, well-behaved lady; now I am a nasty and obnoxious old woman. Well, "When in Rome . . ."

25

Paolo doesn't like the new me, DO YOU PAOLO? You see, the new me, I am quite, quite daring! Paolo, I say, I believe I will have another glass of wine. Paolo, I say, my hair, I think I will cut it. Paolo, I say, I will wear the red dress with the lace on the front and you will like it! Oh no! I am not the same woman my husband once married! It was hard for him, for both of us, when we first came here. Paolo worked sun-up to sun-down, his body ached, but we still could not afford to keep house and home together. And so I decided I would get a job. PAOLO, REMEMBER THE DAY I TOLD YOU I GOT A NEW POSITION? YOU WERE SO ANGRY! He was so angry! We had a huge fight, a *confrontation*, if you will, and I was so angry I just stormed from the house, right out into the street, just as they do in the movies. DO YOU REMEMBER HOW I JUST STORMED OUT OF THE HOUSE?! But I would not give up the job.

(Pause)

Let me tell you a secret. Sometimes, when I was shopping in the district near my house, I would find a beautiful thing—a lovely scarf the color of a sunset, or a new perfume with the scent of the ocean, and just for a moment, I imagined myself making love in that scarf, on the beach . . . with someone. NOT Paolo someone. And this someone, he would have sweat on his shoulders and hair falling into his face and only a picture of me in his eyes. Ay, he was beautiful! So beautiful that, sometimes I would forget my love for Paolo. I think he knew. Paolo knew. And let me tell you, when a husband knows that you think of things other than him, well this can be a problem. This can cause *strife*.

You see, I was no longer the sweet young lady that left sleepy little Saltillo with its dusty streets and dusty people. I was here now, completely here; so I kept my job. At first I worked at the Baile Mexicano, an "Absolutely Authentic" Mexican restaurant with fake Mexican food for people who think they are but aren't really authentic-fake-Mexican-food-lovers. All of the dishes came with a side order of American

26

fries. Bean burrito . . . with fries, Tacos . . . with fries, Pollo con mole . . . with *American* fries. ¡Ay! It was an insult to create such garbage but you loved it! There are many things Americans do well, but when it comes to food, you are . . . less than . . . *subtle.*

So, each day after work, to get the stench of refried French fries off my clothes, I would walk through the shopping district of the city. I love sales. If there is one thing that Americans are the best at, it is putting on a sale. White sales, bargain basement, low, low prices, 20 percent off, 50 percent off, 75! I did not really need the very last bottle of *Sophia's Passion* foaming bath salts but, such a price, no? I had my own money; I bought it. I did that a lot, and it always made Paolo furious. Yes, we were struggling in those days, we were always struggling, but he could not understand my need, and so we argued. A lot.

After our fights, I would always take walks, and one day (after a very bad fight), I found myself lost in the city. I had been walking for hours, and my feet hurt. Just as I thought to go back home, I turned a corner into a lovely little garden. There was water running in a small stone fountain and a little marble bench, and I decided to sit for a moment and rest my feet and the thoughts running through my head. It was a blue day in October, and I was feeling, perhaps, a little sorry for myself, and maybe a tear or two flushed itself from my eye. There was a young woman sweeping the walkways in the garden, and I did not notice her until suddenly I felt a soft hand patting my shoulder. "Is there anything I can do?" she said quietly. "I am not sure, where are we?" It was the hotel garden, she told me, of the Casa de las Mañanas. *(Pause)* The Casa de las Mañanas. The House of Tomorrows. I thought the name very . . . *appropriate.* I began working there the very next day.

Do you know what I think? DO YOU KNOW WHAT I THINK, PAOLO? I think that we forget why we are here. Not here, like in this room, but here on the earth. Some peo-

27

ple think that there is no purpose to our being here at all. I think that if that is the case, we should all leave, no? And let the birds and the badgers and the giraffes take over. There is a reason—there must be a reason for us to live and work and die and love. To exist. These things I think about sometimes. And on that bright day in October, I knew that the shopping and the arguments and the walks through the streets were all to bring me to that place. The place of my work; it was here for me; to help me find happiness for myself, and I, Maria Angelica Romero de Martin, I am here for . . . I am here for . . . Paolo. *(She smiles.)* You are surprised? Ay, my Paolo, you must know him to understand. Today, tonight, we are married seventeen years, Paolo and I. And for all that time, when he is here, and when he is not, I am in love with him. *(Pause)*

Sometimes, sometimes I forget things. Sometimes I remember things that are not true. I remember me, standing here on the steps and watching you, your body smaller than I could conceive of, leave for the bus home, and thinking that maybe I should have kissed you good-bye. I remember you, Paolo, so many years ago in a suit standing in the hot Saltillo sun on the corner of the calle Moreno, waiting for a bus to go to work. I had never seen someone so handsome, and so sad. Your sadness touched my sadness, and as I looked through the window of the shop where I worked, I prayed to God to banish all of the mass transit coaches in the city, so that you would stand waiting patiently on the corner of my street, forever. But the bus came, and you got on, and I went back to work. But the next day, you were there waiting. And the day after. And the day after. As was I. And soon, I knew that you were not just waiting for the bus. And each day as I pressed my face to the glass, I imagined the smell of the nape of your neck, and the feel of my hand on the pulse of your throat, and the sound of your breathing. And each day, I waited, waited for you, as you waited for your bus, and for me. Who knows how long we may have waited? I mean after all at that time, I was a shy, young and very proper girl, and you were really still just a boy in men's clothing. Who knows how long we may have waited?

There is fate. There is destiny. There is God. Who is to say if they are different or the same? I cannot. But, one must believe in God. One *must* believe in God, because only God can cause the changing of the seasons, the wind and sun . . . and rain. And God brought us rain. And God brought you to me. As you waited quietly for your bus on the corner, a light fall rain began to drop from the sky, and you turned, slowly and deliberately, and walked into my shop to buy an umbrella. From that moment on, you and I, Paolo, have been together. *(From somewhere in the room she picks up a framed photograph of a man.)* And so tonight, we celebrate seventeen years together, yes? *(She pours one glass of wine.)*

¡Ay! Paolo, this life we lead is so strange and so precious. It is often that we search for pearls on the horizon, not recognizing the jewels at our feet. For a while, you carried the weight of the world for me, and though your hair did not sweep the back of your neck, and the skin on your hands was scarred from your work, and I was sometimes for you, nothing but a trial . . . still I love you, and you loved me. I am your purpose, and you are mine. ¡SALUD! *(She toasts the photograph. She downs the wine.)*

29

Gideon and Josephine

JEANNE DORSEY

(Josephine is on a blind date with Gideon. Responding to Gideon's gesture, the waiter has just placed the check on the table.)

JOSEPHINE: Listen Gideon, you said you wanted to know something about me. That is what you said. You even told our waiter that I should feel free to express myself. "Feel free to express yourself Josephine," you said that and I took you at your word. So, first I told you that I have a great love of literature, especially Shakespeare and you say "Of course, who doesn't, the guy was a genius but I want to know more about *you* Josephine, tell me more about *you*." So I tell you more. I tell you that my heart is bloody and that my eyes were crossed and now they're crushed and I rhymed for you Gideon, I rhymed for you. . . . and you ask for the check Gideon? You ask for the check? That's not fair! I warned you Gideon, I warned you that knowing me would make you not want to know me and you said . . . well you implied, "Oh no Josephine, lay it on me. I love truth. Truth, truth, truth and more truth, lay it on me." So I do. I lay it on you just like you did with me about your poodle Rebecca! I listened to that story Gideon. I listened and I empathized Gideon, damn it, I empathized. Even though, as you know, I have my own problems. I listened with an open, bleeding heart to your problems and I showed concern. But now you've heard my problems and all of a sudden you want the check! I think not Gideon! I think not! *(She takes a revolver from her purse and aims it at Gideon's heart.)* Put the check down Gideon. Put it down! Good. Thank you. O.K. . . . as soon as you catch the

30

waiter's eye I'd like you to order me some dessert. It's clear that we won't be having dinner together but I would like some dessert. I would like you to order an iced decaf cappuccino and a banana flan, is that clear? Oh and of course whatever you'd like for yourself. Do it Gideon! Now!

A Cock. A Dream. A True Story.

LINDA EISENSTEIN

(A woman. Old enough to know better. She addresses the audience. Each numbered section is a change in tempo, a change in position, possibly a lighting change—as she moves from story to dream to story.)

1.

This is a true story.

The names are omitted to protect . . . well—I'm not really sure who.

There's this guy, see.

Yeah, that kind of story.

There's this guy, see. We used to be close. I thought so, anyway. For years, we were partners. Worked together, made things together. Comrades in arms.

Then, for no clear reason, things got . . . ugly. And we don't work together any more. We hardly speak, actually. A vast silence has invaded the space between us. Even in dreams.

This is about a dream.

2.

(She takes a note out of her pocket.)

In my dream I am looking at this note. This note he has scrawled to me. After months of no contact, he has finally managed to scrawl a note. A whole sentence. I'm surprised—surprised, and pleased.

I am standing next to my mailbox at the office, the office I no longer go to, and I am reading this one-sentence note that he has stuck in there for me to find. It is an invitation. I open it. This is the sentence:

IF I CAN BRING MY COCK TO DINNER, WE MIGHT BE ABLE TO WORK TOGETHER AGAIN. *(Double take.)* I read it again, uncomprehending.

IF I CAN BRING MY COCK TO DINNER, WE MIGHT BE ABLE TO WORK TOGETHER AGAIN. Is this a good sign . . . or a very bad one?

3.

All day I keep thinking about this dream. Working around and around it, like a sore tooth. What the hell does it mean, this sentence?

He wants to bring his cock to dinner.

He'll come to dinner, but only if I acknowledge that he's bringing his cock.

He's afraid I'm going to forbid him to bring it.

He secretly wants to work with me again.

He never wants to work with me again, but he wants me to think he does. Therefore he's brought his cock into it, kind of like a chaperone. Bodyguard. Muscle.

All day I ruminate.

I need to tell this dream to someone, so I call up my friends K. and J. and ask them to lunch. They are subject matter specialists. His former employees. Having endured many a royal screwing, they know him and his cock all too well.

Why, I ask them, did he want to bring his cock to dinner?

We ponder it over our couscous.

4.

So, in the dream, I am holding this note in my hand, reading it over and over. It's in his typical illegible scrawl. His handwriting is as bad as a doctor's—he assumes that it's your job to figure it out.

Nevertheless, the prescription was clear. He was planning on coming over. He might want to work with me again. But

33

only if I was ready for him to bring his cock.

I decide I'm not ready for this.

I don't want to deal with it. Not his cock—I mean, Christ, I know he has one—but that he has to *mention* it.

No matter how much I want to work again, I just can't imagine myself trying to open negotiations with somebody who has to make sure my invitation includes his cock.

What did he plan to do with it?

Did he need to bring it along as moral support?

Was he counting on it as a resource? As a crutch? As a negotiating tool?

I imagine him taking it out during a moment of disagreement and pounding on the table with it to make a point. Like Krushchev with his shoe.

5.
"IF I CAN BRING MY COCK . . ."

Why does he feel the need to tell me about it?, I ask K. She knows him well. He has written her hundreds of imperious little notes.

In her last dream about him, just before she left, one of his notes magically appeared on her skin, as a row of angry red blisters. *(She runs her fingers along her arm, her midriff.)* She could read it without looking at it, like Braille.

"It's simple," she says. "He's afraid, of course, that you're not going to let him have one. Or that you'll cut it off."

That could be true. During the last real talk we had, before the Ice Age, he told me he'd been having nightmares all the time about Lorena Bobbitt.

"Or maybe he wants your reassurance," says K. "That you'll pet it and be nice to it. You know how he's always expecting someone to hold it for him."

This is also true. At nearly every meeting there is someone who has this special assignment. The assigned person varies, but the function is imperative: someone must stroke it, or he pouts.

34

But I'm sick and tired of dealing with his cock, I tell K.

"So am I. That's why we don't work with him any more," she says. "Don't you remember?"

I remember. Yes, I most certainly do.

But really, I say, a little defensive now: I mean he *does* have one. And it doesn't just snap off, so he can leave it at home.

"Why not?" says K. "That's why men's suits come with two pair of pants. One to wear with your cock, one for without. Tell him to wear the second pair."

Maybe she's right. I think about the millions of times we women have been asked to check our hormones at the door. Why shouldn't he have to leave his cock at home once in a while?

It really would be pleasant not to have it waved at me all the time.

6.

So, in my dream, when I look up, I see a group of old ladies passing the note around among themselves. They are reading it aloud, clucking noisily. Each one is more outraged than the next.

"Look at this!" they are saying. "Bring his cock to dinner"?!

"He wants her to invite his *cock* to dinner"?!?

"This is outrageous!" says one. "What makes him think he can write such a thing to you?"

They are making Xerox copies of the note, passing it around. I have the distinct impression they're going to turn it into fliers. Oh, God, I think, they're going to make a public protest on my behalf.

"Dearie," they are saying, "Don't you know this is sexual harassment? You shouldn't have to read such a thing in your office correspondence!"

Ohmygod, ohmygod. Now the old ladies are in on it. It's going to go public. I'm going to be walking down the street and there it'll be, this flier, tacked up on the telephone pole screaming:

35

"IF I CAN BRING MY COCK TO DINNER . . . "
And everybody in town will know. Everybody will know that he writes me such notes. Everybody.
And, God help me, that means everybody is going to know my deep, dark, dirty secret: *that I read the goddamn things! And ignore them! And that I was **still** thinking about letting him come to dinner! Him and his fucking cock!*

7.

So in my dream, I start to make excuses to the old ladies. "That's private correspondence, you can't just, uh, make copies of that, you know." I begin gathering up the fliers, as many as I can, examining them.
"Where did you get this?" I ask one crone.
"It was lying right there, on that table, in full view for everyone to see."
Oh my God, I think. Has he left copies around for other people to see? Does he *want* people to read this note?
What am I doing? Why am I trying to hide this?
Jesus, I realize, as I read it again:
"IF I CAN BRING MY COCK TO DINNER, WE MIGHT BE ABLE TO . . ."
Some people are going to read this and think he and I are fucking. There is going to be somebody, SOMEBODY, who will think this is some kind of coy, cutesy, intimate little vulgarity between People. Who. Are. Fucking.
OH-HHHHHMYGOD!! AHHH! ACCCHH!
My heart begins to race. Race so fast, that I start to wake up. Ahhh. *(She pants for a while.)*
Let me go on the record here. We were not actually ever fucking. Ever. Not actually. Well . . . I did get screwed any number of times, that's for sure. And . . . I was seduced, too. More times than I can count, I let myself be seduced. But—so did many others. *Many* others.
No, that's not right, either. How do we get the language right? We were not actually ever fucking. But we managed to

36

fuck each other over all the same. And somehow, we managed to have these children, he and I. And sometimes . . . it was good. Sometimes . . . Ah, hell.

8.

I can't really remember the rest. Eventually, the dream ended. All dreams do. But it's stayed with me, like a hangover, for weeks now.

So I keep telling this story, over and over, trying to make it come out right. Like a shaman, I parse it, stare at its entrails, try to figure out all its meanings. I've come to realize that it's not just about me and him. So I offer it up, this vision, for the health of the whole tribe. It seems important, somehow, for us to understand.

Audience reactions vary. Most men seem to think it's chiefly about my anger. I can see their eyes skate away from mine, as though even my glance had a cutting edge to it.

Now women . . . Most of them laugh. Even though it embarrasses some, I know. Sometimes I can hear a sharp intake of breath, that gasp of recognition, and I suddenly know it's their story, too. Some, even as they rock with laughter, think it's the saddest story they ever heard.

And even as I tell and retell it, trying to erase its hold over me, I'm afraid I might be increasing its power. I long for this dream not to be an omen of more discontent, or covering up, or hard feelings, or misunderstanding. I long for this dream to carry in it not just a truth, but a healing—

So I keep this note. I take it from my pocket, turn it over and over in my hands, open it, and read aloud:

"IF I CAN BRING MY COCK TO DINNER, WE MIGHT BE ABLE TO WORK TOGETHER AGAIN."

And quietly, reluctantly, I fold it up and put it back in my pocket again. And wait. And hope. Someday there might be a different message. A different invitation.

I wouldn't want to miss it.

37

Vagina Monologues

EVE ENSLER

Introduction

I began this piece because I was worried about vaginas. That's how I begin most things—worry. I was worried about what we think about vaginas and even more worried that we don't think about them. I was worried about my own vagina. It needed a context of other vaginas, a community, a culture of vaginas. There's so much darkness and secrecy surrounding them—like the Bermuda triangle. Nobody ever reports back from there.

In the first place, it's not so easy to even find your vagina. Women go weeks, months, sometimes years without looking at it. I mean a man takes it out, there it is. I talked with a high-powered business woman who told me she's too busy, she doesn't have the time. Looking at your vagina is a day's work. You have to get down there on your back in front of a mirror that's standing on its own, full length preferred. You've got to get in the perfect position, with the perfect light which then becomes shadowed somehow by the mirror and the angle you're at. You get all twisted up. You're arching your head up, killing your back. You're exhausted by then. She said she didn't have the time for that. She was busy.

Let's just start with the word vagina. It sounds like an infection at best, maybe a medical instrument, "Hurry nurse, bring me the vagina." Vagina. Doesn't matter how many times you say it, it never sounds like a word you want to say. It's a totally ridiculous, completely unsexy word. If you use it during sex, you kill the act right there. I'm worried about vaginas, what we call them and don't call them.

In Great Neck they call it Pussycat—a woman told me there that her mother used to tell her don't wear panties underneath your pajamas, you need to air out your Pussycat. In Westchester they call it a Pooki, in New Jersey a Twat. There's Powderbox, Derriere, a Poochi, a Poopi, a Peepe, a Poopelu, a Pal and a Piche, Tuckas, Toadie, Dee dee, Nishi, Dignity, Coochi Snorcher, Cooter, Labbe, Gladys Seagelman, VA, Wee wee, Nappy Dugout, a Pajama, Fannyboo, Mushmellow, a Ghoulie, Possible, Tamale, Tottita, Connie, a Mimi in Miami, Split Knish in Philadelphia and Schmende in the Bronx. I am worried about vaginas.

Vagina Workshop

My vagina is a shell, a round pink tender shell opening and closing, closing and opening. My vagina is a flower, an eccentric tulip, the center acute and deep, the scent delicate, the petals gentle, but sturdy.

I did not always know this. I learned this in the vagina workshop. I learned this from a woman who runs the vagina workshop, a woman who believes in vaginas, who really sees vaginas, who helps other women see their own vagina by seeing other women's vaginas.

In the first workshop the woman who runs the vagina workshop asked us to draw a picture of our own "unique, beautiful, fabulous vagina." That's what she called it. She wanted to know what our own unique beautiful fabulous vagina looked like to us. One woman who was pregnant drew a big red mouth screaming with coins spilling out. Another very skinny woman drew a big serving plate with a kind of Devonshire pattern on it. I drew a huge black dot with little squiggly lines around it. The black dot was equal to a black hole in space and the squiggly lines were meant to be people or things or just your basic atoms who got lost there. I had always thought of my vagina as an anatomical vacuum randomly sucking up particles and objects from the surrounding environment.

I had always perceived my vagina as an independent entity, spinning like a star in its own galaxy, eventually burning up on its own gaseous energy or exploding and splitting into thousands of other well meaning smaller vaginas, all of them spinning in their own galaxies. I did not think of my vagina in practical or biological terms. I did not for example see it as a part of my body, something between my legs, attached to me.

In the workshop we were asked to look at our vaginas with hand mirrors. Then, after careful examination, we were to verbally report to the group what we saw. I must tell you that up until this point everything I knew about my vagina was based on hearsay or invention. I had never really seen the thing. It had never occurred to me to look at it. My vagina existed for me on some abstract plane. It seemed so reductive and awkward looking at it, getting down there like we were in the workshop on our shiny blue mats with our hand mirrors. It reminded me of how the early astrologers must have felt with their primitive telescopes. I found it quite unsettling at first, my vagina. Like the first time you see a fish cut open and you discover this other bloody complex world inside, right under the skin. It was so raw, so red, so fresh. And the thing that surprised me most was all the layers. Layers inside layers, opening into more layers. My vagina, like some mystical event which keeps unfolding into another aspect of itself, which is really an event in itself, but you only know it after the event. The layers of the vagina like those courses you had to take in geology where you see the layer charts of the earth, layers of soil, sediment, protective layers and fertile layers, symbolic layers, aesthetic layers, layers that multiply the pleasure, layers that are in themselves masks or false images of layers.

My vagina amazed me. I couldn't speak when it came my turn in the workshop. I was speechless. I had awakened to

40

what the woman who ran the workshop called "vaginal wonder." I just wanted to lay there on my mat, my legs spread, examining my vagina forever.

It was better than the Grand Canyon, ancient and full of grace. It had the innocence and freshness of a proper English garden. It was funny, very funny. It made me laugh. It could hide and seek, open and close. It was a mouth. It was the morning. And then it momentarily occurred to me that it was me, my vagina, it was who I was. It was not an entity. It was inside of me.

My vagina is a shell, a tulip and a destiny. I am arriving as I am beginning to leave. My vagina, my vagina, me.

Spackling in Tongues

DEBORAH LAKE FORTSON

(Helen, a woman of 40-50, is scraping and spackling the walls of her living room in the week of her twentieth anniversary. She gets irritated with some lumps of joint compound on the tools and starts scraping it off. Short irritated gestures.)

HELEN: I have a bump—on my right toe—like my mother's—her bunion on her right foot. It's right on the big toe, and it's soft like a big blister. It's gross. It's starting to mean I can't wear some of my shoes. And my feet are already so big I can't find shoes. This bump is kind of ugly. Last summer I forgot I had it and painted my toenails a purplish red—a mistake. I used the same color this bump is. I mean it was like putting lipstick on when your face is covered with pimples. But I like toenail polish so I left it on. No one said anything and I forgot about how gross it probably looked. People are more polite than they should be probably. No one said, "Yuk! Don't you know you have a gross bump on your foot?" But here it is, you see. Don't worry, I'm not going to show it to you. I showed it to my Aunt, she said, "Oh, that's the kind of thing we used to hit with the Bible and it would go away. Do you want me to try, dear?" You know why I really don't want to go to the doctor? Besides that he'll probably want to cut it, he'll blame me. Somehow it will be my fault. Do you exercise that toe? Maybe you've been wearing the wrong shoes! Your shoes are too tight. Undoubtedly! It's because you won't wear the right kind of shoes and you eat too much fat. It's because your feet are too big to begin with. You don't need such big feet. If your feet were smaller you could wear shoes that fit. Why don't you have smaller feet? *(Stirring paint or cleaning trowel. In a low, agitated voice.)* Fuss fuss fuss don't make a fuss. Just wait. Maybe things will get better? Don't rock the boat. Don't try to change things. It will just make it worse. A fuss will be too painful. Pain, avoid that! A fuss will be more bumpy than the bump. Don't let anyone see you have that bump! It's a defect! You want too much. No no! Don't protest! Don't push us like that! You are ugly when you speak loudly like that. You're too loud—stop shouting! We know what we're doing. Just hold still, stay quiet, and we'll fix it. You're too loud, stop shouting. We know what we're doing. Just hold still, stay quiet, and we'll fix it.

(Quickly) My cousin Gloria went to show them the lump in her breast when she was 32, with one little boy a year old. They said you're too young, you don't have cancer in the family, don't worry. So we stopped worrying. After she got pregnant it was still there, they said the same. Months later it had grown, the doctor told her it was fine, not to worry. But when it was two and a half inches across and she was nine months pregnant, he decided to test it, and yes, it was cancer, but no they didn't tell her until after the baby was born, and then the doctor got the husband to tell her that she was scheduled for a mastectomy and then radiation the following week. Oh! *(She howls.)*

OOHHHH!

Should we just bury it, our intuition? Bury all the deep unfathomable longings. Yes. Pack it all away. Bury it all, down deep, down in the cool and the dark, something new and strong will form and surge and break through. A force, a desire that won't stop at closet doors, at folded arms, won't be numbed by pain. A desire that stays soft and strong at the same time and doesn't force itself but grows like flowering weeds on thick stalks in the jungles of the cities of man's progress until its succulent roots pierce the concrete heart of the matter—break it into pieces and float it away on the bloodstreams of the earth.

Right. RIGHT! *(She throws tools into the air.)*

43

What a mess! What a mess it all is. I want so much to fit in, to make things work. But I don't iron my shirts, I'm always losing my keys. What American dream am I always losing the keys to?

Am I more comfortable in the mess? There must be a reason I can't get it straight. Maybe I'm an alien. I can't really understand what it takes to get it right because there's something real humans are born with that I don't have.

Take shopping—I don't have the gene for it. Listen, if I'm not even fit to shop, what hope is there for me?

Like last Saturday I go to do the shopping in the evening. I am so tired I am losing my concentration. I drift floating sideways through the aisles of that night market, looking for nourishment. Find myself staring at the chicken unable to decide. Unable to purchase! My face feels like it's floating grotesque, in that cold meat section, staring uncomprehending as though I've never seen dead muscles wrapped in plastic, coffined in styrofoam. The meat man thinks it is all proper, all in order and looks at me wondering will I make it, will I hold together. Will I become a problem? I wonder if I have stains on my sweater from making the gravy at dinner. Is my hair too loose or dirty? I want to recover my surface, put on lipstick, snatch my chicken breasts briskly away from the case in a decisive manner. Purchase my Perdue parts! But on the other hand I want to dissolve, I want to lie down on the plastic meat and announce the death of my will power. I want to hug the meat man, ask him to dance down the drafty aisles. Leave all those meaty decisions and come away into the light, collecting salad and potatoes for the years ahead. I want to disrupt the surface—bomb the edges until the lid blows off and sky pours into the aprons of the faithful bag boys, lands on the shoulders of drowsy shoppers and lifts us up!

I want to explode and rain down on the rivers.

In the small market on the corner I used when we were first married there never would have been a problem of Alienation Among the Chickens. The grocer, Mr. Petrocelli,

44

would've said "How are you?" I would have said "Exhausted," and he would have said, "So, take a roaster, it's easy!" There would have been help. Contact. That market is gone. All the markets like it are gone. Shopping becomes the experience a machine could have. Sucking the support from our lives. While we sit still they take away the guts of the thing. We don't notice until later. We don't vote for this kind of compartment life.

I worry about this. I'm worried. We all worry. Isn't there something else to do? What? Who will notice if we're not in line, all lined up in a row? Why do we put the dynamite around our own heads, light the fuse, and hope for rain?

Oh! Suppose we didn't stop the leaks? Suppose we let the cracks gape, let the seams pull apart, let the bones crack with the stretching of the mind. The release of the long pent up paved over flow rolling relentlessly seaward. Is there no place for the torrent? So full of feeling. From every subterranean spring, from the wet banks of underground rivers the currents come hurrying steadily together picking up sand and rock and running with it, rolling over and over itself.

What's lurking? *(A deep laugh.)* Swimming in and out of lungs and skin.

(Helen begins to bash at the wall with a hammer or a crowbar. Whole sections of plaster fall away, creating a big hole.) Suppose I howled with anger and joy and danced whenever I felt like it. In the supermarket, for instance. We could howl at the statehouse and waltz in the supermarket. *(She dances. She laughs. She looks into the hole. She steps back from it, shaken.)*

45

Babe

CAROLYN GAGE

(Babe Didrikson, a young lesbian athlete, is shooting baskets in the deserted gymnasium of Beaumont High in Beaumont, Texas. It's 1930, and she has just been approached by Melvin Jackson McCombs, the recruiter for the Golden Cyclones, a professional women's basketball team in Dallas. Babe has no idea who he is.)

BABE: They wouldn't let me pass the ball . . . Because coach says . . . (*Mimicking*) "Every girl on the team should have her chance with the ball." She'd rather have five girls in a row miss the hoop than have me put those five in by myself. And then she says, "Well, it's only a game, Babe." Hell, don't I know that? And ain't the object of the game to win? I mean if we ain't tryin' to do that, then I don't know what the hell we're doin' out there on the court. How do you think I feel when I have to watch us lose a game I could have won? It's bad enough we gotta play by girls' rules. (*Melvin doesn't understand.*) What do I mean? I mean we're not allowed to play full court, that's what I mean. We gotta stop on his center line like it's a game of "Mother-May-I" or something. You know what I could do if I could play full court? Hell, I wouldn't have to worry about whether or not anybody passed me the ball, because I wouldn't never let nobody else have it. I could play center, guard, and forward all at the same time, and play them a damn sight better than they're gettin' played now by the rest of the team. Do you have any idea what it feels like to have a clear court ahead of you, and have the ball, and see that hoop just shinin' at you like the pot at the end of the rainbow, and then get to that center line and have to put

46

on the brakes, and wait, *wait* for somebody to get in the right position just so you can pass it? Do you know what that feels like? Yeah, pretty frustratin' is right! And I'll tell you another thing that's pretty frustratin'—this business about "traveling with the ball." You don't see no rule like that in the boys' game. They get to have the ball as long as they want and go with it as far as they want. But us, we get three bounces and then it's pass or . . . (*She lets out a shrill, two-finger whistle.*) "Traveling!" (*She whirls her arms, demonstrating the call.*) You just break yourself free, get a little momentum goin', and (*Another whistle.*) . . . there's that whistle! Penalty! What kind of shit is that? Why don't they come right out with it and tie our shoelaces together? And then people have the nerve to say that girls' basketball ain't as interesting to watch, because there ain't no star players, and that's cause girls ain't no athletes. Like to see boys get to be star players with all that stop-and-start shit. That just smokes me. You think that's funny, don't you? And don't give me that crap about the female organs. (*Melvin is taken aback.*) The female organs—you know, the "delicate female organs . . ." which is the excuse for all these stupid rules. I ain't never gonna have no babies, so don't give me that crap about them female organs.

47

Lardo Weeping

TERRY GALLOWAY

(Dinah LaFarge, an intellectual crackpot, recognizes that her continued existence in American culture is less than a given. Fat, frowsy, agoraphobic, and ungainfully self-employed, she's got just five lousy bucks to last her the rest of her life.)

DINAH: Of course I have a weird fix on the world. Look at me. *(She makes a slow pirouette to let them have their fill.)* I am the Anti Fashion, The Destroyer. A walking offense to the well-dressed and the well-heeled. Well, this *(She waves to encompass body and dress)* has its reasons. This is the involuntary response to that phrase, "You can't be too rich or too thin." Whenever I hear that something in me goes boing! I am overcome with a feverish desire to eat the rich! The Hunts, the Rockefellers, the Gettys, the Carnegie-Mellons! *(The word "Melon" rings her food alarm.)* Melon? Mmm, moment. *(She heads for the icebox, gets out a piece of watermelon, consults her chart and is delighted.)* Freefoods.

I despise the idiot rich. But then I despise the idiot poor too. The poor lack the proper anger. If only they could take pride in being exactly the unchic thing. I'm of the school that believes that a fondness for the wrong fabrics is the true mark of genius. Ah, I pity polyester. If I didn't wear it who in god's name would? Now it can't just be me—don't you think that the world has become increasingly populated by well-to-do bimbos who have nothing but excellent taste? And frankly, I think there is something very wrong with a world in which the shoes on a woman's feet are more interesting than the thoughts in her head. But I am one of a vanishing breed. Individuals of my breadth and caliber are going the way of the late great dodo.

Pardon me. For those of you not in the know, the dodo is a now extinct, of course, much maligned, flightless fowl, the size of a hefty turkey with a rather more bulbous bill. I identify with that bird. Cornered by a savage world. Driven into hiding. Losing in the end. But of course she was a good sport about it all. I'm able to imagine her last days all too well . . . *(She takes on the aspect of the dodo. The material in quotation marks is spoken in the voice of the dodo.)*

Nearsightedness made her friendly
"Hello"
Coming up close to see things for herself
"Hello."
Still she suspected the many dangers.
The world was an open jaw.
"Uh-oh."
She retired to the island of Rodriguez
this last noble Dodo
and laid her last
"ack"
exact
"whah"
one egg
"woo!"

And sat with it
long after the yoke had spoiled,
nudging it with her honker of a bill,
whooing, "Come out, come out!
Your mother's waiting!"

But then I suppose
in a certain, clumsy flightless way
all became quite clear.

Dodo's were a sunny sort.
Untemperamental.
Not known to pine away
like super sensitive porpoise
or touchy whale.

Shunning the behavior
of rude panther
shrilling eagle
thuggish bear,
she chose then
just to sit there
a little to the left of her nest
and puzzle over that empty
empty egg.

(A look of alarm passes over her face. She fires off a letter.)
Pressing Correspondence of the Day
Series D Letter One Hundred Twenty-six

To the Environmental Protection Agency:
    I would like if at all possible to be declared an endangered species. I am a rather large, intellectual, quite sexual woman of independent means who absolutely refuses to procreate until the breach in the ozone layer is mended! Please reply ASAP. My biological time clock is running out.
    Hastily,

(She consults the audience.)
Do you think I'll sound like a crank? Hmmph.
    Tis the majority in this as all prevails
        Assent and you are sane
    Demur—you're straightway dangerous
        And handled with a chain!
Emily Dickinson. Another woman who had sense enough to stay in her room and view with alarm.

I have to admit, I worry that I'm becoming less like Emily Dickinson and more like some demented combination of Sylvia Plath and Mommie Dearest—a sort of Sylvia Rath. I could end up in some loony bin shouting invective poetry about my poor, late mother—

Mommie! You! Of course it was you!
Who played the boogie and whooed!
Who beat my soul to a pulp!
Who swallowed my little red heart in a gulp!
Mommie! Mommie! You two bit shit!
When I was young you kicked the bucket!
Fuck it! Fuck it! Fuck it! Fuck it!

Good God. I am going mad. *(She rushes to the icebox, grabs a chicken drumstick, eyes the picture of the dodo.)* Protein. *(She marks that on her chart and eats.)*

Maybe I should make an effort to go out, mingle, become one with the multitudes. Euuuu. No. The last time I became one with the multitudes I was nine. I was a member of a gang. A gang of marauding boys as it were. See when I was nine I was a bit like Little Lotta—unbelievably strong. And because I could beat the shit out of the boys and I had the requisite foul mouth they quickly embraced me as one of their own. Well, one day we boys decided we'd capture a girl. So we captured a weak one and we all took turns sitting on top of her. The idea was to sit on top of her and kiss her hard enough to get her mouth open and then let go with a huge gob of spit. That was all. So we were taking turns sitting on top of her and she was crying for her mother of course but who could understand her? Her mouth was full of spit— "Haolbulb! Haolbulb!" And then it was my turn. I had enjoyed the camaraderie up until then—I'd been sucking on my cheeks to get the longest most drooling piece of spit—it had become something of a contest by then—So I got on top of her and . . . *(She makes as if to spit.)* And of course I knew

51

her. Oh I didn't really know her. But I knew the look in her eyes. I knew the look in her eyes. *(She puts the drumstick down, wipes her fingers.)* Power makes me uneasy I suppose. Just not quite ruthless enough.

And wasn't that Dickinson's problem? Just not quite ruthless enough? And where did her sensitivity get her? Locked in her own attic room. Her talents ignored, her efforts thwarted. The world dismissive. No, worse! The world absolutely indifferent!

Jigsaw

ANDRA GORDON

HAYLEY: On my birthday candles, I wished for Emma. Emma, with eyes the color of swimming-pool water. Emma, smelling of sandalwood and baby lotion. Emma in the morning, in boys Levi's blown out at the knees, trying on one after another of my shirts, and dropping them at the foot of the bed in a big, soft pile. Emma, skin tasting powdery and a little bit sweet. Emma in the afternoon, dancing in the kitchen to that winter's song, all backbeat and vague romantic lyrics. Emma in from the cold, kicking off her shoes. Emma shivering on the ferry, legs pulled up and shoulder blades pressing ridges into her jacket. Emma on the windowsill, painting her toenails.

I wished for her, and I got her, and for three day-glow months I carried the secret of Emma around with me like a silk camisole beneath an old sweatshirt. Walking with Emma down miles of rainy sidewalk, fingers curled around her belt loop, aware of nothing but the nearness of her hip as it stretched and flexed beneath the soft, old denim.

The geography of Emma's body was so new to me, so far from anything I had ever known, that I felt like an explorer, forging a trail from jaw to throat to collar bone, feeling for landmarks and wishing vaguely for a map. Across the warm slope of belly then nowhere to go but down, as if each of my cells were a compass, all pointing in the same direction. And I knew absolutely, knew everything without knowing how. But as soon as I began to wonder, began to feel for a guideline, I felt the ground giving out beneath my feet, the compass spinning in dizzy circles. Emma's body was suddenly all quicksand, all dark swamp with snakes in the water. I was shaking, my teeth slamming together, until Emma laughed, and pulled me level with her, wrapping her arms and legs around me as if it was cold that was making me shiver. She kissed my forehead and whispered: "What's to be scared of, Hayley? I'm just the same as you. No mysteries here." But I only held to her tighter, until the jigsaw fit of my leg around her hip hit me with a new surge of terror that made me pull her even closer, sinking myself deeper and deeper in a whirlpool of understanding everything and trusting nothing. Not even Emma's fingers, strumming up and down the xylophone of my spine as casually as if it belonged to her.

Every morning, I would wake up in the dark, and lie in bed curled around Emma, too tired to move, too wired to close my eyes, and talk to her sleeping back. And every day, I would ask the same question, first in a whisper, then a little bit louder: "How will I go down in your history, Emma?" She would stretch a little bit, and I'd lean in closer: "Your history. Your own personal history. Where will I fit in?" And every time, she'd say the same thing: "I don't know, Hayley. The same place I'll go into yours, I guess." Then she'd close her eyes and slide back into her dream, thinking I would follow. But I wouldn't, couldn't do anything but lie there with my stomach in a snarl, because it wasn't true—I know it now, and I knew it then, and so did she, she was just being lazy. Emma was the beginning of a story for me. I knew that she'd have a chapter in my history, that she'd be right there in the table of contents. And I knew that someone had this same place in Emma's history, someone who was burned into Emma just as she was burned into me. And it made me crazy, because I wanted that place, wanted my mark on Emma. And I knew that whatever Emma said, I might not even be a footnote.

At the restaurant, I said that yes, absolutely, I understood. Outside, I didn't flinch when Emma kissed me on the cheek. I walked home, listened to my messages, and fed the cat. Then I sat down on my bed, took off Emma's boots, and threw them against the ceiling until the paint began to scatter down in thick, dirty flakes, and a chunk of plaster hit me square in the forehead. So finally, I had something real to cry about.

While I was sitting in the coffee shop, the song came on the radio like some sick joke, and I willed myself not to notice, not even to look. Willed my heart to stop beating double-time and my eyes to focus on the two boys laughing by the window, the girl reading at the counter, the baby at the next table, rubbing applesauce into his hair. Anything but the image of Emma in the train station, kissing me full on the lips, then disappearing down the dirty stairs, leaving me with nothing but a closet full of blouses that smelled so much like her, I couldn't wear anything but the thin white t-shirts that I bought in three-packs at the drugstore. I waited for the song to end, paid my bill, and walked out into the morning, shivering Emma out of my body in the brand-new spring.

One Hundred Women

KRISTINA HALVORSON

NINA: There is a place, inside me, where one hundred women live. It is full of light and anything but lonely. I keep Kelly there, and my mother, and my third grade teacher Mrs. Rhodes, and my best friend Christine from eighth grade, and all the other women who have touched me somehow. There are so many. I close my eyes and I imagine them sitting close together in interlocked circles, talking, holding each other, laughing. Inside me, they know one another. Perhaps some of them are the same. When I am alone I laugh along with them, wrap my arms tight around my breasts, hugging myself, drawing them closer to me. It's only when the men invite themselves in—into the room, into the laughter, even into me—that the links of this, this woman-chain are weakened. The men call, and the women come. The circles break apart. I begin to feel like I am coming apart, that my parts are loose and dangling. I hug myself even tighter and re-name, re-imagine my women. There is at least one hundred of me, without them, I think—Nina the scholar, Nina the poet, the student, the counselor, the lover. I wait for the strongest one of me to step forward so that I can find the right words, summon up the elusive courage to bring back the women I've somehow lost.

And yet, despite my frantic attempts to call forth the philosopher, the diplomat, the encouraging friend, somehow it is always Nina the lover who wins out. She gives in to the romance, releases the women to their princes and saviors. Her mother re-marries, her schoolteacher moves away with her husband, her best friend falls head over heels for a ninth grader. And Nina the lover nods; Nina the lover knows. She lowers her head and waits for her turn to come, and in the meantime the women fall away from her one by one by one by one . . .

What can I do but embrace her, this lover who lives inside my chest, and bid farewell to the other ninety-nine of me, who always retreat in silence.

Affair On The Air

SUSAN HANSELL

(A woman, late thirties, sits with her hands in her lap and her legs together at the ankle. As she talks she shifts back and forth in her chair whenever she tells a particularly uncomfortable or embarrassing detail in her story.)

I called a radio talk show last night. *(Pause, shrugging.)* It's not something I'd normally do, but—*(pause)*—I was feeling out of sorts—*(pause)*—and well—*(pause, looking down briefly)*—lonely.

(Shifting, then upbeat.) The show is called Affair On The Air—*(smile)*—and it's similar to the old television program The Dating Game—*(pause, smile fading)*—except that—it's on the radio. *(Pause)* Well, what happens is, a lot of people call up who want to meet someone special—*(pause, then quicker)*—but who just don't seem to be able to do it on their own—*(smile)*—so they talk to the M.C. of the show, and she asks them what kind of person they are—*(pause)*—and what kind of person they'd like to meet—*(pause, smile fading)* — and then she puts them on hold. *(Long pause, then quick again.)* And then a lot of *other* people call up who liked what the *first* people said—*(pause, thinking about it)* —and then the M.C. interviews *them*, and so—*(pause)*—everybody gets to hear their prospective dates talk—*(pause)*—on the radio.

(Smile, shyly, upbeat.) So I won a spot on the show, and the M.C. asked me what kind of person I wanted to meet—*(pause)*—and I told her—*(pause)*—I just want to meet a man who can talk. *(Pause, shifting.)* And she said, is that *all?* *(Pause)* And I said, yes. *(Pause, shifting, and portraying the annoyance of the M.C.)* And she said, don't you care about

what he does for a living? Or what his interests are? Or what he likes to do for fun? Or what he *sleeps* in? *(Pause, shifting, shy again.)* And I said, no, not really. Not as long as he has his own feelings about life and can talk about them. *(Pause, shifting and taking on M.C.'s tone again.)* And then she said, *well,* that's a pretty *tall* order, isn't it? I don't know many men like that myself. *(Pause, quietly.)* And then she didn't say anything for a long time.

(Pause, then upbeat again.) But then she did ask me to talk a little bit about myself, and so I told her, well—*(pause, shy)*—after going through one marriage and divorce and learning from that—*(pause, shifting)*—and then after going through two years of therapy and learning from that—*(Pause, shy, shifting)*—and then learning how to have orgasms and learning from that, well—*(pause)*—I've realized—the important thing is to find someone you can talk to and who can talk to you too.

(Pause. Portraying M.C.'s irritation.) And then she said, *OK*—*(pause)*—but *most* people who call this show want to meet someone who likes to *parachute* and *scuba dive*— *(pause)*—or gourmet cook and backpack in the wilderness— *(pause, irritation increasing)*—or sell computer programs and electrical equipment! *(Pause, shifting, and then down-beat)* And so I said, Well—*(pause)*—I'm just trying to be honest. *(Pause)* And then I heard her talking under her breath about—how did I make it past the screening interview— *(pause)*—but then she said, oh well, what can I do about it now? *(Pause, then smiling a little.)* And so she put me on hold.

(Pause) So I waited. *(Pause, upbeat.)* And *a lot* of *men* called up—*(pause, trying to explain but confused)*—saying they wanted to meet thin women who weren't needy but were wild and crazy. *(Pause)* And so I waited, and then a lot of women called up—*(pause, increasing confusion)*—saying they wanted to meet men who owned their own micro-chip businesses in Milpitas, California, and who were athletic. *(Pause)* And I waited—*(pause)*—and I listened to them while I was on hold.

59

(Pause) And I waited—*(pause)*—and I waited—*(pause)*—but no one called for me.

(Pause) So this morning—*(pause)*—I decided—*(pause, smiling)* I'd buy—*(pause)* —a designer jump suit—*(pause)*—and join—*(pause)*—an aerobics class. *(Pause, smile slowly fades and puzzled look arrives on face as the lights fade out.)*

Don't

SUSAN HANSELL

(Black stage. Quietly, the sound of a music box begins, plays "Hymne L'Amour" for one minute before slowly winding down to stop mid-note. Brief pause, then the box is slammed shut. Light slowly rises to dimly lit stage. A woman sits in a wooden rocker, rocking slowly, rhythmically, for about one additional minute. When she speaks there is no one focal point for her words, no one figure to whom she speaks. Rather, it is a general relationship which she invokes.)

(Softly, with forefinger to lips.) Sssssshhhhhhhhh. Sssssshhhhhhhhhh. Sssshhhhhhhhhh. Ssssssshhhhhhhhhhhhhhhhhhhhhhhhhhhhhh. *(Whispering)* Be quiet. Don't—*(pause)*—don't—*(pause)*—don't talk—*(pause)*—don't talk about it. . . . . . Sssssshhhhhhhh . . . Just sssssshhhhhhhhhhhhh . . .

(Long pause, then rocking suddenly ceases. Woman sits up straight, alert, faces forward, pauses. Then she begins looking about right, left, up, down, etc., as she directs her voice to multiple foci, with harsh, clipped sounds.) Sh! Sh! Sh! Sh! Sh! Sh! Sh! Sh! Sh! Sh! Sh! Sh! Sh! Sh! *(Then falls back into the rocker, exhausted, slowly rocking.)* Sssshhhhhhh . . . Sssshhhhhhhhhh . . . Just . . . close your eyes . . . and . . . ssshhhhhh . . . ssshhhh . . . ssshhhhhhhh . . .

(Pause, rocking, eyes closed.) No. (Soft.) No. Oh, no. No. No-no. No. Oh, no. *(Harsh)* No! NO! NO! *(Pause, sing-song.)* No-no. No-no-no. No-no-no-no-no-. *(Pause, softly.)* No. No. No. *(Pause, angry.)* No! No! *(Sitting up straight, eyes glaring, voice hard)* NO! NO! NO! *(Pause, still mad.)* SH! SH! SH! Be Quiet! Sh! Keep your voice down! Sh! Sh! Keep it down!

61

(Pause, sitting back in the chair again, voice sing-song, but as a warning.) I'm warning you . . . I'm warning you to keep it down. You better be quiet, you better shush.

(Pause, then begins to rock like a little girl, with her feet up on the chair, voice coy, girlish.) Don't wake Daddy up! Don't wake him up! Be quiet, be careful, be quiet! Daddy's sleeping! Don't wake Daddy up! Don't wake Daddy up or you'll get it! You'll get it if you wake him up! *(Voice becoming more shrill.)* You'll get it! Don't wake Daddy up or you'll get it! You'll get it if you wake him up you'll get it! *(Then giggling, wild, almost singing, childishly.)* Ssshhhhhhhh! Ssshh-sshhh-ssshhhh! Sssshhhhh! Ssshhhh!

(Pause, falling back into the chair, tired, rocking very slowly, voice adult, motherly or maternally soft.) Daddy's little girl. Daddy's little angel. Little angel. Daddy's little girl. Little girl. Little angel. Daddy's little girl. Ssshhh baby sshhh. Be quiet now ssshhh baby sshhhhh. Ssshhhhhhh . . . Sshhhhhh-hhhhhh . . . Sssssssshhhhhhhh . . .

(Pause, rising slowly up, rocking stops, she sits up straight, raising voice.) SH! SH! SH! *(Pause, then shouting.)* I warned you! I warned you to keep it down! Why you little . . . *(Pause, furiously.)* I oughta take this wrapper and—you'd like that wouldn't you? Wouldn't you? Wouldn't you? *(Pause, voice lower.)* Now you just shut your mouth.

(Pause, goes back to rocking, muttering to herself. Muttering gradually becomes audible.) Little bitch. Little bitchy bitch bitch. Little bitch. *(Pause, then a quiet litany of clipped, muttered insults.)* Bitch. Whore. Slut. Cunt. Slit. Hole. Bag. Why-you-old-bag. Bag. Old bag. Dry old hole. Old. Old. Old. Old. Old. Old . . .

(Rocks in silence, 15 seconds. Stops rocking. Sits in silence, 15 seconds. Slowly begins rocking again, slowly, rhythmically; voice low and soft.) Ssshhhhhhh . . . ssshhhhhhh . . . ssshhhhhhhhh . . . just . . . close your eyes and . . . sssshhhhhh . . . sssssshhh-hhh . . . sssshhhhhhhh . . . just . . . ssshhhh . . . close your eyes and . . . sssshhhh . . . sssshhhhh . . . *(Pause, rocking, voice*

comforting.) Such a poor, poor thing . . . Such a poor, poor thing. Poor thing, poor thing. Sshhhhhh. Just ssshhhh . . . Such a poor, poor thing. Poor thing. Poor thing. Sssshhhhhhh . . . ssshhhh . . . Sssshhhhh . . . sshhhhhhhh . . . *(Continues, then voice slowly fades, then rocks to silence, 15 seconds. 15 additional seconds sitting in silence, still, then lights slowly fade to black.)*

Eggs and Bones

CONSTANCE C. HAROLD

(In the studio they once shared, filled with African sculptures and the tools of the restorer's art, Delmar reveals to her former lover Richard how his refusal to accept responsibility led to her disastrous abortion.)

DELMAR: It must be nice to simply wipe it away. You know, I waited for you. I shut the door, and pulled the shades, and I waited for you.

I didn't eat. I didn't sleep or take a shower. I waited for you for two weeks, waiting for you to say, yeah Del, let's get married or baby, it's not the right time or even . . . how do I know the kid is mine? I waited for you to say something, do something, be a man. And after two weeks I got up and I took a shower, and I called the doctor. And the next morning on a cold metal table, he dug inside me and scraped out one tiny egg that wasn't even flesh and bone yet.

And I went home and I bled, and I cried, and I nearly died from the pain. But that pain stuck by me, when nothing else did, it clung to me like a dear and dedicated friend, until I couldn't see, and couldn't breathe anything but blood. So they took me and put me back on the table and tore out all the rot, all the infection, and all the eggs, the babies I can never have, and they sent me home where the phone didn't ring and the door didn't open, and you did not come.

And you ask me, what's wrong with me in that self-serving voice of yours, and you ask what I want? I want all the blood, and the ash and the bones of the ancestors you've used for your own small purpose, to suck out your breath and crack open your chest until the beating of your heart becomes a cold dead thing like mine. I want your seed to dry up in your crotch. I want you to bleed. And I want your phone to never ring and your door to never open, and then you come and ask what's wrong with me.

Napoleon's China

ANN HASKELL

(Claire believes it unseemly to speak to others about one's personal tragedy, so she is telling the man she loves about her mother's death while he sleeps. She is convinced he is unconsciously absorbing everything she says and feels closer to her because of it.)

CLAIRE: When my mother died, I was sure it was a dream. I packed my duffel bag to go to the airport, I thought I was packing clothes, but it turned out I packed a wrench, a hammer, four screwdrivers, an electric drill, all the tools I had in the apartment. I must have known what kind of help I needed, but I sure was sorry I didn't bring any clean underpants.

The day she died, hundreds and hundreds of people flooded into the house. I went into the study, and looked out the window. I was looking for someone that I liked, someone I could talk to about her. I had known these people all my life, but I didn't *recognize* any of them. I picked out two or three people, because of their hair, or their eyes, one woman because of the way she held her pocketbook—in front of her, close—some detail that reminded me of her, and made me think, this is the person I should talk to. I brought them back into the study, but the minute I started talking, I knew I'd made a mistake.

It was so hot that day. Everything outside that window was parched and dry. I did wonder if the ground would be too hard for them to dig a hole and bury her. I wanted her back.

I decided to write the eulogy. A nice one. One that she'd like her friends to hear. Vaguely social, high spirited and above all, *dear*. Everybody said I was the one to do it. Nobody could tell a story like me. Everybody said mother would want me to talk, to say good-bye to her. But she was dead. I sat up an entire night and could not come up with one thing to say. I ended up copying something out of Eudora Welty's memoirs of *her* happy childhood, and read it to a huge gathering in a real pious and sweet voice. It was effective. All those friends who really didn't know her squeezed out a few tears.

This is my crime. I let her down. I could not come up with one story. All my life, I'd been filled with stories. And now, when I wanted to give her the best story of her life, I could not write a single word.

You know, I am not guilty for the things I should be guilty for. I'm guilty for failing. I am guilty for my deep silence that day. For that, I can never be forgiven.

The Patient

LOUISE HECK-RABI

(Susannah Lyme is a patient in a mental hospital.)

SUSANNAH: Miz Lydia's house looked good from the alley. Its backside better than the picture of the Courthouse downtown. White, tall up into heaven, clean and good-smelling as the laundry I delivered twice a week in my wagon. The Askew family wash was a precious cargo worth two or three dollars. Ma had a sign in front of our house: WASHING AND IRONING. She boiled the clothes and beat them with the paddle she used on us. She could iron fast! Nine white men's shirts, long sleeves, in an hour.

Miz Askew liked Ma's work. She like me first time she saw me on the veranda off the kitchen, waiting till the housekeeper counted pieces, me wondering 'bout that smell of molasses just baked and warm. I skipped to the veranda corner finding three pans laid out to cool. Raisin-face cookies. Staring and hoping to steal—"What is your name, child?" I turned like a top, bent my knees like Ma said, and looked up at her. "Susannah Lyme. M'am." She was the cleanest, coolest looking lady I'd ever seen. "How many are there at home?" she asked, putting my name after it, "Susannah," like it was special. I lied. "Five," I said, looking at the cookies. The housekeeper come out the door with three dollars in her hand. "Fanny, please. You will give Susannah seven cookies to take home." Fanny gave me the dollars and a hard look, then went back in, letting the screened door slam this time.

"I am Mrs. Askew," she told me what I already suspicioned. I made half a curtsey. "Yes, M'am." The bag in Fanny's hands crackled with the cookies' weight. "How old

68

are you, Susannah?" she asked next. "Twelve," I spoke up, "Miz Askew." My middle grew tight like it did before tests in school. Still, I felt good with her. We stood there awhile just looking at each other till Fanny folded the top of the bag and cleared her throat. Miz Askew thanked her. I got the cookies. And still she considered me like I was something special she could figure out with her china-blue eyes. "On Saturdays, sometimes on Sunday afternoons, I give large dinner parties. Please ask your mother if you could help at table and with Fanny in the kitchen." Even before she finished I blurted out, "Oh, Miz Askew! I'm sure it'll be alright! So long as it don't interfere with my schoolin'." She smiled then and so did I. "You will ask her permission?" Those words soft as dandelion fluff under the smile. I nodded. "Yes, Miz Askew." She turned. So did I. Almost forgot! "Thank you for the cookies, Miz Askew." She really smiled then. "Please tell your mother that you were given two instead of one, as a reward for your work in pulling the wagon." Her face didn't change. I knew we had a special understanding. And I would die if Ma didn't let me wait table for her. Ma did. But I couldn't fall behind in my homework because of my jobs. I still had to deliver laundry on weekdays. But every cent I earned went into my very own bank account. Imagine! An education fund! Ma said I was the best learner in the whole school, about as smart as Waldo, her oldest, never saw him till I was in college.

Waiting table at the Askews made living easier. I took home food and clothes that didn't fit. I took home memories of seven course dinners for twenty guests lasting three hours. Fanny and the rest of us could do without Mr. Askew, a red-faced ox with heavy feet and heavier voice. Miz Lydia said we could call her that. She called me Sukey, saying it suited me. We marveled at her powers of sweetness to endure him. He'd put you straight if the soup was cool! We hated him. Loved her. Those were the best years of my life, so busy I could hardly feel the seasons changing on my face. I sang in the choir, I played a maid in the Senior play. I was elected to the National Honor Society. I was cheerleader, I helped Ma wash and iron clothes, yet I treasured most my hours with Miz Lydia. I deposited my money in the bank (Ma wouldn't let me take any out). I was going to college—at least for a year— I would have to work, but I was used to it. I wanted to be somebody, wanted to raise Ma up out of that cellar, away from the copper boiler forever. But I was afraid to leave Ma and Miz Lydia. I couldn't fathom how I would live without those four o'clock Sunday dinners where the race question was discussed when I was in the pantry or the kitchen, and hushed when I came in. But I heard plenty!

Miz Lydia kept tellin' me I was tops. She wrote letters of recommendation. She said I could be anything I wanted to be, if I sought it and fought for it. She meant working, studying, praying, not messin' around on the front porch on warm spring nights. She meant not having boyfriends like Doremus and Geneva, she meant ignoring the hoot-calls of every man any color who looked you over in the street.

A leatherbound address book with the address of the Askews written in it, and a five dollar bill was my going-away-to-college gift. Miz Lydia gave it to me herself. She looked confused, her eyes clouding up, but still smiling. She took both my hands. "Remember me, Sukey. This door (it had to be the back door, I knew that) is open to you, always. Write to me. Come if you need work or help. My hands are tied in many ways (that was the ox, Mr. Askew, Lord-of-the-Manor, Nigger-hater, who knew Negroes including me hated him). There are times when I cannot do as I choose." I mumbled thanks, stumbled down the steps, my legs too long for the sidewalk. Too long for the undersized desks in the classrooms of Belmont College, one of those all-black little Southern institutions, trying its best, oh Lord, to educate. I worked in the Library. I lived in a room. I studied. Everything came easy. My straight A's put me on the Dean's List. I clipped the List from the paper and mailed it home to

70

Ma. I might get a tuition scholarship! I was lonely and home-sick, but ready for new worlds.

At student mixers I chewed chips, drank beer, got absorbed in discussions of politics, pacifism, civil rights. I attended forums, rallies, symposia. I read about the riots, the Mississippi murders, I boarded the College bus one Friday to go to a sit-in at the Public Library the next two towns over, where stand-up only service was the rule for Negroes. My first taste of violence was the ice water from the firehoses aimed at us. The local jail was crowded and too small, our sentences light, all of us back to Monday classes like nothing happened. I never wrote Ma or Miz Lydia about my adventures, I did write about my job, my profs, about Neal, his friends who organized bus rides to march with banners in D.C. picketing Air Force bases and submarine launchings. My own participation much less—I had to work! I promised Neal I'd demonstrate at home on Easter vacation, for open housing. We heard rumors of real trouble—but Neal claimed, "Always rumors, doll. Don't believe it!" Doremus and Geneva said No when I asked them to demonstrate with us. And meet Neal. I walked alone to the Church basement, seeing the College bus in the parking lot. We got instructions. Neal's words were, "March and sing at the home of the Housing Commissioner." I held a banner and his hand.

Oh No! Not that beautiful white Georgian-style mansion I knew so well! I couldn't walk. I stumbled, swayed. The police watched us. We circled outside that tall iron fence, singing the words Neal had written to the tune of "Dixie." They say they will never know who threw the firebomb that exploded at the front door. Pow! Like that. Seems everybody was just waiting for that sound to let loose, to rampage like animals from opened cages, a signal to throw our candles toward the house, to push through the closed gates, scale the fence, to scream. More explosions—what were they?—shattered my ears. No, no, not this house, not even if old ox-faced Askew was Housing Commissioner! "What's the

71

matter, Sukey? Get with it!" Neal yelled. He rushed me along, police closing in on us, some on horses. I smelled smoke. The house was burning! Staring, I saw servants' faces framed in the windows with flames behind them. Oh, Miz Lydia! I am your Sukey! Do you understand? Do you know I'm not to blame? Brick throwing started. Why? Neal dragged me down. In an ocean, surging, Neal and I, in a body-pressed wave swirling to that pillared veranda double front doors, wood a-smoking, windows smashing. Miz Lydia, where are you? It was Monday. No dinner in the oval dining room for twenty guests today! Run out, Miz Lydia! Go out back! Won't see you! Let old ox-face get his due, but not you! Please, God! Not you!

Crack! A pistol shot stunned the air, stopped Time, as if the voice of God had spoken one holy word. "Look!" Neal pointed, with pride, "That white bastard's shot!" Snowflakes melted in my open mouth, my eyes stuck on old Ox-face himself, in the shrubs at the side of the house! Askew trying to run away! Like flies buzzin' a wave surged toward him, police swinging billy sticks, horses' hooves making muck of the Askew lawn. "Some screwball's got a gun!" someone shouted. I screamed. There was my Miz Lydia! Cool and clean like always, running out from that veranda side door pulling on her coat, dipping her chin against thickening snow. Did she see ox-face? Did the rage of the mob scare her? She paused as if deciding these questions, then ran. I called out to warn her, "Miz Askew! Go back! Miz Askew! Go back!" Her face turned—did she hear me?—Neal turned, angry, astonished. Crack! She fell in a heap! My arms stretched out to her, dropped from my sight by a shot from an anonymous pistol! "I've got to help her! Let me go! I've got to get to Miz Lydia!" I shouted. Neal held on to me. I wrestled him, broke free, struggled through the smell of sweaty bodies, forced myself into the ring of black bodies leaning over her, not helping. Oh God! Let me die so she can live! I struggled closer just as cops rode closer, billy sticks swinging. I held both her hands, blood from her back, when the first blow swished my head. I screamed so hard I could not close my mouth. On my knees I cradled her, the next blow hit harder, blood trickling from my chest. I'm sorry, Miz Lydia, I'm sorry, I whispered in my own echo chamber, I didn't know, I didn't know, I hurt, I hurt! Oh please God, let me die so she can live! Oh please God, let me die so she can live!

What Mary Says After

NAOMI HISAKO IIZUKA
(from *Skin)*

(Mary is a young woman. She waits in the early morning dimness. She has been up all night.)

MARY: And then later, this is way later, after it got dark, we'd go down to this place out by morley field. it was like a meadow, all flat and long grass and empty, nobody anywhere, nothing, and it'd be me and this guy sean I used to know, I forget his last name, and he and I, I was like maybe 14 and I was all wearing my hair all ratted out back then, and this crazy black stuff all around my eyes like I was a real live punk, or something, even though there was no such thing anymore cause that happened like a thousand years ago, before I was born, before I even remember, and I was running all around the city and hanging out by mission bay, ditching and getting high, and everybody was all, do this, do that, in my face, and I was all fuck that, I didn't even want to hear any of that shit, cause you don't know me, you don't know shit about me.

so then, see, sean and me, we'd go, we'd go down to this place out by morley field, out by where the airport was, and we'd smoke some thai stick, and we'd get real high, we'd get so fucked up we couldn't even move, and then we'd lie on our backs for a long time, we'd lie there and watch the planes take off and land right above us, so close, that we could see right into the bellies of these huge planes, right into the engines, and it was the most amazing thing, and the sound was so loud, it was everywhere and inside, like something splitting apart inside me.

and then later, sean would roll on top of me and we'd

make out. it was cold and late, and I'd get gravel and dirt in my panties and little cuts from pressing down against all the rocks and glass and shit on the ground, and I'd think about the planes taking off and landing above me, and above the planes, the clouds and the sky, and above that, all the stars and planets and galaxies millions of miles away, and on and on like that until all there was was black—

Excerpt from *White Noises*

SHANNON JACKSON

(Audience is seated before a playing space that contains a large plexiglass structure, eight to nine feet high, five feet wide, and five feet deep. It is enclosed on three sides. Shannon, wearing a full-length black slip, stands just inside the entrance with a stool behind her. Circles of different make-up colors have been painted on the left and right plexiglass walls. Pieces of lingerie in various "flesh" tones hang on the inside back wall. A paintbrush and some make-up, perfume, lotion, and spray bottles are lined up on the floor. The following monologue is delivered out to the audience, with shifts in focus, voice, gesture, and comportment to indicate changes in character, time, and location. For the most part, it runs at a very fast pace and different voices constantly interrupt and compete with each other. Sometimes these voices are not always directly represented on the page and run counter to the punctuation marks.)

SHANNON: The question of where to begin is an interesting one. Because when you go to tell a story . . . about something that happened to you, I mean . . . you realize that while you were experiencing it, you didn't know you were in a story.

And so consequently, you didn't know it had begun when it all began.

"I think you should have it published. I think you should consider having it published and you should at least send it to the graduate student essay competition at the Black Theatre Network." This suggestion from a professor about a paper I wrote. I was flattered. I sent it.

I sent it to the Black Theatre Network, thinking well if anyone questioned me I could always say that my professor said I should. *(Beat)* My professor said I should send the essay in, and my professor's black . . . so . . . you know . . . that goes to show.

So I sent it.

I sent it to the Black Theatre Network along with my address, phone number, university affiliation . . . and my name.

SHANNON JACKSON *(Writing J-A-C-K-S-O-N in make-up on the plexiglass.)*

JACKSON

The same name that had appeared on an undergraduate mailing asking me to join Stanford's Black Student Union.

The same name that appeared on a graduate student mailing asking me to join Northwestern's Black Alumni Association.

The same last name that appears on countless football and basketball jerseys.

The same name hooted by my parents' white friends at their Super Bowl Parties. *(Pointing to imaginary TV.)* "Oh, Oh. Jackson. A member of the family, Shannon."

(Reading horizontally.) "Dear Shannon Jackson, you have won the graduate student essay competition at the Black Theatre Network. Congratulations. Please join us to accept your award at our annual conference in Detroit."

I had won. I was flattered. I went.

I went to the Black Theatre Network. It was held in Detroit at the Westin Hotel in The Renaissance Center . . . *(In promotional voice while spreading skin lotion all over body.)* "THE RENAISSANCE CENTER! Where you can enjoy luxury accommodations while sampling cuisine from around the world—try Mexican at Cafe Rio, Greek at Dionysos, or for a good old American hamburger, try Hungry Harry's. Plus, the ladies can enjoy shopping at some of the finest designer stores and the expert services of our own health and beauty consultants. All this in one place, thousands of air-conditioned square footage under one glass roof."

77

The Renaissance Center!

(Breaking out of voice, back against the wall, wide eyes staring straight ahead.)

Once you're in you won't want to leave.

(Sits)

This I read in a pamphlet as I rode in a shuttle from the airport to the Westin Hotel. Several other people rode with me—four black people also obviously on their way to the Black Theatre Network. *(Embodying gesture with each verb.)* They were talking with each other, laughing, teasing each other, remembering the last time, and passing out registration forms. They all seemed to know each other. I wondered if I should pull out my Black Theatre Network registration form. You know, wave it in front of my face so that they would know that I was one of them. I decided to re-read the pamphlet.

While behind me were four white women. Four very inane white women also going to the Westin Hotel, for what reason I know not but they were very loud. *(Repeating above gestures with each verb.)* They were chatting with each other, giggling, teasing each other, telling funny stories, and passing out peppermint candies. They all seemed to know each other. I wondered if I should pull out my Black Theatre Network registration form. You know, wave it a little in front of my face so that they *(indicates forward)* wouldn't think that I was one of them *(indicates backward)*.

We all ended up in a line at the hotel reception desk. My black fellow riders going first; the white women behind me—remembering that time she dressed up as Miss America?—Oh, that was hilarious!—

Suddenly, one woman peered at me from behind my shoulder, looked at me and asked,

"Oh, are you undercoverwear?"

"Am I undercoverwear?"

She smiled . . . generously . . . she meant to be inclusive.

I didn't know how to answer the question.

"Ummm. No," I said . . . . "Are you?"

Yes, she is. She is undercoverwear. She is here for the Undercoverwear Convention. Lingerie saleswomen from around the country convene here every year.

"One thousand of us. We take over the place. We have fashion shows, workshops, cabarets, sing-a-longs. And no men. No husband in sight. We're just the ladies here."

They had come from far and wide, from lingerie salesrooms everywhere. *(Picking up perfume.)* Leaving shiny pink department stores where my high school friends and I would go to have women with moussed hair dressed in designer clothing spray us with the latest scent. "Do you want to try it, miss? It's flowery with a hint of citrus. Very feminine."

Where women with moussed hair dressed in white coats to stand behind counters to ask—"What skin type are you?"—and offered potions to suit a woman's individual needs.

(Pointing to left, right, and to own face throughout.)

Number one to tone, number two to tune, number three to tighten—Come on and pamper yourself. Make-up that shrinks pores, removes age spots, and hides unsightly lines all the while evening the skin tone to a healthy glow. Foundations in all colors—buff, peach, cream, rose, beige, ivory—after all, all women are not alike—light beige, dark beige, rose-beige, rose-buff, buff-ivory, ivory-cream, and natural?

(Leaning over to audience.)

After all, all women are not alike.

It was my turn at the hotel reception desk. The hotel clerk smiled at me, her straightened blue-black hair pulled back in a tasteful bun at the nape of her neck—She's kind of . . . a mahogany in color—Look at those nails—She pushed a pen and check-in slip forward for me to sign.

"Are you here for the undercoverwear convention?" she asked.

79

"Are you here for the undercoverwear convention?" she asked again.

She thought I was one of them.

(Beat)

(Smearing painted name on the glass.)

Before the awards presentation, I had to check in at the conference registration desk. To the left as I descended the escalator, I saw a banner saying "Welcome Undercoverwear." High pitched laughs, calls, and giggles bubbled from around a table covered with streamers and pink crepe paper. I walked to the right, to the right to where the Black Theatre Network registration desk was. Several people were already congregating around it. I walked right to it.—Everyone was looking at me.—I walked right to it. And as I came forward, someone turned around, saw me, and pointed me to the Undercoverwear desk.

"Over there," he said, helpfully.

"No," I said. "I'm over here. I'm Shannon Jackson."

"You're Shannon Jackson?"

"Oh, you must be Shannon Jackson."

Ethel Pitts-Walker, one of the competition judges, pulled me aside and introduced herself. "I really enjoyed your paper. Kathryn! I'm going to introduce you to Kathryn Ervin, the in-coming president of the Black Theatre Network."

"Oh, yes, Shannon," said Kathryn. "What a wonderful essay you wrote! Thank you so much for sharing it with us."

She took my hand in both of hers and smiled.

"Really," she said. "I think you're doing great work." *(Beat)*

And you know she was black . . . so . . . you know . . . that goes to show. *(Beat)*

I read my paper, probably in that apologetic style of the white liberal who—doesn't want to be presumptuous, but maybe has something to say—but how could she really have anything to say—even though she does want to be different—but knows that she can't actually, truly be different—so

80

what is she even doing here anyway . . . I can't stand being sorry and white at the same time; it's so redundant in the modern world. *(Sits)*

Afterward, a wine and cheese reception followed on the Mezzanine level in the Promenade Room. I sipped my drink and ate my cheese and introduced myself to the people gathered there. Some wearing suits, some in jeans, some in silk, some in dashikis. There was this other white woman there, this other white woman moving through the conversation bouquets. Eventually, she stopped and introduced herself to me; she was a casting director.

(Painting a face on glass in make-up, sparingly indicating cheekbones, nose, mouth, and eyes. The image looks something like one of those pale, characterless Marie Laurençin faces.)

"I am casting a movie about Americans who go to Africa to start a basketball team to help the African uh youth there. And so I'm here looking for my basketball players. But you know it's interesting I've just been making my way through here and hm there seem to be quite a few uh older black men and a fair sprinkling of uh young black women but where I ask you are the young black men? . . . I mean there just doesn't seem to be many . . . Well anyway don't worry about me and my problems hm where are you from? . . . Oh, Chicago! Chicago, that's actually my next stop. Wonderful! yes I'll be looking for black men there, too. And you know it's interesting. I only have one or two days there, very limited time. So I need to be very efficient about this, so I was wondering if you could tell me what neighbor— . . . hm . . . I don't want to offend anyone I mean after all black people should be allowed to live wherever they want, but I don't think you'll be offended . . ."

She smiled . . . generously . . . she meant to be inclusive.

"I don't think that you'll be offended if I ask what neighborhoods might I find the most black people?"

(Beat. To audience.)

The question of where to begin is an interesting one.

81

(To casting director and face in plexiglass.)

"I don't know if I can answer that question."

"Oh well, you needn't. I mean don't worry about my problems. Actually though. Perhaps you know some yourself . . . well of course you probably know uh some black men. But do you know any young black men who can hold it together in front of the camera I guess is what I'm asking? . . . We have a bunch of different kinds of roles. There's an adorable Mutt and Jeff duo who are kind of the comic relief. One really tall and skinny and one you know kind of uh rolly polly. And for the lead hm for the lead we want a slightly narrower face you know high cheek bones, doe eyes. More of a milk chocolate rather than a dark chocolate . . . shows up better on camera that way. And uh smaller nose and mouth . . . Not one of the larger featured faces . . . Do you know anyone? I mean it's a golden opportunity for a young black actor. Think of the money he could make. What a way to start off a career. And this is part of what we're committed to doing, to getting more black faces out there in the mass audience. Do you know anyone?"

(Beat. To audience.)

"Well, I know that Malik is auditioning now."

"Malik? Malik, did you say? That sounds wonderful. Malik!! Ah, I love it."

(Pause)

The question of where to begin is an interesting one.

(Spraying water over the make-up on the glass.)

The next morning I packed my bag and left my Westin Hotel room. As I went out into the corridor, I was assailed by the smell of ammonia. The Westin Hotel housekeeper was there. She had been waiting for me.

(Turning out to housekeeper.)

"Oh, uh. You can go in now. I'm finished."

(Turning back to plexiglass wall; begins wiping.)

"She's finished. You can go in now," says my mother to our housekeeper. I'm four years old and I do not understand why we have to clean our rooms for the cleaning lady.

82

(Spreading and wiping the smeared make-up with hands. Wiping it off glass and hands onto the black slip she is wearing. Repeats, trying to get make-up off the glass entirely. Slows down. Gradually stops to face audience again. Black slip stained with make-up.)

I don't know, I might have wondered . . . you know when I was a little girl . . . I'm not sure, but I might have wondered . . . when I was four years old . . . how someone with such dark skin could have gotten things really very clean anyway.

(Pause)

I don't remember her name—the housekeeper. I was going to ask my mom what her name was since, you know, I was doing this piece. And I thought she might fit in somewhere.

(Beat)

The question of where to begin is an interesting one. Because when you go to tell a story . . . about something that happened to you, I mean . . . you realize that while you were experiencing it, you didn't know you were in a story.

And so consequently, you didn't know it had begun when it all began.

Aisle 12-B, Sundries

DINAH L. LEAVITT

(Rose Rose, over 60, stands in the aisle of the supermarket with her shopping cart. Although she is not wealthy, one notices that she is impeccably dressed. It is Sunday morning.)

ROSE: I always wear a girdle to the Food King. I'm glad they're back—girdles. Oh now they call them body shapers and they make them out of lycra, not rubber. I don't want to jiggle when I walk in the aisle. People who know me, I know everybody at the Food King, are often behind me. I want to glide like my grocery cart. If I get a cart with a gimpy wheel, I trade it in right away. Don't you?

It's so beautiful here. "Clean and well lighted." I feel at peace here. I remember Mr. Khayat's market when I was a girl. Dark, dark and the meat section smelled. And they didn't sell any of the nice things they sell here like candles, reading glasses, tiger balm.

Creamettes are up three cents.

But in the old days you dressed to shop! Oh not hats and gloves, but you wore a clean ironed dress. Lady shoes. Now I see the most awful side of humanity. Started out with curlers in the 1950's. Pink and green mixed, sometimes without even a scarf over them. Not even all the same color . . . Now it's athletic wear, that or blue jeans. No self respect. And I tell you I know some of these people are not athletic. Look at them; they look awful!

Now and then somebody comes in from the old days and I follow them. They never know I do it cause I switch directions in the aisles or skip soda and chips. That way I can see them coming and going—admire the besom on their jacket pocket or their clicky patent heels, hair cut.

And what most people today buy! Junk, junk, junk. You know you are what you eat and that's not just an old saying. Look! *(Points to another cart.)* Fritos, Nature Valley granola bars—the second ingredient is sugar, Skippy Peanut Butter, Sugar Pops, and yogurt—read the label—half sugar! Microwave popcorn, Kraft singles, Sara Lee—grease and sugar. It's all grease and sugar and so are these people. It's sinful. Their kids are, too. Little fatties.

Oh don't get me started on grocery store children. BRATS. I am sorry but 99% of them are brats pure unadulterated. The good ones must stay at home. Whine, cry and fight the whole time. Yesterday I saw a young boy roll a loaded cart over his little sister's leg. Deliberately. Oh don't get me started. And the check out. Have to have every piece of junk up there. Lifesavers, gum, artificially flavored juice in those waxy container bottles. Squeezits! One boy went into hysterics yesterday because his mama wouldn't let him have a copy of *Better Homes and Gardens.* He wasn't old enough to read. My mama would have popped me one good. She didn't buy him the *Better Homes* but I say it's too late by the time they get to the point of public tantrums at the check out. Brats. I was trapped in the checkout line with more than ten items so I couldn't change to Express.

That's Mr. Thornhill; he's the manager; he knows me. Since I reported the cigarette thief he knows my name. "Hello Mrs. Rose," he says. You'll hear him when he notices me. A man was stealing a carton of Kools. If it had been a frozen meat pie I would have thought twice but KOOLS. And I have to pay for the shoplifters in higher prices throughout the store. Even with EDLP's, coupons, TPR's, and specials, things cost. I watch now. May God let this place be safe from thieves.

HiDry paper towels are two rolls for a dollar.

There's Grady Parker, he's vegetables. Joe Marino, meat, Pat Leavy does the flowers—she says she isn't Jewish. Mike, the boy with palsy says he got a raise on Wednesday. I know

85

all the delivery schedules by heart and he loves to hear me rattle them off. This is Sunday morning so there won't be any deliveries until eleven thirty.

I wouldn't say we're all friendly; we don't visit outside the grocery store, but in a way, we are like a family. I shop every day. I love it here. If Jesus came back I think he'd be a stock boy not a carpenter. Mr. Parker in vegetables always comments on all the mouths I must have to feed. I just smile. This is the only mouth I feed. Been alone for sixteen years. As long as I have the Food King, I'm not lonely. I was 'til I started coming every day, but if you come every day you see everybody—everybody has to eat. A lot of ladies go to the shopping mall, but I like this better. It's of a higher order. It's food.

Listen, they're playing PAPER MOON. *(She hums the melody.)* The music here is such a lift. Sometimes I dance down the aisles. This would be a foxtrot, of course. *(Rose begins to sing the song and to sway as the lights fade to black.)* It's only a paper moon, adrift on a cardboard sea. But it wouldn't be make believe . . .

Grace, Honey

SHARON LENNON

(On the day that Grace's youngest daughter, Lucy, is moving out of the house, Grace reflects on her own life choices in a room of her own: the bathroom. She responds to a question her middle daughter, Denise, has asked her.)

GRACE: The other day I was on the phone with Denise; oh we had a nice talk, and she asked me how it felt when I met her father. Oh, I didn't tell her all of it, ya know. Just the basics. *(Laughs)* I didn't tell her, about *(laughs)* when we kissed for the first time, Artie and I. Well, it wasn't the first time. It was the first time that really counted. We had this date, dinner and a movie in Palisades Park. There was this terrific little Italian restaurant—it's not there anymore, but we ate there, and then took a stroll over by that nice view of Manhattan. Well, when we sat down on one of the benches, he leaned over, and I thought he was gonna kiss me, ya know on the mouth. But, he stretched his neck way out and kissed my eyebrow. *(Laughs)* And that was it, that's all he wanted to do. He told me he was looking at my eyebrows all evening, and he thought they were beautiful and very expressive and he wanted to do that all night. He said that my eyebrows revealed me and who I was more than any other part of my body. It sounds kind of funny now. Well, he really threw me for a loop, because I wasn't particularly crazy about him, ya know. But, oh, that little kiss, it was amazing, and I thought I was gonna jump right out of my shoes. To think, I could've made a whole different decision if he'd kissed me normal, like other men did. But, Arthur kissed me there, in just that way . . . . Funny, how such a small touch can move you in just a

87

way that it changes how you see an entire situation. It's so small sometimes, but it can shape the rest of your life. *(A few beats. Grace starts to clean the sink.)*

After we were married a couple of years, I started to shave my eyebrows. Cause, ya know, it was real fashionable then. *(Wiping sink.)* Well, do you know, Artie never said a thing about it. I don't think he even noticed. Really. And maybe, you know, somewhere in the back of my mind I was thinking he wouldn't want me to do that. Never said a thing. Sometimes, when I hadn't put them on with pencil, he'd say, *(Imitating voice.)* "Grace your lookin pretty tired, honey. Why don't you hit the sack early tonight." Now, how can you sleep next to someone every night for years and not notice when their eyebrows suddenly disappear.

Making a Community

JOAN LIPKIN

(Kylie, an African-American woman who is middle-aged or older, talks to a visitor.)

KYLIE: There's a million memories in a lifetime but it seems like some of them just stick out brighter than others. Like the ferris wheel from when the carnival came to town. I saved for weeks. Drove my poor mother to distraction talking about that ferris wheel. *(Remembering childhood, excitedly, to her mother.)* "Can you really see *all* the way to Webster?!" *(Then, more nervously.)* And, "What if it *stops* at the top?"
(Beat)
But it didn't make any difference. Because I got stopped at the *bottom.* See, when I got there, there weren't any rides for sunkissed children.
(Beat)
Sunkissed. A private language for a public pain. *Sunkissed.* For *after* we were colored and *before* we were Negro.
I was just a little girl. I didn't know what to do so I just cried. I cried and cried. My mother held me in her arms and said not to worry. That some people didn't know how to share *their* toys. My mother.
(Beat)
My mother. Now *she's* the one you should be talking to, God rest her soul. Smartest woman I ever knew and she never made it past the eighth grade. My mother was a domestic. Put bread on the table for the whole lot of us after my father passed, mopping other people's floors. She used to say, "There ain't no work that's bad work, if you do it honest and decent." But she wanted us to have an easier time of it than

89

she did. She used to say, "If you get schooling, even if your back is broke, you can still use your mind."

See, my mother thought that education was a way out and she believed that no matter what the law said, her children had a right to it. One day she took off from work and got all dressed up like she was going to see Jesus and sat down at the State Capital all day until they would see her. You ever hear about that? Mmmmhmmmm. Guess that's another one they left out of the history books. *(Only half joking.)* Well, maybe we can get it into the *bicentennial* edition.

Can you imagine what it must have been like for this little burnt black lady to sit there in Jefferson City all day while people shushed her away like she was a fly?

I was so young, I didn't think too much about it at the time. But looking back, I can only wonder, "Were you scared, Mamma? Were you scared?"

(Beat)

But she never did brook too much by the law, since she said it was *white people's law.* She was following a *higher* power, the law of God.

Now, my mother was a *real* Christian. So, she just sat there and sat there until they gave her the answer she wanted to hear. God only knows why they changed their minds. She always thought it was because they wanted to do the right Christian thing. *(Only half joking.)* I always thought it was because they wanted her to hush up and go home.

So we got to go to school alright. But I still can't tell you after all these years if she *won.*

See, the State Legislature decided that we had a right to go on with our education, but it wasn't going to be here in Kirkwood. Uh uh. This fine Christian community wasn't about to have their high school spoiled with *our* sunkissed faces.

No, we had to take the street car all the way into the city to go to Sumner. And the Kirkwood School District would pay. Or some of it, anyways. Just to make sure we went some place else. *(Joking)* Maybe we should have said we wanted to go to *Paris*, instead! But Sumner it was.

Only the ten dollars they paid for our tuition was not enough so I was usually sent home in the middle of the term. I had to come up with an additional seventeen dollars and fifty cents every quarter. So Mamma got me housework or washing to do. And let me tell you, back then, when my mother only made three dollars a day, working from seven to seven, that was a lot of money.

(Beat)

I can still remember taking the street car past the white kids going to their high school. Me looking at them. Them not looking at me. And being sent home every quarter when the school didn't pay its share. Full of pain for something I couldn't name.

(Beat)

What do you think all this shooting up and gang banging and tagging is from, anyway? It's just pain that doesn't have nowhere else to go.

(Beat)

I thought about going some place else. But where would I go? You think it would have been better someplace else? Kirkwood. Odessa. Tuscaloosa. New York. It was all the same back then. Our real crime was to get caught in a moment in history. *Theirs* was to let it happen.

(Beat)

But Kirkwood is my home. I got memories of the limestone quarry and the Greentree Festival and old St. Joes's, too. I didn't want anything fancy. I liked it here for the same reasons you do. I wanted a place that was small and safe. Where I could raise my babies and not worry. Where I knew folks and they knew me. Where there's garbage pick-up on a regular basis.

(Beat)

Even for sunkissed folks.

(Beat)

91

I guess, I never have understood why making a community, keeping folks in together, always means leaving someone out.

Rosie

JESSICA LITWAK
(from *Reincarnation*)

(Rosie is standing on 52nd Street in New York City. She is in her thirties. Slightly overweight. With thick glasses, an ill-fitting suit and torn pantyhose. Her posture is not so good and her self esteem is clearly lacking. She holds a styrofoam coffee cup.)

ROSIE: Since the summer I was ten, I have been seeking the remedy for chagrin; inner peace or a boyfriend. In between suicide attempts I have diligently pursued these goals at any price.

I have experienced the humiliating results of personal advertisements and computer dates. I have tried singles clubs, singles bars, singles volleyball games, and singles supermarket shopping. I am a lifetime member of the Swinging Singles Secretaries Association all paid up through next July.

When the search for true love proves futile, I dedicate myself to the quest for serenity and mental health. I have analyzed my nightmares as archetypes and I have beat my parents to a pulp with a tennis racket in a small room filled with pillows. I have every Louise Hay tape ever recorded and have spent hours and hours naked in front of a mirror chanting, "I love my upper thighs." Last year, I went to an intensive workshop in self-hypnosis. I went six weeks without urinating. I believed myself to be a grapefruit. Before I did that I tried a few other self awareness techniques: EST, direct centering, women sex and power, women and corporate climbing, women and primitive mythic syndromes, women who love too much, women who eat too much, women who watch too much TV. I've done Gestalt Therapy, Freudian therapy, primal therapy, re-birthing. TMA, DMA, REM, Silva mind control. I was rolfed and discovered that my disconnection with my legs has to do with my sterile relationship with my father. That didn't surprise me—he's a Republican. I have studied Judaism, Hinduism, Zen Buddhism, non-denominational Christianity. I even danced and rang bells with the Hari Krishnas in Times Square for a few months. It was nice but I was allergic to the incense. I've had my colors analyzed, my chart read, I've done workshops in aroma therapy, crystal healing, foot massage. I did bioenergetics and the therapist told me I had a masochistic character structure. That sounded very unattractive so I quit. I've tried raising my endorphins with strenuous exercise and raising my blood sugar with Entemanns chocolate chips. I decided I was chemically unbalanced so I went on Prozac for thirteen months. For some reason it depressed me. I have done everything I can to better myself, expand myself, explore myself, command myself. Nothing pans out.

And here I am in America, surrounded by homelessness and gang warfare, by AIDS and poverty, by hypocrisy and misogyny and watery overpriced coffee . . . and I still don't have a boyfriend. And as for finding inner peace, well . . . sometimes it seems easier just to kill yourself!

Excerpt from *Mad Love*

JENNIFER MAISEL

(Diane believes she is a snake and tries to kill her husband by biting him; she speaks only to the audience.)

DIANE: The miracle of birth. I'll explain it to you just as my mother told me. The rabbit dies. In the woods there are thousands of rabbits. You've seen them. They eat all the lettuce in our garden, nibble at tomato plants and sunflowers. Still, except for that little jaw mulching away. You see, honey, when we set those traps and put the poison around the roots of the plants we are contributing to someone's happiness. Because, in each one of those stiff little fuzzy bodies lies the soul of an unborn child, and every time one of the little suckers winds up belly-up among the rutabaga, some very happy mommy-to-be comes home to break the very happy news to her husband that a little child's soul implanted itself firmly into her stomach the last time she ate a carrot. So now you know. Don't even think of asking how they get out.

I dream about Chinese apples. The kind where you split it open and each seed floats in a red capsule that you break by pressing it with your tongue against your teeth. It's like sucking the blood from a cut before it begins to clot. You spit out the seeds. Word was in the fifth grade that the seeds and the skin and the peel were poisonous and we'd have spitting contests in hopes that a big Chinese apple tree would grow on the school grounds. I dream about Chinese apples. My lips and my fingers drip blood red juice and my tongue is covered with seeds to spit out. To spit out and one gets sucked up into my . . . *(motions to her crotch)* here . . . and this tree full of pomegranates grows out of my belly-button and now I'm

95

happy because if I want a Chinese apple I don't have to go to the grocery store. And I reach to pick the most alluring ripe one off of the tree—and my fingers sink into its flesh and hundreds of roaches swarm over my hand and the seeds I spit out are roaches crawling all over my tongue. I wake up and I know I am pregnant.

I begin to show. My stomach starts to pooch out as if I've gained weight. For some reason it is upholstered with a lush red velvet. The lump is there when I look down, but I haven't looked in a mirror yet. Ted is there, leading tours around the neighborhood, leading tours around my body, pointing out my perineum for those who aren't quite sure what that is. I am naked and he shows the tourists the brown line that is stretching over my stomach. He drew it on with eyeliner early this morning because I didn't have one yet and the book said I should. Ted tells the crowd that he's coaching me through the birth process. What very few people know, he says, is that the only reason women feel pain during childbirth is because they get so tense. If only they would relax. For the next five months he will rigorously drill me in relaxation techniques. I can't zip my favorite jeans.

There are things I wanted to do to him that simply weren't done. I wanted him face down into the mattress. I wanted him flattened under my weight. I wanted him spread-eagled, not able to move and I wanted to pierce him with part of my body and flood him with seed that might take root as a nine month memory of the experience. I wanted him to hold back his cries because they distracted me. I wanted him to breathe back his own breath mingled with sheet sweat and must and Clorox. And I wanted him to wait carefully, feigning sleep until he's quite sure I'm snoring in his ear and extract himself—careful—from my heavy limbs trapping his body. I want him to wipe away the semen and the tears in the bathroom and vow to leave me for good and I want to wake up to him the next morning with breakfast on the table and coffee in the air and the most genuine smile in the world on his face.

Ted's stomach bulges. He develops stretchmarks on his ribs and eats Ritz crackers before he opens his eyes in the morning to avoid nausea. At this stage, he tells me, the larva begins to look like a fish and will move through a walking amphibian period before it descends into his lower belly for birth. Ontogeny recapitulates phylogeny, he tells me, as he struggles to lift his bulging body out of his favorite armchair. I indulge his cravings and rub cocoa butter over his breasts. He has gone up a cup size. In the ninth month we pant in unison with our legs tied to the stirrups. He likens the pain to shitting a bowling ball.

I gave birth to a daughter. There was reason behind it. I fell in love—I did what I was supposed to do. There's always the hope that some part of you will carry on. There's always the hope that love stories have happy endings.

The Mouse and William

DEBORAH MARGOLIN
(from *The Breaks* by Deborah Margolin and Rae C. Wright)

(Betty is a nurse's aide—a "lifer" in the hospital system. For six months she has shared this broom closet as a smoker's refuge with another worker, and for the first time, she speaks about her family. She is cleaning a spot on her sweater with seltzer and paper towels.)

BETTY: I saw him out the window of the bank yesterday. He didn't know I was watching him, he didn't see me. It's strange, Marian, I forget how handsome he is. And he was crazy, kicking up his legs, and you know, in the snow and everything, he was kicking up his legs against the side of the building where the candy store is. And I thought: he's done lost it, all I could think of is, he's going to die, my little boy is going to die. And he kept kicking and kicking, it was so funny, really, Marian, and it was my turn but I forgot, he looked so funny, like he wasn't even mine, Marian, like he wasn't anyone I knew at all. Well I couldn't tell and I wanted to tell the manager of the bank, lock the door! There's a madman. He has a gun! There's a lunatic! I mean there we were in a bank and everything. A bank is Disneyland to a lunatic with a gun, Marian. And I wanted to run out there and give him my jacket, he was just dressed in a T-shirt. Well he was running along the wall of this building, kicking up his feet, falling down, running again, kicking again, and all, looking at the wall, and then I saw a little mouse, Marian, he was trying to kick this mouse to death, and this little mouse is running for its life, and he looked like it was so important to kill this mouse . . . . the two of them running for their lives, the mouse and William. And he had nothing on, Marian, nothing, just a T-shirt, it's twelve degrees, what an asshole, I hate him. And I hated that mouse, I hated it. It scared the shit out of me . . . . . because it couldn't defend itself. It couldn't even fucking defend itself. It couldn't defend itself against a drug addict in the fucking snow. So I went up to the teller and made my deposit and whatever and then I went back out and crossed the street and walked down the sidewalk where he was and saw the mouse, but William wasn't there. But the mouse was lying there in the snow, it wasn't moving. But its eyes were open, and it looked fine, but it wasn't moving. It wasn't moving. *(She holds up the sweater to scrutinize the job she has done cleaning it.)*

House

RUTH MARGRAFF
(from *All Those Violent Sweaters*)

(A narrow woman with an extremely long dark braid sits next to a floral centerpiece exactly in the center of the table. She is on the phone.)

EDITH: Hello, is this Victoria's Secret? Is this London? It's Ohio? Oh but you sound so Victorian! No no no I got it in the mail I have to ask you something on page 6. Where is that house, is that a house? No, no I mean the house she's sitting in, not the clothes, your clothes are terrible, your bras are terrible, and that cover girl is pretty but she looks fat this month. What you should sell is the furniture, I love the furniture on this page, right. Okay so she's on page 6, she's sitting on page 6 in a house, *(chokes up)* in a house, and I want to know where that house is, if it is a house. No this is important. *(Almost crying.)* I don't want the bra, okay, okay, okay, if you—don't hang up please—I'll buy the bra just don't hang up can you ask somebody—London—London might know—Okay. Okay. Okay. Never mind.

    (Edith hangs up. Picks up the phone, puts it down, picks it up again. She idly wraps her braid around the centerpiece as she talks.)

    Hello? Is this Tweeds? Hello. I just have one quick question and it's silly but page 29, okay the girl is wearing heather grey for one thing, but the house that's off like in the distance and there's puddles all around her, you know I think I've been there, right there where she's standing, by that house, the upstairs window . . . Well page 23 is inside of that upstairs window, am I right? I can't tell because she's *inside*, you might have faked something, you can fake things like that I suppose, but those are really puddles on page 29. You've got the puddles and the heather grey and then the house, it's really good, it's worth it going through a lot of bullshit in my mail to get to this picture, it's really getting to me right now, *(sucks her breath in)* it's really I feel like I've been there in this picture, I mean she is selling something to me, you know, I have this house, see I don't know where it came from but it comes into my head and sits there and I can't remember it or anything, I don't know where it is but you know I floated down the stairs a hundred times in that old house with all my wheat pennies down in the shag carpet and the burglar broke in—he broke in and stole our piggy banks and I had *wheat* pennies in my piggy bank, I didn't know wheat pennies were getting *rare* and I never once connected it to that old house. You know I *make* my sweaters, I make all of them myself, I mean I knit them *(choked up)* but I like to see what *you* do, and I like this one, it's so nice. I like the little boxes right beside the sweaters where you show the texture of it up close, and your stitches are . . . your stitches . . . *(Sobbing almost.)* I just really like those little boxes. That's what you should really sell I think. *(Dialtone. She hangs up.)*

The Handwriting, The Soup, and The Hats

SUZANNE MAYNARD

(Annie is an actress searching for someone or something to believe in, but the forces she turns to—such as God and Marlo Thomas—consistently disappoint her.)

ANNIE: When I was young, I loved *That Girl*. Marlo Thomas was my hero. I thought that's what it means to be an adult: you grow up, you get a boyfriend and you wear a lot of hats. There would be wine and drapes and soufflés that fell when Donald came home and slammed the door too hard. You fight with the man you love, and then go to a restaurant, and everything is funny and fine. (*Pause*) Well, rarely are things both funny *and* fine. Like this morning, I went to the kitchen and took out the last can I had in the cupboard; it was a can of Campbell's Chicken Gumbo. So, OK, fine, I need something in my stomach before I go to this audition. But, as I'm looking at it, I start to get nervous, panicky, almost scared of it. Insecure about my ability to put can-opener to can and make a successful go of it. Jesus, how do I market myself when I don't even think I can open a can of soup. OK, the point is, I spent a good part of adolescence emulating *That Girl* and all that it foretold about adult life, only to be told, years later, that *That Girl* was really just a spinoff of *Love American Style*. So who cares, right? I mean, big deal. Well, yes, as a matter of fact it is, a very big deal. It just seems that anything you're taught, or you choose to put your faith in, always turns out to be a spinoff of something else. Like Christ for example. Why'd I have to put all of my faith in

God's son? Why the middle man? Why the go-between? Why not just go straight to the source? I stopped believing in God when I found out Marlo Thomas is not that straightforward after all. *(Pause, looking at the soup can in her hands.)* I had to calm myself down. I will open this can of soup, it's friendly, it won't judge me or tell me I'm too short or too tall or too young or too old for the part. It's soup. Chicken Gumbo. Just what you want at 8 in the morning, before an audition. I dig into the can, twisting with all the conviction my mother used when opening soup. I catch my reflection in the lid: tensed jaw, concentrated brow, a bit of sweat has begun to drip from my temple. I've almost got it, almost. And then the question of when to stop. Do I stop just before the opener has made it all the way around? Or do I allow the opener to meet so the lid separates completely, but then I risk it sinking into the sucking marsh below. Then again, if I don't let the opener complete the circle, there's that little piece of metal that hangs on and hangs on and will not let go, and the metal's all jagged so I'll cut my finger and pass out on the kitchen floor and miss the audition. Alright, so I'm a little indecisive, obsessive, hung up about some things, but so was Marlo! The difference is, she had canned laughter to back her up. Now I'm not saying canned laugh tracks are a good thing, not necessarily, but at least you don't feel so alone. Marlo could spend hours deciding on an outfit, miss her date with Donald, put her entire relationship on the line and she'd be supported by constant admiring chuckles. *(Pause)* All I've got is a couple of cats and a turtle.

103

Waking Women

CASSANDRA MEDLEY

(A closed-in porch of a neat A-frame house in a working-class black neighborhood in a midwestern city. Ms. Edie enters as if coming from the direction of the street. She is a black woman in her mid to late fifties, dressed in a plain housedress and slippers. She is carrying a rattan hand fan in one hand to beat off the heat and a potted plant tied securely with a white ribbon in the other. Her hair is done up in curlers with a hair net tied securely on her head. She has a sorrowful expression on her face as she addresses the unseen woman before her. Throughout the monologue she speaks to the audience as if speaking to her close friend and confidante, Lucille.)

MS. EDIE: Pinkie's in labor! *(Fanning herself with indignation.)* That's *right!* Yeah, girl, Pinkie done been in labor since . . . well, she went in at four this morning and here it is what . . . ? Twelve-thirty? Okay, so she's still, yeah, chile . . . well, you know they say that first baby is always the hardest. So she's in there now and uh . . . took her down at four o'clock, her water broke at three-thirty . . . um-hum . . . Oh, yeah, that's what they say . . . that first one . . . yep . . . count on that to be the hardest. Well, now, course with me, they just "dropped" . . . I was real lucky . . . 'cause I weren't in there *no* time and 'fore I know nothing, I was just opening up m'legs and look like my boys just "dropped" out the barrel, but hon-nee, poor Pinkie, she's up in there now and she's having a time of it . . . (*Pause*)

Shooo! That silly sister-in-law of mine! that Gladys! best good common sense my brother ever had was to *leave* that woman . . . girl, the way she brought up that poor Pinkie!

104

(*Pause*) Oh, chile, I just don't even wanna get into it 'cause you got *enough* on your mind as it is, but hon-nee, do you know, that Pinkie, that child ain't *never* been to a picture show in her *life!* Now you know that's a shame! That's the gospel truth! Fifteen years old and ain't never *ever* been to the movies in her life! I ain't telling no tale. 'Cause my damn sis-ter-in-law, 'scuse my French, 'cause my sister-in-law Gladys just keeps Pinkie all locked up in the house *all* the time! Oh, I don't know *what* be going through Gladys's mind! She think she be sheltering Pinkie or "protecting" her or I don't know what. Keeps Pinkie in the house *all* the time! Don't let her go *nowhere*. Don't let her go out shopping with her little friends . . . *parties?* You better forget it! *Sleepovers?* Forget it! *Dances?* Forget it! Join a club? Forget it! After school home games and whatnot? *(She waits for Lucille to silently answer back "forget it," and she nods "correct.")* You got it! And like I told Gladys, I said, "Gladys," we was sitting out on the porch and I said, "Gladys" . . . 'cause you know me, I speak my mind. I said, "Gladys you just can't keep your daughter locked up under lock and key in the house like that," I said, "Gladys, that ain't right! 'cause *you* know and I know we was all young once, and Gladys, you just can't keep Pinkie under your nose all the damn time."

Now I know for myself, see I'm gonna tell ya, when I was young, see, I was "fast." I'm gonna tell you like it is; I was "fast." And here I was dark skinned and considered "ugly" and the boys was after me? And here Pinkie is, light skinned and with straight hair! Well, now, you *know* the boys gonna be after her! And here she can't even go to the picture show and ain't never been in her life! And I told Gladys, I said, "Gladys," "Gladys," I said, "You know that now we have got to face reality. It ain't like when we was coming up, no, it ain't. It ain't like back when they didn't talk about nothing and you weren't supposed to know nothing and when your first time of the month first come on you, you thought you was bleeding to death and all that, 'cause you didn't know no better and all, like y'know, when we come up. After all, this is 1991 and my goodness, and things have changed and you gotta face up to it!" And I told my ole silly sister-in-law, "Gladys, you just can't rule that girl like that!" I've told Gladys time and time again, "We have got to face reality here, and we have got to tell these kids 'bout birth control and whatnot," and hon-nee, ooohhh! What did I want to say that for? Chile, do you know she looked at me like I was the devil's own *slut*? Oh, yes, she did! (*Pause. She studies Lucille, nodding as to answer a retort.*) Well, now, I know, I *know* that, hon-nee, I know that you mean 'bout "sin," and I'm as religious as the next one, I'm as upstanding as any one of the rest of your friends, Lucille, but keeping these kids *ignorant* ain't keeping them from "sin." How's that s'pposed to "keep 'em from sin" . . . ? (*Pauses*) See what I'm saying? (*Pauses*) I mean, I mean, yeah, I see what *you* saying, but do you see what *I'm* saying? . . . So anyway, okay . . . so I said to myself right there and then, I said, *all right! so be it! lemme just shut up and back off, lemme just shut my mouth!* so I shut my mouth.

See, 'cause these here kids these days, they gonna get out here, they are curious. And a young girl like that? Huh! Pretty as she is? You know she gonna be wanting to find out and to experiment and whatnot . . . with what it's like to have a boy kissing her and—holding her and hon-nee, . . . humph! (*Fans herself vigorously.*) That's just nature, wanting somebody to be rubbing up 'gainst ya and thing. . . . Course, now that ole fool I married, well, my time is now dried up. . . .

Well, now, I'll tell you how it went down, see . . . Here all these weeks and weeks and carrying on, see, and I'm steady coming over visiting Gladys, and here I'm noticing that Pinkie up here always got on the *same* top, day after day, week after week, the same kinda blouselike thing, like a navy blue, you know like them navy blue nylon button-down things, like a jacket, and she's wearing this thing day in and day out, from "can't see to can't see," and I'm steady coming over. Well, one day, Gladys is out of earshot, and I say to

Pinkie, "Say, Pinkie? honey, you gotta change that top, girl, I think you gonna have to wash that blouse, 'cause you know how 'navy' is now, that 'navy' gets that funk in it, and you can't wash it out. . . ." I said, "Well, Pinkie, uh, you gotta change your blouse *sometime* uh . . ." and I'm thinking to myself, well what is going on? And Gladys ain't saying nothing, and I'm waiting for her to notice or say something or *something*. I guess she ain't seen it, 'cause she ain't said nothing. Gladys got her head so stuck in them prayer books— 'scuse me for saying so, Lucille, on such a sad occasion—but she can't half see no way. I mean—I mean, the Lord said for us to "pray," well, okay, but not to go deaf, dumb, and blind in doing it! And then if I try and say, "Gladys, ain't Pinkie got another jacket or something to put on?" Then Gladys think I'm trying to talk bad about her, and she wanna rile up and jump up in *my* face and jump bad with me. And look like to me everytime I turn round here come Pinkie in that same navy blouse, jacket-type blouse thing, so I'm thinking, *What is* with *this child?* and I said to Gladys finally, I said, "Gladys, Pinkie's wearing that thing out"! And Gladys come talking 'bout (*imitating a high-pitched voice*) "Well, if that's what she wants to wear, then that's what she wants, what you trying to make something of it? what you trying to start?" so I said to myself, "Well, hell, I'm gonna just let well enough alone then!" And what happened? The next thing I know Bernadette from 'cross the street come calling me, calling *my* house, talking 'bout how her daughter Carol, who's Pinkie's best friend, told *her* that Pinkie up at the school told *Carol* that she thought she *may* be pregnant and that Pinkie told Carol "not to tell nobody," but that Carol just now *told* her! Well, I said, "*Whaaaaa?*" Say *what?!* Well, hon-nee, I said to myself, *Let me go down here to Gladys's* and see what is what, see just *what* is going on here!" Well, so, hon-nee . . . I couldn't get out m'house fast enough! My phone come ringing off the hook, and who's on it but Gladys, weeping and wailing and having conniptions and pleading with me as the

"Auntie" to come over and "have a word with Pinkie." Uh-hum! *See!?* And far be it for me to say, "I told you so," far be it from me to say, "I told you the pony was gonna jump the stable!"

See, and she wanna jump all up in my face when I was trying to *tell* her something way back, but now, now when it come down to the get-go, you *see* who she called on, now don't you! (*Pauses in fury.*) I'm telling you, girl! see, now, that the monkey's out the bag, now that she finds out the cards done *already* been shuffled, *then* she come calling on me "to deal!"

Well, honey! Get down to the house and what do I find? Gladys sitting up there with Pinkie looking all long face and looking like she been nailed to the cross and Pinkie's all wide-eyed and mystified! And Gladys acting like she ain't never left Sunday school, just hedging and swallowing and ducking and dodging! Don't know what's *with* that woman; act like she ain't never seen the "wee-wee" on a dog! Don't know *how* my brother ever got a child with that woman, my goodness— that's that old sanctified church mess. They ain't like *our* kind of Christian; them people crazy—way she act you'd think she ain't never seen herself "down there," I swear! You shoulda seen her, *(imitating a high-pitched, awkward voice)* "uh . . . uh, P-P-P-P-P-P-Pinkie? P-P-P-P-P-P-Pinkie?" She wanna beat round the bush and hesitate and germinate and I don't know what else. "P-P-P-P-P-P-Pinkie . . . have you—have you *done* . . . have you been doing anything?" And Pinkie she just stares at Gladys wide-eyed and shakes her head back and forth (*She shakes her head in no response.*) "Un-uh" . . . Shit, girl!!—'Scuse me, 'scuse me, Lucille, this is not the place and this is not the time, but I was so outdone, I said, Well, hell! I mean hell! later for all this! Let's get it all out here in front and the hell with beating round the bush and carrying on and acting all prettified and citified. I said, Well, hell, let's just get it out in the open. I said, "Pinkie have you *fucked?!*" I mean, you know, *Let's just get it out here!*

Well, her Mama wanted to have a seizure, but I ain't studyin' that woman. I said to Pinkie, I said, "Pinkie, well, when was your last time you had your period?" I mean, you know, let's call a "trump card" a "trump," let's say it like it *is*, let's bring it all out here! Later for all this shucking and jiving and ducking and dodging and conniving and hiding and carrying on!

Well, hon-nee, I am here to tell you, Pinkie went up to calendar and hon-nee, them pages of that calendar went to . . . (*She illustrates with her hands flipping in the air*) . . . flipping and ah flipping and ah flipping and ah flipping and ah flipping . . . (*Her voice trails off.*) And I said, uh-oh, oh, Lord! oh, Lord ha-mercy! well, well sir, I walked up to her and hon-nee, I lifted up that ole navy blue blouse, jacket, whatever the hell it was, and that belly was ah sitting up there just as pre-tee!

And see Gladys all this time wanna keep hiding Pinkie way from the world and keeping her at home and keeping her under lock and key and keeping her all closed up and keeping her way from the boys and what happened? You *see* what happened! And I said to her, "Pinkie, when did this happen?" Well, it turns out she was sneaking some little boy round here, right in the very house of her so sanctified mama! Honey, it's the gospel truth! (*She throws her hands in the air.*) If I'm lying, Lord choke me! Right there in the basement, right under our own noses. I was probably sitting up there, too, with Gladys upstairs, probably watching tee-vee with her and here Pinkie supposed to be following Gladys's ole-timey rules and regulations, supposed to be "in the bed." Ha, she was "in the bed," all right, "in the bed" down in the basement with that boy!

So anyway . . . yeah . . . Pinkie's laying up there now, she's laying up there in labor, and I'll tell you one thing, my dear. . . . Now she's fifteen and having this baby. . . . Oh, Gladys is gonna help take care of it, and Gladys and me we gonna hog whip that chile if she don't *stay* in school. . . . But honey . . . . (*Her face is suddenly a portrait of sadness, foreboding, and old hidden recollections.*) Her childhood is *over* . . . her childhood is up! Them days of being a little carefree little girl! She can just lock 'em up . . .! (*She struggles to fight back tears.*) . . . 'Cause raising up a baby and raising up a child and being a child your own self and with no man? Trying to raise yourself plus raise something all by yourself? (*Pause*) Talk about being "grounded in the house"? Now she *really* gonna be "grounded"! (*Pause*) She's on the killing ground now . . . yes, Ma'am!! Pinkie's gonna be a mama! She's on the killing ground now . . . !

Other People's Ancestors

DIANNE MONROE

(Dell, a middle-aged Jewish woman, is explaining how her life has become cluttered with the presence of other people's ancestors.)

DELL: I always felt like my roots were shallow. Like I had to cling tenaciously to any soil into which I was deposited.

It was always other people's ancestors who spoke to me.

I was born in Lexington, Kentucky on November 1, 1951. I grew up in a world where TV was still in black and white, and so was everything else. We were beige, and the neighbors didn't quite know what to make of us.

In elementary school I learned to sing, "The sun shines bright on my old Kentucky home. It's summer, the darkies are gay."

In my third grade textbook there was a picture to prove it. A dozen black men and women dancing around a campfire and eating watermelon, grinning broadly. To illustrate a lesson on the pre-Civil War South.

Maybe I have trouble hearing my own ancestors, because the other people's ancestors I grew up surrounded by were all screaming so loudly. Or maybe because all my ancestors went up in smoke—literally. Maybe they were disoriented, lost, confused and didn't know where to find me, because we had traveled so far to arrive at the only one place I knew as home.

I grew up with my parents telling me how fortunate I was to be born anywhere at all. Grew up with the Eichman trials on our grainy black and white TV. Live from Israel, direct to our living room. Grew up with whispered adult conversations about lists sent to some Jewish organization in New York who specialized in locating lost relatives. Like they'd just somehow been carelessly misplaced.

All the other kids went to family reunions every summer. Gleeful occurrences peppered with an amazing, complex, incomprehensible assortment of uncles, aunts and cousins, seconds and thirds, once and twice and three times removed.

"Why can't we have a family reunion?" I demanded. Amazed to see my mother break down in sobs. Surprised to have my father swat me and send me to my room.

I had exactly two grandfathers, two grandmothers, two uncles, and two aunts. And was told I didn't know how lucky I was to have them.

My first lesson in race relations came when I was five years old. The day Carmen, our cocker spaniel, ran away from home and got found at the country club.

We had already searched under every front porch and every bush in the neighborhood. Mama was carrying a clammy wet all beef frank to entice our dog out from behind wherever it was. I was trailing behind, clutching a back-up frankfurter, hoping none of the other kids would come out and see my mother, a grown woman, down on her hands and knees in the dirt, waving a frankfurter under somebody's front stoop, shouting "Carmen! Carmen!"

We were the only people in the neighborhood with a dog named Carmen. Daddy had to name our dog after some lady in the opera. Daddy liked opera. None of the other kids even knew what opera was. They liked Elvis. Daddy wouldn't even let Elvis in the house.

Well, Carmen had one of those little tags with our phone number on it. Some kind of way she got all the way up to the country club. Someone got the number off the tag and called us. Mama hurried me and my sister into the car and on up to the country club to reclaim our dog.

We were stopped at the gate. Mama explained to the uniformed man with ice blue eyes about Carmen, our cocker, and how we had come to take her home.

"You'll have to wait here," snapped the man with the ice blue eyes, "I'll get someone to take care of it." Like 'it' was something dead and slimy and nasty and dirty.

Mama pulled our car over to where the man pointed. We waited. And waited. For a long time.

Finally we saw a man walking down the long, gracefully curved driveway from where the trees discretely obscured a view of the country club. He looked just like a picture negative my father once showed me. Skin the darkest of ebony and hair such a brilliant white that it sparkled where the sun got caught and tangled up in it. He was wearing the uniform of a servant and carried Carmen in his arms.

The man who looked like a picture negative approached our car and placed our puppy in Mama's arms. Not a word was spoken, but I saw something pass between them, under the watchful glare of the man with the ice blue eyes. Something I didn't understand. And knew better than to ask. Because on my mother's face was the same expression I saw when I asked her why we couldn't have a family reunion just like all the other kids.

And right then I knew there was something terribly wrong with the world. And it had everything to do with the man who looked like a picture negative and caught the sun in his hair, and my mother's light beige skin and shiny black hair and the man with the ice blue eyes.

Juice

PATRICIA MONTLEY

(The speaker is in her fifties.)

WOMAN: I was afraid I would dry up. Like the proverbial prune. They say women do, after menopause. But I haven't. Not yet anyway. *(Puzzled)*

The fact is, I feel . . . *steamy*. It's not the hot flashes—they've come and gone. This is different. I wake up in the middle of the night and my whole body is . . . moist. My palms and soles feel like the leaves of lush tropical plants in a greenhouse. It's as though my heart is pumping electric currents into all my fluids—like that metal element I have at the office to heat my tea water. And at that moment, at that moist moment, I feel a readiness—no, a need, an . . . *urgency* . . . to do something . . . to be something . . . more. *(Beat)*

Something strange is happening. My pores are open. Things get in. Light, for example. It invades me. When I drive in the country on a bright morning, the sun passes through my flesh as easily as it passes through the car window. When I walk down the street on a sunny day, the light penetrates my body. I no longer cast a shadow. Last week, I went to a Monet exhibit at the museum and when I saw "Meadow at Giverny," I felt I *was* the light in that meadow—that my breath was the breeze above that yellow-green grass. *(Beat)*

Other things get in too. People. They steam open my pores and come right in. I was sitting in the park yesterday, watching a toddler try to get on her sister's tricycle while no one was looking. She tackled it from the front, from the side, and eventually from the back, until at last she sat precariously but triumphantly on the seat, listing slightly, her feet dangling above the pedals. And suddenly I was crying, heady with my success, for I had become that fearless child; I had had that great adventure, and was ready for another. *(Beat)*

It's really quite exciting. I find now that my senses are more . . . *aroused.* By smells, for example. The leather conditioner I use on my boots . . . the crisp, glossy pages of a new book . . . the delicate spray of an orange as the skin is peeled away . . . the warm, cloying scent of my own body as I bend over the breakfast counter in my nightgown. I'm more aware . . . more *appreciative.* Touching comforts me. I open to it. Nothing to hide, nothing to lose. When I embrace my friends, I enjoy pressing my body close to theirs, feeling the bulges of breasts and bellies, the sturdiness of thighs and shoulders, faces cradled in necks, inhaling affection like a fine perfume. Making love, I am surprised by passion flowing through me like a river of light. I know the dance by heart; yet still the music moves me deeply—until I sing and sing and flood the world with my delight.

Locofoco

SUSAN MOSAKOWSKI

(Clio, a TV reporter, tells her sisters how she was taken off the air.)

CLIO: I was fired last week. I was about to do the 10 o'clock news when the teleprompter went down. Everybody was listening, waiting for me to speak. I felt defenseless because I didn't have their words—I had to defend myself somehow, so I spoke: "WHAT'S HAPPENING NOW? YOU ALL WANT TO KNOW THAT? DON'T YOU? WELL HOW THE HELL AM I SUPPOSE TO KNOW?" I'm sure everyone was floored. I went on: "I only know what they tell me. They give me a mike, a teleprompter, an earpiece and a script and I talk. You can't see the radio in my ear, but it's there. I wear it all the time even when I'm not working. I tried to take it out, but the network said don't worry it's a tight fit and to leave it alone—it was always reassuring until now." *(Pause, as if getting a transmission.)* Just a minute I think I'm getting something—no I guess not. *(Holding on to her ear, trying to transmit to the network.)* OK people—This is not OK people. Come on bozos. If you don't give me some feed I'm getting rid of the plug. Who do you think you are? You aren't some goddamn life support system. Feed me—take me off—SO WHAT! I'm tired of plugging the news. This is not the real news anyway—it's somebody's vision thing. *(Pause)* I haven't talked about this to anyone. But no more. My lips are moving! I'm rolling!

I watched the Olympics and saw the network turn it into a soap opera. I listened to Congress, and heard the vision of the way things could be, while they put the President's dick in the public eye. I watched the real life video of an innocent man getting beaten, and saw the jury unable to convict his assailants because they would not believe their own eyes— they had this vision thing going on. *(She receives a message over the earpiece.)* What? No! I won't go back to HUMAN RESOURCES, I am the human resource! What do you mean I'm not standing here anymore. Listen—I know you're listening—you took me off right?—so I'm not here anymore, right? *(Pause)* Well I've got news for you!

When Our Daddies Come

LESLÉA NEWMAN
(from *Rage)*

(A woman of any age, race, or ethnic background is alone on stage addressing the audience. The lighting is dim, to suggest night. The stage is empty except for a bed.)

When our daddies come
into our room at night
we leave our bodies
and fly out the window
up to the stars
past the houses and the trees
and all the parked cars
past the sun and the moon
and Mercury and Mars
to the Planet of the Angels
which is very, very far
There's an Angel there for everyone
there's even one for me
She has long black hair
and a shiny gold dress
She's pretty as can be
She sits me in her lap
She rocks me in her arms
She sings a little song for me
to keep me safe from harm

I sit on her lap
until my father my daddy my step-father
my grandfather my godfather my papa my pop

my uncle my brother my brother's friend
my sister's friend my sister's boyfriend
my mother's boyfriend my fourth grade teacher
my sixth grade teacher my piano teacher
my babysitter my doctor my dentist
my neighbor my priest my mailman
is finished
then it's time to go home
My Angel cries
and I cry
but she has to send me back
My Angel cries
and I cry
but she has to send me back

A Line of Cutting Women

RITA MARIE NIBASA

(The speaker begins the piece boldly, brashly, and then a necessary softness occurs later, as she grows in understanding, as she learns to separate her life from the lives of those around her.)

CUTTING WOMAN: I come from a line of cutting women, so it was only natural that I took up the knife. My mother's mother cut six men, my mother cut four. At seventeen I had cut only one. You know, men who see their own blood bond too easily for me. Now, my grandmother cut one of her husbands to the bone and dared him to talk about it. Seven years later when she next saw him, he stopped his car in the middle of the street and yelled as she passed on the sidewalk: "Katie, you the meanest thang in Memphis." Now, even my mother didn't have any problems with the men she cut—one of whom was my father, who, afterward, brought his check home more regularly. But me, well, I had to cut a man who saw it as an act of love—tough love, as it were.

It was a Friday afternoon, and I was walking home from school. James, a friend of mine, stopped and asked if I wanted a ride. As I walked toward the car Ricky opened his door and motioned for me to sit between them. An open bottle of beer cradled between Ricky's knees tipped forward slightly, and beer spilled onto his shoes: his prelude to the evening. I told him he couldn't pee on my head and make me think it's rain, and, carrying my mother's and sister's reputations, I opened the back door and climbed in . . . . Before we could even test zero to sixty Ricky wanted to know when he and I would get together. Now mind you, this was only loose talk. I wasn't supposed to take it seriously, and because I had no time for secondary things, I just chuckled. Then he asked me if I knew that in the realm of sexual endeavors he was king. I leaned forward in my seat and said close to his ear that I knew it, but I'd heard his throne was shaky and that all his subjects were imbeciles . . . . Ricky drew back his arm and slammed his fist into my chest, knocking me back. I bounced against my seat a few times and fell on the door . . . . I closed my eyes and saw, smiling meekly at me, the faces of the men my mother and sisters had fought. There too was my father, among the woman-beaters and womanizers I knew. I wondered whether all men were just walls with cracks . . . . What would my mother think? What would she say if she knew I had let the son of a wife-beater hit me? . . . The popping sound of gravel spewing from beneath the tires reverberated in my head like the feet of displaced women and children running. James had turned his car into my driveway. I got out and slammed the door. And then I, who often wore light clothing because I didn't want more pressure on my skin, swayed under the added weight of that blow . . . . I walked into my house, put down my bookbag and took out a knife.

I placed the knife in a brown paper bag and walked out the door. I had no idea where I was going, but evil lying by the wayside joined in and led me across town in a direct line to Ricky. After about a mile and a half, still clutching the bag, I spotted James's car in front of a liquor store, and Ricky sat in the car with his elbow resting on the door and his fingers nervously tapping the hood. I took the knife from the bag, drew it back, and tiptoed up to the car. As Ricky saw the knife coming down, his arms flew up and he gasped. I turned away from the little boy I saw in his eyes and plunged the blade into his upper arm . . . . I dropped the bloody knife back into the bag and ran toward home, scenes from old movies flashing in my mind as I ran like The Fugitive. A mother runs down the street in the night, a baby pressed tightly in her arms, small children trailing . . . . Why can't they go home? Why can't they sleep in their own beds? In a street in the middle of a night compromises are made and years of fight fade bitterly into submission.

As I slowed down I realized that I was running in the street. I looked around me, letting a car pass, and then stepped onto the sidewalk. I turned the final corner toward home, and the car that had just passed was idling next to the curb. Through the back window, I caught a glimpse of some girls I knew. Gloria, who should be graduating with me, dropped out of school at sixteen with her first child; at seventeen, she had her second. Pat, who was also my age, had so many men that she turned into one. And Teresa, sweet Teresa, in and out of jail, lost custody of her children.

My thick hair hung about my face like Medusa's, and a large drop of dried blood ran down the front of my shirt, like a tear on a cheek. Suddenly, I was crying so hard I was heaving. What years on the Mourning Bench had failed to release thrashed about there in my storm . . . . My tears though were not only flesh and blood. A body, you see, is really just a small thing to bury . . . . A dream, now that's something else.

The Lion

KIRA OBOLENSKY

(Katherine, a woman in her late 50s to 60s, is covered with white gauze bandages—wrapped around her head, her arms, her legs. We see the edges of her apartment . . . modest, middle class.)

KATHERINE: I know today is Friday because I went to the Ukrainian church to help the ladies make pirogi. I live in the neighborhood, because it's close to the Gas Company where my husband used to work. I don't go to church and I never eat those things, but I love listening to women prepare food. Now I don't speak Ukrainian, there is no reason on earth why I would, but with all of us at the long table I feel like we are a great big centipede, each of us a leg, and we are crawling to a common destination.

Actually, centipedes are quite extraordinary creatures and I don't mean to take them in vain. *I love animals.* This is what I always say at Easter when everyone is babbling about Jesus on the third day blah blah blah or when the community is up in arms because some vision of the Virgin Mary appears floating in the air: who needs a magic trick when there are creatures in this world with 100 legs.

Television can really show you—up close and personal— the most intimate details. I watch quite a bit of television now, but I am very selective. I avoid anything with people in it. Televsion has given me a real appreciation for the food chain, and not a day goes by when I don't think about it—the birds eating the spiders who eat the gnats, etcetera, etcetera.

Today is Friday. So I show up right at nine and pour myself a cup of coffee and sit down in my customary spot at the end of the table. Irene asks me if the cat got my tongue and I say, "no." I haven't been in for a few weeks and I half expect *a question or two* but Irene won't, because that might imply she's interested in me. She knows I'm not Ukrainian, which for her is a problem.

I pour and then I sip my coffee—it's hard for me to swallow—in fact—*(Katherine clears her throat)* excuse me, I have this—oh this is just awful—I have this *(she coughs something up)* fur in my mouth.

Irene asks me if I want to make prune or kraut pirogis. The prunes leave you with dirty fingernails. Kraut makes your fingertips sour. I opt for prunes. She gives me a platter and I start to scoop little spoons of the dark sticky stuff into round sections of dough. And then Irene, casually, turns, she's on her way down the table and says: "What happened to you?" "What happened to me—I ask?" I answer in the same breath— "I won a contest." Her eyebrows go up.

Next to animals, my favorite thing is contests. They bring meaning and form to my life. Name in a hat, name in a fishbowl, tests of skill, tests of random luck, magic numbers, magic numbers . . . The notion that we exist in a mass and that from that mass someone can emerge—chosen—the winner . . . or the loser I suppose . . . . Now I have won several ice buckets. I have never used an ice bucket, but they come in handy as gifts. And Mel won a naugahyde Barcolounger in an incentive thing at work, which doesn't count for me, although I am the one who lounges in it at night hoping for good public television.

"Yes, I did." I take a sip. "I won a contest." That's all I say. And I pull my attention to the job at hand. Irene tells me that her Ava is coming by today. I manage to nod my head. She's always showing pictures of Ava like she's some kind of goddess. Looks chunky to me.

I go two ways on pictures. I have a picture of Mel in a yellow sweater that was taken just before he retired. Yellow was never his color. His gray head retreats into the blue back-

124

ground, but his torso in that stoplight of a sweater just pops. He looks so simple. You can see the comb marks in his hair and he has a doughy look on his face. His hands are folded in his lap—I never saw that man do that with his great big hands until I saw him embalmed. I had that picture by my bed for ages and soon that's the way he started appearing to me when I was having a memory . . . . Walking up the aisle and there he is waiting for me in that yellow sweater. I never would have walked if I'd seen that waiting at the altar. So I put it away and soon enough he started appearing to me slender and scrubbed and shaking with desire at the vision of me in white satin.

Now I have millions of pictures of Sally all over the house. I've got her as a baby in the kitchen, because that's where we put her highchair. As a toddler in the bathroom. And the gorgeous picture of her sweet sixteen above my bed. Every night, I take it down and I press my lips to her forehead. The other day, I noticed a very strange blemish floating on her face. There on the glass. I scraped at it a bit and figured out that it was the skin from my lips accumulating. I instinctively went to the Windex, but something stopped me at the last minute. I mean, if you've given birth, a little residue from the lips is nothing to be alarmed about.

Father Joseph walks in. He visits us every Friday morning halfway through with cookies, which he has personally purchased. Father Joseph and I have a good relationship. He is aware that I am not a member of his flock, but he doesn't push. When he gets to me, he offers me the cookies which I decline and he asks me, "Katherine—were you in a car accident?" And I say no, "*I won a contest.*" He's listening and so is everyone else, Irene included.

I get another cup of coffee. This is for suspense, to leave Irene and the rest of them hanging. I have read that there is more bad coffee consumed in this state than anywhere else in the world. Once I had an Italian friend. Graziella. I met her in one of those support groups for parents of murdered children. Her good coffee just ate up my intestines.

125

I sip and I swallow and then I answer. "A Make A Wish Contest. One of the charity foundations. I put my name in at the supermarket and at the bank, and sure enough I get a call. Make a wish! the man on the phone said." For a minute, my mind raced—make a wish! . . . . . But turns out it's an experience I won, a local experience like lunch with the anchorman of the news or a drink with the mayor. I get to choose it.

They picked me up on a Monday morning because that's when the zoo is closed. In a limousine. The driver, who is very young, must have heard about my wish. He tells me he wouldn't mind petting a big furry pussy, himself.

Shortly after we drive through the entrance gates, a very attractive young woman greets me. She says "Hi, my name is Sally" and the coincidence makes me think for a minute I've died and gone to heaven. Sally escorts me to the lions and the zookeeper, I think that's what she does, explains to me that Suki is their tamest lion, raised in captivity, comfortable with people. I wash my face and arms and everything exposed with a special anti-bacterial soap. The handler—different than the keeper—asks me if I'm menstruating. Not in 12 years, I say. *(Pause, sip of coffee.)*

Suki is at the far end of the cage. He's got his head on his paws, and if he were smaller it would really be cute. I stick out my hand and I say "Suki, Suki, Suki . . ." He rises. He is the size of a small car. And hot. He sniffs my hand with his giant velvet nose. And I touch fur—thick, spongy, coarse—I stroke his neck, he swipes my feet and I'm down on the cement floor. Oops! He wants to play. He puts his legs in the air and I wedge myself against his tummy. The weight and the sound of his beat and the heat of a living thing sweeps me to a place I haven't been in years. And we're snuggled together and Suki takes out his tongue—the size of a beef liver—his wet sticky hard tongue and he licks me my arms, my hair and I . . . stick out my tongue, I really don't know what came over me, my tongue is totally useless, like painting the house with a toothbrush.

126

Father Joseph is riveted, as are the ladies. I take my time.

One of our audience—the keeper, I think, says "Hey, wasn't she supposed to just pet . . . ?"

Have I mentioned Suki's tail? It slices so sharp that the air falls in splinters around my body. Frozen. Heat turns tides and then this force slams my neck. Everything wet and I fly into the shattered air, riding on a lion's tail, and I hear screams from a place far away. Oh, I remember screaming, screaming so hard my blood hits the moon, but not now . . . Suki doesn't make me scream, he makes me . . . Pour. Drain. Scar. I will have scars. That's a fact. I look for something in Suki's eyes. I know the lion's name. It has eyes. And inside . . . anger? hunger? hate . . . . ? Curiosity. Instinct.

"Well if that isn't the stupidest wish . . ." Irene. Father Joseph . . . "God save and bless you, Katherine." To which I respond with dignity, God hasn't got anything to do with my salvation.

And I walk out, my wounds bleeding, my heart full with my story and my Sally and I come home, where it's oh so quiet.

127

Tipped Uterus

TONI PRESTI (IN COLLABORATION WITH JENNA FREEDMAN)

When I was 15—that's in the tenth grade, I got pregnant. My boyfriend was 20, and we were using the "pulling out" method of contraception. I couldn't make the phone call for the abortion from my house, 'cause it was a secret. So I had to do it at school. I remember going to school that day with about $5 worth of change in my jeans pocket. Calls were ten cents back then. I cut my first class, biology, and I went to this pay phone underneath this stairwell. I had my list of abortion clinics, and I went down the list until I found one that would take me on a Saturday. So I arranged to meet my boyfriend on the corner where we all hung out, and he was 20 minutes late. By the time he got there, my semi-adult composure was just right out the window.

We drove to the clinic. We went up to the reception area and Matthew paid $135, and the nurse said it would be another $50 for anesthesia. We didn't know about that, and we didn't have another $50. But at the time I didn't really know what anesthesia was. I didn't really get it. So I said, "That's alright. Forget it. I don't need that." Next I went into the operating room, and there was a nurse in there, prepping the room. She was a big, solid, black woman, about 60 years old. She was prepping me and the room with this sort of rhythm. And she took me in—lulled me with it. She was talking about her daughter's garden. Marigolds. Then the doctor came in. He looked between my legs, and he smiled. He looked at my face, and he smiled. Then he flipped on that machine, and he smiled.

Afterwards, I went into the recovery room. It was a big room. Unsupervised, with all these young women in there crying, and sort of yelling and walking around. And I just sat there in this green lazyboy chair really quiet. Rigid. About five minutes later this woman, this woman?—this girl—came in and sat down next to me. She was beautiful, and I remember feeling awkward because I felt so ugly, and she was gorgeous. She boldly took my hand, and just held it, really tight. When I think about it now, I realize I fell in love with her, because she was so beautiful. She started to cry, and she said, "It hurts."

And then she passed out. Fell asleep with my hand. I wanted to get out of that room really badly, but I didn't want to let go of her. I did, though. I untangled myself, and I left.

The thing about it is, whenever the subject of abortion comes up—when I hear it from a friend or on the news, or whatever, I feel a tug—and I realize that it's her. It's that girl.

Fireweed

LAURA QUINN

(Fireweed is a wild flower that grows on every square inch of Alaska. It's really beautiful and very tough.)

LORETTA: I used to sell Avon.

I worked out of No Neck, Alaska. I'd set out in my pontoon plane and cover 300 miles, easy, in one day flat. That's how I met Robert. He owned a dog-sled farm about 70 miles out of No Neck, and he used to buy soap-on-a-rope from me pretty regular.

Well, we broke up on the account I didn't shave my legs. Here we were, in a climate that gets to maybe 70 degrees on the fourth of July and he wanted me to remove a significant contributor to my warmth. There are ten men to every woman in Alaska; you think he would have been too busy being grateful to me for sleeping with him in the first place to be worrying about the fur on my knees. But no! Our break up was painful. I sold my pontoon plane, gave up my cosmetics empire, and moved to Seattle where the man-woman ratio is only four to one, and got a job in a gun store.

So, this morning I woke up and it was 85 degrees here in Seattle. I don't need to tell you how hair contributes to sweat. So, I went down to the local drugstore and I bought myself a pink lady's disposable Daisy razor and shaved my legs. Then, during lunch, it occurred to me that I had finally done what Robert had wanted, so why not send him the hair?

I went and picked the hair out of the razor where it had been sitting in damp little clumps. I hoped that when it dried it would resemble hair again, but it just looked like little bits of fuzzy dryer-lint. Robert is not a quick thinker. He wouldn't understand an envelope of former leg hair, especially if it no longer resembled leg hair, so I took some scotch tape and stuck the former leg fluff to the razor package and signed my name.

"To Robert, Love Loretta."

Still, maybe Robert wouldn't be able to figure it out. The subtle symbolism of my pain would be ignored. The delicate irony, like that of an anvil striking Wile E. Coyote again and again and again as the Road Runner "beep-beeped" insanely would be lost on his thick skull.

Bearing this in mind, I took a laundry marker and wrote in two inch letters: "I SHAVED MY LEGS YOU ASS-HOLE!"

And I mailed it.

Girl Gone

JACQUELYN REINGOLD

(Carla, a dancer in a topless bar, tells the other dancers how she feels about a certain group of feminists.)

CARLA: Are you one of those feminists? A bunch of them came in here one night, like a tour group, a hairy leg convention, staring at me like I'm a victim. So I stared right back and started to talking to 'em right while I was dancing. Fucking feminists. Who the fuck are you to tell me what to do? You want to help women? You want to help the women who need help? Don't put us down. Don't say we are adding to the problem by showing our God given breasts. Don't tell me I'm less than you, you elitist bitch. Don't tell me the way I talk is making me a fucking victim, bitch. Don't tell me I can't say bitch, bitch. You act like you're better than me, smarter than me, more enlightened than me, well come from where I come from and see where you would have ended up. You want to be my sister? Get me better working hours. Get me a dressing room I can take a nap in. But don't tell me I'm not worthy. Don't tell me I shouldn't do what I choose to do. I make money with my body. You make money with your narrow mind. You don't want to be me, I don't want to be you. I don't tell you what to think, you don't tell me what to dance. Objectify, my ass. It's my ass. *(She turns around, pulls up her skirt, sticks her butt out.)* I've always been a bad girl. I'll always be a bad girl. That's who I am. That's what I do. It's no better and it's no worse. You want to be a feminist, then don't blame me, and don't try to rescue me.

Flo-Jo Jenkins

DEANNA RILEY

(A woman in her late sixties, Flo-Jo, addresses other women at a club meeting.)

FLO-JO: My name is Flo-Jo Jenkins and I'm here to tell you it's a man's world. Bites your butt, doesn't it? *(Pats her butt.)* Does mine. I see you got a chunk taken out of yours, too. Yes, it's a man's world. I know. I married one. I have seven sons, seven grandsons and seven lovers who were seven sons of bitches. Seven is my unlucky number. I'm none of your damn business years old and tired of being a woman in a man's world. So I decided to change it. And no, I'm not going through the "change." I just got a bad attitude. When I went through menopause, I decided to keep the PMS. It's handy. I get respect and chew out anyone I damn well please. I like it. Leona Helmsley, the Queen of Mean. My hero. She wanted it her way or the highway. Think her husband ever left the toilet seat up? Not a chance. We shouldn't have thrown her in jail, we should have canonized her. Saint Spit-In-Your-Face. My personal change program started at home. Men think with their pinochles in their pocket. My husband, Harold, drops his underwear on the floor. If he's three feet away from the hamper, that underwear still belly-flops on the linoleum. One day he dropped his shorts, the magic maid didn't appear. After forty-three years of picking up his underwear, I got tired. Real tired. So I left it there. His boxers stayed on the floor for two months. Two whole months. So I threw those puppies out the window. His BVDs landed in the gingko tree. Did he pick them up? No. They just flapped in the breeze. Finally, I couldn't take it anymore. I had never burned no bra. Too busy with mildew build-up to contemplate women's lib. But I burned down the tree. To a cinder. Nothing left but a smoking nub. I found that quite liberating. Now, all I have to do is flick my Bic, and you better believe that he picks up that underwear. No jockey shorts throw rugs are only the first steps. I have bigger plans. Bigger plans than calling them *old* instead of *distinguished*. I don't want equality; I want power. And I'm not talking construction workers wearing miniskirts. I'm not a spiteful woman. I want real power. Let my husband be Mr. Flo-Jo Jenkins. I want my name first on the invitations, first on credit cards. I don't care diddly about etiquette. Miss Manners can go faux pas herself. Thought I was going to say something else. Shame on you. I'm a lady, damn it.

Glow in the Dark Woman

ELAINE ROMERO
(from *Living Dolls*)

(A twenty-four-hour cafe. Toni frantically rushes into the cafe, purse in hand, making a beeline for the bathroom. She slams and locks the door behind herself.)

TONI: Oh fuck! He followed me in here. I'm stuck in another goddamn bathroom until he leaves. *(Beat)* Get the fuck out of here! I mean it. *(Toni leans with her back against the door, slowly slipping down until she sits on the floor.)*

Great. I've got better things to do with my life than dodge him all the time. *(Beat)* I told him not to track me down. But did he listen? You know, men. They get all bent out of shape when you think of something besides them. Like yourself.

(Beat) We lived together a couple of months. It wasn't two weeks when I started noticing something. Something strange. *(Whispering)* I was becoming invisible. You really couldn't tell at first. It sort of crept up on me from behind. Like *Invasion of the Body Snatchers*, except it was happening to my body. See, this guy I was with was afflicted with an eyesight problem. He couldn't see me. *(To the guy.)* Hello. He'd talk when I was talking. He'd forget to say hello when he came home from work. He'd change the channel when I was in the middle of a goddamn movie. If I needed the bathroom, he had to use it first. For an hour. Then, my things started disappearing. The little notes I left to myself would get lost under his tools. I started missing appointments. People started calling me irresponsible. I couldn't talk on the phone because he was waiting for a call. Only the call never came. People thought I didn't give a shit. Bit

135

by bit that arrogant sonofabitch was erasing me off the face of this earth.

I had to do something. To get me back. So, I told him. I needed some space. To think. "Space. You want space?" he said. Like I was gonna drift off into the stratosphere. But I just ignored him. 'Cause if I listened to him, I'd disappear altogether. That's when I found this. *(She takes out a yellow highlighter pen.)*

My trusty Glow-in-the-Dark highlighter pen. The second I felt myself turning transparent, I'd sneak into the ladies' bathroom. To start coloring myself in, of course. I started with my foot. *(She takes off her shoe and sock, revealing a yellow-highlighted foot.)*

It felt silly at first, but what the hell. I figured, annihilation deserved a drastic reaction. So, day by day, as he got meaner and meaner, I got brighter and brighter. Until he couldn't avoid me anymore. I glowed at night, so I wasn't afraid of the dark. I glowed and glowed until the whole world knew who I was. *(Beat)* I started doing little things for me. Like leaving him. I got myself a place. A phone that he could not occupy. He was not pleased.

Suddenly, he started showing up everywhere. The man turned love-obsessed. Every time I stopped at a stoplight, he was there, giving me flowers and shit. Every time I went from the frozen foods to the produce, he was there, stretching out his arms, begging for a hug—for forgiveness. Why oh why had I left him. He just couldn't understand. He was so confused.

(Beat) I'm trying to be alone. But will he let me? No, he's begging, pleading, crying, "Baby this. Baby that. Baby, I'll change." Like that's gonna make me lay down and die.

The other day I got this idea—a real lightning-charged kind of brainstorm. There must be someplace where I can escape that he wouldn't be caught dead. And then it hit me. The ladies' bathroom. I'll stay in here all day if I have to.

(Beat) All I ever wanted was—I don't know—someone

who notices you when you need him to, but he also stays away sometimes, too. Someone who doesn't get all worked up about what you're doing or not doing. He just leaves you be because—'cause he knows you've got your world under control. *(She peers under the door. She stands up, brushing herself off.)* That's all I ever wanted. An in-between kind of guy. Who doesn't try to make me disappear. *(She slowly opens the door. Checks both ways. Exits.)*

Based on a True Story

DONNI ROSE

(Nora believes she is being stalked. She is standing outside her apartment bathroom, which is occupied by her friend Kathy.)

NORA: I'm a good person. I'm a relatively good person. *(Looks around the place.)* Not a neat person, but a good person. I don't hunt. I don't even step on cockroaches. And that's mainly, I don't know, about ninety percent, because I don't want to kill them, not because I don't want insect guts all over my shoes. Well, maybe seventy-five percent. I don't hang up on solicitors. Of course, I don't buy from them either. No, I just make them go through their spiel and then I say no thank you ever so politely. It would be better if I hung up on them, wouldn't it? Well anyway, I don't ask my parents for money. Of course my parents bug the shit out of me. Jesus, what's good about me? I stay and watch the credits at the end of movies. WHO CARES? I gave money to a street person the other day. Of course street people ask me for money every day and I don't give every day. Actually, I don't give more than I do give. But, I'm really going to re-examine my money to the homeless policy. I really am. Damn, I did fucking shoplift when I was a teenager.

Oh god, come on, come on get on the track here. I'm a good person because . . . . I'm a good person because . . . . Shit, I think I'd rather do . . . How I spent my summer vacation. I, I ah I recycle. I almost always recycle and I don't drive aggressively. Those are for sure. Like I'm really never bitchy; I'm hardly ever bitchy. I'm letting Kathy live here until she finds a place. Of course she's my best friend. Everybody takes in their friend. What else? What else? I share. *(Points to the bathroom.)* I share my hot water. *(Looks at bathroom again.)* What is she doing in there?

I tell people things. Like yesterday. Just yesterday, in fact, I called up Naomi and said, listen Diet Coke's a dollar forty nine at Walgreens. That was a nice thing to do . . . . . . WHO AM I KIDDING? For every little piddly ass okay thing I might do, there's probably ten self-absorbed, greed-mongering acts of rebuttal. I give ten dollars to PIRG and spend fifty seven dollars on Italian romping shoes. Like I'm going to Rome to romp?

I kick Smoka when he starts snoring sometimes; I just reach out and kick him because I want him to stop snoring so I can get to sleep because I place the importance of my nine hours over his deviated septum's right to self expression. That is so . . . callous of me. I deserve to have a maniac stalking me. I just don't feel bad enough when I hear about tragedies. It upsets me more to find out the Teflon Sisters aren't playing at El Rey on any given night, than it does to read about kids drowned by their parents because they can't afford to feed them anymore. You know, I deserve to have a crazed maniac stalking me. In fact, this guy's probably too good for me. It should be Charles fucking Manson out there by my car. *(She looks out the window.)* In my car. *(To him.)* Christ. Who do you think you are? Why don't you just get it over with? Whatever you're going to do, would you please do it already? Carve me up and feed me to the homeless.

Boxes

SHARON HOUCK ROSS

(Elaine enters pushing a grocery cart toward the audience. She stops and anxiously looks past them for a moment.)

ELAINE: I just parked my car in a wheelchair parking space. I've been shopping at the HyVee for three years and I've never seen a crippled person park there—not one. Much less six of them at the same time. *(She looks at her watch.)*

I haven't gotten caught. 'Course I'm not getting much shopping done, standing here in the foyer staring at my Honda hatchback. I should get in there and browse through the red meat for Mr. Sudder. He's my principal. He's coming to dinner tonight. Home visits with the faculty. "Sudsey" they call him in the teachers' lounge. He likes to sneak his Heineken between fifth and sixth periods. Mr. Sudder likes rump roast cooked slow in a crock pot until it falls off the bone. I wanted fish. But he said I needed the iron.

Fifteen minutes. This could be a first. I have always gotten caught. In high school, I was stuck in fifth hour study hall with Coach Judy who stuttered and had a glass eye. He used his other one to look up all the girls' dresses with the rest of the boys. Every day, somebody got out of that study hall by lying. Everybody did it. Everybody. Everybody but me. I never lied. I never broke rules. But one day, like today out there in that parking lot—I don't know. Something just snapped. I stared Coach Judy straight in his good eye and said, "Mrs. Wheeler wants me to do her bulletin board in the English room." And then I took off for the cafeteria for a Dr. Pepper and peanuts. And got caught. *(She furiously arranges the items in her cart, stacking them into neat squares.)*

You know what that feels like? Getting caught every time you so much as *think* about doing something? Like living in a box. That's what. A Chinese box. You climb out of one and there's another and another and another. I'm trying to deal with my anger.

My senior students keep writing essays about that movie. You know. The controlling principal, the rigid father, the liberating teacher who jumps on top of a desk and yells, "Seize the day." Seize the day. He gets fired in the end and a kid shoots himself in the head. "Get a clue, for crying out loud"—I want to say to them. "You live in a box—I live in a box—he, she, it—lives in a box! A desk is just another box, whether you're sitting behind it or standing on top!" Mr. Sudder would get me for that one. He doesn't like *his* box rattled—or theirs. But I'm real tired of reading those essays. They give me headaches. I have headaches all the time now. *(Absent-mindedly, she picks up a package of peanuts from her cart, opens them, and eats.)*

Did you hear? We have our first woman serial killer. I wonder what took her so long. *(Beat)* She got caught. *(Staring at the parking lot.)*

Uh oh. Here it comes. That man is walking awfully slow. Right toward my Honda. I bet he's the parking police. He's looking in the window. This is it. He's going to turn me in. I knew it! Maybe if I run real fast to the meat department, I can grab that rump roast and check out before they announce it over the P.A. system. Before I'm publicly humiliated in front of all these people I don't even know. Good God, I bet they even print it in the newspaper with the drunken drivers, don't they? It's a law. A federal law, isn't it? Mr. Sudder's going to kill me!

Well. He's walking away. Didn't even write down the license number. Huh. Guess he's just some ordinary man. Guess he's just some ordinary, every-day sort of man who happens to have a fascination for foreign cars. Whew. *(Consulting her watch.)*

Seventeen minutes, thirty-three seconds. No ticket. No tow truck. Maybe I should scoot out there real fast and move it while I'm ahead. What do you think? *(Beat)* No. No, I'm waiting it out. Can you believe this? I'm standing right here in broad daylight—*getting away with it!*

Okay then. I will not brush my teeth a second time every night with that fluoride stuff.

I'm through obeying the speed limit on 12th Avenue. Nobody else does.

There will be no more essays about movies.

And I am not going to register my dog with the city. Fifteen bucks because she's not spayed. They don't charge more for boy dogs like that, do they? No. Just thinking about it gets me mad all over again. That's where I was before I came here today. City Hall. Getting mad. *(Beat)* Maybe that's the difference in getting caught. Before I was always scared. Now I'm mad.

And I'm through with the smiling and the nice. I am not a nice person. Fuck it.

And now I'm marching directly to the HyVee frozen food section and I'm buying the biggest slab of halibut I can find. "Sudsey" is getting fish for dinner tonight . . . and liking it. *(Elaine whirls her shopping cart around and exits.)*

Vegetable Love

TAMMY RYAN

(April is talking to her sister, Moira, who is pregnant. April is drunk.)

APRIL: You know what scares me? Not human catastrophes like relationships and nuclear war—we can avoid those if we're smart—we probably aren't, but if we were—we have some measure of control over those decisions—some human's finger is on the button, and it's up to him *or her*—it's up to *us* in a larger sense—to decide if we are fucking stupid or not. And that's pretty frightening too, actually, now that I'm talking about it—but not in the everyday sense. I'm able to live on some level of denial about *that*. But what punctures through the everyday veil of denial—what really really scares me in waking moments and in sleep—including a really good drunk—like now—is Mother Nature. There's no way to protect yourself from a really big earthquake—or an out of control tornado, a hurricane—or a—a *typhoon*. I mean, there's no reckoning with that kind of power. Struck by *lightning?* It can happen at any time. And if we venture out further—like imagine Outer Space: *Billions* of meteors cruising like ballistic missiles, missing us by *inches?* How do we know? You know what wiped out the dinosaurs? A fucking *rock*. A big one. It's insane. We can be wiped out by the mindless whim of Mommy Nature skipping stones through the galaxy. Even though her picture is on Hallmark cards, Mommy gives away how terrifying she is with every move she makes. I mean, do you *realize* what kind of force has been unleashed in you? To set life in *motion?* Not just sex—two men can have sex, two women can have sex, but they'll never unleash that *force*

143

needed to start life. ZAP! Like lightning striking. Do you know there's only about fifteen minutes in a month that we can get pregnant? And really when you get down to it, it's about the battle between one tiny microscopic egg and one teeny weeny tadpole sperm cell—sperm *whale*. Now where did that come from? They named a whale, the biggest creature known on the planet after a tiny microscopic—makes you wonder. Anyway, it all comes down to a difference between one moment, really, and another, for *every person that's alive*. It's a miracle. That kind of power—is impressive—and absolutely horrifying.

Making It (Part 1)

LISA DIANA SHAPIRO

When I was about twenty, I did something completely
    unheard of.
I told my mother I had lost my virginity
when I actually
hadn't.
I grew up in Miami, Florida
in the 1970s
when disco was king.
My boyfriend was named
Isaias Alvarez Gonzalez Goldberg.
His father was Jewish.
At least, that's what I told my mother.
Isaias was in love with me.
I wanted to get laid.
All my friends had.
So he rented a hotel room at the Sonesta Beach hotel,
and we stayed there for a weekend,
trying to lose my virginity
unsuccessfully.
I couldn't do it.
I was convinced that at any moment,
the sky would crack open
and my mother would appear.
My mother, you understand, is Jewish.
When I was eight, I asked her about the facts of life.
She said,
"Go practice the piano."
At eighteen, I asked her about birth control.
She said,

"Say no."
So I realized
(virgo intacto)
that telling my mother I had done it
was the same
as actually doing it.
So I lied.
And I was free.

where the unknown god abides

S.A. SIZEMORE

(Margaret, one of the first women to be made a priest in the Catholic Church, is having difficulty coping with the estrangement of her daughter, Elizabeth. She is arguing with Kate, a friend and fellow priest, who has criticized Margaret's recent parental and spiritual ambiguity. Margaret is almost in a hysterical tirade.)

MARGARET: Don't you dare judge me until you've fought the same demons that grapple me!! The doubts. Lapses of faith. Questions. Unbearable questions. Why should *I* be allowed to be a priest if it makes someone else feel rotten? Why am I supposed to have such spiritual authority if I have so many doubts and animosities?! The demons come at night with selfishness and uncertainty. Tempting the power I have. I question things now that I *never* would have questioned before! What if—What if God is sitting up there laughing at us?! No, not laughing. Pitying! Pitying our pretentious conventions, our ignorance hugging the hope of purity and peace. Maybe even angry at our arrogance. *We* created all this! We created this institution of Church and priesthood. And we had to lace it with gold and crystalline repetitions. Make it grand and mystical. Theatrical. *That* is the legacy I left my daughter to contemplate?! How can I expect her to justify my life with *that?!* How can I expect her to accept me when I *chose* this collar over her?! I took away her faith and left her to be alone with the demons and the questions! She can't possibly have faith in an infallible Church if she knows full well just how fallible I am! So would someone please explain to me what to do now before my head explodes?!! (*She calms down as she realizes she has whipped herself into a fury.*) I'm sorry. I'm not making any sense. I'm tired.

Alchemy of Desire/ Dead-Man's Blues

CARIDAD SVICH

(Simone is standing, barefoot. In the background, a bone-yard looking on to a wide expanse of sea.)

SIMONE:
I got up this mornin and said to myself,
"I'm gonna find me some shoes.
I'm gonna find me some shoes
so I can walk this earth and see where my feet land,
see what my feet see that my head can't."

You need shoes
cause bare you're just another part of the earth—
not on top of it, not above it—
ain't no way you can own a part of this world
if you don't got shoes.

So, I set out. My toes wigglin.
Set out in search of what would find me.

Not long before walkin became too much.

I got on my knees
rubbed my hands in the ground
and said to myself, *"Find them*
And if you don't *find them*—
don't look back.
Cause what is waitin for you

is the foot-print of every other mad soul
who lost their wiggle on the search for a bit of stride."

And as I was rubbin, my hands raw with motion,
I found this spot,
where there was nothin.
n in this spot, I found myself a piece of card-board
had belonged to a bucket of chicken.

I looked at it. Looked at it hard. Took my nose to it.
But it didn't smell no more.
Didn't smell like nothin cept the dirt it come from.
Thought, "The underneath of the earth must be littered
for miles and miles with pieces of card-board from
buckets of chicken that have been buried—*cast off*—
by those that have loved, lost, or seen too much
of the earth's ways to believe in them."

I got off my knees.
And as I stood there
somethin came over me:
and I just took a blade to it,
a sharp blade of grass,
and with it, I cut myself some soles
some soles to walk this earth,
n strapped them to my feet with a piece of chicken wire
til my feet bled—
bled
but navigatin the world.

The Bird

NAOMI WALLACE

I get out of the truck and get back in on the passenger side. She moves over behind the wheel.

I say: "Like I said. It sticks in second gear if you're not easy. You've got to lift it up and out of first and then slide it into second. Don't hesitate. If you do, it will stick."

The truck inches forward, then bumps hard and stalls. She tries again. She is wearing a gold ring on her middle finger with a stone in it that must be a diamond. Tony is the first girl I've ever sat this close to who wears a diamond. I better remember to never get her a ring because I could never match a diamond like that. But maybe she won't be my first one after all and then I won't have to buy her a ring.

We bump into first again. Then we ride smooth for a few seconds. When the engine strains she slides into second without a hitch. Too bad. Now I won't get to go through the gears again with her hand under my hand.

"You drive like you've driven a stick before."

"Never," she says.

"How old are you?"

"Fifteen."

"You mean you've got no license and you're fucking driving my truck?"

"You didn't ask me if I had a license. You asked me if I wanted to drive your truck."

"Pull over."

"Why?"

She is laughing now. The sound of it pours into my ears like sand and plugs me up. For a minute I can't hear anything but the laughing. She pulls over on the side of the road and we change places again. We drive down River Road and park at the water's edge. It's broad daylight. I wonder if I should kiss her in broad daylight. Maybe that would be stupid. We both look out at the river and the sun's hitting it so hard it throws up a glare that makes both of us squint. "I'll take you home," I say. "Wait." Her hand stops my hand as I pull the stick into reverse. Her hand is cold and surprises me. I feel it in my gut.

"My father knows your father," she says.

"Yeah."

"My father's a liberal man," she says. "He doesn't judge people by what they've got in the bank."

I put the key in the ignition. The river looks cold. I shiver. When the sun hits the water head on it looks like ice.

"And neither do I," she adds.

"Well then, Tony, you should be right proud of yourself. Like father, like daughter."

"I knew you'd get touchy if I brought it up."

I let go of the key and turn to her. I feel tired.

"Brought what up?"

"Money." She doesn't want to look at me and she's biting her bottom lip. "You know. Come on, it's not a secret that you and your family are poor people."

Poor people. I think about those two words, what they would look like if I wrote them down.

I say: "Sounds like you've got a real special Dad."

(When she tells the following she now exaggerates and mimes driving.)

I put the truck into reverse and this time she doesn't try to stop me. Coming off the bank my tires spray gravel up behind us. I want to be cool, really cool now so I drive fast, too fast, down River Road. The rear end of the truck skids on the curves. She doesn't seem to scare and I want to scare her. I want it more than I want her. But she leans her head back and closes her eyes. I can hear she's breathing fast, but I don't know if it's because I'm doing sixty in a thirty-five. *(She quits miming.)*

Then there's a smack against the windshield like a tight-packed snowball, only it's mid-June. She opens her eyes at exactly the same time the bird makes contact with the glass. I look in my rear-view and it's rolling down the road like a ball. When I look back at her, she's closed her eyes again.

I drive her up the long private drive to her house that stands like a ski-lodge on the hill. When I get to the top and stop the truck, she doesn't open the door to get out. She leans close to me and asks: *(Whispering)*

"Does it get you wet to drive fast like that?"

It's like a glass of water in my face. I'm not even mad, I just don't know what to say. She gets out of the truck and slams the door shut and walks. I roll down the window and call her name: "Tony." She doesn't turn around but she stops and listens to me: "It didn't feel a thing. It was dead on contact."

She walks back to the truck. She almost touches my forehead like she wants to check for a fever that I haven't got. For years afterward, I remember that moment, her cool hand moving towards my face, my forehead almost under her fingers, the blood rushing up to the front of my skull to welcome her. But then it doesn't happen. The touch is withdrawn.

"And what will happen to us on contact?" she asks.

She is looking at me now as one might look at a face in the dark, as though there is something she wants to see but can't. *(Beat)* She kisses me suddenly and hard. It isn't a nice kiss, the way I would have liked it.

"Don't worry." Tony laughs as she moves away.

"We won't feel a thing."

153

Waiting for the Big One

PENELOPE A. WEINER

(Sister Burns is a dignified, seductive televangelist. She has occasional three-minute spots on a local cable access channel.)

SISTER: The older I get, the more I am drawn . . . to the floor! It's gravity. It's obsession! It's inevitable! I had to be very diligent in order to overcome my mother's obsession with floors. Her compulsive behaviors held me hostage. Prisoner, in my own body. I'd find myself cleaning, scrubbing, sweeping floors against my own will! But I broke that compulsion. I broke through that pattern. I broke it all down and found . . . my own desire. Now, I am drawn to the floor but it is not as a captive. I love floors. I love them when they're dirty. I love all varieties! I love to clean them. But I love most . . . ! What I desire, the thing I must DO!!! . . . is lay on them. I am drawn to floors!!!!

It's desire at its most fundamental. I lay on the floor and . . . ! *(She has an impulse.)* I want you! All of you!!! . . . No! NO! Women only! . . . to lay on the floor. Get down on the floor and feel gravity. Up and at 'em girls! LAY ON THE FLOOR! Close your eyes. Feel yourself moving down . . . gravity pulling you, blood surging through veins, pushing you . . . your molecules . . . the motion of your being. The essence of movement urging you to look closer, merge, melt, break through, break down . . . break something!!!! Stay down on the floor!!!!

Can you feel it? It's desire. Reach out. Touch someone if you can. If you can't, imagine someone. Imagine where their hand lay. Feel their presence. Feel that sort of prickly inclina-

154

tion to react. That's desire!!! Your desire. *(Mysteriously, seductively.)* You are being drawn out.

I don't know why . . . exactly why I suggested only women go down . . . to the floor. But I suspect it was the man in the audience, second row, on the left. Just as I opened my mouth to let those words out . . . "Go to the floor!" I saw him look at his watch. I glanced up and could have sworn I saw at least two other men . . . doing the same thing and I thought . . . if they can't listen for three minutes, three minutes! . . . what's the point of telling them to go to the floor?

If time weighs that heavily upon them how could they understand the implications of lying on the floor where all movement generates up and out, where expansiveness is truly possible. Where time itself is part of that law which dictates the explosiveness of the universe. Where the unrelenting urge . . . the action of all being . . . the internal motion of all growth and desire . . . demands that things get increasingly and increasingly more complicated . . . *(Stopping abruptly.)* It happened again!! You sir! You had to look at your watch. Why? Where is the time going that you must watch it so carefully? Is it going to slip away from you?

MEN. Men too, must sit on the floor!!! They must take off their watches . . . they must let time stop . . . Let it go. Sit on the floor!!!! *(Sister sits on the floor. She is silent for a long while. Some evidence of discomfort occurs.)*

But I'm forgetting, this is TV. You don't "do nothing" on TV! But you must in your life!! Once I urged you to "do something" but now I see that what you must do is nothing! If you haven't done it yet, let it go. Take it off!!! Give it up!!! Men . . . women. Do less!! . . . and less!!!! . . . and less!!!! . . . and less!!! . . . and less!!! . . . and less!!

Desire. Time. Push us, pull us, drop us through holes, lead us to brilliance! But we're not just pawns. We have dreams . . . dances of our own . . . which push us! . . . pull us! This morning I heard a voice. It said, "Sister, you're giving your best but you haven't given your most. You haven't given it all!"

I said, "What? What must I give?"

The voice said, "Give it up!"

"Desire?" I said.

"Let it go."

"Time?" I asked.

"Take it off!" said the voice.

So, now I say, we must now! HERE AND NOW!!! Every single one of us! Men, women, children, all of us together we must . . . Sit on the floor . . . Get off of that couch . . . Get out of those clothes . . . TAKE THEM OFF!! Break your clocks. Throw them in the hot tub! Dance! Dance. Dance with desire . . . Dance with your dreams! Lose track of time. It doesn't matter. Dance with disarmament! Take off your armor. Dismantle! Dislodge! Deconstruct!

If it doesn't fit, don't wear it. If it doesn't nourish, go hungry. You can't protect yourselves, stop trying. Put down the phone, give up your jobs, send me your cars, liquidate your assets. Give up your guns!!! YES!!! Give up your guns! Eat off your sofa. Dance on your TV! Urinate on your expensive Scandinavian dining set!!! Make love to your pistols, your shotguns, your Uzis, your switchblades, play with your mace!!! . . . AND TAKE OFF YOUR CLOTHES!!! (Sister begins shedding clothes, wig, etc. She tries to get out of the TV.)

156

Southern Utah: Another Tragedy

ERIN CRESSIDA WILSON
(from *Hurricane)*

(Esther sits in a bar in southern Utah. She smokes and drinks a lot. Esther is in a tube of light, speaking to us.)

ESTHER: I saw my first mushroom on a field trip. Miss Hansen took us to the edge of town and had us put our ears to the glass windows as we watched the mushroom cloud in the distance. I thought right there and then, I thought, "I'm marrying a man who works on those clouds, gonna hitch myself up with a fella who works those sky mushrooms." And that's exactly what I went and did. Yup. So now I'm worth one hundred thousand dollars! If I get the right kind of cancer that is. But then I'll never see that money. My family might, but I got no kin to speak of.

Now I don't claim to know much because I don't, but you know, they asked a bunch of kids, down there at the Hurricane Junior High School, they asked these kids, you know, if they believed that there was such thing as the Holocaust. Well, you know their answer was "No." "No, no, no" was the firm answer of theirs. They thought it was a myth like the Easter Rabbit or Santy Claus. Well, they used their skin for lamps, made shades with human flesh, knocked out their teeth for gold, you know, and they would take their hair and make wigs. But how you gonna convince a kid from Hurricane, Utah that that really happened? We're good at forgetting. Painting over the sore spots. Hey, but I'm stupid.

Well, now, this is something, you know, Graham, my husband, he excavated the ground after the nuclear tests used to go off, you know, cleared the area, and brought cans of water to the soldiers. Water's the best thing to wash off with in cases of radiation exposure. Just plain water. That's right. And sometimes, there'd be these days when they'd stop him from entering. They'd stop him in his car. They were waiting for the wind to shift, that's right, they were waiting for the wind to change. So it could blow east. Towards Southern Utah, Hurricane, St. George, and the likes. But not towards California and Los Angeles. That's a fact. Because California was a real place, a real place back then where things were happening. But in any case, the point is that this land here, in Utah, that my grandfather homesteaded and had took away from him in the Great Depression, this land was designated by the United States government as, and I know this now, as perfect and useless, yes. Disposable. The land. The people. A place you might throw out your used razor blades.

It's not my husband I mourn so much, but don't get me wrong, cause I do, it's my daughter, born with her heart outside her body.

Now you know I'm stupid cause I don't know why, but I always return to this land, return to Hurricane, where the rocks have faces and the wind is hot, where the dry heat and the sulfur springs make you high. Around here the streams bubble hot, there are prehistoric fossils, the bottom of the ocean was here once, you can find shells up there, and there's a good road up there you can go up to the mesa with a six pack and watch the meteors. But what I love the most is that underneath this beauty lurks the memory and reality that the grass will turn brown under your feet and that if you hold your fingers up you can see your bones. And you can taste it, sure, taste it on your tongue, like metal . . . like sex, the sky is pink. And now the moonlight is even too bright for me and these eyes. You think I got a hair left on my head? You think my teeth ain't real? They discovered they were hollow, that's right, no nerves, no blood, as they pulled them out, one by one, and gave me a new set to drop into a glass of water each night.

Oh, it's silly, but I remember learning, in the encyclopedia it was, I remember learning that crocodiles, they make hundreds of teeth their whole life, hundreds of teeth—wish I did—they just fall out and grow back, fall out and grow back, and they uhm, they, the men, they would take the teeth, this was back at the turn of the century or some such time, they used to take the teeth and cause they were hollow, they filled them with gunpowder, this is a fact, and used them as ammunition, as bullets, imagine. Crocodile teeth as ammunition. I feel like they stuck those crocodile teeth in my head and turned my skin the color of the rainbow, pulled my scalp up with the comb and cut my voice box, cut it right out of me.

Can you imagine burning rabbits running across a field, and sheep, homes split down the middle and cattle on fire, poison milk, children born with no faces, just large holes, the heat of seven suns, 125 atomic blasts detonated in Nevada between '51 and '62, each one about the same size as that Chernobyl. And my voice box cut right out of me. I never was a very good talker anyway, but I always knew how to think, quietly, to myself, stupid, but I thought, as I straightened the cuffs on Graham's pants leg before throwing them into the washer, the poison dust from his cuffs on my fingers, the taste of the pink cloud, like sex, and I am quiet, and I think you can hear me Claire, hear my loud whisper, your heart I touched in my hand when you were born, outside your body and how you did not live to see twenty-four hours . . . your face, a hole . . . . . . your heart, in the stones, your touch, in the stream, your torso in the stars, your hair in the wind on my lips, your face . . . . .

I think she'd be thirty years old now, she would be. He'd be sixty. Ha!

One dusk I saw a flock of mourning doves flying. A flock of mourning doves. And they had just flown by the light of a mushroom, that spitfire light of the mushroom, and they just dove, these mourning doves, they just dove straight into the light and died, kamikazied, a whole flock of mourning doves were blinded by this light that they relentlessly stared at. Maybe they was smart. You see, they thought the light was water, that it was the water that would hold them. But you could say I was one of those mourning doves. Or just stupid. Just staring into that light over and over and over and over again. Proud to be a part of it I guess. Or just proud to be able to accept anything that comes my way. I'm worth one hundred thousand dollars with the right kind of cancer. But don't listen to me. If I knew then what I know now, well . . . when you're dumb you're dumb. Right?

Claire, I'm happy. I don't watch the news, I don't take no bull, I'm a survivor and you know, Honey, do you know, you never got to see that mushroom, but it was like heaven, it was like heaven above. In that trailer, next to that butte, the glass and the heat of the day, the shudder of the window and the look of heaven, man-made heaven in the sky, in the south of Utah, in the mid-1950s, the baldness of neighbors, things you could not conceive, squinting our eyes up to Salt Lake City as we wondered the half life of atoms. And I think in this tiny town, I think about how we marvel at the news of war and in a way feel filled by it cause it's over there, over there, and Hitler, he's not just over there, he's way back then. Why it is that they chose this land I will never know and why it is that we don't count I'll never know, but we bombed our own country. But when you're dumb you're dumb, right. Hey, I'm no activist. I'm just sitting in this bar, right, drinking this beer, right, quiet as a mouse. Shhh.

(Esther downs her last beer. She lights another cigarette.)

160

Andie

ELISABETH ZAMBETTI
(from *Andie & Swain*)

(Andie, a young woman from a small mid-western town, is in her sixteenth hour on a Greyhound bus heading east with her boyfriend Swain. She is readying herself to leave him and their obsessive relationship. She is turned to face the window and leans forward as if to press her forehead against the cold glass.)

ANDIE: When it's day, there's something weird about windows on a bus. You don't notice it at first but after a while . . . like four or five hours after you been staring through them, they start to bend. To sorta melt at the edges. You pass by a field, outta the corner of your eye you see a farm house coming up. It gets closer and closer, picks up speed and just before you think it's gonna blur on by . . . it slows down like it's hit water and yeah . . . it bends across the window. The glass warps and stretches the image, magnifies it for the briefest suspended second, then releases it. *(Headlights and a loud car shifts into fifth and passes the bus.)*

There's something hypnotizing about it. It's hard to pull your eyes away when something comes swimming past. It doesn't matter if the window is dirty either, if it's got road dust, birdshit, mosquito guts on it . . . the bending still happens. Well, at least it always happens when I'm looking. *(Inhales)* But when it's night . . . there's nothing. Just my black eyes and mouth. I can't see those little farmhouses, those little lives. But I know they're there, just warpin' on by. I feel them pass. If they would just leave a light on for me then I would see them. *(Yells)* Turn on your lights you motherfuckers . . . ah . . . Christ. *(Her cry disturbs Swain, who has been asleep in the seat beside her. She murmurs to him as more headlights pass by. She strokes his cheek.)*

I first met Swain in a laundromat in Spearfish. I was feelin' sick to my stomach. I had been staring into my dryer for too long and everything was all blurry. My head was full of this humming from all the electricity. I stood up to go buy a Coke from a machine that looked like somebody had tipped over a couple of times to get their change. I had almost staggered to it when a voice said, "It don't work, sonavabitch took my dollar." I turned to see two cowboy boots propped up on the folding-table. They were attached to two denim legs, a greasy gray tank and . . . a comic book which hid his face. He was lounging in front of a dryer a little ways down from mine. I knew it would be a mistake . . . but I couldn't help it . . . I looked into his dryer. *(Inhales)* At first all I saw was a flopping mess of wet clothes. Then I leaned over the folding-table with a hand over my throbbing forehead, and I saw it begin to change. A faded blue plaid shirt took shape and sailed by, its arms outstretched to me . . . a white bathtowel rolled itself over and I saw it slipping down a pair of narrow hips, some black Levis danced past and I saw them astride a wild pony. I covered my eyes, in an instant I could see his life. Everything he had been until this moment. Until the moment before he met me. And I wondered how my clothes would look dancin' and spinnin' around with his. I looked over at the man, and the comic book was down . . . and some very familiar eyes looked into mine. I looked down at the bottom of his boots. They were worn down and I found myself wanting to walk where those treads had been. Walk in footsteps that were bigger than mine. His eyes said, "I see you . . . I know." That was six months ago and we been walking ever since. But I'm getting off at the next stop and going alone.

I wasn't gonna tell him I was going. I don't wanna fight or scream or cry anymore. I was just gonna get off and not look back. But he knows . . . he can smell it on me . . . *(She*

162

laughs.) Sway, baby, you are one crazy motherf . . . Keep dreaming, Sway. I'll be your dream girl forever, just keep your eyes closed. Your eyes know too much. They keep me. *(She sees a sign through the window, cranes her neck to read it. She whispers with hope and desperation.)* Twenty more miles twenty more miles twenty more miles. Keep dreaming, dream man.

Biographies

ELLEN K. ANDERSON is the author of *Hula Whores, Barbed Wire Under Your Armpits, Listen for Wings, Liz Istrata, Inflatable Girls,* and *Three Tits.* These works premiered in Santa Barbara at the Center Stage Theater, Access Theatre, and the University of California. Her awards include The Santa Barbara Independent Theatre Award, a Santa Barbara Arts Commission New Works Grant, and Best New Play in the Washington, DC Theatre Festival. She currently teaches playwriting at the University of California, Santa Barbara.

DOROTHY ANTON is an actor, director, and comedienne. Her plays include: *Cafe Divadlo; Girls' Dreams; Turk and Taylor; Divvying up the Pie;* and *Sex, Drugs & Apple Pie,* from which "Mamma" is excerpted. Her work has been presented in Los Angeles, San Francisco, Chicago, Cleveland, and Prague, Czech Republic.

DORI APPEL is an award-winning playwright, poet, and fiction writer. Ten of her fourteen plays have been produced, and *I'd Know You Anywhere,* the spirited tale of a reluctant mother-daughter reunion, won the 1994 New American Comedy Competition. *Girl Talk,* a revue-style play co-authored with Carolyn Myers, is now available from Samuel French. Other plays include: *Fun House Mirror; Kitchen Tables; Mother, Tree, Cat;* and *Freud's Girls.*

DEBORAH B. BALEY is a member of New Dramatists. She has also been a company member with the Perseverance Theatre in Juneau, Alaska since 1980 where many of her plays have been produced, including *Signs of Life* (also produced at Company One in Hartford, Connecticut) and *The Last Frontier Club* (winner of the Alaska Repertory Theatre's Drama Quest contest). Her latest play, *Into the Fire,* was presented at the 1995 O'Neill Conference. She is also author of *Blue Moon Over Graceland* (a Noh drama about Elvis Presley), *Covered Dishes* (a screenplay), and *Coyote Goes Salmon Fishing* (in collaboration with composer Scott Davenport Richards). She has received grants from the National Endowment for the Arts (NEA), Alaska State

Council on the Arts, Brown University, and Banff Playwrights' Colony.

SUSAN BRABANT has published poetry and prose in *The Family*, *Poetry of the People*, and *The Willow Creek Journal*. In 1990, her first full-length play, *Blossom's Wedding*, won second prize in the Purgatory National Play Contest. Her other works include *Gracie and Butch*, *The Warbride*, *Confessions of the Chaff*, and *Booth and Company* (a play with music). In addition to works produced at various theatres around the country, she was commissioned to write a piece for the Jerry Brown Presidential Campaign of 1992.

JENNIFER CORLEY is a junior English major with a concentration in playwriting at the College of Charleston in South Carolina. She has lived her entire life in the South and finds it to be fertile ground for dramatic and comedic material. Her plays include *Turbulent*, *The Shady Creek Cafe*, and numerous short pieces.

BRENDA CUMMINGS produced her one-woman show, *Momscare*, in 1994 and her Country/Western revue, *Petty Cash and Small Change*, in 1991. For many years, she has been an actress with the Obie Award-winning children's theatre company, the Paper Bag Players. Her acting credits include Georgette in *The School for Wives* at Yale Rep, Lizzie in *Linda* with the Ridiculous Theatrical Company, and various roles in *Hot Keys*. In addition to domestic and international tours, she has performed in New York at The Kitchen, PS 122, BACA Downtown, Naked Angels, Manhattan Class Company, HERE, NADA, La Mama, and Dixon Place.

LIZZY DAVIS is a junior at Brown University studying Theatre Arts. Her focus is acting. Her theatrical studies include a focus on theatre anthropology and inter-cultural studies. This interest has led her to studies of India, South America, and Africa. She will soon spend three months studying in Bali. Additionally, she leads theatre workshops in the Adult Correctional Institution for Women in Cranston, Rhode Island and hopes to continue similar work throughout her life.

CASEY DEFRANCO lives in California in the Santa Ynez Valley. She is a radio and TV commercial performer and the mother of a son, Joey. She wrote *In Rap With Dance*, which received the first Emmy ever awarded for a cable television show. She also wrote *Arrow Bay* and *Lady Jane*, two radio drama series which ran for five years in the southern U.S. markets. She is the author of four plays; *Angel's Share* was her first.

CHRISTINA DE LANCIE wrote and directed *A Larger Night* in 1988. This short film was featured in national and international festivals including the Edinburgh International Film Festival, the Chicago Film Festival, the San Sebastian Film Festival, and Women in Film, Los Angeles. It received numerous gold and silver awards. *F-64* is her first stage play, also written in 1988. It received the 1993 Jane Chambers Playwriting Award and was a finalist for the 1993 Susan Smith Blackburn Award. *F-64* was workshopped in the 1994 Carnegie-Mellon Showcase of New Plays.

LISA DIXON is an actress and playwright currently living and working in Chicago. She studied playwriting with Naomi Wallace in the graduate program at Illinois State University.

JEANNE DORSEY is a writer and actress living in New York City. Her plays (*At the Movies With Vera and Vivian Vigilante, Birthday Vigilance, Gideon and Josephine, Once Upon a Family*, and *Stepping Out with Mr. Markham*) have been seen and/or heard at Ensemble Studio Theatre, NADA, Naked Angels, New Georges, and the Westbank Cafe. Ms. Dorsey is a Participating Artist at Alice's Fourth Floor and an Affiliated Artist with New Georges.

LINDA EISENSTEIN is a playwright and composer whose plays and music theatre works include *Three the Hard Way, Star Wares: The Next Generation* (with James A. Levin), the opera *Street Sense* (with Migdalia Cruz), and *The Last Red Wagon Tent Show in the Land* (with Teddi Davis). She lives in Cleveland, Ohio.

EVE ENSLER's plays *Extraordinary Measures* and *Floating Rhoda and the Glue Man* recently opened in acclaimed productions Off-Broadway. She is currently writing a new play on Bosnian women refugees for the Joseph Papp Public Theatre, and has been hired to be head writer for Kathy Najimy's television series and to write a new screenplay for Goldie Hawn. Her other works include *The Depot* (directed by Joanne Woodward), *Ladies, Scooncat, Chamomile Tea, Cinderella/Cendrillon* (with Anne Bogart), *Coming from Nothing*, and *Reef and Particle*.

DEBORAH LAKE FORTSON studied acting and theatre with Jacques LeCoq in Paris, and made theatre pieces in Boston and New York. She studied playwriting with Derek Walcott and Kate Snodgrass at Boston University. She is married with children, and she often writes about the dilemmas, pitfalls, and peculiarities of women finding their way in relation to self, family, work, and joy. Her produced plays include *Baby Steps, Crazy Jane, A Clean Slate*, and *Her Dream Kitchen.*

CAROLYN GAGE is a lesbian-feminist playwright and activist. Her collection of plays, *The Second Coming of Joan of Arc and Other Plays*, was a National Finalist for the 1995 Lambda Literary Award in drama. She has written the first manual on lesbian theatre production, *Take Stage!*, to be published by Scarecrow Press in 1996. Her lesbian musical, *The Amazon All-Stars*, was published by Applause Books in 1995. She is the recipient of an Arch and Bruce Brown Foundation Grant, which will fund publication of her play *The Last Reading of Charlotte Cushman.*

TERRY GALLOWAY is a deaf writer, performer, and Texan who now lives in the part of Florida that is not Miami Beach. In the early seventies, she helped found Texas' longest running comedy cabaret, Esther's Follies. In the early eighties, she began presenting her one-woman shows at W.O.W., Limbo Lounge, P.S. 122, the Women's Project, and American Place Theatre. Her work has been produced all over the United States, England, Canada, and Mexico. She has also co-written a PBS children's series and published a play, a performance text, a handful of articles, a collection of poetry, poems, and many monologues. Currently, she's the head of the Mickee Faust Club jolt theatre group.

ANDRA GORDON has had readings of her work at The Miranda Theatre, New York Stage and Film, Alice's Fourth Floor, and the Win Atkins Theatre Project. New Perspectives Theatre Company will be producing her scripts *Jigsaw* and *TWO* in the coming season. Ms. Gordon's directing credits include *The Tempest* at New York Stage and Film/Powerhouse, *The Incident, Dead Men We Love* and *Twister* at La Mama, and her own adaptation of Beat poetry at The Open Eye. Ms. Gordon is a graduate of Harvard University.

KRISTINA HALVORSON is an administrator, teacher, and writer with The Playwrights' Center in Minnesota. She served as the playwriting grants consultant for the 1994 Kentucky Foundation for Women and was a member of the 1993-94 Actors Theatre of Louisville Apprentice/Intern Company as literary management intern. *One Hundred Women* was first performed in the 1993 Winter Apprentice Showcase at ATL and has since been published internationally and performed across the country. Ms. Halvorson received her B.A. in Theatre from St. Olaf College in Northfield, Minnesota.

SUSAN HANSELL was born in Stockton, California. She graduated from Berkeley in 1981 and got her M.A. in English from San Francisco State in 1987. Professional San Francisco productions of her work include *Pink Rope, A Day In,* and *14 Ladies in Hats.* Her new plays include *My Medea, Rollover Othello, Calling Jana,* and *Life by Jana.* Ms. Hansell has also published numerous poems, essays, translations, stories, and journalistic pieces. She currently resides in Brooklyn, New York.

CONSTANCE C. HAROLD directed the premiere production of her drama *Eggs and Bones* for the 1995 Colonial Plays One-Act Play Festival, where it appeared with her play *Another New Year's Eve.* A former graphic designer and illustrator, she uses her training and experience in the visual arts as a major element in her plays, screenplays, and essays.

ANN HASKELL is a poet and writer who lives in the Hudson River Valley. *Napoleon's China,* her first play, was written in collaboration with Sherry Kramer and composer Rebecca Newton. It has been produced at the Salt Lake Company.

LOUISE HECK-RABI, a native Detroiter, earned a Ph.D. in English at Wayne State University and taught English and Library Science there. Among her publications are two plays, many poems, and the book *Women Filmmakers: A Critical Reception* (Scarecrow Press, 1984). A Michigan Council for the Arts grant assisted the completion of *Hungarian Village,* a play with music. She co-wrote and produced *Jumpstart,* a sixty-minute theatrical video about teen illiteracy. She died in October 1995.

NAOMI HISAKO IIZUKA is a founding member of Theatre E, a San Diego-based theatre group. Her plays include *Skin* (directed by Robert Woodruff at the University of California, San Diego and since produced at Soho Rep and Dallas Theatre Center), *Carthage* (read at New

York Theatre Workshop and The Public, and produced by Theatre E), *Tattoo Girl* (produced at Seattle's Annex Theatre, the Off Center Theater in Tampa, and San Diego's Sledgehammer Theater), and *Coxinga*. Her most recent play, *Marlowe's Eye*, was workshopped at Playlabs. She is the recipient of a 1995-96 Jerome Fellowship.

SHANNON JACKSON is an assistant professor of English and Literature at Harvard University where she teaches performance studies, theatre, and cultural studies. She has performed and been published in several venues and has received fellowships from the Spencer Foundation and the National Endowment for the Humanities. "White Noises" is an excerpt from an ongoing project on the racialization of whiteness and the performativity of white racism.

DINAH L. LEAVITT is Professor of Theatre at Fort Lewis College. She has performed more than fifty roles and directed almost as many shows. She has published several articles as well as *Feminist Theatre Groups*. Her plays include *Aisles, Durango, CO!, Butter Beans* (which won the Dayton (Ohio) Playhouse's Blackburn Award of Excellence in 1993), *Anglers* (the 1995 winner of the International Competition for a New Play sponsored by Southern Illinois University), and *Christmas Presence*. She is the co-founder of the Boulder Feminist Theatre Collective and produces the Anaszi Pageant in Farmington, New Mexico.

SHARON LENNON is a writer and director of film and theatre. Her work has been performed at the Samuel Beckett Theatre, West Bank, Innerspace Theatre, and The Julliard School. Her plays include *Alone Time* and *Tummy Tucking*. Her film work includes *Eat Your Heart Out Goody Two-Shoes* and *Skin Deep from the Knees Up*. Her essays and other writing have been published in *Listen Up: Voices from the Next Feminist Generation, Ms.* Magazine, and *The New York Times Book Review*.

JOAN LIPKIN is the Artistic Director of That Uppity Theatre Company in St. Louis, where she founded the Alternate Currents/Direct Currents Series and After Rodney, a poetry performance group of white women and women of color. Her plays include *Some of My Best Friends Are . . . , He's Having Her Baby* (co-written with Tom Clear), *Love & Work & Other Four-Letter Words, One Sunday Morning, The Pornography Letters, Stories from Generation X, (Y, Z . . . .)*, and *Small*

169

Domestic Acts (taped by the BBC). She is a lecturer in the Performing Arts Department of Washington University.

JESSICA LITWAK has performed her one-woman plays *Fire Dreams* and *Holiday: A Year in the Life* at the Westbank Theatre in New York. *Emma Goldman: Love, Anarchy, and Other Affairs*, another one-woman play, was produced by The Women's Project in New York, San Francisco's Gumption Theatre, and the Storefront and New Rose Theatres in Portland, Oregon. Ms. Litwak's *Between Wind* was directed by Anne Bogart for the Music Theatre Group. Her play *Pirate's Lullaby*, conceived at the Eureka Theatre, was produced at Artists Repertory Theatre in Portland, Oregon, where it won the Drammy Award and the Oregon Book Award. It will be produced at the Goodman Studio Theatre in 1996. *Reincarnation* received its world premiere in 1995 at Portland's Echo Theatre. As an Equity actress, Ms. Litwak has performed Off-Broadway and regionally.

JENNIFER MAISEL's full-length plays include *Eden*, *Mad Love* (PEN West Literary Award finalist, California Playwrights Competition finalist, Jane Chambers Award honors), and *Dark Hours* (winner, Center Theater International Playwriting Contest in 1992). She is also the author of several screenplays and one-acts including *Storyteller*, *Welcome to Nuclear Beach*, *Wooden Horses*, *Objects in the Mirror are Closer Than They Appear*, and *Animal Dreams*. She received the Roger L. Stevens Award for Playwrights of Extraordinary Promise from the John F. Kennedy Center's Fund for New American Plays. Jennifer's works have been produced for regional houses, off- and off-off-Broadway houses, and in Los Angeles theatres.

DEBORAH MARGOLIN is a founding member of the Split Britches Theatre Company. She is also a playwright and performance artist with five full-length solo pieces in repertory. She is currently teaching in the Performance Studies Department at NYU. She has received numerous awards for her work and is a member of the Board of Governors at the New York Foundation for the Arts. She co-authored *The Breaks* with Rae C. Wright, an Obie Award-winning playwright and performer.

RUTH MARGRAFF just received her M.F.A. from Paul Vogel's Playwrights Workshop at Brown University. *All Those Violent Sweaters* was first developed by the Public Theater and produced at the Medicine Show Theatre in New York in 1993. Her other plays include *Flags Unfurled: 1976*, *Gat Him to His Place*, *Wallpaper Psalm*, and *Kissing Herself: A Gable of Songs*. They have been produced in New York at New Georges, the Greenwich Street Theatre, Joe's Pub at the Public, BACA Downtown, the Courtyard Playhouse, as well as in Rhode Island, Iowa, Minnesota, and Texas. She is presently working in Minneapolis as a Jerome Fellow at the Playwrights Center.

SUZANNE MAYNARD is a Seattle playwright whose work has been seen in Seattle at the Annex Theatre, A Contemporary Theatre, and Seattle Children's Theatre, as well as in New York at New York Theatre Workshop, New Georges, and The Miranda Theatre Company. Ms. Maynard is an active member of Annex Theatre where much of her work receives formative workshops and readings as well as full productions. Ms. Maynard is also a member of Seattle Writers' Kitchen and Seattle Playwrights Alliance. Her other plays include *Abigail's Atlas* (published by Rain City Project), *Popsy and Lorraine*, *8 Bit Divinity*, and *Hyenas*.

CASSANDRA MEDLEY's plays include: *Dearborn Heights*, *Ma Rose*, *By the Still Waters*, and *Ms. Mae* (one of the sketches which comprise *A...My Name is Alice*). *Alice* received the 1984 Outer Drama Critics Circle Award and is still touring. Her screenplay for *Ma Rose* was awarded the Walt Disney Screenwriting Fellowship in 1990. She has won a New York Foundation for the Arts Grant, New York State Council on the Arts Grant, National Endowment for the Arts Grant in Playwriting, New Professional Theatre Award, and the Marilyn Simpson Award. She teaches playwriting at Sarah Lawrence College and Columbia University and has been a guest artist at the University of Iowa Playwrights Workshop.

DIANNE MONROE has written plays, fiction, and literary non-fiction. She has worked as a journalist, writing feature articles and columns on social issues, education, and the arts. She is co-author with Nguyet Lam of *Scattered Children*, a collection of stories retracing the journeys of Vietnamese and Amer-Asian refugees now living in Atlanta. Recently she has been teaching creative writing to E.S.O.L. (English for Speakers of Other Languages) students to enable them to share their stories with others.

171

PATRICIA MONTLEY teaches theatre at Chatham College. Her published plays include: *O My Goddess!*, *Alice in Collegeland*, *Valley Forgery*, *Shakespeare Goes to First Stage*, *The Prodigal Daughter*, *Bible Herstory*, *Not So Grim Fairy Tales*, and *Founding Mothers*. Her play *Sisters* won several awards including First Place in the Wo/man's Showcase New Play Contest, the Colonial Players Playwriting Contest, and the ATA Women's Program Playwriting Contest. She is the Director of the Chatham Players Touring Company.

SUSAN MOSAKOWSKI is the Co-Artistic Director of Creation Production Company. Among her plays are *Ice Station Zebra*, *The Rotary Notary and His Hot Plate*, *Cities Out of Print*, and adaptations of *The Cabinet of Dr. Caligari* and *The Inferno*. Known for her visually striking productions, her recent work *The Tight Fit* was critically acclaimed in Los Angeles and at La Mama in New York. Her work has been presented in theatres and museums in the United States and Europe. She has received an NEA Playwriting Fellowship, a Rockefeller Foundation Fellowship, three Northwest Area Fellowships for her trilogy based on Marcel Duchamp's *Large Glass*, and numerous other NEA Inter-Arts Grants.

LESLÉA NEWMAN is an author and editor with twenty books to her credit including *Sweet Dark Places*, *The Feminine Mystique*, *A Letter to Harvey Milk*, and *Writing from the Heart: Inspiration and Exercises for Women Who Want to Write*.

RITA MARIE NIBASA holds an M.A. degree in German Literature from the University of Illinois and has studied at universities in Regensburg and Tuebingen, Germany. She has published poetry, essays, and translations. Her first play, *Stories Like Ours*, was produced at Parkland College Theatre in 1995. "Cutting Woman" comes from a longer piece, *A Line of Cutting Women*. At present Ms. Nibasa is writing fiercely and is experiencing the pleasure of her fingertips in bloom.

KIRA OBOLENSKY is a core member of the Playwrights Center in Minneapolis. Her plays include *The Leek Eaters*, *Chapman's Seed*, *The Stendahl Syndrome*, *Eugene Onegin*, *The Adventures of Herculina*, and *The Last 60 of '99*. They have been staged or workshopped at the Public Theatre, the New York Theatre Workshop, the Philadelphia Festival for New Plays, the Denver Center, the Oregon Shakespeare

Festival, the Atlantic Theatre, and the Juilliard School. Her adaptation *The Return of Don Quixote* will open in 1996 at Trinity Rep in Providence, Rhode Island. She is a two-time recipient of the Jerome Fellowship and has received grants from the McKnight Foundation, the Minnesota State Arts Board, and Lincoln Center's Le Comte de Nouy Foundation. She is the Associate Artistic Director at Classic Stage Company in New York.

TONI PRESTI has collaborated on many ensemble pieces including *Tipped Uterus*. She has toured with Martha Boesing and crossed the Atlantic with the Shoestring Players performing at the Edinburgh Festival. She lives and works in New York. She collaborated on *Tipped Uterus* with Jenna Freedman. Ms. Freedman has worked with David Cale, Morty Pottenger, and other artists at spaces including PS 122, Dance Theatre Workshop, and Mabou Mines. For now, she is concentrating on writing poetry.

LAURA QUINN is a native of Washington, DC currently living in New York City. She received her B.A. from the University of Virginia and her M.F.A. from the Iowa Playwrights Workshop. Credits include *Home to Tara* (Source Theatre), *Cielo Drive* (Zena Theatre Group), *Well Done Poets* (Love Creek productions; published by Dramatic Publishing), and *To Save the Human Race* (Love Creek Productions and Offstage Theatre Co.). "Fireweed" was broadcast by American Public Radio.

JACQUELYN REINGOLD's play *Girl Gone* received the Kennedy Center's Fund for New American Plays Rogers Stevens Award, was a finalist for the Susan Smith Blackburn Prize, was produced by the MCC Theatre in New York, and was published by Dramatists Play Service. Her other plays include *Dear Kenneth Blake, Tunnel of Love, A.M.L., Lost and Found, Annie and Andy, Creative Development, Joe and Stew,* and *Freeze Tag.* They have been seen in New York at Ensemble Studio Theatre, MCC, Naked Angels, the Circle Rep Lab, and the Working Theatre. They are available from Samuel French and Dramatists Play Service. Ms. Reingold is a member of EST, MCC, and New Dramatists.

DEANNA RILEY's work has been produced Off-Broadway by Polaris North Theatre, in Richmond at Firehouse Theatre Project, and in

Milwaukee at Playwrights Studio Theatre's Festival of Ten-Minute Plays. Her monologue, *Help Me, I'm Becoming my Mother!* was published in *Play It Again!* She has garnered many awards including three Emmys and a Delaware State Arts Council Established Professional Artist in Playwriting Grant. She has an M.F.A. in Playwriting from Indiana University and teaches at Goucher College in Baltimore.

ELAINE ROMERO is the author of thirty plays including *Fat-Free Chicana and the Snow Cap Queen, Walking Home, Dream Friend, If Susan Smith Could Talk, Refugees, Living Dolls, Undercurrents, Forced Entry,* and *Smashed!* These works have appeared at TENAZ '95/Festival Latino III (LATA), Borderlands Theater, the Invisible Theatre, the Portland International Performance Festival, and the Planet Earth Multi-Cultural Theatre among others. Also a screenwriter and fiction writer, her awards include first prize in the 20th annual Chicano/Latino Literary Contest (1994), a Tucson-Pima Arts Council Playwriting Fellowship (1991), and the 1995 Society of Southwestern Authors' Short Story Award. *Living Dolls* was commissioned and produced by the Invisible Theatre in Tucson, Arizona.

DONNI ROSE is originally from New York, now living in New Mexico. She has a B.A. in Sociology from the University of New Mexico, where she also studied theatre. Her works have been produced by the University of New Mexico and a local theatre in Albuquerque, where she makes and sells costume jewelry.

SHARON HOUCK ROSS is Playwright-in-Residence and Literary Manager for the Women's Project and Productions in New York where she teaches and coordinates the Playwrights' Lab. Her plays include: *Trapped Daylight* (produced by New Georges), *11 Shades of White: The Story of Veronica Lake* (Women's Project and Open Stage Theater in Pittsburgh), *Game!* (Circle Rep. Lab), and *Entry Points* (Iowa Festival of New Plays). Her new full-length play, *Flooding,* received a reading at the Women's Project. She is a graduate of the Iowa Playwrights' Workshop at the University of Iowa.

TAMMY RYAN is a graduate of Carnegie-Mellon University and a recipient of a Pennsylvania Council on the Arts Fellowship. She works with Pyramid Productions developing playwrights in Pittsburgh. Her work includes: *Pig, The Boundary, Vegetable Love,* and *Souls on Board.* She is currently at work on a series of short plays inspired by Japanese senyrus entitled *The Hidden Life*. She lives with her husband and daughter in Pittsburgh.

LISA DIANA SHAPIRO's award-winning first play, *Aces Wild*, premiered in 1994 in Los Angeles. Actor, writer, and East Coast native, Ms. Shapiro is currently expatriated to Los Angeles to write for television. "Making It (Part 1)" bears absolutely no resemblance to her real life.

S. A. SIZEMORE was born in Santa Monica, California and educated at California Lutheran University. Her plays include: *A Prison for Elizabeth* (which received a Meritorious Achievement Award in Playwriting from the Kennedy Center/American College Theatre Festival), *A Good English Gentleman* (published in *The Morning Glory* literary magazine), *Robin in the Hood, Sadeness, Anne Hath a Way* (produced by Plaza Players Theatre), *where the unknown god abides*, and *Under the Glass Table*.

CARIDAD SVICH, a playwright and translator of Cuban, Croatian, Argentine, and Spanish descent, was born in Philadelphia and now lives in Los Angeles. *Alchemy of Desire/Dead-Man's Blues* received its premiere at the Cincinnati Playhouse in the Park, as winner of the Rosenthal New Play Prize. It was also staged as part of the New Play by American Writers Festival at the Royal Court Theatre, London. Other plays include *Scar* (at T.W.E.E.D. New Works Festival), *Gleaning/Rebecca* (at Beyond Baroque Literary/Arts Center), *But There Are Fires* (Women's Project), and *Any Place But Here* (INTAR, Theatre for the New City, and Latino Chicago Theatre.)

NAOMI WALLACE's theatrical pieces have been produced in both the United States and Great Britain. *In the Heart of America*, a Gulf War drama, premiered in London at the Bush Theatre, then appeared at the Long Wharf Theatre in New Haven. It was awarded the 1995 Susan Smith Blackburn Prize. Her most recent drama *One Flea Spare*, set during the London plague of 1665, premiered at the Bush Theatre and will be produced in the Humana Festival in 1996. *Slaughter City*, a Mobil Award winner that concerns labor struggles in the American work place, will be produced by the Royal Shakespeare Company. Ms. Wallace's first book of poems, *To Dance in a Stony Field*, was published in Great Britain in 1995.

PENELOPE A. WEINER is a writer, director, and performer who teaches theatre at Washburn University in Topeka, Kansas. *Waiting for the Big One*, her fifth full-length play, earned her a Kansas Arts Commission Playwriting Fellowship in 1991. It was produced at Vortex Repertory Theatre in Austin and by Chameleon Productions in Lawrence, Kansas. Her play *Is There a Murderer Here?* was recently produced at Quality Hill Theatre in Kansas City.

ERIN CRESSIDA WILSON is an award-winning playwright, performer, and a professor of playwriting at Duke University. She is the author of eighteen plays produced in New York City, regionally, and in Europe. Her work is published by Smith & Kraus.

RAE C. WRIGHT co-wrote *The Breaks* with Deb Margolin and *Flesh!* with Tim Kirkpatrick. She was a leading member of the ensemble and lyricist for the Obie Award-winning New York Street Theatre Caravan for sixteen years, during which time they toured Appalachian coal-mining communities, Indian reservations, prisons, migrant camps, labor union halls, and to major festivals in seventeen countries. She has received numerous grants and commissions for her solo works including *She is Just Away!* She recently directed *Miss Ruby's Blues* at the New York Shakespeare Festival Public Theatre.

ELISABETH ZAMBETTI is from the San Francisco Bay Area. At The Western Stage Theatre in Salinas, she helped develop the original stage adaptation of Steinbeck's *East of Eden* with Alan Cook. Her one-act *Wasstree* was presented as part of The Western Stage's New Vision Festival. Her one-act play *Andie & Swain* was a finalist in The Turnip Festival Theatre Company's 15-Minute Playwriting Festival in New York. Her one-act *Belle Fourche* will also be featured there in the Moving On Festival. Her full-length play, *The Number 45*, was presented at The 42nd Street Theatre Collective's Summerfest.

Performance Rights

Professionals and amateurs are hereby warned that the monologues in this volume, being fully protected under the copyright laws of the United States of America, the British Empire, including the Dominion of Canada, and all other countries of the copyright union, are subject to royalty. All rights, including professional, amateur, motion picture, recitation, lecturing, public reading, radio and television broadcasting, and the rights of translation into foreign languages are strictly reserved. Particular emphasis is placed on the matter of readings and all uses of the plays by educational institutions, permission for which must be secured from the authors or their agents, as listed below. For those to be contacted in care of Heinemann, the address is 361 Hanover Street, Portsmouth, NH 03801.

Ellen K. Anderson, c/o Heinemann. Dorothy Anton, c/o the Dramatists Guild, 234 West 44th Street, New York, NY 10036. Dori Appel, c/o Heinemann. Deborah B. Baley, c/o Helen Merrill, 435 W. 23rd Street #1A, New York, NY 10011. Susan Brabant, c/o Heinemann. Jennifer Corley, c/o Heinemann. Brenda Cummings, c/o Heinemann. Lizzy Davis, c/o Heinemann. Casey DeFranco, c/o Heinemann. Christina de Lancie, c/o Peregrine Whittlesey, 345 East 80 Street #31F, New York, NY 10021. Lisa Dixon, c/o Heinemann. Jeanne Dorsey, c/o Heinemann. Linda Eisenstein, c/o Heinemann. Eve Ensler, c/o Carol Bodie, Three Arts Management, 9460 Wilshire Boulevard, Beverly Hills, CA 90212. Deborah Lake Fortson, c/o Heinemann. Carolyn Gage, c/o Heinemann. Terry Galloway, c/o Heinemann. Andra Gordon, c/o Heinemann. Kristina Halvorson, c/o Heinemann. Susan Hansell, c/o Heinemann. Constance C. Harold, c/o Heinemann. Ann Haskell, c/o Heinemann. Louise Heck-Rabi, c/o Judson Robb, 1605 Ford, Wyandotte, MI 48192-2303. Naomi Hisako Iizuka, c/o Helen Merrill, 435 W. 23rd Street #1A, New York, NY 10011. Shannon Jackson, c/o Heinemann. Dinah L. Leavitt, c/o Heinemann. Sharon Lennon, c/o Heinemann. Joan Lipkin, c/o Heinemann. Jessica Litwak, c/o Bruce Ostler, Fifi Oscard Agency, 24 West 40th Street, New York, NY 10018. Jennifer Maisel, c/o Susan Schulman, A Literary Agency, 454 W. 44th Street, New York, NY 10036. Deborah Margolin and Rae

177

C. Wright, c/o Heinemann. Ruth Margraff, c/o Heinemann. Suzanne Maynard, c/o Heinemann. Cassandra Medley, c/o Heinemann. Dianne Monroe, c/o Heinemann. Patricia Montley, c/o Heinemann. Susan Mosakowski, c/o Heinemann. Lesléa Newman, c/o Heinemann. Rita Marie Nibasa, c/o Heinemann. Kira Obolensky, c/o Jason Fogelson, The Gersh Agency, 130 West 42nd Street, New York, NY 10036. Toni Presti and Jeena Freedman, c/o Heinemann. Laura Quinn, c/o Broadway Play Publishing, 56 East 81st Street, New York, NY 10028. Jacquelyn Reingold, c/o Dramatists Play Service, 440 Park Avenue South, New York, NY 10016. Deanna Riley, c/o Heinemann. Elaine Romero, c/o Heinemann. Donni Rose, c/o Heinemann. Sharon Houck Ross, c/o Heinemann. Tammy Ryan, c/o Heinemann. Lisa Diana Shapiro, c/o Robert Myman, Esq., Myman, Abell, Fineman, Greenspan & Rowan, 11777 San Vincente, Suite 880, Brentwood, CA 90049. S.A. Sizemore, c/o Heinemann. Caridad Svich, c/o The Tantleff Office, 375 Greenwich Street #700, New York, NY 10013. Naomi Wallace, c/o Carl Mulert, Joyce Ketay Agency, 1501 Broadway, Suite 1910, New York, NY 10036 (U.S. rights) and Rodd Hall, A. P. Watt Ltd., 20 John Street, London, WC1-N2DR (U.K. rights). Penelope A. Weiner, c/o Heinemann. Erin Cressida Wilson, c/o George Lane, William Morris Agency, 1325 Avenue of the Americas, New York, NY 10019. Elisabeth Zambetti, c/o The Dramatists Guild, Inc., 234 West 44th Street, New York, NY 10036.

THE
15-Minute
ORGANIZER

Emilie Barnes

HARVEST HOUSE PUBLISHERS

EUGENE, OREGON

1973, 1975, 1977 by The Lockman Foundation. Used by permission. (www.Lockman.org)

Verses marked NIV are taken from the HOLY BIBLE, NEW INTERNATIONAL VERSION®. NIV®. Copyright © 1973, 1978, 1984 by the International Bible Society. Used by permission of Zondervan. All rights reserved.

Verses marked NKJV are taken from the New King James Version. Copyright © 1982 by Thomas Nelson, Inc. Used by permission. All rights reserved.

Verses marked KJV are taken from the King James Version of the Bible.

The material in this book has appeared in somewhat similar form in *Virtue* magazine.

Cover by Terry Dugan Design, Minneapolis, Minnesota

THE 15-MINUTE ORGANIZER

Copyright © 1991 by Harvest House Publishers
Eugene, Oregon 97402
www.harvesthousepublishers.com

Library of Congress Cataloging-in-Publication Data

Barnes, Emilie.
    The fifteen-minute organizer / by Emilie Barnes.
    ISBN 0-7369-0450-6
    1. Time management—Religious aspects—Christianity.   2. Women—Conduct of life.   3. Women—Religious life.   4. Christian life—1960–   I. Title.   II. Title: 15 minute organizer.
    BV4598.5B37 1991   90-20593
    640'.43—dc20   CIP

Over the years countless women have sent me household hints that have helped them be more efficient as "household engineers." This book is dedicated to the many women I have learned from: my readers, my friends, my mother, my Auntie Evelyn, and the older women who mentored me as a young mom and Christian.

These women have been my Titus women. I'm so thankful that God has given me a teachable spirit, and because of that I'm able to learn and to teach my readers. I'm so grateful for the many ideas that I can pass on to the next generation.

Emilie Barnes

Acknowledgments

Thank you Harvest House Publishers for being so faithful for printing all my books since 1980. From the very first book you have recognized that my ideas are transferable to my readers.

Contents

Finances

Holidays

Foods and Kitchen

Organization

Introduction

We live in a very hurried-up society. There is not enough time for love, marriage, children, vacations, listening to music, and reading a good book. Our television programming has to fit into a 30-minute time allotment; a TV character must go from birth to death within this time period! In a sense we are all in a hurry to get life over with. We demand instant cures, fast-food eating, and fast-forward buttons on our DVD players.

The purpose of this book is to provide brief but effective solutions to many of our basic organizational questions. Each chapter is short and to the point, especially designed for the person who has limited time to read a book.

This book can be read cover to cover, or else it can be used as a reference book to be placed on your bookshelf, to be read when you are looking for the answer to a particular question.

I have developed each chapter out of my own needs. Over the years I have met many people at our seminars who have had the same organizational needs that I have solved in my own life. I think you will find these ideas to be an encouragement to you as you become frustrated and cry out, "I can't seem to get organized, and my world is falling apart!"

Our motto is: "Fifteen minutes a day and you're on your way to having more hours in your day!" Make this a battle cry in your home, and you'll see how well it works!

This book can change your life and give you more hours to do the things you really want to do. Enjoy what you learn in this book and be willing to pass it on.

Part 1

GETTING
STARTED

one

Goal-Setting Made Easy

While they are still talking to me about their needs,
I will go ahead and answer their prayers!

Isaiah 65:24

o you want to set goals but shy away from it because of past failures in following through with your goals, or just because you don't know how to set a goal?

With a little information you can learn how to properly set goals for your life. Proverbs 29:18 states that if we have no vision we will perish. You are either moving ahead or falling back; there is no middle ground. I label the meaning of a goal as *a dream with a deadline.* Sometimes our goals aren't very achievable because they aren't very measurable. We have goals such as "I want to lose weight," "I want to eat better," "I want to be a better wife," or "I want to be more spiritual." These are all good desires, but we can't measure them and they don't have any deadlines.

There are two very important parts to goal-setting. Goals must include:

- ◆ A statement of quantity (how much)
- ◆ A date to complete (deadline)

A proper statement of a goal would be "I would like to lose 15 pounds by March 15. This way I can determine whether I have reached my goal." But remember that goals aren't cast in concrete; they just point you in the right direction. You can always rewrite, restate, or even cancel any goal.

13

As the beginning point of goal-setting, I recommend that you write down your goals that you want to accomplish within the next 90 days. As you get proficient in 90 days go out to six months, then nine months, then one year. Bite off little pieces at first; don't choke on a mouthful.

You might ask the same questions that a lot of people ask who come to my seminars: For what areas of my life should I write goals? In my own goal-setting I try to concentrate on eight areas:

1. Physical goals
2. Marriage/family goals
3. Financial goals
4. Professional goals
5. Mental goals
6. Social goals
7. Community support goals
8. Spiritual goals

These are not listed in any special priority, but are randomly listed for consideration when I want to get a grip on my life. An example of a 90-day goal for each of these areas would be:

1. I want to do 50 sit-ups by March 1.
2. I want to plan a 25th wedding anniversary party for my parents by April 15.
3. I want to save $250.00 by February 28.
4. I plan to enroll in an accounting class at the community college by April 2.
5. I plan to memorize the state capitals by May 5.
6. I plan on inviting the Merrihews, Planchons, and Hendricksens to a roller skating party on March 26.
7. I will take the Red Cross fliers to my neighbors on February 14.
8. I plan to read the Gospels of the New Testament by April 1.

Notice that each goal states a quantity and gives a date for completion. Each goal is measurable. As you complete each goal, take a pen and draw a line through that goal. This action will make you feel good about goal-setting.

As you complete each goal, you might want to write a new goal to take its place for the next 90 days.

two

Establishing Daily Priorities

*Never be lazy in your work,
but serve the Lord enthusiastically.*

Romans 12:11

"I've got so many things to do today that I don't know where to begin!" Is that how you feel on many days? This statement is shared by many people because they have never learned to establish daily priorities.

This chapter will give you tools for solving the dilemma "what do I do next?" Tools needed for this exercise are:

- ◆ Sheet of paper
- ◆ 3 x 5 cards
- ◆ Pen or pencil

Label your sheet of paper "TO DO" and list all the things you have been requested to do for today. When you are requested to do something, you need to ask yourself two basic questions:

1. Do I want to take advantage of this opportunity?
2. Shall I take part in this particular activity?

After asking the two questions you may answer in one of three ways:

15

✓ Yes

✓ No

✓ Maybe

You only want to deal with the items which you have written YES next to. The NO or MAYBE items can wait for another day. Deal only with the YES items today.

Using one 3 x 5 card for each activity, write out the activity you will do. Such activities might include:

- ◆ Get a haircut
- ◆ Go to the bank
- ◆ Pray for ten minutes
- ◆ Spend 30 minutes cleaning the kitchen
- ◆ Write a thank-you note to Sally
- ◆ See Mary's soccer game
- ◆ Prepare dinner for tonight

After all your activities have been written on separate 3 x 5 cards, sort them by the order of priority (what needs to be done first, second, third, etc.). Concentrate on only one activity at a time. After each has been completed, you can either toss out the 3 x 5 card or place it on the bottom of the stack of cards. When your children or mate come home and want to know what you've done all day, you can read off the various activities and they will be impressed!

Every request that comes your way doesn't have to be answered YES. It's okay to say NO. *You* need to control your schedule and not let others plan it for you.

One of our family mottos is to say "no" to the good things and save our "yeses" for the best.

three

12 Ways to Put Off Procrastinating

*It is far better not to say you'll do something
than to say you will and then not do it.*

Ecclesiastes 5:5

The National Procrastination Club was scheduled to meet in San Francisco in early 2003, but the meeting was canceled because they weren't able to plan it. Does that sound like you or a good friend of yours? Most of us are caught up in the no-action mode of not getting started.

Many of us self-talk ourselves into procrastinating. We say things like "I work best under pressure" or "The easy way is the best way" or "I can still go shopping and get the assignment completed on time." Does this sound familiar?

It's hard to measure procrastination because we measure performance by what we *do* and not by what we *don't do*. Procrastination becomes a problem when we neglect or delay doing those things that are important to us. Procrastination is the universal "effectiveness killer." Putting things off takes an enormous toll. Some of these include:

- *Continuous frustration.* We are always under the stress of frustration. We say things like "I hope," "I wish," "Maybe things will get better," and other such negative self-talk. We're always going to get it together *tomorrow.*

17

- *Boredom.* Boredom is a way of life, and a great escape for not using present moments constructively. Choosing boredom as a way of life is merely another way that the procrastinator structures her time.

- *Impotent goals.* We never get around to accomplishing our goals. Our speech is loaded with "I'm gonna's." But we never get around to actually putting into action our gonna's.

- *Always having unsolved problems.* We feel like a fireman trying to put out new fires. As we have one almost out, another one starts. We don't actually put any fires all the way out, and we're always tired because nothing is resolved. Unsolved problems tend to create more problems.

- *Waste of the present.* The past is history and tomorrow is only a vision, but the procrastinator wastes *today.* She is always living for tomorrow, and when tomorrow comes she starts waiting again for tomorrow.

- *Unfulfilled life.* Procrastination is an immobilizer that blocks fulfillment. There is always tomorrow, so today never has to count for anything. We fill our daily voids with less desirable things just to fill the void.

- *Poor health.* We put off next month to have a checkup for that lump in our breast. Then it is too late. Or we drive too long on bald tires, until we have a costly accident because we have a blowout on the freeway.

- *A life of indecision.* When we put off decisions we are forfeiting important opportunities. By not being able to make decisions we allow ourselves to become slaves to our future rather than masters of it.

- *Poor human relationships.* The people in our family, at our church, and at our work become restless around us if we aren't capable of doing anything. People don't want to be around us. We become the object of jokes and insults, which damage our relationships over time.

- *Fatigue.* With all the above energy drains working against us, no wonder we're tired at the end of the day!

How to Roll into Action

A human body at rest tends to remain at rest, and a body in motion tends to remain in motion. Procrastinators have a difficult time getting in motion, but once we get into motion we tend to stay in motion. If we gain momentum the task is well on its way to completion.

The following are a few ideas for creating momentum.

1. *Recognize the futility of procrastination as a way of living.* Do you really want a life of frustration, fatigue, and boredom?

2. *Break down overwhelming tasks into small tasks.* Try to limit them to five-to-ten-minute tasks. Write them on 3 x 5 cards for easy referral. Hardly anything is really hard if you divide it into small jobs.

3. *Face unpleasant tasks squarely.* Ignoring unpleasant tasks doesn't make them go away. Not doing it today only ensures that you will feel equally burdened about it (plus other tasks) tomorrow.

4. *Do a start-up task.* Pick one or two of those instant tasks from number 2 above and begin to work on those. Just get started.

5. *Take advantage of your moods.* If there are tasks you don't feel like doing today, find those tasks you *do* feel like doing today. Take advantage of your moods. Get started.

6. *Think of something important that you have been putting off.* List the good things that could possibly happen by doing the task. Now list the disadvantages that could come about as a result of inaction. You will usually find that the advantages outweigh the disadvantages.

7. *Make a commitment to someone.* Enlist a friend to hold you accountable for getting started. Choose someone who is firm and won't let you off the hook.

8. *Give yourself a reward.* Find an important goal that you have been dodging and decide what would be a fitting reward for you when you achieve it. Make your reward commensurate with the size of the task.

9. *Give yourself deadlines.* Color-code the due date on your calendar so you can visually see that date each day. You might even color-code a few immediate dates along the way to make sure you are on track. Write down the due date.

10. *Resolve to make every day count.* Treat each day as a treasure. Self-talk yourself into accomplishing something new each day. Live for *today* without always anticipating tomorrow.

11. *Be decisive and have the courage to act.* Many times we're crippled by "what if," "I'm gonna," "I wish," "I want," "I hope," and so on. Make something happen!

12. *Refuse to be bored.* Get out of the rut you're living in. Buy some flowers, cook a new dish, replace the familiar with the unfamiliar. Take time to smell a new rose.

13. *Practice doing absolutely nothing.* When you're avoiding getting started, go sit in a chair and do absolutely nothing until you are motivated to begin. Most of us are poor at the art of doing nothing. You'll soon find yourself eager to get moving.

14. *Ask yourself, "What's the best use of my time and energy right now?"* If that's not what you are doing, then switch to a higher priority. What you are doing might be good, but is it the best?

15. *Ask yourself, "What is the greatest problem facing me, and what am I going to do about it today?"* Plan your action and get into motion.

As Christian women, we are directed in Proverbs 31:15, "She gets up before dawn to prepare breakfast for her household, and plans the day's work for her servant girls." This means we are to be women of action. Treat each day as being precious. When it's gone, it never comes back to you.

four

How to Stop Saying "I'll Do It Tomorrow"

*Commit your work to the Lord,
and then it will succeed.*

Proverbs 16:3

Are there things you really want and need to accomplish but keep putting off for another day? Do you often let little things slide until they pile up and become large problems? Guess what—there is hope. There are steps you can take to get going and get organized.

In reality most procrastinators suffer from nothing more than simple laziness. They just delay doing things that bore them.

The perfectionist puts off projects because if she cannot do it perfectly she won't do it at all. Susan is a typical example of a perfectionist. The things she does are exact, perfect, and "spit-shined." She analyzes her project, gathers her tools and materials, sets a time, and goes for it. However, Susan's house can be a total mess much of the time because she doesn't tackle part of a job. If she can't do it all and do it perfectly, she'd rather not do it at all. So because she doesn't have large blocks of time in her life, she gets very little accomplished.

We all at times put things off for later, but later may never come. Who loves to rake leaves every day? But if they don't get raked we may never see the front yard until spring. Reward yourself after those "hate-to-do" jobs. Take ten minutes to read a magazine or have a cup of tea or hot cocoa.

21

Arrange some flowers or do something fun and something you love to do. Remember, life sometimes isn't easy; we have many responsibilities we may dislike doing.

Here are a few tips to help you get going.

1. *Set goals.* Set manageable goals. Start with small ones so that you feel a sense of accomplishment. If it's the hall closet that needs cleaning, plan to do it in three- to 15-minute segments. If it's answering letters, don't do them all in one day; set a goal of 30 minutes a week until you're all caught up. Remember, break things up into small steps.

2. *Make a schedule.* Block out time for each day on your calendar to complete a task. Perhaps it's ironing; allot 30 minutes for the day, then STOP. Before long you will be all caught up. What you thought would take one whole day will only take 30 minutes a day for four days.

3. *Be realistic.* If you find that 30 minutes a day is too long, cut down the time by five or ten minutes. If you find that 30 minutes is not long enough, add ten or 15 minutes. Remember that interruptions take place (children, phone, etc.), so be sure to allow for these.

4. *Take it easy.* If you feel overextended, trim down your commitments until you get caught up and have a workable, manageable load you can feel comfortable with.

5. *Get help.* Incorporate your family. Perhaps the garage or attic needs reorganizing. Ask, "What can you do to help mom and dad?" Plan a fun day working together, then reward the kids with their favorite chocolate cake and apple cider.

6. *Do it now.* Remember, it is more important to just *get it done now* than to do it perfectly later. *Now* gets results, and you'll feel great for accomplishing something.

7. *Be flexible with your goal.* Nothing is set in concrete. You may need to adjust your goals. Remember, setting a goal is a step in conquering procrastination.

8. *Remember to reward yourself along the way.* After that project is completed, all the letters answered, and the garage cleaned, get excited and take the family out to dinner or take a friend to lunch.

How about an afternoon at the mall? Or feed the ducks with the children, ride bikes, fly kites, or cut pumpkins and make a pie. You know what you and your family love to do, so do it! Give yourself time off. Even procrastinators deserve a little fun.

Thank the Lord each step of the way. God is interested in our successes and guides us through our failures.

five

Putting Everything in Its Place

There is an appointed time for everything.
And there is a time for every event under heaven.

Ecclesiastes 3:1 NASB

With spring cleaning around the corner, it's time to consider doing something about the piles of stuff that have accumulated over the winter days of holiday rush.

While we were busily celebrating Christmas and the New Year, our closets, shelves, and drawers were mysteriously attracting all sorts of odds and ends. These things have meaning to us and we don't want to give or throw them away. But we do need places to put them away. Here's a system that will get us organized.

The necessary basic equipment:

- 3 to 12 large cardboard boxes approximately 10 inches high, 12 inches wide, and 16 inches long, lids preferred.

- One 3 x 5 plastic file card holder with 36 lined cards and seven divider tabs.

- One wide-tipped black felt marking pen.

- 8½ x 11 file folders

Take the large cardboard boxes and begin to fill them with the items you want to save and store for future use.

Mark the front of each box with a number. Assign a 3 x 5 lined file card for each box. For each box write on the card what you have stored in that box. For example:

Box 1—Scrap sewing fabric

Box 2—Chad's baby toys and clothes

Box 3—Jenny's high school cheerleading uniform

Box 4—Ski clothes

Box 5—Gold-mining gear

Box 6—Snorkel gear with swim fins

Save Number 15 for your income tax records (April 15):

Box 15A—1998 records

Box 15B—1999 records

Box 15C—2000 records

Box 15D—2001 records

Box 15E—2002 records

Number 25 is a good one for your Christmas items:

Box 25A—Wreaths

Box 25B—Outdoor lights

Box 25C—Indoor lights

Box 25D—Tree decorations

Box 25E—Garlands & candles

By labeling your boxes A through Z you can add to your number sequence and keep all your items together. (It saves a lot of time when you need to retrieve those items.) Every two or three years go back through these boxes, cleaning them out and consolidating them.

On your 3 x 5 card write in the upper-right-hand corner where you have stored each box. Ideally, store these boxes in the garage, attic, or basement. If you don't have the luxury of lots of storage space, spray paint or wallpaper the boxes to fit in with the decor of your home (such as the laundry room, bedroom or bathroom).

When you get to the bottom of the "put away" pile, you will probably find many loose items of papers and records that need some type of storage for quick retrieval. This is where your 8½ x 11 file folders come in handy.

Label the folders with the following headings and then place each paper or receipt in the corresponding folder:

Insurance Papers

◆ Auto

◆ Health

◆ Homeowner's

Homeowner Papers

◆ Escrow papers

◆ Tax records (for current year)

Receipts

◆ Auto repairs

◆ Major purchases

Store these folders in a metal file cabinet or a storage box. If possible, keep these boxes near the office area in your home. Close accessibility to these files will save you extra footsteps when you need to get to them.

Give your young children storage boxes, file cards, and file folders to help them keep their rooms organized. This provides an excellent model for their future personal organization.

Just think of your satisfaction when a member of your family comes to you and asks where something is and you pull out your box, flip through your cards, and tell him or her to look in Box 5, which is located under the attic stairs. Won't he be impressed with the new organized you!

six

Four Tools to an Organized You

To fail to plan is to plan to fail.

Unknown

Do you ever look around your home, room, or office and just want to throw up your hands in disgust and say, "It's no use, I'll never get organized"? The old saying "Everything has a place and everything in its place" sounds great, but how do you make it work for you? Here are four simple tools to help you get your home organized for the new year.

◆ "To do" list
◆ Calendar
◆ Telephone/address list
◆ Simple filing system

A "To Do" List

Use the same size of paper for the first three tools (8½ x 11 or 5½ x 8½). This way you won't have to fight with different sizes of paper. After choosing your size of paper, write the words TO DO at the top of a piece of paper. Begin writing down all the things that you need to do.

27

When you finish each item during the day, relish the pleasure of crossing it off the list. At the end of the day, review your list and update any new things you need to add. If you have accomplished something that day that wasn't on your list, write it down. Everyone's life is full of interruptions, and you need to applaud yourself for what you *did* accomplish!

At the end of the week, consolidate your lists and start again on Monday with a fresh page. Eventually you will want to rank your TO DO items by importance. This added technique will help you maximize your time to it fullest potential.

A Calendar

I recommend two types of calendars. The first is a two-page "Month at a Glance" calendar. One glance will give you a good idea of the overview of the month. Details aren't written here, but do jot down broad engagements with times. For example, write down meetings, luncheons, basketball games, speaking engagements, and dental appointments.

The second type of calendar is a page for each day—"Day at a Glance." On this calendar you write down more specific details, such as what you will be doing on the hour or half-hour. Be careful that you don't overload your calendar and jam your appointments too close together. Remember to schedule in time alone and time with God.

As a guideline, I suggest that if you've been someplace before and you know where you're going, allow 25 percent more time than you think it will take. If you estimate that a meeting will last one hour, block out one hour and fifteen minutes.

A Telephone/Address List

This list will become your personal telephone and address book. Using the same size paper as your TO DO list and calendar, design your own directory of information for home, work, and play. You might want to list certain numbers by broad headings, such as schools, attorneys, dentists, doctors, plumbers, carpenters, and restaurants. This helps you look up the specifics when you can't remember the person's last name. Use a pencil in writing down addresses and telephone numbers, since it is much easier to correct than ink if the information changes.

If you have a client or customer listed, you may want to mark down personal data about the person to review before your next meeting. Some items to include are the client's spouse and children's names, sports of interest, and favorite foods and vacation spots. Your clients will be impressed that you remembered all that information about them.

The same system works well with guests in your home. Include some of the meals you served them, any particular food allergies they have, and whether they drank coffee or tea.

A Simple Filing System

The motto in our home is "Don't pile it, file it." This tool will make your home look like a new place! At your local stationery store, purchase about four dozen colored or manila 8½ x 14 file folders. I recommend colored file folders because they help you categorize your material and also add a little cheer to your day. I find that the legal-size folders (8½ x 14) are more functional, since they accommodate longer, nonstandardized pieces of paper.

Label each folder with a simple heading, such as Sales Slips, Auto, Insurance, School Papers, Maps, Warranties, Taxes, and Checks. Then take all the loose papers you find around your home and put them into their respective folders. If you have a filing cabinet to house these folders, that's great. If not, just get a cardboard storage box to get started.

After you have mastered these four tools to organization, you can branch out and acquire more skills. Remember, though, to give yourself time, since it takes 21 consecutive days to acquire a new habit.

seven

How to Find More Time

*All of us must quickly carry out the tasks
assigned to us by [God]...for there is
little time left before the night falls.*

John 9:4

"If only I could get organized!" "I just don't have enough time in the day!" Do you ever hear yourself making these statements?

Don't we all at some point in our lives find ourselves waiting until the last minute to fill out tax forms, wrap Christmas presents, or send a belated birthday card?

Here are a few ideas that will help you find more time for yourself and enable you to get all those little jobs done.

1. As you make a TO DO list, set small, manageable deadlines for yourself. For example, by October 2 I'll clean two drawers in the kitchen. By October 8 I'll sort through papers in my desk. On October 28 I'll select my Christmas cards.

   Some other bite-sized chunks that will take 15 minutes a day are answering a letter, cleaning a bathroom, or changing the linen on one bed. If it helps, set a timer for 15 minutes. When the timer goes off, go back to your regular schedule.

30

2. Plan ahead for guests. Sometimes having guests come to your home can be overwhelming when you think about the preparation involved. Doing things in 15-minute increments works wonders for your preparation. Write out a TO DO list about a week before your party, Sunday brunch, or arrival of weekend guests. Plan to do a little each day until your guests arrive.

   For example, one day make up their bed with clean sheets. Wait until the next day to do the vacuuming and the following to do the baking. Remember, reward yourself or give yourself a break after each accomplishment. Pick some flowers, take a walk, polish your nails, or give yourself a facial.

3. Watch out for interruptions. They will be there, but try to avoid them. If you have an answering machine, turn it on. If you don't have a machine, tell the caller you will call back later, when you finish the project you're involved in. Wait until the baby is sleeping for certain projects. Put a note on the front door that reads "Available after 3 P.M."

4. Learn to say no at least until you've completed what you set out to do on your list. But remember to keep your list realistic and obtainable. Don't load yourself to the point that you feel overwhelmed and then give up and do nothing at all.

5. Get your family to help with odd jobs by giving them a chart. TO DO BY 5 P.M.: a) Sweep the driveway; b) Rake the leaves in the backyard; c) Set the table for the next meal; d) Take an apple break.

   Let your family in on your 15-minute plan. They'll love working against time; it becomes a game. Reward, praise, and compliment them for a job well done. If each child works 15 minutes a day toward an organized home, look how many hours it will save you! This will give you time for yourself and at the same time teach your children to be responsible young people.

6. Reward yourself when projects are complete. Go out for lunch with a friend and share what you've accomplished. She'll be excited for you and probably go home and clean out her drawers too! Or sit down with a cup of tea or coffee and read a magazine or the Bible.

Part 2

CLEANING

eight

How to Get Housework Done in Record Time

Teach us to number our days and recognize how few they are; help us to spend them as we should.

Psalm 90:12

For the busy woman today, housework is a nuisance and not necessarily her real concern. Today's woman does not have time to devote her full time to cleaning, as did her grandmother or great-grandmother. However, dirt doesn't just blow away and seven dwarfs don't appear at night while we sleep to clean up our messes. Wouldn't it be wonderful to have time to do things with family and church instead of spending all day Saturday cleaning, cleaning, cleaning? Here are some speedy tips to get the job done and feel great about doing it.

Start with collecting the right supplies.

- ◆ Pail or bucket and mop.

- ◆ Broom and dustpan.

- ◆ Squeegee. Professionals use these exclusively. Never use newspaper or paper towels, since they contain fibers that leave the windows messy. A good squeegee works fast and easy: Use a spray bottle with rubbing alcohol; spray on window and squeegee off.

- ◆ Billy's old football knee pads. These are great protectors which can be purchased at sporting goods stores (or similar work pads at hardware

35

stores) for cleaning floors and tubs. Soft pads keep knee work less painful.

◆ Clean dustcloths. Diapers are great, and so are 100 percent cotton dishcloths (well-washed and dried).

◆ Carry-all tray. A must for storing cleaning items such as wax, window spray, etc.

◆ Feather duster. A super item for moving small amounts of dust from a higher level to a lower level, where most of it can be vacuumed up. I have lots of cobwebs and knickknack items, and this is my quick lifesaver of dusting each item every time. Invest in a good ostrich duster. You can purchase one at a hardware or janitor supply store.

◆ Pumice stone. It gets that ugly ring out of the toilet bowl caused by rust and mineral deposits. It's amazing how fast a pumice stone will remove the scale; just rub it on the ring gently and it's gone. It also cleans ovens and removes the carbon buildup on grills and iron cookware, as well as removing paint from concrete and masonry walls and scale from swimming pools. Pumice stones can be purchased in hardware stores, janitor supply stores, and beauty supply stores.

◆ Toothbrush. Great for cleaning the hard corners of floors and showers and around faucets at the sink.

◆ Vacuum cleaner. An absolute must!

◆ Ammonia. An excellent cleaner (not the sudsy type) for floors.

◆ Powdered cleanser. For sinks and bathtubs.

◆ Oven cleaner.

◆ Rubber gloves. To protect your hands from the chemicals in household cleaners and detergents.

◆ Scraper. Use the razor-blade type to remove paint from tile or glass and decals or stickers from the shower door. Also, remove dried-on food after it gets hard, such as pancake batter or eggs. But be careful not to scratch the surface.

Fill your carry-all tray with many of the above items. It's ready to work when you are!

When you work, be sure to use the *speedy easy method:*

1. Put on some music with a very fast beat. This will help your cleaning go faster plus take your mind off the drudgery.

2. Go in one direction. Work around your room from top to bottom and from right to left or left to right—whatever feels good to you. Also start at one end of your home and work toward the other end. Don't get sidetracked with this mess and that mess.

3. Before cleaning windowpanes, wipe or vacuum sills and wood cross-frames. Use your spray bottle with alcohol and squeegee and cotton cloth. Use a horizontal stroke on the outside and a vertical stroke on the inside. That way you'll know if you missed a spot because you can tell which side the streak is on.

4. Use your hair dryer to blow off the dust from silk flowers. Your feather duster will work well to dust off soft fabric items, plants, picture frames, and lampshades. Remember, we're working from top to bottom in each room, so you'll be vacuuming up this dust soon.

5. After wiping clean your wastebaskets, give the inside bottom a quick coat of floor wax. This will prevent trash from sticking to the bottom of the wastebasket in the future.

6. Change your air conditioner and heater filters every six months for best performance. This will keep the dust and dirt from circulating through your rooms.

7. Wipe off the blades of your window and/or room fans quarterly to keep dirt and dust from flying around.

8. Try to avoid interruptions; take the phone message and call back when it is convenient.

9. Big question: Should you vacuum first or last? Last, of course.

Having the proper tools helps. Don't feel that everything has to be done in one work session. Set your timer and then work in 15-minute time slots. Work fast, but after each time and/or project, treat yourself to a cup of hot chocolate or iced tea, or put a mask on your face and enjoy a hot bath.

Then go to the garden and pick a fresh bouquet of flowers for your beautiful clean house.

nine

Are You a Pack Rat?

*She watches carefully all that goes on
throughout her household, and is never lazy.*

Proverbs 31:27

Answer yes or no to each question. You get a zero for every no and one point for every yes.

A zero is a perfect score and probably impossible. If your score is 10, you are a pack rat and you've come to the right place!

1. Do you find yourself complaining that you don't have enough room or space?

2. Do you have things piled up in cupboards and closets or stacked into corners because there is no place to put them?

3. Do you have magazines stacked around the house waiting to be read? Are you saving them for the day when you'll sit down and cut out articles, recipes, and patterns?

4. Do things often get "lost" in your house?

5. Do you think, "I'll just put this here for now and put it away later"?

6. Are things collecting on top of your refrigerator, dresser drawers in the bedroom, counters, end tables, coffee tables, and bookshelves?

7. Do you have things around your home that you haven't used for a long time or possibly don't even want?

8. Do you ever buy something you already have at home because you can't find it or don't want to look for it?

9. Do you often say, "It might come in handy someday"?

10. Do you have to move things around in your closet or cupboards to find a certain item?

Let's see how you did.

0–3   You're in pretty good shape.

4–7   You could use some improvement.

8–10   It's never too late, pack rat. However, I'd start with prayer. Philippians 4:13 says, "I can do all things through Christ who strengthens me" (NKJV).

Begin with a family meeting, saying that you have discovered a problem. Let them know that you are a collector of things and need help from all of them, along with their support, to help you get your house in order.

When we admit our problem, somehow it helps us to get started in organizing.

You didn't get to this problem point by yourself; surely the whole family is as guilty as you are. But *you* are the one admitting it, so let's start with you. You take the responsibility and work toward getting control. (Altogether too many homes today are controlling us instead of us being in control of our homes.)

Step 1 is to think of what area of your clutter is bothering you the most. Is it the top of the refrigerator?

Step 2 is to set a 10-to-15-minute time slot to take care of that clutter. Set your timer on the oven and go at it. You'll be surprised at what you can get done in 15-minute intervals!

Repeat steps 1 and 2 above with each area of your home clutter. It may take weeks to finish the project, but at least you'll be working toward organizing your pack rat clutter.

Begin to file away the piles of papers, letters, articles, etc. into a file cabinet or cardboard file box, keeping in mind *don't put it down, put it away!* This will help you in the future to put things in their proper place.

If you have a difficult time deciding whether to *throw* something away or *store* it away, put those difficult-decision things into a box or baggie and put it in the garage, attic, or basement. Then if something is so important to you that you would go to the extreme of retrieving it from the box or baggie, that item should be stored nearby. But if those boxes or bags sit for several months untouched, it's a sure indication to give them away or throw them away.

"Out of sight, out of mind" is a good saying to remember. So *throw away* and *give away*.

After attending one of my seminars, one woman told me that in five weeks she had organized the things in her home into 62 cardboard boxes! She said, "I'm a pack rat, but at least I'm an organized one!"

ten

Key to a Clean House

In everything you do, put God first, and he will direct you and crown your efforts with success.

Proverbs 3:6

Do you have the type of home where every room you go into contains so many odd jobs to do (picking up yesterday's paper, washing off the refrigerator door, folding the last load of clothes) that you rush around all day never completing any one job?

If you struggle with getting household chores done, try this time-tested technique: *Break down big jobs into little jobs.* Here are a few ideas.

♦ Commit yourself to accomplishing a chore that shows. Start by picking up and putting away items in the living room that don't belong there (i.e., last week's TV listings or your son's Tonka truck). It will help you feel better if, as you walk into the house, at least the living room is in order. Take a minute to make a bed or pick up dirty dishes scattered throughout the house. The idea is to organize *at least one thing*, since this will take you only two minutes or less.

♦ *Buy a timer or use the one on your oven.* A woman once told me that she hated to mop her kitchen floor. It caused her anger and stress every time she thought of doing it, and even more stress every time she walked across a sticky floor.

41

I recommended that she time how long it took her to mop her floor. She reported that it only took her three minutes! Now when she thinks of mopping that floor she thinks of taking only three minutes to do the job, and she feels less stressed about it. We have many jobs around our homes that can be done in three to ten minutes.

◆ *List on a piece of paper the jobs that can be done in 15 minutes or less.* This will be easy to do once you get into the swing of timing your chores.

Because our normal tendency is to group work into big jobs, we make the excuse that we don't have time to do certain chores. For example, we may figure it takes 30 minutes to clean the refrigerator, and if we don't have 30 minutes to do it, we won't do it at all.

In reality it could take only seven minutes. Once you've timed this job, the next time the refrigerator needs cleaning it won't be that big a deal.

◆ *Profit from the precious minutes usually wasted while you wait for someone.* You are ready for Marci to pick you up for that meeting, but you have ten minutes before she comes. Instead of sitting on the stairs to wait for her, look around and find one simple task you can complete. One glance and you'll find jobs such as unloading the dishwasher, dusting a table, folding a load of laundry, putting a fresh load of clothes in the washer, or wiping around the bathroom sink.

◆ *Divide jobs into segments.* When cleaning the living room, divide it into three segments: dusting, picking up items, and vacuuming. The segment idea also goes for the bathroom: scrubbing the sink, shower, and toilet; mopping the floor; shaking out the throw rugs; polishing the mirrors.

◆ *Improve a room's appearance every time you go into it.* Simply putting the milk away or straightening a bath towel will make the room look better, and then you'll feel better about it. Remember, don't put it *down*, put it *away*.

◆ *Replace an item where it belongs after you use it.* (This is one idea that would be worth training the whole family to do.) Instead of leaving the toothpaste cap on the counter, put it back on the tube and place the toothpaste in a drawer or on the shelf.

Instead of tossing a towel on the floor or clothing on the bed, hang it back up on the towel rack, or on a hanger in the closet.

◆ *Do simple tasks right away.* For example, if you go to the grocery store and buy celery, don't put off cleaning it. Instead, as you're putting away your groceries, clean the celery, cut it up, put it in a container of water, and slip it into the refrigerator. Presto, the job is done!

This week commit yourself to nine things you can do in 15-minute time slots. When you do, you'll have accomplished 1½ hours of cleaning without even noticing it!

eleven

Do I Really Need This?

Teach a wise man, and he will be wiser;
teach a good man and he will learn more.

Proverbs 9:9

I have a friend who has 40 robes. Now one woman cannot possibly wear 40 robes. "It's hard to throw things out," she says. Another woman has saved her plastic baggies from the supermarket and at last count had 320 of them!

We live in a world of mass production and marketing. We must learn to sort and let go of certain things, or else we will need to build a huge warehouse to contain everything, not to mention inventorying the stock of collectibles so we know what we have and where it all is located. Years ago, when we got something we kept it until it wore out. But today it may never wear out before we tire of it. Yet it seems just too good to dispose of.

We often have things not because of an active decision to keep them but because we have not made the decision to get rid of them.

On an average, people keep things several years after their usefulness has passed. Perhaps we overbuy and have supplies, materials, and tools left over. The things we liked years ago are not what we like or enjoy today, but we hang onto them, thinking that someday we may use them again. It's like we're obligated to keep them "just in case."

Toys and baby equipment are saved because someday they may be used for grandchildren. We store things for our adult children "someday." Let's face the job of streamlining our possessions and ask ourselves some questions:

1. How long has it been since you used that item? My rule of thumb is if it hasn't been used in the past year I'm going to give it away, throw it away, or store it away.

   I use trash bags for my throwaway items. A black one is best so *you* can't see in it, *your husband* can't see in it, and *your children* can't see in it. Those 320 baggies can go into the throwaway bags, along with broken toys, torn and stained clothing, and newspapers and jars you've been saving for the "someday" you might use them.

   Keep tax records (including canceled checks) for seven years and then throw them out. (But keep *homebuying* and *homeselling* records permanently.) Throw out most receipts, check stubs, and utility bills after two or three years.

2. The irreplaceable items that I don't use go into storage boxes, such as my honeymoon suit, Bob's high school and college letterman's jackets, baby's first shoes, and other memorabilia. Those boxes I number 1, 2, 3, etc. I catalog these on a 3 x 5 card that is also numbered, and I put it into a small file box. Then these cards are ready to retrieve if I need them at a later date.

3. The only reasons to keep things for long periods should be for memories or perhaps to pass on to another member in the family someday, such as a lace tablecloth, a quilt, granddad's toolbox or pocketknife, or books that can benefit another member of the family or a friend.

   Things you don't need to keep include old magazines (unless they could realistically become collector's items) or magazines that are recent. These could be placed in your doctor's office, convalescent hospitals, etc. Junk mail is a big source of clutter and needs to be thrown away. *"Don't put it away, throw it away"* is a good motto for that junk mail. If you have a pile now, stop and throw it away right now. It's a great feeling, isn't it? But a new pile will return in a few days, so do it again and again until you realize that throwing this junk mail away is not going to affect your life in any way other than making you feel great!

With other mail our motto is *"File it, don't pile it!"* Get some file folders and label them "Medical," "Insurance," "Bills," "Household," "Letters to Answer," etc. As the mail comes in, open it, read it, quickly highlight it with a yellow pen, and then file it into the proper folders. Those folders can then go into a file drawer or box.

Our children's school papers were kept for one week, with two papers chosen at the end of the week and put into a file folder. At the end of the month they were allowed to choose only two special "let's keep" papers. By the end of the year the file folder consisted of those special papers, photos, and report cards. Each year the folder was put into their own "keepsake" box, and by the time high school graduation came each person had a special box filled with special memories. (They still have these boxes.)

On my fiftieth birthday I received over 150 cards, each one from a special friend, with special notes in many cases. They would fill a box just by themselves. Not too many people are interested in those cards except me, and in 20 years certainly no one but me. With those that I could, I cut off the front side of the card and used them as postcards (if not written on). Special notes I kept and put into a memorable photo book with my birthday celebration pictures.

Cards that Bob and the children have sent me over the years I keep in a file folder, being careful only to keep those that are unusual or have notes. Now...hold your breath...I dumped all the others!

If you or your husband or your children are pack rats, use my box and catalog system for storage. You may still be a pack rat, but at least you'll be an organized one!

twelve

Swish, Swash, How Do I Wash?

She is energetic, a hard worker.

Proverbs 31:17

I was talking with a woman who had 15 children (all single births) who told me she pulled 60 socks out of her dryer one day and none of them matched! I was able to tell her about those plastic sock sorters you can buy that scoot onto the end of a pair of socks. Into the washer and dryer they go, and they stay together until you are ready to roll them and put them in a drawer. I have also had women tell me they keep a good supply of large safety pins by their laundry area so they can safety pin the socks together in pairs before putting them into the washer.

It has always amazed me how socks get totally lost from the washer to the dryer, and come out single and perhaps lost forever. I'm beginning to think that our appliances feed on socks, since they seem to get eaten in the laundry process!

The laundry needs organization as much as any other area of our homes.

In raising our children, I delegated much of the chores to the children themselves. By the time Jenny was ten years old she was doing all the laundry from sorting to ironing. It took time and training to get her to that point, however. I didn't just dump the laundry responsibility in her lap at ten years old and tell her to go to it. I began when they were two and three

47

teaching both Jenny and Brad to sort the dirty clothes into three laundry bags. One was a colored bag made out of some bright calico print fabric that had lots of colors on it; all the *colored* clothes went into that bag. Another laundry bag was all white for the *white* clothes, and another one was navy or dark solid for the dirty *dark-colored* clothes.

Make a rule that what goes in the wash inside out (such as socks, underwear, and T-shirts) comes out inside out. Have everyone straighten his or her own clothes. King-size pillowcases make great laundry bags. You can string some shoe laces around the top and you have laundry bags—fast, simple, and not too expensive, if you buy the pillowcases on sale. Colored plastic trash cans make great laundry sorters also. With a fat felt pen you can write on the outside "COLORED," "WHITE," or "DARK." That way the family can simply sort their dirty clothes as they dump them in the proper bins.

Now that the clothes have been sorted and the socks paired up with your sock sorters, you can plan your washday.

Young mothers with several children may need to wash every day, others one to three times per week. But it is important to schedule your laundry days ahead and begin early in the day, or better yet, put in a load the night before. Many days I would have a load started the night before. On your way to bed, simply dump in one of the bags of sorted clothes. By morning they are ready to put into the dryer or basket for hanging out today, and you will be one load ahead of the game. When it was Jenny's responsibility for the laundry, I would put a load in on my way to bed as a little surprise to help her out with the chores.

If at all possible, use cold water, especially on colored clothes. The colors stay sharp longer and don't fade as quickly.

Wash full loads rather than small loads. That saves on energy for both you and the appliances. Remember, *do not* run the washing machine or dryer when no one is at home. If the machine leaks or short-circuits, you could have some big problems.

As soon as the dryer stops, take out the permanent press articles. Think toward no ironing, and that way you'll have less ironing than otherwise. Many articles can go without the iron if you remove them immediately from the dryer and put them on hangers. So...keep a good supply of hangers close to your laundry area!

Now let's talk about hangers. The plastic colored-type are really the best. They help prevent marks and creases on your clothing, plus you can color-code your whole family. If you have several children at home, plus mom and dad, you will use a lot of hangers.

An easy way it worked for us was to give each person in the family a color. Brad had blue, Jenny had yellow, mom had white, dad had red, etc. When the shirts or blouses were taken out of the dryer, they were hung on the appropriate-colored hangers. Then when the children came in from school, they picked up the hangers of their color, took them to their room, and hung them up.

You can also color-code underwear and socks as much as possible by giving each family member his or her color or pattern. Another great idea is to sew onto the garments (with a thread or embroidery thread) the person's color so he or she can identify the items. Color-coding also works well with folded clothes. One mom told me she had a shelf built in her laundry area, and on this shelf she placed colored plastic bins (the dishpan type). So if Brad's color is blue he gets a blue bin, Jenny gets yellow, etc. All the folded-type clothes go in at the time of folding and are taken to the person's room. If the bin is not returned to the laundry area, then no clean clothes until it is!

Another mom went a step further and gave each person his own colored towels. Again, Brad would now have blue towels. If a towel is left lying around and it's blue, we know who didn't hang up his towel or put it away!

Put a few hooks near the laundry area so they will be handy to hang the colored hangers on. If your laundry area is in the garage, a long nail works great. Or string a line from one rafter to the next. (It also makes a great clothesline for those drip-dry articles or rainy day hangups.)

Fold each load as you take it out of the dryer. Should you forget a load and it sits awhile, simply throw in a well-dampened towel and let it dry again for about ten minutes. The dampness from the towel will freshen up the load and take out any set wrinkles.

Set aside at least one day a week for ironing. Keeping ahead of ironing is the only way to keep your mind free of those "need to do" lists that grow longer and longer.

One husband shared with me that anytime he needed a fresh shirt to wear, it needed to be ironed. Have a catch-up ironing day! How happy you and your spouse will be when you go to the closet and see those shirts beautifully ironed and on colored hangers! Then keep it up. No more hurried ironing at 6:00 A.M. so you or your spouse has a clean shirt to wear to work.

When folding linens and towels, fold them all in one direction. When they are placed on the linen closet shelf, they can be piled up neatly in an organized fashion.

Label your shelves in the linen closet so that whoever puts the linens away will know the right spot.

Buying different patterned sheets for each person's bed is great for instant recognition. One mother told me she buys solid sheets for twin beds, stripes for full or queen, and floral for the king-sized beds.

Let's Review

- Teach and delegate some laundry responsibilities to your family.
- Start washing loads early in the day or the night before.
- Color-code the family.
- Aim toward having no ironing.
- Fold each load as you take it out of the dryer.
- Iron weekly to prevent ironing build-up.
- Have family members put away their own laundry.
- Label linen-closet shelves for quick identification.
- Thank the Lord we have appliances to help us save time!

thirteen

Household Remedies for Stubborn Stains

A home is built of loving deeds.

oliday time is busy enough without having to fight spots and stains. Do you wonder how you can get stubborn stains out? If the holiday tablecloth is stained and so are the cloth napkins—with lipstick—this can cause added stress for the holidays as well as any day.

Here are some hints on getting those stubborn stains out.

Candle wax. To remove from fabrics, simply place a paper towel under the spot and one on top of the spot. Press with a warm iron until the paper towel absorbs the melted wax. Move the paper towel frequently so it doesn't oversaturate.

Coffee or tea. Can be removed by rubbing the stain with a damp cloth dipped in baking soda.

Lipstick. Here are three ways to remove lipstick from fabric: 1) Rub it with a slice of white bread; 2) dab the smear with petroleum jelly, then apply a dry-cleaning solution; 3) pat with salad oil on the spot and launder the fabric after five minutes.

Makeup marks disappear from dark clothing if they are rubbed with bread.

Nail polish spots. If they get on fabric (which happens often to women with small children), lift the spot by applying remover to the fabric

51

underside. (But first check on an inconspicuous place to make sure you won't damage the fabric.)

Grease. Remove grease from fabrics by applying cornstarch or dampening and then adding salt dissolved in ammonia.

Food stains. There are several ways to remove chocolate or cocoa stains from fabrics. You could soak the stains thoroughly with club soda before washing or else rub talcum powder into the stains to absorb them. Try applying milk to the stains, since milk keeps them from setting. A fourth way is to rub shortening into them, then launder. Remove fruit stains by pouring a mixture of detergent and boiling water through the fabric or sponge the stained area with lemon juice. You can also rub the cut sides of a lemon slice over the stain. To remove egg stains from fabric, soak the fabric for an hour in cold water before laundering.

Hardened stains. These can sometimes be loosened up by placing a pad dampened with stain remover on top of the stain and keeping the top pad damp by adding more stain remover as needed.

You can remove shoe polish from clothing by applying rubbing alcohol. If traces of polish remain, add a teaspoon of borax powder to the water when laundering.

To eliminate a tar spot on fabric, apply shortening and let the tar soften for ten mintues. Scrape it away and launder.

Hints on Treating Spots and Stains

Work fast! Treat the stains right away. The longer a stain stays on a fabric, the more likely it is to become permanent.

Handle stained items gently. Rubbing, folding, wringing, or squeezing can cause the stain to penetrate more deeply and may damage delicate fibers.

Keep a cool approach to stain removal, since heat can set a stain. Keep stained fabrics away from hot water, a dryer, or an iron. After washing a garment, be sure all stains are completely removed *before* ironing. Heat-set stains are often impossible to remove.

Remove as much of a stain-producing agent as possible before treating it with a stain-removal product. That way you'll avoid the possibility of enlarging the stain.

Steps to Success

Pretest any stain-removing agent in an inconspicuous spot, such as the seam allowance or hem of a garment, the part of a rug that is hidden under a table or chair, or the upholstery under a seat cushion. Always run a sample test, since even water may damage some surfaces.

When you flush a stain, especially on a nonwashable fabric, carefully control the flow of flushing liquid with an adjustable plastic trigger spray bottle.

When stain-remover instructions call for sponging, place the fabric stained-side-down on an absorbent pad. Then dampen another pad with water or a stain remover and blot lightly from the center of the stain outward to the edge to minimize the formation of rings. Change the absorbent pads when there is any sign of the stain transferring to them so the stain won't be redeposited on the fabric. For ring-prone fabrics, barely touch the stain with the sponging pad so the stain absorbs the cleaner slowly. When the spot has been lifted, use a dry pad on either side to blot up as much excess moisture as possible.

Tamping is a good way to remove stains if the fabric is sturdy enough. Use a small dry brush or toothbrush. Use it as a small hammer with a light action until the stain is removed.

An effective way to loosen many stains is by scraping with a teaspoon. Place the stain directly on the work surface and grasp the spoon by the side of its bowl. After adding a stain remover to the stain, move the edge of the spoon's bowl back and forth in short strokes, without pressing hard on the spoon. This procedure shouldn't be used on delicate fabrics. You'll get best results if you work from the center of the stain outward.

If, in the cleaning process, you have to use more than one stain-removal agent or method, thoroughly rinse after each one before applying the next.

Homemade Spot Removers

A soapless spot cleaner can be created by mixing two cups of isopropyl rubbing alcohol (70%) with ¾ cup of white vinegar. Pour the mixture into a clean bottle and cover tightly. *Label* the bottle. To use, blot the soiled area until it is dry, apply the cleaner with a cloth or sponge and let stand for several minutes, then blot the area dry again. Repeat if necessary. Blot with water after using.

To make a wet spotter for nongreasy stains, combine one cup of water with two tablespoons of glycerin and two tablespoons of liquid dishwashing detergent. Stir in a small bowl until the mixture is thoroughly blended. Pour into a clean bottle or squeeze bottle and cover the container tightly. *Label*. When using, blot the soiled area dry, apply the spotter, let the spotter stand for several minutes, and then blot the soiled area dry again. Repeat if necessary.

fourteen

Tips for Easier Spring Cleaning

Wisdom has the advantage of giving success.

Ecclesiastes 10:10 NASB

As winter begins to melt away, we get excited and motivated to get our homes in order. But it takes a bit of organization and a few tips in order to get started toward completing the job. Just remember, it can take less time than you think. Jobs that you anticipate taking two hours can actually take only a few minutes.

So let's get started with these three thoughts in mind:

DO IT!
 DO IT RIGHT!
  DO IT RIGHT NOW!

Cleaning Products to Have on Hand

- ◆ All-purpose cleaner
- ◆ Floor products (waxes plus cleaners for vinyl or wood floors)
- ◆ Bathroom products (disinfectant, tile cleaner, mildew remover)
- ◆ Furniture polish
- ◆ Cleaning pads
- ◆ Scouring powders
- ◆ Metal polish

- Silver polish
- Window cleaner
- Dishwashing detergent or powder
- Rug and carpet cleaners
- Upholstery cleaners (Scotchguard after cleaning to protect against staining)
- Bleach, liquid or dry
- Fabric softener, liquid or sheets
- Prewash stain removers
- Oven cleaner (be sure to use rubber gloves with this type of cleaner)
- Drain cleaner
- Toilet bowl cleaner (a pumice stone is a must for removing the ring around the bowl)
- General cleaners (vinegar, ammonia, baking soda)

Cleaning Tools to Have on Hand

- Rubber gloves
- Vacuum cleaner, plus attachments for those hard-to-reach places (blinds, baseboards, radiators, shutters, corners in furniture, mattresses, ceilings, and walls)
- Dustcloth (100% cotton is best, such as towels, flannel, etc.)
- Feather duster
- Brushes for corners, tile, barbecue, etc.
- Paper towels
- Bucket
- Rags
- Broom and dustpan
- Stepladder or stepstool
- Mop
- Floor polisher or shampoo rug cleaner (optional)

Methods to Try

- Do one room at a time. Don't hurry; be thorough.
- Make a chart and delegate some of the jobs to the family: a) dad: windows; b) son: barbecue; c) daughter: pantry.

- Each week reward your family by making their favorite pie, cake, or dinner.

- Take short breaks and eat an apple or have a cup of tea or chocolate milk and cookies.

- Take cleaners with you from job to job and room to room by putting them in a bucket, a plastic type carry-all, or a basket.

- Turn on the radio for music to work by. Make it lively music so you can work faster.

- Time yourself by setting a timer. It's amazing what you can accomplish in 15 minutes.

- Upholstery furniture pieces can be brushed and vacuumed clean. This removes surface dirt and should be done four times a year.

- Drapes can be sent out for cleaning, or, depending on their fabric, they could be washed. Once-a-year cleaning is generally enough.

- Miniblinds can be removed and hosed down with sudsy water and ammonia. Then they can be maintained monthly with a feather duster.

- Wash windows quarterly (more often if needed).

- Baseboards should be checked monthly and cleaned if needed.

- Check air conditioner/heating unit. The filters need to be checked and replaced at least twice a year. These must be kept clean for maximum efficiency and lowest cost. Check with your local air conditioning/heating professional to find out how often you should do that in your area.

- Barbecue grill can be scrubbed with a hard brush. Oven cleaner works great, but make sure to use rubber gloves. Remember to remove ashes after each use.

- Keep your awnings clean by scrubbing with a long-handled brush. Use water and a mild soap. Rinse with a hose.

- Garage and cement driveways can be cleaned and scrubbed with detergent. Scrub with a stiff broom dipped in thick detergent suds. Repeat over the oil stains. Rinse by hosing with clean water.

fifteen

Organizing Your Summer to Prevent Trouble

They that wait upon the Lord shall renew their strength.
They shall mount up with wings like eagles.

Isaiah 40:31

The National Safety Council estimates that more than half of all summer accidents could be prevented if people took simple, common-sense precautions.

Summer brings varied schedules and activities: day and summer camp, skiing, swimming, biking, and many other activities which may result in animal bites, heat exposure, sunburn, cuts, insect bites, and much more. Unpredictable situations may be prevented by following these helpful hints:

- ◆ Post emergency phone numbers in plain view by the telephone for you and your children and the babysitter.

- ◆ Plan ahead by taking a first-aid class including CPR (cardiopulmonary resuscitation) from your local Red Cross chapter. Many chapters offer the classes at no charge.

- ◆ Give your children swimming lessons at the earliest possible age. Many YMCAs and YWCAs offer great programs for children.

57

- If you are in an area where no swimming classes are offered, work with your children yourself. We started with our children at a very young age by pouring water over their heads and having them hold their breath and blow bubbles underwater. Make it fun, and at the same time you will be helping them become comfortable in water.

- Common water-safety violations often result in injury. These include running, jumping, or sliding around a pool deck, diving without checking the water depth, and leaving a child unattended beside a pool, lake, or bathtub. (Purchase a cordless phone to keep with you at home so you won't leave the children unattended by pool or bathtub.) Go over safety rules with the family *often:* no running, never swim alone, etc.

- Purchase (or put together yourself) a first-aid kit for car travel. Keep it in a suitcase at the lake or pool area. This will keep it handy for you but out of the reach of children.

- Sunburn is very common, so use extra precautions. Sunscreen lotions are a must; keep them handy for small children and light-skinned people. Sunscreens are rated from 1 to 30+; the higher the number, the more protection they give. A sun hat, visor, or bonnet is also recommended to prevent sunburned noses.

- Poison ivy, poison oak, and poison sumac are often found in uncultivated fields and wooded areas. Touching one of these plants (whose leaves often cluster three to a stalk) usually results within 24 hours in an oozy, itchy rash that may spread over much of the body. The trouble comes with infection caused by scratching the area. If your summer plans include hiking or picnicking in wooded or mountain areas, review with the family the facts about these poisonous plants. You may want to go to the library and find photos of the plants. Ask questions and inquire about these and other potential dangers in the area you plan to go to. Educate yourself and your family for a safer outing.

- Insect bites or stings can cause swelling, pain, redness, burning, or itching which can last from 48 to 72 hours. If you know you are allergic to bee stings, before leaving town be sure to consult your doctor about any medication you may need to take along. This is a good item to keep in your first-aid kit.

A honey bee leaves its stinger imbedded in the skin. It's best to remove the stinger with tweezers or by scraping with a fingernail. Wash the sting area with soap and water and apply ice or flush with cold water to reduce swelling and pain. Calamine lotion is available over-the-counter in drugstores. Baking soda works well by mixing with water to form a paste. (Baking soda is another good item for your first-aid kit.)

◆ Think ahead and plan ahead in order to be prepared for emergencies. When taking various foods on picnics, remember to keep the perishable items in coolers with lots of ice. Any food item containing mayonnaise is likely to go bad quickly. Don't let any food items sit in the hot sun. Eggs and uncooked meats need to be kept especially well-cooled.

◆ Take a car emergency kit. Some very good kits are available at auto parts stores. Or you can make up your own kit consisting of: flares, jumper cables, "HELP" sign, "CALL POLICE" sign, fire extinguisher, nylon rope, towel, flashlight, fuses, and an approved empty gasoline can. All of these can be put together in a plastic dishpan, which can also be used to carry water in an emergency.

◆ Buy and use a "Hide-A-Key" box. After the first time I locked my keys inside my car, the time I lost and the stress I endured sent me directly to a store to find a "Hide-A-Key" case and attach it to the car in a hidden place. (This makes an especially good gift for teen drivers.) For some reason keys locked inside a car cause lots of trouble to lots of people. So think ahead and prevent this kind of trouble!

sixteen

Fall Family Organization

Don't act thoughtlessly, but try to find out and do whatever the Lord wants you to.

Ephesians 5:17

Is getting the children organized a problem for you after a summer of irregular schedules? Here are a few steps to help you!

Step 1

Plan a back-to-school organizational day with each child. For the working moms it may need to be a Saturday or an evening.

Step 2

With a child, go through his or her drawers and closets and throw or give away summer clothing and outgrown shoes. A lot of the summer clothing can be stored away for next summer. Put clothing in boxes and label the boxes according to size, so when next summer arrives, the clothing can be given to other members of the family or to friends whom they will fit. That way you can recycle the children's perfectly good clothes. The boxes can be stored in the basement, garage, attic, or closets.

Step 3

Take a wardrobe inventory! Use the checklist chart (Figure 1, page 61).

60

Wardrobe Inventory

Blouses	Pants	Skirts	Jackets	Sweaters

Dresses	Gowns	Lingerie	Shoes	Jewelry

Figure 1

Step 4

Now comes the fun. Plan a time alone with each child to go over the inventory chart and to discuss needed new clothing to fill in the chart.

For moms who sew, take the child with you when picking out patterns and fabrics. If shopping from mail order catalogs, sit down and discuss the purchases with your child. Make it a togetherness time, and then he or she will feel part of the new wardrobe and the "I hate to wear that" syndrome will be eliminated. This method also teaches your children how to make decisions responsibly. Later on you'll find this guidance and time pay off as your children grow older and shop capably for themselves.

Step 5

Plan a family meeting to discuss home responsibilities. Make up a "Daily Work Planner Chart" (see Figure 2, page 63). Notice that mom's and dad's names are also listed on the chart. This shows that you work together as a family. Especially if mom is working outside the home, the family needs to support her all they can.

Step 6

Make a list of jobs the family can do to help around the house. (See Figure 3, page 64 with suggested jobs.) Put each item on a separate piece of paper and put each into a basket. You may need two baskets, one for children's jobs 3–7 years old and one for children 8–18. Then once a week the children will draw out two to five jobs. These jobs are put on the "Work Planner Chart."

As the children do their job, a happy face can be drawn by their name (or a sad face if they dropped the ball and neglected to do their job). Stickers or stars can also be used. This makes for a colorful chart.

If they complete their jobs easily, they may draw another job from the basket and get extra credit or double stickers, stars, or happy faces. Children become excited about duties around the house and work toward a colorful chart for each week of the month.

At the end of the month you can plan a special family surprise as a reward for jobs well done. You might say, "This month we've worked together as a family. Now we're going to play together as a family." Plan a fun Saturday bike ride ending with a picnic lunch, or a Friday evening by the fire popping corn and playing a favorite family game.

Organizing for fall can be a creative and productive time in your homes. Let's begin.

Daily Work Planner Chart

Day of Week	Mom	Dad	#1 Child	#2 Child	#3 Child	#4 Child	#5 Child
Saturday							
Sunday							
Monday							
Tuesday							
Wednesday							
Thursday							
Friday							

Figure 2

Daily Work Planner Chart

Day of Week	Mom	Dad	#1 Child	#2 Child	#3 Child	#4 Child	#5 Child
Saturday	Clean House	Clean Garage	Bathe Dog	Mow Lawn	Clean Refrigerator		
Sunday	Plan Upcoming Week	Plan Upcoming Week	Set and Clear Table	Do Evening Dishes	Do Evening Dishes		
Monday	Menu Planning Grocery Shopping	Pick Up Dry Cleaning	Do Evening Dishes	Set and Clear Table	Empty Garbage Feed Dog		
Tuesday	Wash Clothes	Pick Up Rooms (Clutter)	Fold and Distribute Clothes	Do Evening Dishes Feed Dog	Set and Clear Table		
Wednesday	Mop Floors	Clean Bathroom(s)	Set and Clear Table	Iron Clothes	Do Evening Dishes Feed Dog		
Thursday	Shopping Drop Off Dry Cleaning	Vacuum	Do Evening Dishes Feed Dog	Set and Clear Table	Empty Garbage		
Friday	Change Bed Linens	Water Plants	Dust Furniture	Do Evening Dishes Feed Dog	Set and Clear Table		

Figure 3

- *Wallpaper scraps.* It's always a good idea to save wallpaper scraps in case sections of the paper need to be repaired later. To make a patch, tear (don't cut) a scrap into the approximate size and shape needed. The irregular torn edges will blend better with the paper already on the wall, making the patch less apparent than it would be if cut.

- *Paint splatters.* Here's an easy way to erase paint splatters from a brick fireplace. Get a broken brick the same color as the brick on the fireplace and scrub it back and forth over the spattered areas. Brick against brick will abrade away most of the paint. Any remaining paint will pick up the brick color and thus be camouflaged.

- *Clutter.* Work better and faster by tossing out things that are no longer needed or have lost their usefulness, such as stacks of old magazines or receipts. If you don't want to throw them out, store them in a box.

- *Unfinished work.* Don't let work pile up. Decide which projects need to be completed.

- *Lots of choices.* Since your time is limited, choose to do things that you enjoy or find useful. Don't overload yourself with tasks or responsibilities. Always strive to simplify your life.

- *Procrastination.* Do the jobs you dislike *first*. Once you've got those unpleasant tasks out of your way, you'll find that the rest of the work will be somewhat easier.

- *Racing through each day.* Try to work smarter, not harder. Plan your day. Pace your energy and skills through the day like a disciplined athlete getting ready for the Olympics. At the end of the day you will have achieved more and won't feel so tired and stressed.

- *Cleaning the grout.* To clean the grout between the tiles in your kitchen or bathroom, mix up a paste of scouring powder and hydrogen peroxide (just enough to make a paste.) Apply with an old toothbrush, let sit 20 minutes, then wash off with hot water and a scrub brush. (Keep the windows open as you work!) Try a mildew stain remover you can buy in the hardware store or supermarket and apply according to the directions on the container.

- *Whitening a porcelain sink.* First fill the sink with two or three inches of warm water. Add detergent and half a cup of chlorine bleach. Let sit 15 minutes, then wash the entire sink with the solution. Rinse thoroughly with hot tapwater.

◆ *Cleaning glass or plastic shower stall doors.* Just put a little lemon oil furniture polish on a soft clean cloth and rub the doors clean. Be careful not to get any of the lemon oil polish on your tiles. (The whole problem of keeping the shower stall doors clean can be avoided if everyone wipes the doors dry after taking a shower!)

◆ *Speeding up a sluggish drain.* First run hot tapwater down the drain, then pour in three tablespoons of baking soda and half a cup of distilled white vinegar. Stop up the drain and wait 15 minutes. The baking soda and vinegar will foam up, reacting with each other and eating away at whatever is slowing the drain. Finally, flush the drain with hot tapwater.

◆ *Removing candle wax from a tablecloth.* Place the waxy section of the tablecloth between two thicknesses of paper toweling and press with a warm iron. If a greasy spot remains, treat it with a dry cleaning fluid.

◆ *Removing candle wax from a candlestick.* Try pouring boiling water into the candlestick socket to melt the wax. Once melted it will wipe out easily.

◆ *Getting white rings off furniture.* Dampen a cloth with a small amount of mineral oil and dab it in fireplace ashes. Wipe gently on the ring, then polish or wax the wood as usual.

◆ *Eliminating cooking odors.* Boil 1 tablespoon white vinegar in 1 cup water over stove. This will eliminate unpleasant cooking odors.

◆ *Eliminating tobacco odors.* During and after a party, place a small bowl of white vinegar in the room.

◆ *Freshening laundry.* Add ⅓ cup baking soda to wash or rinse cycle. Clothes will be sweeter and cleaner smelling.

◆ *Removing water spots from fabrics.* Sponge entire stained area with white vinegar; let stand a few minutes. Rinse with clear, cool water and let dry.

◆ *Removing lipstick, liquid makeup, or mascara from fabrics.* Soak in dry-cleaning solution and let dry. Rinse and then wash.

- *Freshening lunch boxes.* Dampen a piece of fresh bread with white vinegar and put it in the lunchbox overnight.

- *Making your blankets fluffier.* Add 2 cups white vinegar to a washer tub of rinse water.

- *Removing dark or burned stains from an electric iron.* Rub with equal amounts of white or cider vinegar and salt, heated first in a small aluminum pan. Polish in the same way you do silver.

- *Removing decals.* Paint them with several coats of white vinegar. Give the vinegar time to soak in. After several minutes the decals should wash off easily.

- *Deodorizing refrigerator.* Place one opened box of baking soda in the back of the refrigerator or in a shelf on the door. Change every other month.

- *Freshening drains and garbage disposal.* Use a discarded box of baking soda previously used in your refrigerator.

- *Removing burned or baked on foods from your cookware.* Scrub with baking soda sprinkled on a plastic scouring pad; rinse and dry. You might also try warm soda paste soaked on burned area; keep wet, then scrub as needed.

- *Deodorizing your carpet.* Sprinkle dry baking soda on the rug. Allow to set overnight, then vacuum. (Test for color fastness in an inconspicuous area.)

- *Deodorizing cat litter.* Cover the bottom of the litter pan with 1 part baking soda; then cover baking soda with 3 parts litter to absorb odors for up to a week. Litter won't need replacing as often.

- *Disinfecting wood chopping surfaces.* Scrub with a mild bleach solution, then rinse and rub it with a thin coat of mineral or salad oil.

seventeen

Year-Round Clothing Care

*She looks for wool and flax,
and works with her hands in delight.*

Proverbs 31:13 NASB

With the cost of clothing and fabrics these days, we need to know what we can do to keep our clothing fresh and new, especially if we are spending money on fairly expensive clothing.

We live only one hour from the Los Angeles garment district, and 90 percent of all my clothing is bought from 40 to 70 percent off. I don't have time to shop very often, so I need to take especially good care of my clothing so it will look new and fresh for several years. Here are some fun ideas and tips to do just that.

First of all I start with three basic items in a solid color:

1. A blazer or jacket
2. A skirt
3. Pants

To these three basics I then add blouses in prints or solid colors that will coordinate. Next I add a few sweaters and several accessories, such as scarves, ribbon ties, boots, jewelry, and perhaps a silk flower. Finally I

68

purchase two pairs of shoes, one for casual wear and one pair for dress (the church type).

Since I do a great deal of traveling, I take these six to nine items and a few accessories (plus one all-weather coat) and coordinate them into approximately 12 to 16 outfits that will last 7 to 14 days.

How to Make Clothing Last

1. Dry clean your garments every eight to ten wearings (or longer if possible). Dry cleaning is hard on fabrics.

2. Rotate your various items of clothing as much as possible so they can regain their shape. I have a friend who rotates her garments by hanging them after each wearing at the right end of the closet. The next day she picks the skirt or pants that are on the left end of the closet. That way she knows how often they are worn. This works especially well with men's suits.

3. As soon as you take off your garments, empty the pockets, shake the garment well, and hang up immediately.

4. Have you ever thought of Scotchguarding your new fabrics? It's very effective and will last until the garment is cleaned or washed. (Then just spray it again.) You can also use Scotchguard on your fabric shoes.

5. Mend your garments as soon as they are damaged. Sew on those buttons and repair those rips and loose hems. My Bob has a tendency to tear out the seat of his pants, so I triple-stitch and zigzag the seams when they are new, even before they are worn. That keeps embarrassing moments to a minimum.

6. Keep from snagging your hose by using hand lotion to soften your hands before putting your hose on.

7. Hang wrinkled clothes in the bathroom while showering. The steam will cause the wrinkles to come out.

8. Let perfumes and deodorants dry on your body before getting dressed in order to prevent garment damage.

9. I put a scarf over my head before pulling a garment over my head to prevent a messed hairdo and makeup smudges and stains.

10. Hang blazers and coats on padded hangers to avoid hanger marks.

11. Keep sweaters in a drawer or shelf rather than on a hanger (to prevent stretching).

12. Skirts and pants are best hung on hangers with clips; or you can use clothespins on wire hangers.

13. Even very good jewelry can discolor your clothing, so just dab the backs with clear nail polish. The polish can also be painted on jewelry with rough edges that could pull fibers of fabrics.

14. Some stickpins can make holes in delicate fabrics, so be careful and don't wear them if you are in doubt.

15. Be sure to have your good leather shoes polished to retain their shine. It also feeds and preserves the leather.

16. Brush suede shoes with a suede brush that brings up the nap. You can use a nail file to rub off any little spots.

17. Replace heels and soles on your shoes before they wear down completely.

18. If your shoes get wet, stuff them with paper towels or newspaper and allow to dry away from direct heat.

19. Shoe trees are great to keep the shape in your shoes.

20. When storing leather handbags or shoes, never put them into plastic bags, since this can cause the leather to dry out. Instead, use fabric shoe bags or wrap the shoes in tissue and put them into shoeboxes.

eighteen

20 Washday Hints to Relieve Laundry Stress

She makes coverings for herself;
her clothing is fine linen and purple.

Proverbs 31:22 NASB

Does washday come when there is nothing clean left to wear? Does your clothing need to be ironed before you can go out of the house, or do you go anyway looking wrinkled or crumpled? Do your children dash madly about in search of matching socks but are not able to find them because your washing machine ate them up or they fall out of a fitted sheet two weeks later, after you've thrown out the single one?

Sorting laundry can save time, stress, and energy. Children can be taught simple organizational techniques to save the family washday stress.

1. Divide your laundry into three cloth bags. These can be made from fabric or three large king-size pillowcases with a drawstring. Bag 1 is white for the soiled white clothes. Bag 2 is dark (brown, navy, black) for the dark soiled clothes (jeans, washcloths, etc.). Bag 3 is multicolored for the mixed-colored clothes. Colored plastic trash cans can also be used. Label the cans "colored," "white," and "dark." Show all members of the family how to sort their own dirty clothes by putting them in the proper bags or cans. Each child or bedroom could have its own laundry bag. From there they take the clothes to the central sorting area, then sort

71

their own into the three bags. (Or each day *all* dirty clothing goes to the sorting area.) On washdays or whenever the bags become full it's a simple matter of dumping bag 1 into the machine and swish, swash, the wash is done. To solve your missing-sock problem, invest in plastic sock sorters. These can be found in drug or variety stores. Safety pins are also great to keep socks paired during the wash and dry cycles. One mom purchased only white socks for the children, one size fits all. Remember, it's not what you *expect* but what you *inspect*. So be sure to teach the method and then inspect from time to time to see if they are doing it properly. Whatever goes *in* the bags inside out will come *out* inside out.

2. Each family member can also have his or her own bright-colored bin for clean folded clothes. Christine's is pink, Chad's is blue, Bevan's is white, mom's is red, and dad's is green. Or you can use all white bins (or dishpan-type bins) and color-code them with stick-on dots or colored felt markers with each family member's name on them.

3. Whoever folds the clothes places each person's items in his or her proper bin. It is then the responsibility of each family member to take his own bin to the drawers and empty the bin. Should the bin not return to the folding area, no clothes will be folded for that person.

4. Plan your washing days and start washing early in the day.

5. On washing day use cold water if possible, especially on colored clothes, as this will help them to stay bright longer.

6. Wash full loads rather than small ones. This saves energy and your appliances as well.

7. Never leave the washer or dryer running when you aren't home. A machine leak or short circuit can cause damage or, worse yet, start a fire.

8. If using a dryer, remove the clothes as soon as it stops, then hang and fold. This will save wrinkled items and many times save ironing items.

9. Forgot to take out the clothes in the dryer? Simply throw in a damp towel or washcloth and turn on the dryer again for five to ten

minutes. The dampness from the towel will freshen the load and remove any wrinkles.

10. Hang as many clothes as possible on hangers, especially permanent-press garments. This will also help cut down on ironing. Put up a few hooks near the laundry area or string an indoor clothesline.

11. I recommend using plastic-colored hangers rather than metal ones. They prevent marks and creases on your garments. Using colored hangers can also color-code your family. Assign each person a different color. Then when you take the clothing out of the dryer, hang it on the appropriate-colored hanger: mom, white; dad, brown; Kevin, blue; Susie, yellow; etc.

12. Schedule at least one day a week for ironing, or three 15-minute slots per week. Keep ahead of your ironing; this will relieve your stress level and eliminate having to iron at the last minute before you leave the house.

13. To help ironing time go quickly, pray for the person whose clothing you are ironing. This way ironing can become a real joy and blessing.

14. Label your linen closet shelves so that whoever puts the sheets and towels away will know just the right spot for them. This prevents confusion, keeps your closet looking neat, and saves time in finding king-size or twin-size.

15. When your iron sticks, sprinkle a little salt onto a piece of waxed paper and run the hot iron over it. Rough, sticky spots will disappear as if by magic.

16. Always wash your throw rugs in cool or lukewarm water. (Hot water will cause the rubber backing to peel.) Let the rug dry on a line instead of in the dryer. You can fluff it up when it is dry in the no-heat cycle of your dryer.

17. Here's a little trick to make ironing easier: Using pieces of wax candles in an old cotton sock, swipe your iron every so often while ironing. The wax makes it glide smoothly, and your ironing goes faster.

18. Instead of using expensive fabric-softener sheets, pour one-fourth cup *white* vinegar in the last rinse of the washing cycle. This eliminates static cling, helps remove wrinkles, gives clothes a fresh smell by removing soap, and cleans the drains of the washer by removing soap scum and lint.

19. Another way to remove garment wrinkles: Hang wrinkled garments on the curtain rod in your bathroom and run very hot water from the shower. Close the bathroom door and let the water run for a couple of minutes. The steam will fade the wrinkles from your clothing. Great for those who travel!

20. If your steam iron clogs up, fill it with a mixture of one-fourth cup of vinegar and one cup of water and let it stand overnight. Heat the iron the next day. Remove the mixture and rinse with clear water.

Part 3

CHILDREN

nineteen

How to Get Your Children to Help Around the House

*Train up a child in the way he should go,
and even when he is old he will not depart from it.*

Proverbs 22:6 NASB

As a mother of five children under five years of age, at one time in my life it was easy to become overwhelmed and frustrated at trying to be Supermom. I needed help, and the help came from my family. I found a way to get my husband and children to help with the housework cheerfully. Even the toddlers helped.

Your children will benefit by one day becoming independent, responsible adults who are pleased with their accomplishments. So make the housework fun, give clearly defined directions, keep the jobs realistic, and avoid criticism. Above all, praise, praise, praise!

I wrote the jobs that they could do on individual pieces of paper and put them in a basket. Then they got to choose two or three jobs from that basket once a week. These jobs went onto a Daily Work Planner Chart (see page 64), which was posted. When jobs each day were completed they were marked with an "X" and a happy face or a sticker. By the end of the week the chart was full of marks; each child used a different-colored marking pen, and each loved to see his or her color appear often. Rewards came at the end of the week, with lots of praise!

Toddlers respond well to marks on a chart, and teens like to work on a point system. (So many points per job; add them up on Saturday and reward accordingly.) When our children got into junior high school, even their friends wanted their names on our Work Planner Chart. Why? Because we had a well-defined plan, we made it fun, and they were rewarded.

If you want your children to grow up believing that the mess belongs to the person who made it, don't teach them that they are helping mommy. Instead, applaud them for making *their* bed, dressing *themselves*, and putting *their* clothes away. Praise your children for keeping *their* room neat and putting *their* toys away. Thank them for doing a good job because they are such good workers. Help them to feel good about being a part of a family effort. Then they will learn that they are part of a family team in which each person contributes and each person appreciates the other.

Have the mindset that the child's room belongs to the child. Teach your children from an early age (one, two, three years old) to be responsible for their own clothes, bed, laundry, and toys. This way they will find out early that if they wish to live in a neat and clean room they will have to do the work themselves.

You ask, "What if they like to live in a mess?" You are still the winner because you are spared the time, energy, stress, and aggravation of doing it all.

At an early age, when they make their bed praise them for it! Praise will get you everywhere, and they'll want to do it again and again.

When they're ready to put away their toys, have boxes, bins, or low shelves available for them to use. Let them do it their own way, arranged by them and not you. Provide low hooks so they can hang their own sweaters, jammies, and jackets. Whenever possible, make a game of putting these things away.

One mom installed a wooden pole that went from the floor to the ceiling. Then she screwed cup hooks into the pole and sewed a plastic curtain ring onto each of the children's stuffed animals so the children could easily hang up their animals when they were finished with them. This arrangement also provided a creative decorator item, and the children loved hooking their teddy bears to the pole.

Make the chores fun and games. The children will want to work if you make it a happy time!

A toddler can set the table. Make a placemat out of paper and draw the shapes of the fork, plate, spoon, and glass. The child gets to put each item in its proper place. Soon Susie or Timmy will want to set the table for everyone.

Let them play policeman or trashman. Give them a pillowcase to pick up toys, trash, and papers around the house and even in the yard.

Toddlers can feel important this way and can learn to like the feeling of work. Congratulations are in order for a job well done!

Help your child dress independently. Keep solid bottoms in a low drawer with printed tops. If you buy coordinates, any top will go with any bottom. Even a young child can choose what to wear within reason and limitations.

Avoid uncomfortable or difficult clothing. If you want to have children who can dress themselves, they certainly can't cope with tight collars or fancy buttons. Snaps and loose tops help them not to feel frustrated. The Velcro used on shoes today is great for little fingers and makes the children feel proud of themselves as they put on their own shoes.

Yes, children can learn to love to do their fair share around the house!

twenty

How to Teach Your Children About Money

Steady plodding brings prosperity;
hasty speculation brings poverty.

Proverbs 21:5

We live in a world where adults often find themselves in financial woes. Where do we learn about money? Usually by trial and error, since few families take the time to teach their children how to be smart with money. Yet at an early age, children should know about money and what it can do for them.

Children who learn about money at an early age will be ahead in this mystery game. Learning to deal with money properly will foster discipline, good work habits, and self-respect.

Here are eight ways in which you can help your children get a good handle on money.

1. **Start with an allowance.** Most experts advise that an allowance should not be tied directly to a child's daily chores. Children should help around the home not because they get paid for it but because they share responsibilities as members of a family. However, you might pay a child for doing *extra* jobs at home. This can develop his or her initiative. We know of parents who give stickers to their young children when they do something that they haven't specifically been asked to do. These stickers may then be redeemed

for 25 cents each. This has been great for teaching not only initiative but also teamwork in the family.

An allowance is a vital tool for teaching children how to budget, save, and make their own decisions. Children learn from their mistakes when their own money has been lost or spent foolishly.

How large an allowance to give depends on your individual family status. It should be based on a fair budget that allows a reasonable amount for entertainment, snacks, lunch money, bus fare, and school supplies. Add some extra money to allow for church and savings. Be willing to hold your children responsible for living within their budget. Some weeks they may have to go without, particularly when they run out of money.

2. **Model the proper use of credit.** In today's society we see the results of individuals and couples using bad judgment regarding credit.

   Explain to your children the conditions when it's necessary to use credit and the importance of paying their loan back on a timely basis. You can make this a great teaching tool. Give them practice in filling out credit forms. Their first loan might be from you to them for a special purchase. Go through all the mechanics that a bank would; have them fill out a credit application and sign a paper with all the information stated. Let them understand about interest, installment payments, balloon payments, late payment costs, etc. Teach them to be responsible to pay on time.

3. **Teach your children how to save.** In today's instant society it is hard to teach this lesson. At times we should deny our children certain material things so that they have a reason to save. As they get older they will want bicycles, stereos, a car, a big trip, etc. They need to learn the habit of saving so they can then buy these larger items.

   One of the first ways to begin teaching the concept of saving is to give the children some form of piggy bank. Spare change or extra earnings can go into the piggy bank. When it gets full you might want to open an account at a local bank.

   When your children are older you might want to establish a savings account at a local bank so they can go to the bank and personally deposit money to their account. This habit of depositing money will help your children begin thinking about saving.

In the end, children who learn how to save will better appreciate what they've worked to acquire.

4. **Show them how to be wise in their spending.** Take your children with you when you shop, and show them some cost comparisons. They will soon see that with a little effort they can save a lot of money. You might want to demonstrate this principle to them in a tangible way when they want to purchase a larger item for themselves. Go with them to several stores to look for that one item, writing down the highest price and the lowest price for that item. This way they can really see how much they can save by comparison shopping.

   Clothing is an area where a lot of lessons on wise spending can be made. After awhile your children will realize that designer clothes cost a lot more just for that particular label or patch. Our daughter, Jenny, soon learned that outlet stores were great bargains for clothes dollars. To this day she can still find excellent bargains by comparison shopping.

5. **Let them work part-time.** There are many excellent part-time jobs waiting for your child. Fast-food outlets, markets, malls, babysitting, etc., can give valuable work experience to your children. Some entrepreneurial youngsters even begin a thriving business based on their skills and interest. These part-time jobs are real confidence boosters. Just remember to help your child keep a proper balance between work, home, church, and school. A limit of 10 to 15 hours per week might be a good guideline.

6. **Let them help you with your budgeting.** Encourage your children to help you budget for the family finances. This gives them experience in real-life money problems. They also get a better idea about your family's income and expenses. Children can have good suggestions about how to better utilize the family finances, and their experience can give them a better understanding of why your family can't afford certain luxuries.

7. **Give them experience in handling adult expenses.** As your children get older they need to experience real-life costs. Since children normally live at home, they don't always understand true-to-life expenses. Let them experience paying for their own telephone bill, car expenses, and clothing expenses. Depending upon the situation,

having them pay a portion of the utility and household bills can be an invaluable experience for children who have left school and are still living at home.

8. **Show them how to give to the Lord.** At a very young stage in life, parents and children should talk about where things come from. The children should be aware that all things are given from God and that He is just letting us borrow them for a time. Children can understand that we are to return back to God what He has so abundantly given to us. This principle can be experienced through either Sunday school or their church offerings. When special projects at church come up, you might want to review these needs with your children so they can decide whether they want to give extra money above what they normally give to their church. Early training in this area provides a valuable basis for learning how to be a giver in life and not a taker.

Your children will learn about money from *you*, so be a good model. If you have good habits, they will reflect that; if you struggle with finances, so will they. One valuable lesson to teach them is that money doesn't reflect love. A hug, a smile, a kiss, or just time spent together is much more valuable than money.

twenty-one

Summertime Projects to Keep Your Children Busy

Children are a gift from God;
they are his reward.

Psalm 127:3

One July afternoon our Brad and Jenny echoed, "There's nothing to do, Mom. What can we do to have some fun?"

With a quick prayer and a lot of creativity we came up with our Summer Project Box. We scurried around the house to find just the right box. (The right box should be sturdy and made of cardboard. A shoebox, hatbox, or even a file-type box will do.) To keep our projects separate we made cardboard dividers (file folders will also do). On these dividers we listed summer projects which the children were interested in exploring. I found that they were very creative in their ideas.

Here are some of our projects that were successful. Your children may have other projects, depending upon their ages and interest.

Sports/Games

Set up a file on your favorite sports star. Include photos (you can send for them), articles from newspapers and magazines, and autographs. Also include copies of letters which your children write to their favorite stars in football, baseball, hockey, skating, etc.

84

Organize a Summer Olympics in your neighborhood. Time the running events and relay races, and measure the long jumps. Design and create medals and/or rewards.

Set up a bowling alley in your backyard by using milk cartons for pins and a large rubber ball. Tell the children they can ask neighbors to save their milk cartons to contribute to this project.

Garden/Nature

Plant and care for a vegetable garden or flower garden. Children love to watch the plants come up and to eventually harvest the vegetables and pick the flowers. Keep records on plant growth, watering, and fertilizing.

Make a study of insects. Keep a record of what they eat and how they live. Make sketches of them. Take your children to the library and find books about insects and how to identify them.

Press wildflowers to use for art projects, Christmas cards, and/or thank-you notes.

Find rocks—smooth, round, and odd-shaped. Make creative items with them by painting them with flowers, people, and animals. One summer the children filled their wagons with the rocks they had painted and sold them door-to-door as paperweights.

Food

Set up a lemonade stand for the neighborhood. This is a great way for younger children to learn about running a small business. Have them make the posters, set the cost, and stock the stand with such items as lemonade, ice, and cups, and perhaps such additional items as muffins, cookies, licorice, and nuts. Garden vegetables could also be sold (corn, carrots, radishes, pumpkins, etc.).

Have your children choose a recipe and make something from scratch. Have them file a copy of the recipe in a box, with notes on how it came out.

Beach/Lake

Take pictures or make sketches of various kinds of boats. Collect shells and devise your own classification system. Take a field trip to the beach and discover the tidepools. List the different kinds of crabs, snails, starfish, etc.

Go lake or ocean fishing and bring home the catch for dinner.

Study nature, balances of life, tadpoles, and frogs.

Go sailing, canoeing, rowing. List the activity and what was learned. Put into the Project Box.

Vacations/Short Trips

Conduct research to find places in your area that would make good family trips. Write a short description of each place and include, if possible, a photo or drawing of the spot. Share your research with the family.

Make a file of activities for car, plane, train. List necessary items to take along. Include clothing, camera, etc. Collect maps, brochures, and postcards from your travels and file them in the Project Box.

The children may come up with more project categories to add to the Project Box. They will be excited by simply putting together their box. The summer will be fun, exciting, and a real learning time for your children as they choose a project on those days when they would otherwise say, "But, Mom, there's nothing to do!"

twenty-two

Organizing Fun Ways for Your Children to Earn Money

Much is required from those to whom much is given, for their responsibility is greater.

Luke 12:48

To be industrious is what Proverbs 31 tells us women to strive to achieve. But do we teach that to our children? As our own children grew up, we thought of all kinds of ways to create money-earning ventures. One of the very first projects they did was at ages five and six. We lived in a beach area in Southern California and spent time collecting shells and rocks. We had so many that they overflowed the bedrooms. So one summer we had a rock-painting session in the garage with acrylic paints. The children made creative, colorful rocks and shells, and when they were finished they displayed their creations in their wagon, walking the neighborhood and selling their rocks and shells for five cents each. They were really excited to sell rocks and shells for cash!

It's hard for children to earn money by doing chores around the house. Even for money it just isn't the same as earning it independently. When children earn money for themselves it gives them a sense of responsibility. When the jobs are fun and helpful, everyone benefits.

How much should mom be involved? Plenty at first. Make sure you know the people who are hiring your child. Help match your child's age

87

and ability to the job in question, and be sure the child is realistically paid for his or her time. After that pull back, relax, and watch your child blossom with the satisfaction of earning money for a job well done.

Over the years we came up with many moneymaking ideas. Here are some of the family-tested ones that WORK!

1. **Toy Sale.** This children's version of the garage sale works especially well when the prices are kept low, since most customers will be other children. Put pricetags on everything, post a sign at the bottom of the driveway, and place the most eye-catching items up front. Let the children take it from there. They will learn about making change, negotiating, and (after sitting for hours between customers) perseverance.

2. **Pet-Sitting.** Many owners of birds, cats, and goldfish (and other pets that don't need walking) hire a sitter to come in every day to feed the animals, change what needs changing, and give the pets some love and affection. Depending on the child's age, you may have to help lock and unlock the pet owner's doors or gates. But once inside, it's the child's job, and it's a good one. Standard rates of pay for this service are between $1.50 and $4.00 per day.

3. **Yard Work.** Even before they're old enough to handle power equipment, children can help garden in other ways. Their young backs don't get nearly as tired from pulling weeds and planting flowers as adults' do, and children make great scouts for hidden rocks and branches that play havoc with the lawnmower. Rates should be a penny per rock for the tiny tots and more when the work is harder.

4. **Dog-Walking.** The size of the dog may dictate the size of the walker, but most kids can handle this job. People are surprisingly eager to pay someone else to walk their dog, especially when the weather is sloppy. Today's busy person is usually happy to pay $2.00 per walk.

5. **Assisting at Children's Birthday Parties.** The hired helper should be only a few years older than the party group. He can help pass out food, round up trash and wrapping paper, oversee the games, and provide a vital extra set of eyes and hands for those guests who wander off and search for something breakable. Rate of pay: $5.00 per party.

6. **Cleaning Out Crawl Spaces, Storage Sheds, Etc.** The more cramped the space, the better little bodies can help to clean it. Children are surprisingly strong and endlessly curious about cluttered nooks and crannies. Though they can't sort through the things you've accumulated, it may be worth paying a few cents just for the company. Rate of pay: $1 per hour.

7. **Child-Walking.** An older child can walk a younger child to school every day, to a music lesson, or to the playground for a time of teeter-totter or swinging. Estimated rate of pay: $1 per day.

8. **Summer Stock.** This is always a fun time for children to express their talents. Plan a show where several children put on an act or talent show. Sing a song or lip sync to a record, tell a few jokes, play an instrument, juggle, write and then read a poem, do a dance, or teach the dog a trick and then have the dog do tricks. Sell tickets to the show. Suggested ticket price: 25¢ to 50¢ each, depending on the talents.

9. **Summer Camp.** This is great fun for several children to help in. Together they can supervise up to eight children—making crafts, running relay races, and conducting a story read-aloud hour.

   Two hours is usually the maximum attention span for most children. Rates: from $2.00 to $4.00 per child, depending on the cost of necessary craft items, such as Popsicle sticks, yarn, paints, cookies, juice, and other goodies.

10. **Car Wash.** Always a hit. Cloths, whisk broom, buckets, and window spray will be the equipment needed. Children can go door-to-door and make appointments. After the winter weather has thawed out and the spring rains are over is a good time to canvass the neighborhood. If they do a good job they could very well turn this into a weekly job. Rates range from $4.00 to $5.00 per car, depending on the size of the car and how well the job is completed.

11. **House-Sitting.** Many people like their home taken care of when out of town or on vacation. This is a good opportunity for the child to learn responsibility. The lawn and potted plants (indoor and outdoor) need watering, paper and mail taken inside, and lights turned on and off to make the situation seem normal. Pets can also be fed and watered. The rate of pay will depend on the amount of work done. Range: $1.00 to $5.00 per day.

twenty-three

Child Safety

*In everything you do, stay away from
complaining and arguing.*

Philippians 2:14

Charcoal lighter fluid may not taste good, but a thirsty child may easily grab a can, put it to his mouth, and down a swallow in a matter of seconds.

I was reminded of this type of household accident (and others) shortly after our three grandchildren were born. I realized once again the importance of making my home safe for small children.

Accidents happen when we least expect them, and they are most common within our own homes. The National Safety Council estimates that there is a home accident every seven seconds.

Even if you don't have children, making your home safe for visitors with small children is very important.

I've compiled a list to help you get started.

Kitchen Safety

- ◆ Keep knives in a knife holder on a wall or in a higher drawer.

- ◆ Put knives in dishwasher point down.

- ◆ Store cleaning items in a plastic bucket or a carry-all with a handle. Place it on a shelf in the garage or the hall closet.

The bucket or carry-all can then be taken from room to room for cleaning and will free up the space under the kitchen sink for storing paper towels, napkins, paper plates, and cups.

◆ When cooking on your kitchen range, keep the handles of your pots turned *away* from the front of the stove. If you don't do this, children can easily dump a pot of boiling water or food on their heads by pulling on a handle or swinging a toy overhead.

◆ Always wrap broken glass in paper or place it in an old paper bag before throwing it into the trash. This goes for razor blades and jagged metal lids as well. A child may drop a toy into the trash and try to retrieve it, or may be taking out the trash and see an item he wants to look at or take out.

◆ When wiping up broken glass off the floor, use a dampened paper towel. This will ensure that you get all the pieces and will also protect your hands.

◆ Teach your children how to pour hot water slowly and to aim steam away from them so it doesn't gush out and burn them. Be sure to check the lid of a teapot or kettle to see that it fits tightly and won't fall into the cup and splash boiling hot water all over.

◆ Any poisons or extremely dangerous products should be kept in a locked cabinet on a very high shelf.

◆ Never store products in unlabeled jars or cans. It's just too easy to forget what's inside.

◆ For all electrical outlets, purchase cover caps for your child's safety. The caps are very inexpensive and can be purchased at drugstores, hardware stores, and even children's shops.

◆ Never leave a cord plugged into a socket with the other end exposed for a child to put into his mouth. Use an empty toilet paper tube to wrap your cords around, and place the tube in a safe drawer.

Bathroom Safety

◆ Never leave children in the bathtub unattended; a lifeguard needs to be on duty at all times. Falling is just one of the hazards that younger children face in the tub. Don't answer the door or telephone without taking the child with you.

- Check the water temperature carefully before putting children in the tub or shower. It can start out warm but then get really hot if you accidentally bump the faucet handle with your hand. Never allow children to fiddle with the faucets. Scalds can happen very quickly.

- Never add hot water to the bathtub when the baby is in it. Be sure the hot water faucet is turned off tightly. Wrap a washcloth around the faucet for safety when the child is in the tub.

- Tell the whole family that shower valves should be turned to "OFF" after use. Otherwise a bather or bathtub cleaner may get scalding water on his or her head.

- Store all medications in a cool, dry place somewhere other than the bathroom. This way there is no danger of little hands reaching your medicine, and it will not be damaged by moisture.

Door Safety

- If you have small children in your home, keep your bathroom doors closed at all times. A latch placed up high where toddlers can't unlatch it should do the trick.

- Be careful of bathroom doors that lock from the inside. Be sure you have an emergency key that will open the door from the outside should junior become locked in and you locked out.

- Door gates can be used across bathroom or bedroom doors, stairs, and many other places that you want to keep away from children. These gates can be purchased in most stores that have baby departments. Look for them also at garage sales or in want ads in newspapers.

Miscellaneous Safety

- Post emergency phone numbers near your phone for both yourself and babysitters.

- Take a first-aid class that includes CPR (mouth-to-mouth resuscitation) at your local Red Cross chapter.

- Give your children swimming lessons at a very early age and/or teach them in the bathtub how to hold their breath underwater. Many community pools offer swimming lessons.

- If you don't already have a first-aid kit, get one or make up your own. Store it out of children's reach.

- Use side rails on small children's beds to keep infants from falling out. These can be purchased out of catalogs or in children's departments at most stores.

- Keep scissors, plastic bags, icepicks, and matches away from the reach of children.

- Warn children not to touch an electrical appliance plug with wet hands.

Remember, safety saves lives!

twenty-four

Preparing for Vacation Travel

*If you refuse to discipline your son, it proves
you don't love him; for if you love him
you will be prompt to punish him.*

Proverbs 13:24

Believe it or not, it can be a joy to travel with your children!
Granted, the preparation for a trip sometimes seems exhausting, and you may wonder if it is worth it all to leave the house, the pets, and a regular routine. But the excitement and wonder of children as they experience new sights will truly be ample reward for the effort involved.

Here are some hints for making your trip smoother for the whole family.

◆ **Prepare your children for the exciting adventure.** Talk with them about where you are going and what you will be doing. As children grow out of the infant and toddler stages and as their world expands to include friends, some verbal preparation becomes very important.

Tell your youngsters about the fun that is in store for them. Show them books, maps, and photographs about your route and destination. Be sure to reassure that you will soon return home and that the toys they didn't take with them will still be there when they get back.

- **Watch your tendency to overpack.** The rule of thumb for experienced travelers applies to children as well: *Take just what you need and no more.*

  The length of the trip (adjusted for the dirt factor for your children) should give you a reasonable handle on the amount of clothing they will need each day. Bear in mind that a public laundromat will probably be available during your travels.

- **Pack only clothing that your children like.** Let them help you pack. Even a three-year old can learn to help. Lay out five items and let them choose two to take along. This is a great teaching tool.

  In our family, our children eventually did all their own packing. I merely checked their items to be sure all the bases were covered. Sometimes we had to leave items behind because, as time and experience taught us, we learned we were wearing only half of what we took. However, always take a sweater or sweatshirt, since temperatures can sometimes change very quickly, even in tropical areas.

- **Take toys that your children enjoy.** Again, let your child help in this area. A toy that you consider mundane might provide considerable amusement to your child.

  It's also a good idea to stash away a couple of new attention-getters—maybe a special surprise like a new toy that he or she has always wanted. But don't forget the tried and true, either. A special pillow, favorite blanket, cuddly stuffed teddy, or special doll are often comforting for a child sleeping in a strange bed for the first time.

- **Consider a backpack for the preschooler and older child.** This is a great way of limiting items or toys taken. Make a rule that your children can take along whatever fits into their backpack.

- **Bring along a surprise box.** Children love it when mom and dad have secrets for them. Your box can include such items as toys, food snacks, puzzles, books, and word games. Be creative but keep it a surprise, and when things get hectic or a child gets irritable, pull out the surprise box.

- **Remember car seats.** If you are renting a car for your trip, request a car seat for any child four years old and younger or a booster seat for five- through eight-year-olds. Many rental agencies provide these seats, but the availability is sometimes limited, so it is important to reserve one.

- **Plan frequent stops.** This is very important if you are traveling by car with small children. Cramped legs and fidgety children will be the cause of many arguments if not taken care of sensibly.

  Give your children plenty of opportunities to get out and run, skip, and jump for a few minutes, and also to use the restroom.

- **Always carry a small cooler with you.** Keep a cooler filled with milk, fruit juice, snacks, and fruit. This will be a pick-me-up, and the refreshment is always welcome. It will also prevent too many fast-food stops. Picnic whenever possible; it's cheaper and children love it.

- **Invest in a first-aid kit.** Fill an empty coffee can with Band-Aids, children's aspirin, antiseptic, thermometer, scissors, safety pins, tweezers, adhesive tape, gauze, and cotton balls. Try to cover all bases. Don't forget a good supply of handy wipes and a blanket.

- **Bring a flashlight.** Be sure to check the batteries before leaving home. When all else fails, children love to play with a flashlight. Take along an extra set of batteries.

- **Throw in your bathing suits.** Keep these in an easy-to-get-to place. Many motels and hotels have pools that are usable even in the winter months. They may also have hot tubs or Jacuzzis. Also, you may find yourself stopping by a lake or beach for a quick swim.

- **Give your children their own map.** Depending on the age of your children, give them a map so they can follow the route and tell you how far it is to the next stop or town. Older children can also keep a journal of the trip.

- **Send up a prayer for safety and patience.** Before we drive out of our driveway, we always offer a prayer for protection and patience. Prayer during the trips also helps to calm a tense situation.

Some of your most memorable times together as a family will come from traveling on vacation. With a little planning and preparation, those memories can be truly happy ones.

twenty-five

Off to School

Let the little children come to Me, and do not
forbid them, for of such is the kingdom of God.

Mark 10:14 NKJV

I can vividly remember when my niece, Keri, was living with us. We had done everything possible to make sure that she knew how to walk to school on that first day of kindergarten. We had even made dry runs, with her walking without us and us following behind in a car to make sure she got there. And in practice she did well.

On that first morning to school she left the house all dressed with new clothes, little knapsack, and a lunchbox. We were so excited on that first day of school. We kissed her goodbye, took a picture, and said goodbye. Off she walked in the direction of her new school. But in about 30 minutes the principal of the adjoining elementary school called and said, "Your niece Keri is here at the wrong school!"

No matter how hard we try, our efforts sometimes go unnoticed. However, there are certain steps we can take to make sure that the first school experience is at least somewhat successful.

Walk with your child to school or the bus stop at least once before the school year starts. Be sure the child understands any special arrangements you have made for his or her going to school and returning home. Practice the proper way to cross the street at every opportunity.

Be sure your child has seen and used a public toilet (including a urinal for boys) so that the school restrooms won't seem strange. Teach your children to use the correct words to ask to "go to the restroom or toilet." Emphasize the need to wash hands even when grownups are not around with reminders.

If your child will be eating lunch in the school cafeteria, take him or her to eat at a cafeteria-style restaurant, so that the procedures will be familiar. Let your child practice at home carrying a loaded food tray or using a lunchbox. Remind him or her to bring his lunchbox home each day.

It is very important for your child to know his or her full name, address, and home and work telephone numbers. (At least Keri did know how to get in touch with me.) An excellent way to teach these numbers is to set them to the tune of a nursery rhyme or a popular song. Be sure to give the school office your *work* number as well as your home number, plus the name and number of a parent substitute to call if you're not available in an emergency.

Make a safe place to keep any notes "to" and "from" the teacher. I inserted a manila envelope with holes punched on one side into my child's loose-leaf notebook. This way the notes to home didn't fall out and get lost.

Sick Days

Is your child too sick to go to school? This is a common cry heard by mom and dad. Talk to your child and carefully listen to what he or she is saying. The problem may not be stated in words but instead may be hidden beneath several unrelated answers. If you decide to allow your child to stay home from school, have a quiet talk showing a lot of love from mom.

If your child has too many pleas for sick days, consider causes other than illness, such as being teased, or frightened, fear of parental separation, etc. If you choose to keep your child home from school and in your judgment the child is not truly ill, staying home should not be a fun time. Put the child to bed for the day to "get well." If his pleas continue, make an appointment with your family doctor and your child's teachers. Both professionals might give you valuable feedback to why your child wants to stay home.

Reasons to Keep a Child Home from School

- ◆ A fever of 101 degrees or greater.
- ◆ Nausea and/or vomiting.

- Abdominal cramps.

- Diarrhea.

- A cold, when it is associated with a fever, frequent coughing, or heavy nasal congestion.

- A cough, when its symptoms aren't due to any allergy or the after-effects of a recent illness.

- A sore throat, with fever.

- Any unidentified rash. This should be checked promptly by your doctor for the possibility of measles, chicken pox, or other infectious disease.

- Any infectious disease that your doctor has diagnosed.

- An earache.

- Conjunctivitis (pinkeye).

- Your own visual test or gut feeling that tells you your child really isn't well.

- Your child is overly tired or emotional.

Send your child off to school with a hug and a smile!

Part 4

FINANCES

twenty-six

Keeping Your Utility Bills Down

My health fails; my spirits droop, yet God remains.
He is the strength of my heart; he is mine forever!

Psalm 73:26

nergy bills are never fun to pay. Although some factors may be beyond your control (extreme weather conditions, home location, or illness in the family), there are ways to make your use of energy more efficient and to reduce your energy bills. Here are some tips and ideas to help stabilize those bills.

Heating

Your heating system is probably your home's biggest energy user in the winter. It can be an energy waster if you don't use it wisely.

1. Leave the thermostat alone. During the day set it at 65 degrees or below. You raise operating costs 5 percent every time you raise the thermostat two degrees. Turn it down to 55 degrees or off at bedtime for more energy savings.

2. Proper insulation keeps your home warm in winter and cool in summer. In fact, up to 20 percent of your heating energy can be lost through an uninsulated ceiling.

3. Cut more heat loss by weatherstripping doors and windows. Close the damper when not using the fireplace or else heat will escape. Close off rooms not in use, along with heating vents, though not in more than 30 percent of the house. (Make sure you leave the vent open nearest the thermostat to ensure proper temperature sensing.) Turn off individual thermostats.

4. Close draperies at night to keep out the cold. Open them during the day to let the sun shine through.

Lighting

Although individual lights don't use much energy, because houses are full of them and they get so much use (especially in winter), lighting costs can add up. Here are some ideas on keeping lighting costs down.

1. Fluorescent lights provide three times the light for the same amount of electricity as incandescent lights. They are very economical for bathrooms and kitchens, last ten times as long as incandescent bulbs, and produce less wasted heat.

2. Dimmer switches can multiply bulb life up to 12 times while they reduce electricity use.

3. Turn lights off when you're leaving a room and advise your family to do the same.

4. Let the light shine through. Lampshades lined in white give the best light. Tall, narrow shades or short, dark-colored ones waste watts. (Dirt and dust absorb light too, so add bulb-dusting to your cleaning list.)

5. One properly situated light in a room will do the work of three or four carelessly placed fixtures. Rearrange your room so the light is used more efficiently. If you're redecorating, use light colors. Dark colors absorb light.

6. Don't use infrared heating lights for night lights or general lighting.

7. Use lower-watt bulbs.

8. Turn off all outdoor lights except those necessary for safety and security.

Hot Water

Although hot water is the third-largest energy user in the average household, its use can be cut down painlessly.

1. Consider flow-restricting devices. These devices can cut water consumption in half.

2. Buy a water heater insulation blanket. This saves up to 9 percent of your water heater costs.

3. Fix the drips on all faucets. One drip a second can waste up to 700 gallons of hot water a year!

4. Take showers instead of baths. The shower's the winner for less hot water use if you keep your shower time under five minutes. (If you need to wash your hair, do it in the sink. A shower just to shampoo is a hot water waster.)

5. Monitor the use of the dishwasher. Run it once a day or less. It uses about 13 gallons each time instead of the 10 gallons each time you wash dishes by hand.

6. Use cold water for the garbage disposal. It solidifies the grease and flushes it away easily.

7. Turn down the temperature on your hot water heater to 140 degrees. (That's a "medium" setting if your dial isn't numbered.) If you don't have a dishwasher, 120 degrees may be adequate.

8. When you go away on vacation, set the pilot setting on "low" or turn it off altogether. If you have an electric water heater, it may be the type on which the upper thermostat can be set 10 degrees lower than the bottom one.

twenty-seven

Energy-Saving Tips Around the Home

Always be joyful. Always keep on praying.
No matter what happens, always be thankful,
for this is God's will for you.

1 Thessalonians 5:16-18

It sometimes seems surprising how those energy bills can jump around from month to month. What can you do to stabilize those bills and hold down the energy costs?

Some factors may be beyond your control: extreme weather, location of home, illness in family, old or less efficient appliances, etc. Additional houseguests, entertaining, building around the house, special projects, and vacations can often contribute to fluctuation in your energy usage.

Most energy users in the home are easily recognized, and many times you can make these more efficient. Here are some tips and ideas to help you stabilize those energy bills.

Refrigerator/Freezer

Your refrigerator/freezer is probably one of the biggest energy users in your home. Here are some ways to beat the cost of keeping things cool.

1. *Keep it clean.* In a manual-defrost model more than half an inch of frost can build up and make the appliance work harder, so *defrost*

regularly. Vacuum clean the condenser coils below or at the back of the refrigerator/freezer three or four times a year. Clean coils keep it running efficiently and help save energy.

2. *Keep it closed.* The time for decisions is not when you have the door open. Get everything you need for a sandwich or recipe in one trip.

3. *Keep it full.* Frozen food helps keep the air cool in your freezer. But don't overpack food in either refrigerator or freezer, or the cold air won't have space to circulate properly.

4. *Heat has no business in the refrigerator.* Cool dishes before you store them so your appliance won't have to work so hard.

5. *Investigate before you buy.* A frost-free refrigerator/freezer may use 30 percent more electricity than a manual-defrost unit. Also, be sure to choose the correct cubic footage for your family, since a too-full or too-empty refrigerator/freezer wastes energy.

6. *Unplug your second refrigerator.* Refrigerators are big energy users, so if your second refrigerator is not being used to full capacity, unplug it. It could save you $20 a month or more, depending on its size.

Range/Oven

Your food budget shouldn't stop at the checkout counter. These days the cost of preparing the food can add up. Here are some tips on holding down cooking costs.

1. *Pots and pans are important.* Pans with flared sides or that are smaller than your burner let heat escape. If they're too big or have warped bottoms, food won't cook evenly. (For most foods, a medium-weight aluminum pan cooks fast and efficiently. Save your heavy pans for foods that require slow, steady cooking.)

2. *Cover up.* Use pan covers, since trapped steam cooks food quickly. Also, thaw foods completely before cooking.

3. *Preheating is out.* Unless you're baking things like breads and cakes, preheating isn't necessary and is very costly. Casseroles and broiled foods don't need it.

4. *Plan all-oven meals.* A meal like meatloaf, baked tomatoes, scalloped potatoes, and baked apples can all cook at the same time and temperature.

5. *Limit your boiling.* Water doesn't get any hotter with prolonged boiling. Therefore when you need to bring water to a boil (e.g. for making drip coffee), turn off your range once the water has started to boil.

6. *Keep that oven door closed.* Every time you open the door, you lose 25 degrees of heat. Get yourself a timer and just be patient.

7. *Use your free heat.* A gas oven retains heat for up to 15 minutes, an electric oven for up to half an hour, and an electric range-top element for three to five minutes. Use that free heat to warm up desserts or rolls or to freshen crackers and cookies.

8. *Keep it clean.* A range free of grease and baked-on residue works better and costs you less.

9. *Use a microwave oven.* A microwave oven uses about the same amount of energy per hour as a conventional electric oven but cooks most foods in less than half the time. This can mean big savings on the cooking portion of your bill.

10. *Use your electric skillet,* broiler oven, or toaster oven instead of your electric range's oven for cooking and baking in small quantities. These can use as little as half the energy and won't heat up the kitchen nearly as much.

Washer/Dryer

Here's how to get the most out of that costly hot water.

1. *Wash full loads.* Washing two or three large items (like sheets) with a number of small ones (but don't pack them in) will give you a clean wash without taxing your washer's motor. If it is necessary to wash less than a full load, adjust the water-level settings accordingly.

2. *Sort by fabric, color, and degree of soil.* Use hot water only for whites, hard-to-clean items, and sterilizing. Use cold and warm water on all the rest. Your clothes will be just as clean, will fade less, and will have fewer wrinkles (which might save you some ironing).

3. *Check hose and faucet connections.* If the hose is cracked or the faucet connection is loose, you're probably losing hot water.

4. *Don't overkill.* Don't overdo it on soap, washing cycle, or drying. An oversudsed machine uses more energy. Regular clothes need only a 10- to 15-minute washing cycle. And overdrying will age your clothes and make them stiff and wrinkled.

5. *Get the lint out.* Clean the filters on the dryer after every use. Besides making your clothes more attractive, a lint-free machine works more efficiently.

6. *Use your clothesline.* It will save you 100 percent of the energy otherwise consumed by your gas or electric dryer. This could amount to between $4 and $18 of the average $120 bill paid monthly in some areas of the country.

Small Appliances

Some small appliances can do the same jobs with half the energy use as their full-sized counterparts. Use them whenever practical.

1. *Use small appliances.* Small appliances use less energy if you remember to turn them off when you're through. Pull the plug on your coffeepot, iron, electric skillet, and curling iron. (A memory lapse will waste energy and might ruin the appliance.)

2. *Little appliances are okay.* You needn't be guilt-stricken about enjoying the luxury of an electric toothbrush or carving knife. (A continuous-charge toothbrush usually uses less than five cents a month and a carving knife less than ten cents a year.) Cut down instead on the *big* appliances. They're the ones that add up on your electric bill.

Air Conditioning

In many areas keeping cool in summer can cost a lot more than keeping warm in winter. Here are some things you can do to hold down the cost.

1. *Watch your degree of comfort.* Set your thermostat at 78 degrees or above. A setting of 78 instead of 73 saves 20 to 25 percent of your AC operating costs.

2. *Keep the cool air inside.* Close doors and windows. Check the weather-stripping. Seal up cracks. Insulate. These measures will help cut heating costs in the winter as well.

3. *Don't block vents.* Move furniture away from vents and window units. Trim shrubbery outside, too.

4. *Close drapes or blinds.* This helps keep the sun's heat out. Solar screens and shades can also effectively block a large amount of the sun's heat before it enters your home.

5. *Check your filters.* Do this once a month during cooling season. Vacuum or replace them as necessary.

6. *Grow deciduous trees.* Plant them where they will shade your house from the sun's hottest rays in the summer and let warming sun through in the winter.

7. *Check the EER before you buy.* Some systems use less energy than others—sometimes only half as much. Find the Energy Efficiency Rating (EER) on the yellow energy-guide label. The higher the EER, the more efficient the unit. An EER of 10 will consume half the energy of a similar unit rated 5.

Swimming Pool

If you have a pool, a major portion of your energy outlay is the cost of operating it. Here are some ways to get control of swimming pool energy costs.

1. *Lower your pool's temperature.* Lowering your pool heater setting just two degrees can reduce your pool heating substantially. (A reduction from 80 degrees to 78 degrees could save up to 20 percent of heating costs.) The lower temperature saves on chemicals, too.

2. *Use a swimming pool cover.* You can save as much as 80 percent on your summer pool-heating bill by using a pool cover.

3. *Heat early in the morning.* The sun and the pool heater work together most efficiently during the morning hours.

4. *Protect your pool from wind.* Wind has the same effect on your pool as blowing on hot soup: It cools it. Hedges, fences, and cabanas help keep wind down.

5. *Don't overfilter.* Most pools require only four to five hours of filtering a day in summer and two to three hours in the winter. Reducing your filtration by 50 percent may save you more than $20 per month. Be sure to filter before 11 A.M. and/or after 5 P.M.

6. *Keep filter, skimmer, and strainer basket clean.* When your pump motor doesn't work as hard, it costs less to operate.

7. *Don't overclean.* Automatic pool-sweeping devices can usually get the job done in three to four hours a day in the summer and two to three hours a day during the off-season. But remember to set the cleaner to start 15 minutes before you filter. Again, try to operate the sweep outside the hours of 11 A.M. to 5 P.M.

Waterbed

Improperly controlled, waterbed energy costs could make you lose sleep. These tips will save you a lot of money.

1. *Don't unplug the bed during the day.* Getting the bed up to temperature every night uses more energy than operating the bed continuously with thermostat control.

2. *Make the bed every morning.* Controlled tests have shown that beds with mattress pad sheets, cotton quilt, one blanket, and one-inch foam rubber mat between mattress and pad save about $15 a month over one covered by just sheets.

As you begin to put these various tips into practice, you will begin to see real savings on your monthly energy bills!

twenty-eight

Saving Time and Money

A man who refuses to admit his mistakes can never be successful. But if he confesses and forsakes them, he gets another chance.

Proverbs 28:13

ime and money: We never seem to have enough of either of them, do we? Actually, we can control both time and money so that they work efficiently for us.

Here are some practical household tips that can help you save both time and money on a daily basis.

Saving Time

1. Plan a weekly menu and base your shopping list just on those menus. Then add to your list those staples which are getting low. Make sure your list is complete before you go shopping; it will save you time and gasoline.

2. Avoid trips to the market for single items.

3. Never shop for food when you're hungry; you may be tempted to deviate from your shopping list!

4. Plan your timetable for meal preparation so that your broccoli is not done ten minutes before the chicken and thereby loses color, texture, flavor, and nutritive value.

5. If you have such conveniences as a microwave oven or food processor, take advantage of them by incorporating them into your time schedule and menu for the week.

6. Organize your kitchen and save steps. Keep your most-used cookbooks and utensils in an area close at hand.

7. Save salad preparation time by washing and tearing salad greens once a week. Store them in an airtight container such as Tupperware.

8. Learn to do two things at the same time. When talking on the telephone you can: load the dishwasher, clean the refrigerator, cook a meal, bake a cake, mop the floor, or clean under the kitchen sink. I do recommend getting a long extension cord on your telephone or better yet, get a cordless phone.

9. Shell and chop your fresh pecans and walnuts while watching television. Then store them in the freezer or refrigerate them in airtight bags. When baking day arrives you'll be all set.

10. Convenience foods are worth their extra cost when time is short. A stock of frozen pastry shells, for example, will enable you to make a quiche or cream pie in very little time.

Saving Money

Here are some tips to keep in mind when planning your weekly menu.

1. Seasonal produce is usually your best buy. Green beans, in season, cost less per serving than canned beans and offer much more nutrition. Fresh produce also has better flavor and fewer additives.

2. High-ticket items are placed at eye level at most grocery stores. Check the top and bottom shelves for similar items with lower pricetags.

3. Avoid impulse buying; if it's not on your list, don't buy it.

4. Check your local newspaper ads for sales, especially in the meat section.

5. When things are on sale, consider buying them in larger quantities. For example, a dozen cans of tuna can be stored indefinitely.

6. Stay within your budget. Take a small notepad or calculator to the store so that you can keep a running total.

7. Take advantage of coupons, but only buy the product if it is already on your shopping list. Although this seems tedious, I know women who save $5.00 and more on their weekly grocery bill by using coupons.

8. Buy cheese in bricks. Slice or grate it at home to save the cost of handling and packaging.

9. Compare prices. For example, whole chicken breasts with ribs are about half the price of boned chicken breasts. If you want boned chicken, buy whole chicken breasts and parboil them for 10 to 12 minutes, and the meat will peel right off the bone.

10. Turn your unused bread crusts or not-quite-fresh bread and crackers into crumbs by using your blender. Use your crumbs in stuffing, casseroles, and meatloaf.

11. Save the oil from deep-frying. Strain it through cheesecloth and then refrigerate it.

12. Citrus fruit yields more juice when stored at room temperature.

13. Look into using special services and conveniences that don't cost extra money. For example, shopping from catalogs is one way to streamline your schedule and save time.

By putting even half of these ideas into action, you'll be surprised at how much time and money you'll save!

twenty-nine

Great Fund-Raising Ideas

*Happiness comes to those who are fair to others
and are always just and good.*

Psalm 106:3

any of us are members of churches, clubs, fraternities, or sororities that are looking for ways to raise funds. About the time we realize there is a need to raise funds, we scratch our heads to think of creative ways to supplement our budget. Our minds go blank! Some of these ideas from our readers can help you.

- ◆ **Service, Time, and Talent Auction.** In this auction you don't sell material possessions but pledges for service, time, and talent. Items you might include: babysitting, a resort area condominium, home-baked cookies once a month for a year, car service to and from the airport for a future plane trip. Each donation is the generous giving of self.

- ◆ **Cleanup Crew.** A great high school or teenage project is to take the place of professional street cleaners when you need to clean the streets of the fall leaves. Charge the neighbors or business tenants a fair wage scale. It doesn't take many students to earn a substantial amount of money for their special project.

115

◆ **Hill of Beans.** Here's a fund-raiser that's literally a hill of beans—kidneys, pintos, lentils, split peas, garbanzos, limas, and more. Members of your club can donate these beans. Combine them into a colorful, flavorful mix, which are then bagged in plastic baggies of two cups each and sold for $2.00 along with instructions for rinsing, soaking, and making soup. Tie a colorful ribbon at the top of your bag to provide eye appeal.

◆ **Lip Sync.** Hold a lip-sync show. While a recording of a real singer plays, each child performs one or two songs, imitating the artist's style and mouthing the lyrics. Have rehearsals so the students can pool the songs, tapes, records, and lyrics. You can even make costumes with materials on hand and such finishing touches as feathers or jewelry. Sell tickets or take a freewill offering. This is a good source for added funds.

◆ **Krazy Kalendar.** For your special fund-raiser, make up a unique calendar where you can preprint for specific days of the month specified money to put away for this fund-raising idea. For example, during a typical week in July ask for 50 cents on Sunday "if you didn't go to church tonight," followed by "one cent for each year of your age above 21" on Monday, "ten cents if you have a patio or deck" on Tuesday, "25 cents if you turned on the air conditioner" on Wednesday, "five cents for each glass of water you drank" on Thursday, "one cent for each page of a book you read" on Friday, and "ten cents if you drank lemonade" on Saturday. Deposit the money in a jar and contribute jointly for your special fund-raiser.

◆ **House Numbers.** Raise extra money by painting street numbers on the curbs of your neighborhood streets. Be sure to clear the idea with your local police department. Call on the neighbors to presell the orders. Depending on the economic level of your neighborhood, a fair price would be in the $3.00 to $5.00 range. Stencil black numbers in white 6 x 10 inch rectangles on curbs, steps, and sidewalks. You might even have local merchants donate the paint. You will find that the police and fire departments are usually delighted with the easy-to-read addresses.

◆ **Tasting Bee.** If you are passing up the usual barbecues, fish fries, pancake breakfasts, etc. you might want to try something different to make money—a "Tasting Bee." At theme tables decorated with flowers, flags, and costumed dolls representing various parts of the world, you can serve portions of a variety of American, European, Mexican, and Oriental foods. For a fixed price you can sample food from as many tables as you wish. The dessert table could be an extra cost if you wish. The only eating utensils needed should be teaspoons and toothpicks. You could also preprint the food recipes and sell them for a nominal cost.

- **20 Talents.** Give your group of 20 youngsters $1.00 each to purchase supplies for a craft or baking project. You can also pool your money for larger projects. You can even contribute a little extra money on your own if you like. You can also use materials found around the house. In three or four weeks you can bring the crafts or baked goods to a central area in which they can be sold. You can turn the original $20.00 into much more than this by selling or auctioning off cookies, cakes, holiday decorations, aprons, stuffed toys, baby quilts, or covered photograph albums.

- **Seesaw Marathon.** Schedule a seesaw contest within your group and seesaw from a Friday afternoon until Sunday afternoon. You can presell pledges from your neighbors, friends, and family based on the number of hours the students can keep going. The students can teeter-totter in three-hour shifts.

Use your own creative imagination in creating your fund-raising projects. These efforts bring out the organizational ability of the various members and tend to bring the members closer together. Those who participate in these projects also become more familiar with the sponsoring group's purposes.

Fund-raising can be fun!

thirty

Organizing and Retrieving Records for Your Income Tax Report

*Better is a little with righteousness
than vast revenues without justice.*

Proverbs 16:18 NKJV

"Jenny, where are the canceled checks for Dr. Merrihew?" Does this sound familiar around your home as you prepare for the annual April 15 deadline? Much unnecessary stress is caused in our households when we don't properly plan organizational details to help us as we prepare for our yearly IRS reports.

For many of us, we can complete the short form and claim the standard deductions and mail the forms off. However, for those who itemize our deductions, we have the responsibility to keep thorough detailed records.

Each year we find ourselves adapting to new tax laws (and it looks like the changes will continue). For those of you who have figured your own tax forms in the past, now might be the time to look into a professional tax-preparer.

Years ago my husband, Bob, and I searched for a qualified tax professional, and we have been pleased with the additional refunds we have received because that person thoroughly understands the tax laws. With the coming changes, a professional preparer can more than save you the service charge to properly figure your new tax forms. Since his or her time usually costs by the number of schedules to prepare and the length of time it takes, you will save many dollars by having your records complete when you meet for your appointment. A little planning will save you a lot in the end.

Many of us have different styles of organization. Sally Sanguine can't be bothered each month to keep accurate records, so she tosses all her receipts, pay stubs, bank statements, canceled checks, and receipts (cash and charge) into a drawer or shoe box until tax time. At the end of the year she dumps all her materials on a tabletop or the floor and begins to sort. This type of record-keeping takes four to six hours to process. If you have several schedules with a small business, rental property, stock transactions, etc. you might spend up to three or four days to complete the forms.

If this is your style (and it can work) you can simplify the task by filing the receipts in an accordion file folder or large 9 x 12 envelopes. Total each category and write the total on the top sheet of the category. Then record your totals on a worksheet. At this point you are ready to complete your own tax forms, or you can meet with your tax-preparer. Treat yourself to a bowl of ice cream or popcorn. In order to function under this method you have to have the right mindset. You are making a trade-off of small increments of time each month for a larger block of time once a year.

Many of us function better by staying on top of our record-keeping in smaller blocks of time. Some people prefer daily, some weekly, and some monthly. Whatever your desire, you need some basic tools to start your record-keeping.

- ◆ Regular or legal-size manila file folders (multicolored make the task cheerier and brighten up the task).

- ◆ A metal file cabinet (two-drawer minimum) or standard-size boxes to house yearly records or an accordion-type file folder.

- ◆ Regular or legal-size envelopes.

- ◆ Wide felt pen for labeling your headings.

- ◆ Highlighter pen for marking receipt totals (for ease in identification when summarizing).

There are several ways to categorize your records. Select one that best fits your style of organization. Make a list of all items that will be income items and all expenses that are tax-deductible. Some suggested categories are:

Income
- Salary—both spouses
- These records must include total wages, federal tax withheld, FICA, and state and local taxes. This information is on your W-2 form.
- Income listed on a 1099 form.
- Alimony received (excluding child support)
- Interest and dividend income
- Income from sale of property, stocks, mutual funds, etc. Consult your tax-preparer for short-term or capital-gains implication.
- Royalties, commissions, fees
- Bonuses and prizes
- Tips and gratuities
- Annuities, pension income, retirement benefits
- Lump-sum distribution from retirement plans
- Unemployment compensation.
- Rental income
- Social Security benefits
- Business income
- Other income—including hobby income

Expenses and Deductions
- Contributions to an IRA or other pension plan
- Social Security benefits
- Adoption expenses
- Alimony paid
- Casualty losses. Include auto accidents, fire, theft, storms, property damage, etc. List the loss, the value, and insurance payment, if any.
- Charitable work. Document expenses such as transportation, special clothing, and food and lodging if out of town.

- Work-related childcare and dependent-care expenses; note name and address and social security number of provider.

- Contributions, including tithes and offerings. List the name of the organization and the amount. Keep a canceled check or receipt if over $250 to one organization.

- Interest paid on all loans or mortgages secured by your residence.

- Investment expenses. Include supplies, publications, transportation, cost of safe deposit box.

- Expenses to operate your business

- Expenses related to your rental property

- Job-related expenses. This could include auto, special shoes, tools, uniforms, union dues, education expenses, professional dues and journals, safety equipment, transportation to a second job, job-seeking expenses, and employment agency fees.

- Medical insurance (premiums), doctor and dentist bills, prescribed medication and drugs, eye exams, eyeglasses, ambulance, artificial limbs, hearing aids, lab tests, X-rays, acupuncture, chiropractors, nursing care, miles driven, lodging, etc.

- Job-related moving expenses

- Tax (income, sales, state, and cancelled checks for estimated taxes paid during the year)

- Tax-preparation costs

This list is not all inclusive, so check the IRS instructions carefully each year.

Once you have determined which of the income and expense items relate to your family's organizational needs, you can:

- Label a file folder or envelope for each income or deductible topic. When you have an item to file away, you can use the front of the envelope as a journal for writing down the date, to whom, and the amount of the entry. At the end of the year you just total the items listed on the front of the envelope and you have the totals for that entry. Inside your envelope you have all the receipts and stubs to back up your final total.

- Store these envelopes in your metal file folder, your cardboard box that you purchased from the local stationery store, or your accordion file.

Although not needed for taxes, I have found that household receipts can be organized in a very simple way by using a regular legal-size folder. Just open it flat and glue onto each side of the folder three legal-size white envelopes. Label each envelope for the receipts:

A. utilities   D. entertainment
B. donations   E. insurance
C. credit cards   F. food

Set up one of these file folders for each month of the year, using your wide felt pen to label one folder for each month of the year. Each month as you pay bills, just slip the receipts into the proper envelope and file away. One added step speeds up the year-end process: Total the receipts in each envelope each month and write the total of the contents on the front of each of the individual envelopes.

The IRS requires that you keep your records for a minimum of six years for most records. However, you will need to keep real estate and investment records for as long as you own the item and a minimum of six years after you've sold it. Take particular care when storing your records. You do not want to lose these records! In case of an audit you will find the reconstruction of your records to be very time-consuming and in some cases quite costly.

Before the end of each year, call the IRS (1-800-829-FORM) and request your free copy of Publication 17. This book explains many of the tax laws in language fairly easy to understand (have a soda and popcorn snack while studying).

With a little thought and preparation you can have a system that is easy and that reduces stress and tension when your spouse asks you to find where Dr. Merrihew's canceled checks are. Review together if you are married, because none of us knows when an emergency might occur for the other partner. Let's not keep our records a mystery!

thirty-one

Seven Steps to Financial Cleanup at Tax Time

*A prudent man foresees the difficulties
ahead and prepares for them.*

Proverbs 22:3

You can do a great financial cleanup yourself by breaking the job down into logical steps. Throwing everything out and making a clean start isn't the answer. Discarding salary stubs, last year's tax return, or current receipts for medical or business expenses will only bring you problems further down the road.

One of the biggest mistakes people make is not retaining records. Throwing away records that later turn out to be important cause people a lot of unnecessary work and worry. Well-kept financial records will pay off during emergencies. Should an accident occur, a friend or family member can quickly locate your insurance policy and the papers needed for vital information.

Here are seven steps to help have "More Hours in Your Day" during tax-return time.

1. *Know what to keep.* Keep permanent, lifetime records. These would include personal documents required for credit, job-qualification

123

papers, Social Security and government program papers, birth and marriage certificates, Social Security number cards, property records, college credits, diplomas, and licenses. Also keep transitory records. These pertain to your current circumstances: employee benefits, receipts for major purchases (auto, stock, jewelry, art), tax returns, insurance policies, credit union information, and canceled checks relating directly to home improvements.

The IRS has the right to audit within three years. Let this be a measure of how long you keep receipts, etc.

2. *Set up your personal system* according to your natural organization. If you are disorganized, your system should be simple. Keep it uncomplicated.

   The less time you have, the simpler your system should be. If you like working with numbers and are good in math, your system can be more complex. The simplest way to begin is outlined in Chapter 30.

3. *Set aside a spot for your records.* Obtain a safe deposit box for permanent documents plus a fireproof and waterproof file cabinet for home use.

4. *Let someone know where your records are kept.* Make a list of the location of your insurance policies and give it to a family member, a friend, or even your pastor.

5. *Get professional advice when you need it.* Expert advice can go a long way and in the long run save you time and money. Accountants are a great source of information and many times save much more than their cost. Financial planners are helpful if your past history has been a financial disaster, and they can benefit you by helping you avoid future mistakes.

6. *Review your will and insurance policies annually.* What worked last year may need some revisions this year. Make sure your family understands your final goals.

7. *Record-keeping requires time set aside.* You must discipline yourself to set aside a time each month on a consistent basis to go over your financial records so you won't be overwhelmed in April when you

have to file your tax return. Some people update weekly when paying bills or when reconciling checking accounts.

Great record-keeping gives mental benefits as well as more hours to do things you enjoy doing. God will honor and bless you as you keep order in your financial life.

Part 5

HOLIDAYS

thirty-two

Holiday Safety Survival Checklist

*Suddenly there appeared with the angel a multitude
of the heavenly host, praising God and saying,
"Glory to God in the highest, and on earth peace
among men with whom He is pleased."*

Luke 2:13-14

The holidays are supposed to be fun, relaxing, spiritual, and festive. This Christmas safety checklist will help you and your family have a safe and merry Christmas! Taking these simple safety precautions throughout the season will prevent mishaps and help you enjoy the holidays even more.

Tips

- Don't overload electrical circuits.

- Use only the replacement bulbs and fuses recommended by the manufacturer.

- Replace broken or burned-out bulbs in old strings of lights, unplugging them before you do.

- Keep strings of lights unplugged when hanging them on the tree.

- Use clips specially made for hanging lights on the house. Misdirected nails and staples can damage or expose wires.

- Don't use indoor lights outside.

- Do not use lights with worn or frayed cords, exposed wires, broken or cracked sockets, or loose connections.

- Check all electrical lights, cords, and connections before you decorate.

- Use a heavy-duty extension cord with a ground, and never string more than three standard-size sets of lights per single extension cord.

- Follow the directions and heed the cautions on the packaging of any lighting products you purchase.

- Safety experts recommend using electrical fixtures that carry the approval label of Underwriters Laboratory (UL).

- The Red Cross warns that many holiday plants are poisonous and can cause serious illness. Holly, mistletoe, yew, and Jerusalem cherry plants should never be chewed or swallowed.

- All parts of poinsettias also are dangerous; they contain toxins that can irritate the mouth, throat, stomach, and eyes. If swallowed, seek prompt medical attention. Keep all holiday plants out of the reach of children.

- To avoid electrical shock, do not use electrical decorations on trees with metallic needles, leaves, or branches. Use colored spotlights above or beside a metallic tree.

- Burning evergreens in a fireplace is dangerous; flames can flare out and send sparks flying about the room. Give your tree to the garbage collector.

- Equip your home with a UL-listed, ABC-rated fire extinguisher and smoke or heat detectors. They make good stocking stuffers.

- Be careful with fire salts, which produce colored flames on wood fires. They cause severe stomach disorders if swallowed. Keep them away from children.

- Make sure your tree is fresh when you buy it. As the needles turn brown and begin to break off easily, the tree becomes a greater fire risk. Keep the tree-base holder filled with water at all times. Place the tree in a location away from the fireplace, radiator, and other heat sources. Be sure it is out of your home traffic pattern and doesn't block a doorway.

- Never use lighted candles on a tree or near evergreens or draperies.

- Never use aluminum foil or differently-rated fuses to replace burned-out electric fuses.

- If you buy an artificial tree, make sure it has been UL-tested for flammability.

- Buy toys for infants and toddlers that are too large to fit into their mouths. Be sure the eyes on dolls and the buttons on stuffed animals are secure.

- Buy toys appropriate for a child's age and development.

- Be sure electrical toys are tested for safety. Look for the UL mark.

- Throw away gift wrappings immediately. Don't burn them in the fireplace. They can ignite suddenly and cause a flash fire.

- Always turn off tree lights before leaving home or going to bed.

- When removing your tree lights, wind them around the tube from a roll of paper towels. Start collecting tubes now. It will make for fast, easy storage and easy tree trimming next year.

- Store ornaments in apple-type boxes; layer newspaper or tissue paper between ornaments to prevent breakage.

- Store extension cords in toilet paper tubes and keep them with your tree lights so you'll have them when needed next year.

- Don't forget wrapping paper, cards, and Christmas ribbons go on sale the week after Christmas at 50 to 70 percent off, so stock up for next year and save money.

Blessings for a happy holiday and a safe New Year!

thirty-three

Fall Harvest Pumpkin Times

If we are living in the light of God's presence,
just as Christ does, then we have wonderful
fellowship and joy with each other.

1 John 1:7

*S*ummer is about over and as the nip hits the air and the leaves begin to turn burnt red and orange, it's time to hang the corn on your door and put Mr. Pumpkin in place for the fall season.

Even though we live in the city our home is country. By mid-September our corn season is about over and the stalks from our summer garden are tied and placed around the front door of the house. One year a package of pumpkin seeds planted the previous May gave us an over-abundant supply of fresh, bright orange pumpkins. We not only had enough for our home but enough to supply the neighborhood. We then made Mr. Scarecrow out of an old pair of Bob's blue jeans and a plaid shirt stuffed with newspapers…so easy. A pair of garden gloves for his hands and a pumpkin for his head—we painted the face and placed a straw hat to top it off! All the children loved our harvest scene and it was enjoyed until late November.

Harvest ideas are a treat to create. Take your pick of these ideas and establish your own family traditions.

132

1. If you are proud of your carved harvest pumpkins and want to keep them in firm shape indefinitely, simply spray their insides and outsides with an antiseptic, repeating periodically as necessary. The antiseptic destroys the bacteria that normally grow and soften the pumpkins.

2. Don't throw out the pumpkin seeds when you are through carving. Salt the seeds and dry them in the oven on a cookie sheet for a tasty, nutritious snack the whole family will love.

3. A hollowed pumpkin makes a creative punch bowl for apple cider. It can also be used for a harvest soup tureen.

4. Many local churches, parks, recreation departments, and community centers provide fun harvest activities. A phone call can get you the schedule of events.

5. Take your family to a local pumpkin patch. There are many commercial pumpkin fields in various areas across the country. Often you can harvest your own pumpkin right from the grower's field. If not, consider planting your own patch next year.

   No thumping is necessary to determine pumpkin ripeness: Once it is orange a pumpkin is ready to use. It will last for months if not cut or broken or cracked. It's best not to lift pumpkins by the stems, as they often break off.

   Take home several for Halloween carving and Thanksgiving pumpkin pies.

   This is a fun outing particularly for city families. Many of these patches will have cornstalks, gourds, and Indian corn, which make excellent materials for harvest decoration both at the front door and dining room table. Ask the farmer if you could bring a picnic lunch and share a family time in the midst of the vines.

6. Carving faces on the pumpkins is a fun experience for the family. Children love to be involved in making funny faces, but care needs to be taken when carving. A sharp knife used by either a child who is too young or by a child who hasn't been shown the proper use of a knife can ruin a good time. Colored paint-pens are a great option and can be purchased at craft and art supply stores.

7. Plan a neighborhood pumpkin carving or pumpkin painting party:

- Spread several layers of newspapers on the driveway, kitchen countertop, garage floor, or basement (depending on the weather).

- Carve or draw faces on the pumpkins, each person creating his or her own masterpiece. Children can use the paint pens or felt marking pens.

- Cut into the pumpkin and separate seeds from pulp. (See number 2 on how to roast seeds.)

- After each pumpkin is carved, put a candle inside. In the bottom of the pumpkin carve a shallow hole so the candle will fit in an upright position. A little melted wax in the hole will also help secure the candle. A votive candle in a glass container works best if available.

- Display your pumpkin in the window, on the table, or on your front porch. Make sure there is no fire danger near the candle.

- After the carving session you might want to finish off the evening with hot apple cider, popcorn, and your roasted pumpkin seeds. Truly an evening to remember.

- For baby pumpkins use oranges. A fun project is to decorate with faces using, again, the marking pens. The decorated oranges can also be used as a nutritious snack and put into lunch sacks during the harvest season.

- Make pumpkin faces on a cheese sandwich. Cut the jack-o'-lantern face on one side of bread. Add cheese and second slice of bread. Serve plain or toasted under the broiler. A cleaner combination is dark rye bread with yellow cheese.

- Create these and other fun memories during this special harvest pumpkin time. Plan several harvest walks as a family and collect leaves, acorns, pods, and berries. These can all be placed around your pumpkins on the table for your harvest centerpiece.

thirty-four

The Busy Person's Thanksgiving Dinner

Let us not get tired of doing what is right,
for after a while we will reap a harvest of blessing.

Galatians 6:9

Today's busy women just don't have the time to do what great-grandma did. She cooked for days until Thanksgiving arrived. Many Thanksgivings I found myself in the middle of a busy holiday seminar schedule. The thought of roasting a turkey, cleaning the house, and getting the trimmings together for Thanksgiving dinner caused my stress level to elevate to dangerous heights!

Finally, I stopped to take a deep breath and think long enough to come up with a solution to my busyness. I decided to make our harvest dinner a potluck. I made a few phone calls and quickly organized a simple meal.

Here are some of the steps I took. Try them out this year for your best-ever Thanksgiving.

Step 1

Develop your Thanksgiving dinner menu. Here is a sample menu:

Turkey, dressing, cranberry sauce: You will do this.
Vegetable: Auntie Syd
Potato or rice: Grandma Gertie
Rolls: Uncle Blair

Relish dish: Brad
Pumpkin pie: Jenny

Step 2

Phone your guests to invite them for a Busy Person's Thanksgiving Dinner. For your own reference, make a simple chart or list with their name and what item they will be bringing. (For example: Vegetable—Aunt Amy; Relish dish—Sister Sue.)

Ask them to please call an RSVP to you at least 10 days before Thanksgiving dinner. This way you'll still have time to adjust things if someone can't make it after all.

Step 3

Get your family involved. Assign the name cards to one child or to your husband to write a Scripture verse on the back or inside of each individual card. These verses should fit the Thanksgiving holiday; for example, Ephesians 5:20, "Always giving thanks for all things in the name of our Lord Jesus Christ" (NASB).

Use a 3 x 5 card folded in half, placing the name on the front and the Scripture inside. These will be read aloud by each person before your meal.

Step 4

Have another child make cards titled "I'm thankful for...." These should be given to your guests when they first arrive at your home, so they have time to think about their response.

After dinner each guest will read their thankful card. This is a great way to focus on the positive things God provides for us. Or you could have a person interview each guest, asking the question, "What is the best thing that has happened to you this year (month, week, today)?" This exercise has given our family many great times of communication and often brought tears from each of us.

Step 5

Make out your grocery list for what you will need for the big day. As hostess you will be providing the turkey, dressing, and cranberry sauce.

Step 6

A few days before turkey day, make sure you have everything you will need for setting the table—including a centerpiece. Keep it simple by using a pumpkin surrounded by fresh fruit or three candles in autumn colors with designed holders. (Votive candles floating in a glass or bowl of water also work well as a centerpiece.) To save time, try to use something you already have on hand.

Step 7

Prepare your thawed turkey for roasting in the late afternoon on the day before Thanksgiving.

I recommend my "Perfect Every Time Turkey Recipe." I have found it to be a lifesaver for the busy woman. I've adapted the recipe from Adelle Davis' book *Let's Cook It Right* (New American Library, 1947). I've used this recipe for 45 years and never had it fail me yet!

Recipe

Preheat oven to 350 degrees Fahrenheit.

Wash turkey well and remove the neck and giblets. Dry turkey with paper towels, salt the cavity, and stuff with dressing of your choice. Rub the outside of the turkey with pure olive oil. Stick a meat thermometer into the turkey.

Place the turkey breast-down in the roasting pan on a rack (this way the breast bastes itself, keeping the meat moist). Roast the turkey one hour at 350 degrees to destroy bacteria on the surface. Then adjust the heat to 180 or 200 degrees for any size turkey. The turkey can roast in the oven on this low temperature 15 to 30 hours before you eat it. A good rule for timing is to allow about one hour per pound of meat.

For example, a 20-pound turkey that takes 15 minutes per pound to roast would take five hours by the conventional, fast-cooking method. The slow method is one hour per pound, so it would take 20 hours to roast.

I usually begin roasting a 22-pound turkey at 5 P.M. Thanksgiving Eve. I put the turkey in the oven and leave it uncovered until it's done the next day between 1 P.M. and 3 P.M.

Although the amount of cooking time seems startling at first, the meat turns out amazingly delicious, juicy, and tender. It slices beautifully, barely shrinks in size, and vitamins and proteins are not harmed because of the low cooking temperature.

Once the turkey is done, it will not overcook. You can leave it in an additional three to six hours, and it will still not dry out. It browns perfectly and you'll get wonderful drippings for gravy.

thirty-five

Thanksgiving Countdown

Happy is the generous man, the one who feeds the poor.

Proverbs 22:9

The first national Thanksgiving proclamation was issued by George Washington in 1789. In 1863 President Abraham Lincoln made a Thanksgiving Day proclamation to establish this as a national holiday of thanksgiving to be observed on the last Thursday in November. In 1941 Congress changed the day to the fourth Thursday in November, which is where it has stayed.

For the last 100 years in America, we have been developing meaningful traditions to make this one of the most memorable of all holidays.

Thanksgiving is warm hearts, good food, family, and *lots* of conversation.

It is said that 60 percent of our stress is caused by disorganization. If Thanksgiving brings stress to your mind, it could very well be because of disorganization. So let's relieve that stress. Step by step let's count down the things we can do to make this holiday season stress-less. This will give us time and energy to build memories with our families and friends.

First Week in November

Activity

❏ Polish silver

❏ Plan guest list

❏ Send invitations (or a cheery phone invitation is always welcome)

138

Second Week in November

Activity

❑ Plan menu

❑ Begin marketing list

❑ Plan table setting

❑ Plan centerpiece

❑ List what you may need to borrow and reserve those items

Third Week in November

Activity

❑ Make name place cards. As a family you can each find verses with a thankful theme. Take a 3 x 5 card, fold it in half and stand it up on the table. On the front write the name of the person who will sit at that place and inside write the thankful verse of Scripture. When everyone is seated on Thanksgiving Day, each person reads his verse. This can serve as the blessing.

❑ Have prepared 3 x 5 cards and a pen at each person's seat and have the person write something for which they are thankful. These can be read during or before or after the meal.

❑ Begin to buy some of the staples at the market you will need for that Thanksgiving feast. It will help the budget that last week. Canned cranberry sauce, dressing mix, canned green beans, etc.

❑ Plan your baking day.

Fourth Week in November

By now I'm really excited about all the things that I've done and so thankful I've already accomplished so much toward our special day.

Activity

❑ Plan and organize serving dishes.

❑ Make out a 3 x 5 card for each dish and list on the card what will go into the empty dish. This way you don't have to remember at the last minute what goes where. It also makes it easy for guests to help with the final preparations.

- ❑ Check marketing list to be sure you've got on it just what you'll need for each recipe.
- ❑ The day before Thanksgiving set the table and set centerpiece on the table.
- ❑ Place Scripture name cards at each place.
- ❑ Put serving silverware on the table to be put into each serving dish.
- ❑ Bake pies.
- ❑ Check menu and recipes one more time.

Perhaps you are not preparing a Thanksgiving dinner yourself, but may be taking a dish to someone's home. Your organization will be simpler but should also be planned ahead of time. Ingredients purchased and time set aside for preparation and cooking can be planned ahead as well. Even if you aren't taking food, a hostess gift is always nice: a bouquet of flowers, small plant, stationery, jar of jam, crackers and cheese, etc. Remember, even if you gave a verbal thank-you it is always good manners to follow up with a written note.

As you gather around the Thanksgiving table, holding hands can make this a special family and friendship time. "We give thanks to God, the Father of our Lord Jesus Christ" (Colossians 1:3 NASB). Have a beautiful turkey day filled with love and thanksgiving to God—and don't forget to serve the cranberry sauce and garnish the platter with parsley.

Week After Thanksgiving

Activity

- ❑ Put away fall decorations
- ❑ Start thinking toward Christmas

thirty-six

Christmas Countdown

Unto us a Child is born; unto us a Son is given....
His royal titles: "Wonderful," "Counselor," "The Mighty God."

Isaiah 9:6

Being busy homemakers, with many women also working outside the home, puts added pressure on us as the holiday season arrives. However, if we can plan ahead and organize our holidays, we will find it a joy instead of feeling, "Oh no, not Christmas again!" Proverbs 16:3 says that we are to commit our works to the Lord, and our *plans* will be established.

As we begin this Holiday Countdown let's first give these next weeks to our Lord, remembering to give thanks for *all* things and trusting Him to help us establish our holiday plans and priorities.

Take time to share the true meaning of the holidays with your friends and family.

December Countdown

Christmas is a loving and giving time. Take time to love: Send a card to a shut-in; sing a song at a convalescent home; smile a greeting as you shop.

- ◆ Address Christmas cards and mail early in the month.

- ◆ Make Christmas gift list.

- Plan baking days for the month. Include at least one baking day for the children to help with cookies and candies.

- Plan a craft day for the family to make tree ornaments. Felt, noodles, ice cream sticks, pine cones, and thread spools can all be used to create ornaments. String popcorn and cranberries for the tree. Keep in mind the family unit working together.

- Shop early.

- Wrap gifts early.

- Keep in mind giving handmade and homemade items such as jams, breads, pot holders, and tree ornaments as gifts.

- Attend a Christmas boutique. There you will be able to purchase beautiful handmade items at reasonable prices.

- Decorate your home early in the month so you can enjoy the holiday as long as possible.

- Decorate your front door with a wreath made of pine branches, pine cones, and ribbon, and incorporate a small nativity scene keeping Christ in Christmas. Your front door will give a warm welcome to all who enter your loving home, apartment, mobile home, condominium, or whatever place you call home.

Suggested Stocking Stuffers

- Small stuffed teddy bears
- Paint sets and brushes
- Colored pens or pencils
- Art paper for projects
- Puzzles, books, small Bible
- Marbles, jacks
- Subscription to magazine
- Clothing items such as socks, tights, hosiery, belts, barrettes, headbands, or other hair items
- Music CDs
- Photos (framed)

- Posters
- Theater tickets for a special play, amusement park tickets (Disneyland, etc.)
- Balloons with a dollar bill tucked inside
- Nuts and fruits
- Toothbrush, shampoo, curling iron, hand lotion, perfume or cologne
- Kitchen items for mom
- Small garden tools and packaged seeds for dad
- Any hobby items
- Barbecue tools, picnic accessories
- Tupperware
- Flashlight
- Measuring tape
- Apron, kitchen towels
- Golf balls
- Tennis balls
- Etc. etc. etc....This should get you started with suggested ideas!
- Plan a family "Happy Birthday, Jesus" party:
  —Bake a cake with candles
  —Read the Christmas story
  —Share memorable Christmases
  —Have a family communion
  —Sing "Happy Birthday" to Jesus

- Make a Christmas Love Basket filled with food items, toys, clothing, and needed items for a needy family in your church or community. Sharing our Lord's love with others is what Christmas is all about.

thirty-seven

Stressless Christmas

*Not by might, nor by power, but by my Spirit, says
the Lord Almighty—you will succeed because of my Spirit.*

Zechariah 4:6

How fun and relaxed you will be when you have stacked up creative gifts made by you and ready to give throughout this holiday season.

From the time I was a little girl, my mother taught me how to make fun, inexpensive gifts. Here are a few of those ideas to help you get gift-organized for Christmas.

- Give your favorite recipe written on a cute card and include two or three of the ingredients. Example: Chocolate chip oatmeal cookie recipe—include one package chocolate chips, one package nuts and several cups oatmeal in a zip-lock bag.

- Package in a zip-lock bag five to seven different kinds of dry beans and include your favorite bean soup recipe.

- Take baby food jars and apply cute stickers to the front. Three of these make a great gift for storing cotton balls, bath salts, Q-Tips, etc.

- Paint "Honey Pot" on the front of a jar and fill with honey. Tie a cute ribbon around the lid with a bow.

- Make Christmas ornaments out of different kinds of noodles, using Elmer's white glue.

- Cover shoe boxes with wrapping paper, wallpaper, contact paper, etc., and use as a gift box. Fill with stationery items—glue stick, small scissors, paper clips, marking pens, memo pad, and thank-you notes. Any mom, dad, grandparent, or teacher would love such a gift.

- How about covering a box with road maps and filling the box with more road maps, a first-aid kit, a teaching tape or your favorite music CD, jumper cables, flares, or any kind of item associated with travel and/or the car?

- Baskets filled with items make great gifts:

  Bath—soaps, shower cap, bubble bath, bath oil, washcloth

  Reading—book for each family member, bookmarks

  Kitchen—wooden spoons, measuring cups, can opener, etc.

  Toys—games, books, teddy bear, dolls, truck, puzzles, etc.

  Grandma—bib to use for grandbabies, toy, rattle, book of short stories, baby items, etc.

  Gardening—seeds, garden tools, gloves, pruners/clippers, hand shovel, fertilizer, potted plants

  Sewing—measuring tape, scissors, pins, jar of buttons, elastic lace, ribbon, tape, etc.

  Laundry—bleach, laundry powder or liquid, fabric softener, spray spot remover, small spot brush

  Automobile—car wax, chamois, ArmorAll cleaners, trash bags, litter bag for car

Food items always make great gifts. Use resources that are in your area and available to you. Every year we receive a bag of raw peanuts. Oh, how we love and enjoy them for several months! Here are more food ideas:

- Popcorn
- Breads—banana, zucchini
- Nuts—almonds, walnuts
- Caramel corn

- Pure natural maple syrup
- Fruits—We have several orange trees on our property, so I fill a box or basket with oranges and send them to my uncle. He especially loves this gift and looks forward to it.
- Avocados
- Dried fruits
- Basket of natural foods such as granola mix, raisins, three- to seven-grain cereal mix
- Bread starters

Many of these gift ideas can be prepared far ahead of time so that you will be able to relax and enjoy the holidays. Organization of gifts is one of the keys to a stressless Christmas. So plan and prepare ahead for a pleasant, organized holiday.

thirty-eight

Holiday Hints for You and the Children

This is the day which the Lord hath made;
we will rejoice and be glad in it.

Psalm 118:24 NKJV

*H*oliday times can be a fun time for children. It can also be a very hectic time for parents. What with presents, entertaining, cooking, and shopping…the children get so-o-o excited and seem to have more energy than at any other time of the year. This can be a season of learning for those energetic little ones as we channel that energy into helping us relieve the stress of the holiday "frenzies." Here are some Holiday Helps to bless you and the children.

Plan one or two baking days when the children help with holiday breads, cookies, or pies. Christ-centered cookie cutters such as stars, angels, crosses, and even Christmas trees are available. As you cut the cookies discuss with the little ones the Christmas story from the star to the wise men to the gifts the wise men brought. You can relate that one of the reasons we give gifts to others is to give our love to others as did the wise men to the Christ child. The Christmas tree and lights signify the shining stars and a place to put the gifts. As they decorate the cookies you can sing Christmas carols or play a holiday musical CD.

The cookies can be frozen for later use. A plate of cookies given to friends or neighbors can teach the children to give of their talents and the

147

fruits of their labor. Plus what an outreach to those who receive Christ-centered cookies.

Depending upon the ages of the children they can help wrap presents. Comic strip sections from newspapers make good wrapping paper, or use white paper or tissue paper the children can rubber-stamp. Again, find a Christ-centered stamp with a manger scene or perhaps stars. Glue on candy kisses, candy canes, M & M's. Get creative—anything goes. If the gift is a cookbook or kitchen item, wrap it in a tea towel. If it's an educational book, use roadmaps as the paper. If it's handsewn, a measuring tape makes a cute bow. Get out lace pieces and rickrack to glue on and decorate the top. The children can design a lace collar for mom's gift, and for dad, a tie or bow tie. The children will be excited and invent all sorts of unusual gift wraps.

Make your own gift tags out of wrapping paper pieces or construction paper in red, green, or white; rubber-stamped to match the papers. You can also use wooden spoon ornaments, paper dolls, cookie cutters, key chains, shells, bookmarks, etc. Paint pens (which can be bought at craft or art supply stores) will write on almost anything and the color and print won't come off.

Capitalize, if possible, on the hobby or vocation of the person whose gift you are wrapping. For the golfer, use golf tees tied onto the bow. For an artist, a new paint brush. For the mechanic, a new tool; the gardener, a new pair of gloves or seeds. For the craft lady or knitter, knitting needles or embroidery thread tied onto the bow.

Children will love this gift idea: Roll up a dollar bill and insert it into a balloon. Mail it along with a card and instructions to blow up the balloon and then pop it. Out comes the bill!

When planning your holiday party, buffet, open house, or family dinner, let the older children extend themselves by helping out with the little ones to give you extra time to shop and prepare. They can then have the privilege of taking part in greeting the guests, taking their coats, being polite, and using manners with a smile. They should also remember to say thank you and please. They can pass out hors d'oeuvres, pour water, coffee, tea, clear off tables, serve dessert, and blow out the candles. Cleanup help can also be part of learning. Throw some coins into the bottom of the kitchen sink beneath the sudsy water as a reward. One hundred pennies, four to eight quarters, 20 nickels, etc. On their pillow pin a big thank-you note saying, "Good job, well done!"

If you don't have children, borrow some just to help teach them manners and proper ways of entertaining.

A great gift that children can make is a personalized pillow or pillow-case. They can use paint pens in assorted colors or nontoxic acrylic paints to list a friend's important personal dates and memory places or perhaps his or her favorite Bible verse on the pillow. Grandparents' names can be put along with the children's handprints. Aprons also make great person-alized gifts with the grandchildren's names printed on and/or their hand-prints. This is also a nice idea for teachers at school or Sunday school.

Homemade Christmas cards that children have cut out or colored are always appreciated. Last year's cards can be cut up and glued onto con-struction paper. Children can use stencils, rubber stamps, or their own cre-ative designs. These cards can also be made into placemats. I've found that heavy-duty plastic, oval-shaped placemats (on sale) in a variety of colors work well. Or make the placemats out of heavy poster board and cover with clear plastic contact paper.

Let your and the children's creative juices flow as you guide them into helping you relieve some of the stress the holiday brings.

They will receive the blessings and you will be blessed as you watch their talents develop.

thirty-nine

Organizing Holiday Meals

*The more lowly your service to others,
the greater you are. To be the greatest, be a servant.*

Matthew 23:11

The crisp days of late autumn bring on memories of holiday happenings, roast turkey, cranberry sauce, hot apple cider, family gatherings—and lest you forget, a lot of hard work. But with a bit of organization, holiday planning can be more stress-free and a lot of fun.

I've prepared a Hospitality Sheet for you (Figure 4, page 152) that can be clipped out or easily reproduced for your convenience.

To show you how the chart works, here are a few ideas about how to fill it in.

One Week Before
- Prepare your menu.
- Make your shopping list.

Three Days Before
- Polish silver.
- Clean house as needed.

150

One Day Before

- ◆ Shop for groceries.
- ◆ Clean and prepare vegetables, grate cheese, and chop nuts.
- ◆ Set table and also place centerpiece, candles, and other decorations.

Day of

- ◆ Cook your meal.
- ◆ Give yourself time to relax and dress before the guests arrive.

Last Minute

- ◆ Check your menu to see that you haven't forgotten anything such as the cranberry sauce or pickles.
- ◆ Enjoy your time with family and friends.

Hospitality Sheet

Date _____ Place _____

Time _____ Number of Guests _____

Event _____ Theme _____

Menu	Recipe Preparation Time	Things to Do	✔
Hors d'Oeuvres/Appetizers		One Week Before	
Entreé		Three Days Before	
Side Dishes		One Day Before	
Salad		Day of	
Dessert			
Drinks		Last Minute	

Guest List	RSVP Yes | No		★ Notes ★	Supplies
				Tables/Chairs
				Dishes
				Silver
				Glasses

Figure 4

forty

Holiday
Kitchen Hints

The Lord himself will choose the sign—
a child shall be born to a virgin! And she shall
call him Immanuel (meaning, "God is with us").

Isaiah 7:14

*T*he holiday season is a great time to renew old acquaintances, reconcile broken relationships, and reinforce existing friendships. It's a time for growing—growing through giving, through sharing, through serving. But most of all, it's a time to give thanks to a loving Father for all the little things we take for granted.

Hints

- If bread or cake browns too quickly before it is thoroughly baked, place a pan of warm water on the rack above it in the oven.

- To prevent icing from running off cake, dust a little cornstarch over the cake before icing.

- To add a new taste to oatmeal cookies, add a small amount of grated orange peel to the next batch.

- If you cover dried fruit or nuts with flour before adding them to the cake batter, they will not sink to the bottom during baking.

153

- The yolk of an egg will keep for several days if it is covered with cold water and placed in the refrigerator in a covered dish.

- Either parboil sausages or roll them in flour before frying to prevent them from bursting.

- If you have used too much salt while cooking, add a raw potato. This will absorb much of the salt.

- Tie herbs and spices in a piece of wet muslin or cheesecloth before adding them to soup or stew so that they may be easily removed when finished.

- Save the rinds of the oranges you squeezed for breakfast. Pile mounds of mashed sweet potatoes on them, then brown them in the oven.

- To keep old potatoes from darkening when they are boiling, add a small amount of milk to the cooking water.

- Pancakes will remain hot longer if the bottle of syrup which is to be served with them is first heated in hot water.

- Adding a pinch of salt in the basket will relieve some of the acid taste in perked coffee. For clear coffee, put egg shells in after perking. And remember, always start with cold water.

- Adding about 1½ teaspoonfuls of lemon juice to a cup of rice while cooking will keep the kernels separated.

- Baking apples or stuffed peppers in a well-greased muffin tin will help them keep their shape and look more attractive when served.

- Combining the juices from canned vegetables with soups will increase the quantity and flavor.

- Lumpy gravy? Pour it in your blender and in seconds it will be smooth.

- You'll shed fewer tears if you cut the root end of the onion off last.

- To eliminate spattering and sticking when pan-frying or sautéing, heat your pan before adding butter or oil. Not even eggs stick with this method.

- Muffins sticking to the tin pan? Place the hot pan on a wet towel. The muffins will slide right out.

- To tenderize tough meat or game: Make a marinade of equal parts cooking vinegar and heated bouillon. Marinate for two hours.

- To stew an old hen, soak it in vinegar for several hours before cooking. It will taste like a spring chicken!

- Instant white sauce: Blend together one cup soft butter and one cup flour. Spread in a 16-cube ice cube tray and chill. Store cubes in a plastic bag in the freezer. For medium thick sauce, drop one cube into one cup of milk and heat slowly, stirring as it thickens.

- Unmolding gelatin: Rinse the mold in cold water and coat with salad oil. Your molded salad will drop out easily and will have an appealing luster.

- Ridding the ham of the rind: Slit the rind lengthwise on the underside before placing ham in the roasting pan. As the ham bakes, the rind will pull away and can be removed easily without lifting ham.

- To keep olives or pimentos from spoiling, cover them with a brine solution of one teaspoonful of salt to one cup of water. Then float just enough salad oil over the top to form a layer about 1/8-inch thick. Store them in the refrigerator.

Blessed holidays to all!

forty-one

Surviving the Stress of Shopping

I will call upon the Lord, who is worthy to be praised; he will save me from all my enemies.

2 Samuel 22:4

Many of us who keep a busy schedule right through the holidays usually don't find time to shop for Christmas until after Thanksgiving.

With limited time to spend shopping, every minute must count—and organization is a key. Before you begin, plan your shopping strategy so that you can accomplish the majority of your shopping in one trip.

1. Review all the stores in the mall or downtown area you plan to shop in—such as jewelry, clothing, book, china, and hardware stores. (If you are really ambitious, write them all down.)

2. Decide before you go out what types of gifts you plan to purchase this year. For example, are you going to buy one big gift for each person or lots of little things? Each year I do things a bit differently.

3. Make your gift list based on the order of the shops within the particular shopping area you choose. Work your way around mentally, jotting down specific people and gift ideas.

156

4. Take advantage of wrapping services and/or gift boxes with ribbon and tissue. As much as possible, take home gifts that are ready to place under the tree.

5. Do two things at the same time. If, for example, you purchase clothing for more than one person at a store which offers gift wrapping, allow the clerk to finish the packages while you visit other shops. Circle back at the end of the day and collect your packages.

6. Think in categories. How many golfers, skiers, or tennis players are on your list? When buying for one, buy for the others. What about duplicate gifts? Can you give all your neighbors gourmet cheese in a can or spiced mustard in a jar? Why not?

7. Make use of your phone. Call your florist to make up a silk flower arrangement or a basket of soaps and hand creams. Or order a pretty holiday arrangement with a candle for the Christmas table centerpiece. Many times a florist will wrap and deliver your gift for you.

8. Give gift certificates to the hard-to-please people who have everything. Certificates for restaurants, ice-cream shops, and fast-food drive-ins (children love those) are always a hit.

9. Present a magazine subscription. Often magazines offer a gift subscription at a reduced price for the holidays. Include a current issue with your gift card.

10. Take a few breaks during your shopping to review your list and thoughts. Plan a coffee, tea, or lunch break. If you find yourself weighed down by too many packages, make a trip to lock them in the car.

11. Avoid retracing your steps or making second trips by not leaving a shopping area until you are sure you have accomplished all you wanted to do in that spot.

12. Assign shopping to a teenager or a friend who loves to shop.

13. Remember to keep your shopping simple. It is the love you put into each gift that will last rather than the gift alone. And more importantly, remember to make Christ the center of all your activities this Christmas.

forty-two

Gift Wrap Organization for Gift-Giving

Today in the city of David there has been born for you a Savior, who is Christ the Lord.

Luke 2:11 NASB

ift giving really goes on all year. It is one of the major parts of our lives. The love of giving gifts goes on and on and on and on throughout the year.

Being creative with gift wrap is easy and can be inexpensive—like using newsprint to wrap dad's gift. The stock market, sports, travel, comic, or business section with Christmas ribbon is easy and original.

Perhaps you've saved those little pieces of wrapping paper thinking someday you would use them. Use them now! Simply tape together the pieces and make a patchwork gift wrap. Creative, original, and inexpensive.

Your plain paper or butcher paper can be used as a background for rubber-stamping, stickers, or vegetable prints. To make a potato print, cut a potato in half and carve a design into the potato; a heart, an angel, a Christmas tree, a star, a teddy bear, etc. Dip the potato into acrylic paint thinned with water, then stamp onto the brown paper. Thumbprint designs are unique and handprints are always fun. Collages can be made from old Christmas cards, pictures cut out of magazines, and newspapers. These can be taped or glued to plain paper and used as gift wrap.

Instead of bows on kitchen gifts, use a colored plastic or copper scouring pad, or colorful plastic measuring spoons. The name tag can be a wooden spoon with the "to" and "from" written on the handle with a felt pen.

Baby's gift can be wrapped in a clean disposable diaper or a cloth diaper. An ornament for baby's first Christmas can be tied to the package.

Gifts for sewing buffs can be wrapped in a remnant of fabric, tied with a tape measure, and pinned together (rather than using tape).

At the after-Christmas supplies sales you will find most gift wrap supplies marked down at least 50 percent. This is the time to buy—try to hit the sales this year and relieve the stress for next year. Talking about stress, let's take the pressure out of gift wrapping by organizing all the supplies we need to do the job creatively and quickly.

The perfect tool to help the busy woman out of the gift wrapping dilemma is a "Perfect Gift Wrap Organizer." (This can be purchased mail order. See information on page 309.)

This organizer is the center of your wrapping experience and should include the tools needed to wrap those instant gifts. So begin to collect the following products:

- Shelf paper
- Wallpaper
- Newspaper—funnies, sports page, stock market section, travel section
- Fabric
- Tissue paper—white (great for rubber-stamping), colors, plain, pin-dot, graph, or patterned
- Gift boxes—enameled, fold-up, acrylic, or Lucite
- Gift bags and totes—lunch bags, enamel bags, cellophane bags, window bags, small bottle and jar bags
- Tags or enclosure cards
- Ribbon—satin, plaid, taffeta, curling ribbon, curly satin, fabric, rickrack, shoelaces, measuring tape, lace, jute
- Stickers
- Mailing labels
- Glue gun, glue sticks

- Chenille stems—use on your make-ahead bows and store in a Perfect box
- Rubber stamps, stamp pad, or brush markers

Hints for Use of Old Wrapping Paper and Bows

- Make used wrapping paper new again by lightly spraying the wrong side with spray starch and pressing with a warm iron.

- Run wrinkled ribbon through a hot curling iron to take out old creases. I keep an old curling iron in my "Perfect Gift Wrap Organizer."

- Ribbons—Make your own with pieces of leftover fabric. Almost any type of fabric can be cut to the desired width and length. Striped materials are great to cut into even widths. Press fabric strips between sheets of wax paper with a hot iron. This will keep the strips from unraveling and provide enough stiffness for the ribbon to hold its shape when making it into a bow.

More Wrapping Ideas

Cellophane

- For those "How am I going to wrap that?" gifts. It will always get you out of a jam.

- For a basket, bucket, pail, or small wagon toy filled with goodies—tied with a fluffy bow and a sprig of holly or pine, or decorative stickers.

- For your gifts of food—cookies on a Christmas plate, breads wrapped with cellophane and Christmas ribbon, a homemade quiche, a basket of muffins in a checked napkin or muffins in a muffin tin.

- For a plant.

- For fresh bouquet of flowers—tied with a beautiful bow and a special note inside.

Gift Bags

A wonderful idea for a quick, easy, and decorative way to wrap! They are reusable too!

Line bag with contrasting tissue or wrap your gift item or items in tissue. Add a bow to the handle with a gift tag. Add Tissue Toss on top for a festive look. (Tissue Toss: Use any color combination of tissue depending on the time of the year. Cut tissue into ¼-inch strips, then toss like a green salad and you've made Tissue Toss.)

Decorate bag with stickers, banners, or cutouts from old Christmas cards.

Large silver or black or green plastic garbage bags may be just the thing to hide a large gift. Add a banner, large bow, and stickers. It will look just like Santa's pack. Reuse your smaller bags for lunches or to hold your needlework.

Gift Boxes and Containers

- The decorated ones need only a ribbon! Always get a courtesy box, tissue, and ribbon whenever you buy anything at a department store or where the gift wrap is free. Save them in your gift wrap center for the times you need them. Usually they fold flat and are easy to store.

- Wrap a lid separate from the bottom to use again and again.

- Use tins, ceramic containers, Lucite or acrylic boxes, flowerpots, buckets, pails, and baskets.

Gift Certificates

- Purchase from stores

- Make your own with calligraphy, sticker art, or rubber-stamp art and then laminate them. Have certificates redeemable for:

Babysitting	Day of shopping and lunch
Dinners in your home	Trip to the zoo
Frozen yogurt	Plays

These ideas should help to stimulate your creative juices in making the gift wrapping in your life a happy, pleasant experience.

Part 6

FOODS & KITCHEN

forty-three

How to Save Money at the Supermarket

Plans fail for lack of counsel,
but with many advisers they succeed.

Proverbs 15:22 NIV

Today in our busy society we find that much of our stress is caused by how we provide nutrition for our family. At one time in our society there was much emphasis upon the family spending quality time around the dining room table. Many times in years gone by we could expect to have at least two of the three meals (breakfast and dinner) together. The dinner table was a great place to have a "summit conference" or just to catch up on the day's happenings.

Today with our hustled, hassled, and hurried society, we have stopped or seriously neglected this tradition. I encourage each family to seriously evaluate their family time and see if at least one meal can be shared together. If you do make this commitment, try to make the meal a pleasant time for the family. You want it to be a rewarding experience. This is not the time to be negative. Make it an uplifting time, one where everyone will go away wanting to get back together again.

Many busy families have surrendered to the fast-food phenomenon and very rarely cook at home. This is fine occasionally but should be viewed cautiously for regular meals. Those who find themselves on tight budgets will soon find the fast-food compromise most expensive. In many cases, it also deprives your family of balanced nutrition.

Don't view food preparation as drudgery, but delight in providing meals for your family. There are excellent cookbooks available that simplify food preparation. To ease your planning you might make up 3 x 5 cards giving you about seven different recipes for breakfast, lunch, and dinner. By rotating the cards, you can have variety and not get bored with your meals. Try to introduce a new recipe occasionally. If you have teenagers, they can be of great assistance. They can set the table, shop, clean vegetables, start the meal, serve the food, clean the table, and load the dishwasher. This is an excellent opportunity to teach your children many lessons for the adult life: meal planning, shopping for bargains, budget preparation, nutritional balance, table etiquette, time management in cooking meals, and meal cleanup.

I have a friend who took one summer to teach her teenage sons how to survive—she called it "Survival Summer." At the end of the summer she felt comfortable and self-assured that her boys could take care of themselves in an emergency. An added benefit is that she now has help to relieve her of her expanding responsibilities.

One word of caution is that busy teenagers carrying a heavy college-prep academic load must have time for their studies; however, this doesn't mean that they don't carry some responsibilities for family functions.

To help you save money at the supermarket I have listed several helpful hints for you. These should not only make shopping more efficient, but also save you some money.

1. *Shop with a purpose and with a list.* Plan your menus for the entire week (or two) and then organize your shopping list so that you have to pass through each section of the supermarket only once. You might even make a list of standard products, arranged to correspond to the flow of your normal supermarket. (See page 180 for a sample of a marketing list.) If you have to return to the first aisle to pick up just one thing, you may find yourself attracted by other items. This will push you over your food budget and cause you added stress.

2. *Try to control your impulse buying.* Studies have estimated that almost 50 percent of purchases are entirely unplanned (not on your list). Be especially careful at the start of your shopping trip when your cart is nearly empty. You're more susceptible to high priced, unplanned purchases then.

3. *Get your shopping done within a half hour.* This means you don't shop during rush hour. Shopping at busy times will hurry you up, and you will have a greater tendency to just pull items from the shelves without really shopping comparatively for the best product. Supermarkets are often very comfortable places to linger, but one study suggests that customers spend at least 75 cents a minute after a half-hour in the store.

4. *Shop alone if you can.* Children and even spouses can cause you to compromise from your lists as they try to help you with unplanned purchases. Television advertising can cause great stress when your children go with you. They want to make sure they have the latest cereal, even though it is loaded with sugar and has very little nutritional value.

5. *Never shop when hungry.* Enough said. The psychology is obvious.

6. *Use coupons wisely.* Food companies often use coupon offers to promote either new products or old products that haven't been selling well. Ask yourself if you would have bought the item had there been no coupon, and compare prices with competing brands to see if you're really saving money.

7. *Be a smart shopper.* Be aware that grocery stores stock the highest-priced items at eye level. The lower-priced staples like flour, sugar, and salt are often below eye level, as are bulk quantities of many items. More and more specialty stores are carrying bulk food, which can give you excellent cost savings if you are buying for a large family or joint-purchasing for several families or even for a picnic. One word of caution is that even though you might save money on bulk buying, you might really spend more because your family doesn't consume the item fast enough; you find that it spoils and you end up throwing away excess. This can be expensive and not a savings. Also, be aware that foods displayed at the end of an aisle may appear to be on sale, but often are not.

8. *Use unit pricing.* Purchase a small, inexpensive pocket calculator to take with you to the market. This way you can divide the price or the item by the number of units in the package to find the cost per unit. This way you can compare apples with apples. The lowest-priced container does not always have the cheapest price per unit.

9. *Avoid foods that are packaged as individual servings.* Extra packaging usually boosts the price of the product. This becomes too expensive for families. In some cases a one- or two-member family might be able to buy in this portion; however, for the general buying of American families you would not find this an economical way to purchase food.

10. *When buying meat consider the amount of lean meat in the cut as well as the price per pound.* A relatively high-priced cut with little or no waste may provide more meat for your money than a low-priced cut with a great deal of bone, gristle, or fat. Chicken, turkey, and fish are often good bargains for the budget buyer.

11. *Buy vegetables and fruits in season* since they'll be at their peak of quality and their lowest price. Never buy the first crop; prices are sure to go down. You might even want to consider planning an "old-time canning weekend." Canning produce yourself gives you the greatest economy and lets you enjoy these delicacies all during the year.

As an informed consumer you need to become more and more aware of what the labels on your products mean. Remember that manufacturers have to add additives and preservatives to give color and longer shelf-life to their products. As a buyer you may not be willing to make that trade-off. There are a lot of natural foods on the market and these can certainly help protect your family from the side effects of additives. Labels can tip you off to what's in the jar or the carton, so it's wise to know how to read them.

What Food Labels Tell You

- *Ingredients.* Ingredients must be listed in descending order of prominence by weight. The first ingredients listed are the main ingredients in that product.

- *Colors and flavors.* Added colors and flavors do not have to be listed by name, but the use of artificial colors or flavors must be indicated.

- *Serving content.* For each serving: the serving size; the number of calories per serving; the amount of protein, carbohydrates, and fat in a serving; the percentage of the U.S. Recommended Daily Allowance (USRDA) for protein and seven important vitamins and minerals.

◆ *Optional information.* Some labels also contain the following: the percentage of the USRDA for any of 12 additional vitamins and minerals: the amount of saturated and unsaturated fat and cholesterol in a serving; and the amount of sodium furnished by a serving.

What Food Labels Don't Tell You

◆ *What standardized foods contain.* Over 350 foods, including common ones like enriched white bread and catsup, are classified as "standardized." The Food and Drug Administration (FDA) has established guidelines for these products and manufacturers are therefore not required to list ingredients.

◆ *How much sugar is in some products.* Sugar and sweeteners come in a variety of forms (white sugar, brown sugar, corn syrup, dextrose, sucrose, maltose, corn sweeteners), and if they're all listed separately, it's nearly impossible to know the true amount of sugar contained in a labeled product.

◆ *How "natural" a product is.* The FDA's policy on using the word "natural" on a food label is loose. The product may, in fact, be highly processed and full of additives.

◆ *Specific ingredients that may be harmful.* Because coloring or spices that don't have to be listed by name can cause nausea, dizziness, or hives in certain people, people with food or additive allergies may have trouble knowing which products they need to avoid.

As an informed shopper you have more control over your purchase style and habits. Much of your budget goes to food. Become a good steward of God's money and get the most in return for it. Be knowledgeable in all phases of living.

forty-four

Turning Coupons into Cash

Trust in your money and down you go!
Trust in God and flourish as a tree!

Proverbs 11:28

Many smart women are saving money by couponing. Today's household is certainly concerned with finances.

I've talked with several women who are a part of a coupon club in their church. They meet monthly to exchange coupons and rebate forms. These women have a well-organized file system for their coupons. They bring in magazines and newspapers given to them by other people so the time can be spent in cutting out coupons and filing away or exchanging them with each other.

I've found that an accordion 9 x 5½ file is a great tool for organizing your coupons. Your topics could include:

Personal/health	Mixes
Laundry	Frozen
Poultry/meats	Cleaners
Cereals	Baking products
Baby	Soda pop
Dairy	Dry goods

170

Breads	Snacks
Garden	Cookies
Charcoal	Salad seasoning
Soups	Package mixes
Sauces	Jams
Rice	Coffee/tea
Lunch meats	Pet food
Paper products	Miscellaneous

When cutting out a coupon, run a yellow highlighter pen over the expiration date. That way your eye will catch the date quickly.

I met a beautiful young mother who told me she saved $850.00 one year by couponing. Another working woman saved $1,100!

These women struck my interest and I asked them to share with me some of their ideas that helped save them that kind of money. Here are some of those ideas:

◆ A store will run a special ad in the local newspaper; for example, coffee at $1.99. You have a coffee coupon for 50 cents off. This week you also cut out a coupon that entitles you to a double discount on any coupon. You then can purchase that $1.99 can of coffee for only 99 cents.

◆ Whenever possible use double coupons. If your market is not honoring double coupons, it could be worth driving to another local market that is.

◆ You can cut out coupons for "luxury" items (freezer baggies, an expensive brand of disposable diapers, pie crust mix, etc.) and many times end up finding these things on a clearance table, either discontinued by the market or the manufacturer, or damaged. Then, with your coupon doubled you can get it free or at a minimal price. (Homemade-type mix for rye bread, clearance priced at 90 cents, with a 40-cent doubled coupon cost me 10 cents.) On items used a lot that are costly (disposable diapers, soda pop, or coffee for some people) *drive* to another neighborhood market for a great deal. The savings are far worth it. Stock up as much as your budget and number of double coupons will allow. When a meat item is priced well, stock up on it at a different store. If you eat a lot of poultry and prefer breast meat only, go elsewhere when you can save 60 to 70 cents per pound. Because you stock up, you won't have to do this very often. Also, there are many poultry coupons available; double them for more savings.

♦ What is hard to understand is that in double-couponing the *smaller* quantity is usually the better buy because you can get it for a few cents, if not free. Just buy two or three dish detergents, and you'll have enough until another brand goes on special.

♦ Switch brands of most items regularly. Couponing lets you try lots of products. Obviously there are some things you won't care for, so don't buy them again. But on the average you can switch peanut butter, jelly, rice, margarine, coffee, soda pop, paper towels, toilet paper, etc. You might find a better product in the sampling. Because of couponing, generic is *not* always the best buy. If you can get a superior product for the same price or less, then use a coupon. Stock up on staples and paper products. (If you don't have very much storage, you can put things in the garage or even under the beds.) Most important is getting hold of coupons and filing them. Throw *nothing* away, even if you get two major papers on Thursday (or whatever day is food section day for you!). Tucked into our throwaway neighborhood advertising paper is Safeway's advertising circular. My market is currently doubling *all* other market's coupons, so I cut out Safeway's coupons and keep them for that week. Friends and neighbors can even give you leftover coupons that are mailed to them. You can use many of these as well. However, go through your file once or twice a month to discard those which have gone beyond their expiration date.

♦ Refunding is complicated, or can be, so you may set up rules for yourself. Get all refunding forms from newspapers or magazines because most markets don't stock them. Don't buy the required number of products *unless* you have the refund form. (It's easy to have the advertiser say the refund form is available at your grocer's, but it rarely is, unfortunately.) Try to combine your refunds with purchasing the item on sale, with a doubled coupon, or, better, both! It must be something you use often, not a new, untried product. (Who wants three boxes of terrible-tasting cereal in your cupboards with another free one on the way!) Many people save all box tops and wrappings. I've tried it and it simply was not worth it. Most refunds are for combinations of foods I don't buy or use. Therefore, wait until you see the requirements and then decide if it is worth the effort and postage.

Where can you get coupons? Many places—a lot come through the mail. I used to throw out junk mail and not even look at it. Now I quickly finger through the pages and cut the coupons—before tossing the rest.

Major and local newspapers run coupons every week.

Friends can cut coupons and save them for you. My auntie cuts coupons; it gives her a purpose to help plus any coupons she doesn't use she passes on to me, and any I don't use I then pass on to our married daughter, Jenny.

Grandmas and grandpas use couponing as a great project.

Neighbors', friends', and relatives' cast-off magazines are also a great source of coupons.

Cutting out, filing, and organizing will take you no more than a half-hour per week, and this could very well save you $13.00 to $20.00 per week on your grocery bill. It's fun and very rewarding.

Try it—you'll love it. It's another way of being a good steward of your money.

One woman shared with me that she would write her check at the checkout stand for the total amount and then pocket her savings from coupons, thus giving her money that she spent on Christmas presents. Her husband was so excited about what she did that he told everyone how proud he was of a wife who looks well into her household, being a Proverbs 31 woman.

Remember, coupons give savings!

forty-five

Planning Meals Saves Stress

Let each of you look out not only for his own interests, but also for the interests of others.

Philippians 2:4 NKJV

The average woman cooks, plans, markets, chops, pares, cleans up or eats out over 750 meals a year. If this is anywhere close to true, doesn't it stand to reason this is an area we need to organize? Feeding our families certainly is a big part of our lives—not to mention feeding them with good nutrition. We will gravitate to foods that have been planned and prepared. Here are easy steps and hints to successful meals.

1. Make a simple meal-planner chart. On an 8½ x 11 sheet of paper list the days of the week. Start on the left side from top to bottom. Then across the top list "Breakfast," "Lunch," "Dinner." These will form an easy chart as you draw lines dividing each day and meal time. A sample chart (Figure 5) is included on page 175.

2. From your meal planner, make out a marketing list. Start by listing items needed as they appear on the aisles in your supermarket. This will prevent backtracking in the market. You want to get in and get out. A study showed after the first half-hour in the market a

Weekly Menus

Date _May 5_

Day of Week	Breakfast	Lunch	Dinner
Monday			
Tuesday	Hot cereal	Salami sandwich	Chicken
Wednesday			
Thursday	Granola & bananas	Turkey- cheese sandwich	Lasagna casserole
Friday			
Saturday	Pancakes	Turkey hot dogs	Tacos
Sunday			

Figure 5

woman will spend at least 75 cents per minute. Stick to your list and use coupons.

3. Post your meal-planner chart so all family members can see it. Should you be late arriving home, older family members can check the planner and start dinner for you.

4. Don't forget Tupper Suppers—premade meals that have been prepared ahead of time and are stored in Tupperware or containers in the freezer or refrigerator.

5. Plan family favorites into each week.

6. Remember to include things still in the freezer from previous month plan-overs or leftovers.

7. Also listed on your menu planner you can schedule which person in the family sets the table that day or week; also who clears off. Our rule was whoever set the table also cleared it off.

8. Teach creativity in setting the table by allowing each person, when it's their turn, to use paper or cloth napkins, paper or glass dishes, a candle, a few fresh flowers, teddy bear, a pumpkin, or whatever they think of for a centerpiece.

9. To quickly remove water from the lettuce greens that you have just washed, simply put into a clean pillowcase or lingerie bag and spin in your washing machine for two minutes. Remove from the bag and tear lettuce, making a big salad. Store in refrigerator for up to two weeks.

10. Make up your own TV dinners. Use containers purchased in your market for microwave or regular ovens. Then put your leftovers in sections of the trays and freeze. Great for dad and children when mom's away.

11. Keep parsley fresh and crisp. Wash the parsley and put a bunch of sprigs into a jar, stem ends down. Pour in an inch or two of cold water, enough for the stems to stand in without the leaves touching the water. Tighten the lid, set the jar in the refrigerator, and enjoy crisp parsley for up to two weeks.

12. To speed up baking potatoes in a conventional oven, simply put a clean nail through the potato. It will cook in half the time.

13. A piece of lettuce dropped into a pot of soup will soak up the excess grease. Remove the lettuce as soon as it has absorbed the grease.

14. Our family loves BLT (bacon, lettuce, and tomato) sandwiches. Whenever I fry or microwave bacon, I cook a few extra pieces and put them into a plastic freezer bag and freeze. They are ready for the next BLT sandwich.

15. Leftover pancakes or waffles? Don't discard them—pop them into the toaster or oven for a quick and easy breakfast or afterschool snack.

16. For the two of us I bake six large potatoes. We eat them baked the first night. The second serving is sliced and fried in a bit of butter. The last two potatoes are cubed and served in a cream sauce with some cheese.

17. To get more juice out of a lemon, place it in a microwave oven for 30 seconds. Squeeze the lemon and you will get twice as much juice. Vitamins won't be destroyed.

18. Frozen foods have a definite freezer life; it is important to use the food within the specified period of time. The easiest way to mark meat and other frozen foods is to put a "use by" date on a label or on the package. Your market does this and it makes good sense.

19. Freeze lunchbox sandwiches. They can be made up by the week. Put on all the ingredients except lettuce. It will save time and trouble.

20. You can make your own convenience foods. Chop large batches of onion, green pepper, or nuts, and freeze them in small units. Grate a week's or month's worth of cheese, then freeze it in recipe-size portions. Shape ground meat or ground turkey into patties so you can thaw a few at a time. Freeze homemade casseroles, soups, stews, and chilies in serving-size portions for faster thawing and reheating.

21. No need to boil those lasagna noodles anymore! Just spread sauce in the bottom of the pan, place hard, uncooked noodles on top and spread sauce on top of noodles. Continue with the other layers, finishing with noodles and sauce. Cover with foil and bake at 350

degrees Fahrenheit for 1 hour and 15 minutes. This will probably be the best hint you'll ever get.

22. Before freezing fresh bagels, cut them in half. When you're ready to use them, they will defrost faster and can even be toasted while they are still frozen.

23. Fruit prepared ahead of time will keep well if you squeeze lemon juice over it and refrigerate. The juice of half a lemon is enough for up to two quarts of cut fruit.

24. *Turning one pound of butter into two pounds with gelatin.* Let the butter stand at room temperature until soft. Into 1¼ cup cold milk, soften one envelope of unflavored gelatin. Add 1¾ cups hot milk; stir until gelatin is dissolved. Cool until lukewarm. Whip into butter with electric mixer. Keep covered in refrigerator. Use within one week as a spread, not for baking.

By spending a little time preparing your food and planning your meals, you'll save even more time for the other things you need to do.

forty-six

Pantry Organization

*You must love and help your neighbors
just as much as you love and take care of yourself.*

James 2:8

The last time I visited my aunt's house, I was looking for the dry cereal one morning. "Oh, you'll find it in the pantry next to the cat food," my aunt said as she nodded her head in the direction of a colorful blue door.

I opened the door, ducking just in time to narrowly miss an avalanche of half-folded grocery sacks that came tumbling down. I wasn't as lucky with the mop handle which bopped me a good one! Buried deep in the recesses, I did manage to locate a box of Cheerios.

Although my aunt's pantry seemed more like a war zone than a pantry, your pantry can be a storehouse of confidence at your fingertips.

All it takes is some simple planning and organizing and the pantry will become your best friend.

I suggest stocking your pantry primarily with staple foods including starches, sweets, condiments, and canned or bottled items. These will last for six months or longer.

Perishable goods can also be stored in a pantry. The only difference is, of course, that they will have to be replenished more often. The chart (Figure 6) on page 180 will help you keep track of the basics.

179

Pantry Stocking List

Date _____

Qty.	Cost		Qty.	Cost	
		Starches	___	___	Jell-O®
___	___	Flour	___	___	Pudding mix
___	___	Cornmeal	___	___	Soup
___	___	Oatmeal	___	___	
___	___	Pasta	___	___	
___	___	White rice	___	___	
___	___	Brown rice			**Condiments**
___	___	Potatoes	___	___	Ketchup
___	___		___	___	Vinegar
___	___		___	___	Capers
___	___		___	___	Brown mustard
___	___		___	___	Yellow mustard
		Sweet-based staples	___	___	Oil
___	___	Brown sugar	___	___	Tabasco sauce
___	___	White sugar	___	___	Worchestershire sauce
___	___	Powdered sugar	___	___	
___	___	Honey	___	___	
___	___	Maple syrup	___	___	
___	___	Jams/jellies			**Perishable Foods**
___	___		___	___	Fresh garlic
___	___		___	___	Ginger
___	___		___	___	Green peppers
		Canned & bottled goods	___	___	Celery
___	___	Tuna	___	___	Eggs
___	___	Juices	___	___	Nuts
___	___	Peanut butter	___	___	Green onions
___	___	Tomato sauce	___	___	Yellow onions
___	___	Tomato paste	___	___	White onions
___	___	Dried fruit	___	___	Tomatoes
___	___	Dried mixes (i.e. salad dressing, taco mix)	___	___	Carrots
___	___		___	___	White cheese
___	___	Canned vegetables	___	___	Yellow cheese
___	___	Canned fruit	___	___	Lemons
___	___	Pancake mix	___	___	

Figure 6

Arranging Your Pantry

1. When stocking your pantry, organize your staples and canned goods by category. For example, put canned fruit in one row and dry cereal in another, or organize everything alphabetically.

2. To help keep your food items in the right place, label your pantry shelves accordingly. This is also an excellent way to keep your spices in order.

3. Sort your packaged items such as dry taco mix, salad dressing, and gravy mix in a large jar or small shoebox covered with contact paper.

4. Store as much as possible in jars—everything from tea bags to flour and noodles to coffee filters. Products are protected from moisture and tend to stay fresh longer when placed in jars.

5. For convenience, save one shelf for appliances and group them according to function. For example, keep your mixing bowls, mixers, and measuring cups together.

6. As you plan your weekly menus, check your staple and perishable foods and replenish if necessary.

Other Helpful Hints

◆ Use freezer and storage space well. If you take advantage of sales and coupons to stock up and save money, you can avoid many of those "emergency" trips to the supermarket when unexpected company arrives.

◆ Plan a "cooking marathon" with a friend or your family. Bake or cook a few entrees such as breads, cakes, casseroles and soups. Freeze the items, some in family portions and some in individual servings. Remember to date and label each item. Now, on a day when mom's sick or there's no time to cook a meal, you can open your freezer and take your pick!

◆ Make your own TV dinners by using a sectional paper plate or pie tin and adding leftovers to each section throughout the week. Then freeze the whole plate. Your kids will be able to fend for themselves on the nights you can't be home.

You'll be surprised at how a little organization in your pantry will not only save you precious time, but will relieve a potential area of stress as well.

forty-seven

Kitchen Organization

Happy are those who are strong in the Lord,
who want above all else to follow your steps.

Psalm 84:5

American kitchens are busy places. Today's women spend an average of 1,092 hours a year there, along with everyone from husbands to friends to teenagers to dinner guests to babysitters. That little room puts up with a lot of traffic, and organization is essential. But how, how, *how* do we do it?

It takes time, but it is well worth it. Organization frees you from your kitchen mess and gives you total rest in this big area of your life. Here's a plan to get you started.

What You Need

Jars (assorted sizes), covered plastic containers, lazy Susans, large cardboard box marked "kitchen overflow," contact paper, trash bag, markers, and labels. Most important, you need a two-to-three-hour slot of time and some help from your family. When family members help get the kitchen in order, they're more likely to help keep it that way.

Cupboards

Begin with the cupboard closest to the sink and methodically go around the kitchen. Take everything out of each cupboard. Wipe shelves and repaper if necessary. Throw away or set aside anything that is not used daily or every other day. Pile the seldom-used items in the "kitchen overflow" box.

Put "prime time" equipment such as frequently used spices, glasses, dishes, and pots and pans back into the cupboards, placing seldom-used items toward the back or on the highest levels. Set broken appliances aside to be repaired or thrown away.

Overflow, such as odd vases, dishes, platters, pans, canned goods, seldom-used appliances, and camping equipment (which could be boxed separately) should be stored in the garage or basement to reduce kitchen clutter.

Gadgets and utensils such as wooden spoons, ladles, long-handled spoons, forks, and potato mashers can be stashed into a crock or ceramic pot to save space. Either sharpen dull knives or throw them out. Try a plastic divider (usually used for flatware) in the junk drawer for storing a small hammer, tacks, screwdriver, nails, batteries, glue, etc.

Pots and Pans

To keep pots and pans in neat order, try lining the shelves with plain or light-colored paper and drawing an exaggerated outline of each item. Then store each pot or pan in its designated space. You'll be surprised at how easy it will be to find things.

Refrigerator

Don't let your refrigerator intimidate you; just think of it as another closet. Store fruits and vegetables in covered plastic containers, baggies, or refrigerator drawers to ensure freshness. Keep meats and cheeses on the coldest shelf, and rotate eggs so that you use the oldest first. Lazy Susans are great refrigerator space-savers and can be used to hold sour cream, cottage cheese, jellies, peanut butter, mustard, and whatever else is cluttering up your refrigerator. You can also buy dispensers and bottle racks which attach to refrigerator shelves.

Freezer

The cardinal rule for freezer organization is to date and label *everything*. Be sure to avoid mystery packages! Shape hamburger into patties, freeze on a cookie sheet, and then transfer to plastic bags. They won't stick together and will thaw quickly for meatloaf, burgers, tacos, casseroles, or spaghetti. Keep ahead of ice cubes by periodically bagging up a bunch. Frozen packaged vegetables go together in the freezer as do ice cream and frozen desserts. Potato chips, corn chips, nuts, breads, muffins, wheat flour, and tortillas (corn and flour), even candies, all freeze well. Your freezer can be a real time-saver if you make dinners ahead. Lasagna, noodle and cheese casseroles, soups, beans, spaghetti sauce, and enchiladas are yummy freeze-ahead meals. If you're freezing in jars, be sure to leave 1½ inches at the top for expansion.

forty-eight

Planning Your Kitchen

I will reject all selfishness and stay away from every evil.
I will not tolerate anyone who secretly slanders his neighbors.

Psalm 101:4-5

A well-planned kitchen is the envy of all those whose kitchens are an obstacle course to efficient cooking. No matter how large or small, any kitchen can be tailored to suit your lifestyle if thought is given to your cooking habits and needs.

Here are some helps for a well-planned kitchen.

1. Invest in a good selection of pans and utensils to accomplish your culinary pursuits. These should include:

- One 10-inch skillet w/lid
- One 8- to 10-inch omelet pan
- A set of covered casserole dishes
- A roasting pan with rack
- Bread pans
- Two cookie sheets
- Double boiler
- One muffin pan with 6 to 12 cups
- Dutch oven or similar type of pan

Basic Utensils

Begin with a good set of knives. Bob and I were married for almost 35 years before we invested in knives. We wish we had done it sooner! These items are all great ideas for shower and wedding gifts for the bride and groom. Be sure to include a steel knife sharpener for proper maintenance of your knife set investment.

Other Necessary Items for the Kitchen

- A set of measuring cups
- Wooden spoons—a variety of sizes
- A mallet for tenderizing less expensive cuts of meat
- Spatula—I like the rubber type
- Shears—great for cutting parsley, green onions, and meat
- Rolling pin
- Storage bowls (such as Tupperware)
- Cleaner
- Cheese slicer
- Tongs
- Garlic press—I use this often

Gadgets

- Grater
- Colander
- Sifter
- Vegetable steamer
- Food grinder
- Eggbeater
- Whisk
- Egg slicer—makes pretty slices for salads

Optional Larger Gadgets

- Mixer
- Blender
- Food processor

- Toaster oven
- Microwave oven
- Freezer

2. Plan a logical work space for yourself and be sure that all utensils have a definite place. For example, if you bake a lot, set up a baking center. It could be on the counter top near a convenient cupboard, or even on a mobile kitchen worktable.

Your mixer, baking pans, utensils, and canisters should be readily accessible to that area.

Things that work together should be stored together. This is a good rule to remember when organizing your kitchen. Think through your daily work pattern and plan your space accordingly.

Items seldom used, such as a turkey platter, deviled egg dish, roasting pan, seasonal tableware, serving dishes, and picnic gear should be kept on higher shelves.

If you get a new set of flatware, keep the old to use for parties or to loan out when friends have buffets or church socials.

Spices can be retrieved quickly if stored in alphabetical order: Store on a "lazy Susan" or have your helpful handyman make a wooden spice rack to hang on your wall.

Here's a cute idea for that bridal shower. Have each guest bring (or tie on the top of their package) a spice. Specify a name brand so the spices will be uniform. You could even specify the type of spice on the invitation to prevent repetition.

Use a crock to store your utensils; place on the stove for quick retrieval. It's also a space saver that can take the place of a drawer. It can include your wooden spoons, whisks, meat mallet, ladles, and spatula.

Appliances

The many compact appliances available today are perfect for newlyweds looking to use time and space in the kitchen efficiently.

Mini food-processors and compact mincer-choppers, for instance, are suited for cooking meals for two or three people and are easier to clean than their full counterparts. They also take less space and less time.

Toaster ovens are handy for small meals. To save space they can be mounted under a cabinet. Rechargeable, hand-held beaters can be mounted on the wall. And some new coffee makers on the market brew a single mug at a time.

Several factors should be considered when purchasing appliances:

◆ Space: If you are short on counter space, look at undercabinet models.

◆ Convenience: Look for cordless products. They rest in a recharger base and are always ready to use.

◆ Weight comfort: Make sure hand-held appliances such as mixers and cordless knives are lightweight and easy to grip.

◆ Ease of operation: Push-button controls simplify use. Certain controls, such as a pulse control, regulate the amount of processing.

◆ Automatic shutoff: For peace of mind and for added safety, look for appliances that shut off automatically, including irons and coffee makers.

◆ Dishwasher safety: For maximum convenience, look for products with parts that can be easily disassembled and put into the dishwasher.

Other Handy Tips

◆ Glue a 12-inch square of cork to the inside of the cabinet door over your kitchen work area. On the cork tack the recipe card you are using and newspaper clippings of recipes you plan to try within a few days. It keeps them at eye level and they stay spatter-free.

◆ When using your electric can opener, help save your fingers from cuts by placing a refrigerator magnet on top of the can before opening it. This magnet will give you a good grip when you lift off the lid.

◆ Increase your efficiency with an extra-long phone cord that will reach to all corners of your kitchen. Instead of wasting time while on the phone, you can cook, set the table, or clean out a drawer. A cordless and/or speaker phone provides similar freedom.

◆ Meat slices easier if it's partially frozen.

◆ Want to mix frozen juice in a hurry without using the blender? Use your potato masher on the concentrate.

◆ You can peel garlic cloves faster if you mash them lightly with the side of the blade of a chef's knife.

- To keep bugs out of your flour canister, put a stick of spearmint gum in the flour.

- Mark your bowls and their covers with the same number, using a marking pencil. Then you won't always be looking for a matching cover for the bowl when you're putting away leftovers. All you have to do is match the numbers.

- Arrange your kitchen for maximum efficiency. Position often-used utensils in convenient drawers and cupboards. Make your dishes do double duty. Use a saucepan as mixing bowl; then use the same pan for the cooking.

- Cut the lid off an egg carton and place the cups in a kitchen drawer. You can organize your cup hooks, small nails, paper clips, thumbtacks, and other small items. No more junky drawers.

- When you are in need of extra ice cubes for party or summer use, simply fill your egg cartons with water and freeze.

- If wax has built up on the felt pads of your floor polisher, place the pads between several thicknesses of paper toweling and press with a warm iron. The towels will quickly absorb the old wax.

- Place the plastic lids from coffee cans under bottles of cooking oil to keep cabinets clean. When the lids get dirty, just throw them away.

- A rubber jar-opener (or rubber gloves) gives you easy access to anything in a tightly closed jar.

- To cover kitchen cabinet shelves, apply easy-to-install vinyl floor squares by just peeling off the backing. They are particularly good for lower shelves where pots and pans are usually stored. They cut easily and do not tear or wrinkle.

- One of the best appliances you can have for your busy schedule is a slow cooker (crockpot). Prepare the meal early in the morning and when you come home from shopping or work, you will find your main dish for dinner ready.

- At least once a year pull the plug on your refrigerator and give it a thorough cleaning. Rinse with clean water after cleaning with baking soda (one tablespoon baking soda to one quart water). Let it air-dry.

- A trash can under the kitchen sink takes up some very valuable storage space. Take a large decorative basket and line it with a plastic bag. The bag is easy to lift out when full. Train several family members to take the trash out.

Remember, your kitchen is for cooking, *not clutter!*

forty-nine

Eggs, Eggs, and More Eggs

*I will also meditate on all Your work,
and talk of Your deeds.*

Psalm 77:12 NKJV

ue gregg and I in our book *The Busy Woman's Guide to Healthy Eating* (Harvest House) wrote a chapter dealing with the misunderstanding about eggs in our diet. The controversy and confusion over eggs focuses on the high cholesterol content of egg yolks. Media advertising, news articles, magazines, nutrition books, cookbooks, doctors, and nutritionists would have us believe that food cholesterol raises blood cholesterol. Yet there is no adequate research to substantiate this claim. Researchers are not agreed at all on this issue. The classic study that relates egg yolk cholesterol to blood cholesterol was conducted in 1913 by Nikolai Anichkov, a Russian pathologist, on rabbits. He fed rabbits the equivalent in human consumption of 60 eggs per day. The rabbits developed cholesterol deposits on their arteries. But rabbits are total vegetarians and do not eat eggs. There is nothing in their metabolism to handle eggs.

No human study shows a clear relationship between food cholesterol content and blood cholesterol, whereas research does indicate a clearer relationship to total fat consumption, especially to saturated fat. Yet eggs are lower in saturated fat than both meat and poultry, about the same as

191

lowfat yogurt, and contain one-third of the amount that is in ¼ cup of cheddar cheese.

Advertising and popular news articles repeatedly reinforce the notion that food cholesterol raises blood cholesterol levels. "No cholesterol" labels are printed on vegetable oils and advertised everywhere. The message is effectively communicated, "Cholesterol in foods must be bad!"

Time magazine, March 26, 1984, reported the most extensive research project ever conducted on cholesterol in medical history. This project was declared "...a turning point in cholesterol–heart disease research," because it clearly demonstrated that high blood cholesterol contributes to heart disease and cardiac deaths. Ten years and $150 million were spent on 3,806 men, ages 35 to 39 with cholesterol levels of 265 milligrams. A cholesterol-lowering drug was used in the study. Those receiving the drug experienced an 8.5 percent drop in cholesterol, 19 percent fewer heart attacks, and 24 percent fewer cardiac deaths. Yet nothing was changed in their diets. The study had nothing to do with the cholesterol content of any foods.

The editors of *Time* magazine placed a "sad-face" picture on the front cover of this same issue, using two fried eggs for eyes and a slice of bacon for the mouth, with the overcaption: "Cholesterol...And Now the Bad News." The article was titled, "Hold the Eggs and Butter" (page 56). The message conveyed to the reader was "Eggs and butter contribute to heart disease." Yet the research project reviewed by *Time* had nothing to do with the effects of food on cholesterol! This kind of media influence confuses important nutritional issues of the American public. Of this research project Edward Ahrens, researcher at Rockefeller University, said, "Since this was basically a drug study we can conclude nothing about diet; such extrapolation is unwarranted, unscientific and wishful thinking" (*Time* magazine, March 26, 1984, page 58).

Only 20 to 30 percent of our cholesterol comes from food. Our bodies manufacture the rest. There are many other influences on blood cholesterol levels besides total fat intake, such as exercise, stress, inherited genes, prepackaged foods high in fats and refined carbohydrates, lack of dietary fiber, and inadequate vitamins and minerals. Rather than focus on egg yolks as a dietary disaster, we should develop a balance of real whole foods.

Eggs are a real food. They can readily be used in baking and a couple of times a week for meals. Two breakfasts or an egg main dish will not raise the total fat intake to over 30 percent of daily calories. Eggs are our best protein source because their amino acid pattern most nearly matches that needed for human growth and health. They are excellent sources of trace minerals; unsaturated fatty acids; iron; phosphorus; vitamin B-complex; and vitamins A, E, K, and even some D. Most of these reside in the egg yolk! Yolks also are the highest food source of choline, a component of lecithin that assists in keeping cholesterol liquid in the bloodstream. There is some question as to whether the lecithin is effective in this way, however.

If you do not want to eat egg yolks or are allergic to eggs, be encouraged. There are easy alternatives! You can use two egg whites in place of a whole egg in almost any baking recipe. Unfortunately that wastes the egg yolks, so we prefer using ¼ cup tofu in place of an egg. Mixing it in the blender with other liquid ingredients works best. If you cannot find a real food to give taste pleasure, we recommend doing without.

Consider the value of fertile eggs. Fertile eggs come from hens, living with roosters, that are allowed to grow and peck on the ground. They receive no drugs as chickens raised in close quarters do. We don't really know what the nutritional difference between fertile eggs and sterile eggs is even though some people make claims for the nutritional superiority of fertile eggs. The clearest advantage is that fertile eggs are free of chemical residues. In general, fertile eggs also taste fresher but are also slightly more expensive. Many health food stores carry them. People who raise their own chickens also often sell them.

Mankind has eaten eggs for centuries. Even Job ate eggs: "…is there flavor in the white of an egg! I refuse to touch it; such food makes me ill" (Job 6:6-7 NIV). Yet heart disease was not reported in scientific literature until 1986. You decide. We still believe eggs are an economical blessing from God given to us to enjoy in moderation.

Part 7

ORGANIZATION

fifty

Telephone Tips to Give You More Time for Yourself

*Set your affection on things above,
not on things on the earth.*

Colossians 3:2 NKJV

How many times have you been stuck on the telephone trying to get off but unable to end the conversation? How often have you been put on hold for what seemed like an eternity and sometimes by people who have called *you?* How many times have you finally gotten a good start on a project at home or work only to be interrupted by a telephone call you really didn't want to take?

Our telephone can be a terrific time-saver. However, it also can rule our lives if we allow calls to interrupt meals or delay departures, causing late schedules, missed appointments, etc.

Here are some tips to help you control the telephone so it doesn't control you.

1. Organize a telephone center so you can make and receive calls efficiently. Next to every phone in your home or business should be a pad and pen. Keep extra pads in a drawer or on a shelf and pencils and/or pens too. It's amazing how they wander off, so a supply is important. Your calendar, phone book, area-code map and personal address book also need to be close by for easy reference.

197

2. Organize your calls so that you can make several calls at one sitting when possible. You'll be apt to make your calls shorter and get more done. List your calls, questions to ask, and points to be discussed. Date your calls and take notes for future reference. I have a personal code by each call. If the party I'm calling is not home or there's no answer I put an "O"; if the line is busy I put a wavy line. If I leave a message to call back I put a jagged line. Make up your own code that will work for you.

3. Learn how to end conversations. Getting off the phone can truly be an art. Some people ignore all the signals you give and just keep talking. To free yourself more quickly, warn people in advance that your time is limited. For example, "Your trip sounds exciting but I've got to leave in five minutes, can you tell me briefly?" Or you might insert this, "Before we hang up...." It is a reminder that your call will end soon. You might say, "I really can't spend a lot of time on the phone. Let's speak briefly and meet for lunch [coffee, tea] instead."

4. The investment of an answering machine will be money well spent. You can receive calls when you're away and return calls at your convenience. Some messages will be left as reminders of appointments with no return call needed. You can also screen calls, and if it is urgent you can answer it. If not, return the call later. Let the machine answer while showering, bathing the baby, eating meals, doing homework, or 15 minutes before you must leave for an appointment. That way you won't be delayed by any last-minute calls that can wait.

5. Turn off the phone or unplug it when you don't want to be disturbed during dinnertime, special projects, sewing, ironing, or family meetings.

6. Avoid phone tag. When you leave a message for someone to call you, give a time when you'll be available. If you have to get back to people, ask them when they are able to receive calls.

7. When leaving messages give as much information as possible so you can eliminate another call.

8. Return phone calls. You'll build credibility as you do.

9. If you have children take messages for you, ask them to repeat names and numbers back to callers to be sure the information is taken correctly.

10. Put a long extension cord on your telephone or consider buying a cordless phone. You will then be free to move about, clean a bathroom, check on children, etc. This can help you do two things at once.

Using these ideas will help you to do your work more efficiently and enable you to have more hours in your day to do some things you really enjoy doing.

fifty-one

15 Minutes a Day and You're on Your Way

Seek first the kingdom of God and His righteousness, and all these things shall be added to you.

Matthew 6:33 NKJV

One of the number one frustrations facing all women—single, married, career, homemakers, college students—is how we can get organized enough to eliminate all the mess within our four walls, regardless how little or large those four walls are.

Who wants to spend all their waking hours cleaning their home? Is there a way to live after a messy house? Yes. You don't have to be a slave to your home. Give me at least 15 minutes a day for five weeks and I can have you on top of the pile.

As with any task, you need some basic equipment:

- ◆ 3 large 30-gallon trash bags
- ◆ 3 to 12 large cardboard boxes (approximately 10 x 12 x 16) preferably with lids
- ◆ 1 wide-tip black felt marking pen

You might ask, where do I find these materials? Check with your local stationery store. In some cases your market has leftover boxes of some sort to get you started. Try to have all the boxes uniform in size.

Before you start this project, commit it unto the Lord. Matthew 6:33 is a good verse for this phase of the program. Ask the Lord to provide you with the desire and energy to complete the project. In this program you will clean one room a week for five weeks. If you have fewer rooms it will take you less time and if you have a larger house it will take more than five weeks.

Step 1

Start by marking the three large trash bags as follows:

- ◆ Put Away
- ◆ Throw Away
- ◆ Give Away

Step 2

Start at the front door and go through your whole house. Start with the hall closet and proceed through the living room, dining room, bedrooms, and bathrooms. End in your kitchen because you need all the experience you can get to clean that room.

Step 3

For each room's closets, drawers, and shelves you are to wash, scrub, paint, and repaper everything. Take everything out of and off of these areas and clean thoroughly.

A close friend is a great help at this point in assisting you in deciding what to throw away. Try not to become emotionally attached to any items.

A good rule to help you decide whether to keep an item is if you haven't used it for a year, it must be thrown away, given away, or stored away. Exceptions to this would be treasured keepsakes, photos, or very special things you'll want to pass down to your children someday.

Magazines, papers, scrap material, clothing, and extra dishes and pans must go.

As you pull these items off your shelves and out of your closets, they can be put into the appropriately labeled trash bags. What's left will be put back into the proper closet or drawer, or onto the proper shelf.

After the last room is finished, you will have at least three very fat trash bags.

- The *Throw Away* bag goes out to the trash area for pickup.

- The *Give Away* bag can be sorted out, divided up among needy friends, or given to a thrift store, relatives, or the Salvation Army.

- The *Put Away* bag will be the most fun of all. Take the large cardboard boxes and begin to use them for storage of the items you'll want to save for future use. (See Chapter 5 for a refresher on how to label and store these boxes.)

Just *15 minutes a day* for five weeks has cleaned out all the clutter in your home!

fifty-two

Maintaining Your Five-Week Program

The Holy Spirit helps us with our daily problems and in our praying. For we don't even know what we should pray for.

Romans 8:26

You now have your home clean—washed, dusted, sorted out, and painted through this Five-Week Program—and it feels good. Everything has a place in a cupboard, dresser, closet, or on a shelf; all your boxes are marked and properly filed away. Within a short time you can locate anything. Oh, that feels good. The pressure is off!

It's a big accomplishment, but you're not quite through. It's a matter of maintaining what you've worked so hard on the past five weeks. This is the easiest part when applied.

For this phase of your program you will need:

♦ One 3 x 5 file box
♦ 36 lined 3 x 5 file cards
♦ Seven divider tabs

Step 1

Set-up your 3 x 5 file box with dividers.

203

Step 2

Label the dividers in the file box as follows:

1. Daily
2. Weekly
3. Monthly
4. Quarterly
5. Biannually
6. Annually
7. Storage (You will already have done this from a previous chapter.)

Step 3

Under each tab heading you now make a list of the jobs needing to be done on each file card. Some suggestions are:

A. *Daily*

1. Wash dishes
2. Make beds
3. Sweep kitchen floor
4. Pick up rooms
5. Tidy bathrooms
6. Make meal preparations, etc.

Note: After a very short time these will become automatic and you won't need to write them down.

B. *Weekly*

1. Monday—wash
2. Tuesday—iron, water house plants
3. Wednesday—mop floor, dust
4. Thursday—vacuum, marketing
5. Friday—change bed linens
6. Saturday—yard work
7. Sunday—church, free

Note: If you skip a job on the allotted day, *DO NOT DO IT*. Skip it until the next scheduled time and put that card behind the proper tab in the file. You may have an item listed under two or more days.

C. Monthly
Week 1—Clean refrigerator; clean bathrooms
Week 2—Clean oven; wash living room windows
Week 3—Mend clothing; wash bedroom windows
Week 4—Clean and dust baseboards; wax kitchen floor

D. Quarterly
1. Clean dresser drawers
2. Clean out closets
3. Move living room furniture and vacuum underneath
4. Clean china cabinet glass
5. Clean, rearrange, and organize cupboards in kitchen

E. Biannually
1. Hose off screens
2. Change filter in furnace
3. Rearrange furniture
4. Clean garage, basement, or attic (schedule the whole family on this project)

F. Annually
1. Wash sheer curtains
2. Clean drapes if needed
3. Shampoo carpet
4. Wash walls and woodwork
5. Paint the paint chips or blisters on house

The above schedule is only a sample. Your particular projects can be inserted where needed. Living in different sections of our country will put different demands on your maintenance schedule. Get in the habit of staying on top of your schedule so you don't get buried again with your clutter and stress.

fifty-three

A Place for Everything

I will trust and not be afraid, for the Lord
is my strength and song; he is my salvation.

Isaiah 12:2

raft and sewing projects are fun hobbies, but if you've dabbled in them at all you've probably struggled with where and how to store patterns, leftover fabric, straw flowers, glue, and other odds and ends.

Before you let this clutter overwhelm you, try these simple organizational hints:

- ◆ Begin collecting storage boxes such as shoe boxes, cardboard boxes, or Perfect boxes. (Perfect storage boxes are available from More Hours In My Day—see order information on page 309.)

  Other containers that will work well for storing your craft items are plastic bins or stacking trays, laundry baskets, and small jars (baby food jars are great).

- ◆ Store patterns in boxes organized according to sizes and types: play clothes, dressy outfits, costumes, sportswear, blouses, and pants. Many fabric stores carry cardboard boxes made specifically for storing patterns, and you can buy these boxes at a very low price.

◆ Put fabrics in piles according to colors (prints, solids, and stripes) or types (wools, linens, and polyesters). Then place each pile in a separate cardboard Perfect box and number your boxes 1, 2, 3, 4, etc.

Make out a 3 x 5 file card and list on the card what type of fabric you stored in your Perfect box. On top of the card write the same number that is on the box. For example:

Box 1—Calico fabrics—reds and pinks
Box 2—Solid fabrics—blues, browns, blacks
Box 3—Stripes, polka dots
Box 4—Remnants and a yard or less of scraps

This can also be done with art and craft items. By keeping your 3 x 5 cards in a recipe box, you can quickly retrieve any item simply by looking up its card and finding the corresponding box.

◆ Organize buttons by color or size by stringing them onto safety pins, pipe cleaners, or plastic twist ties, or stick loose buttons and snaps on strips of transparent tape.

◆ Store bias tape, piping, and hem tape in a labeled shoebox.

◆ Keep hooks-and-eyes and snaps in baby food jars and line them up on a shelf or store them in shoe boxes, again labeled accordingly.

◆ String your sewing machine bobbins on pipe cleaners or keep them in a plastic ice cube tray (specialty bobbin boxes are also available at most fabric stores or drugstores).

◆ Organize spools of thread by grouping the spools according to color and laying them on their sides in the lids of shoe boxes. Stack the box tops so that frequently used colors are on top and stick them into a drawer or onto a shelf.

◆ Store fabric fill, stuffing, quilting materials, and straw or silk flowers in cardboard or Perfect boxes by using the numbering system.

◆ Use egg cartons for other odds and ends such as pins, small craft items, paper clips, and stamps.

◆ Clamp pattern pieces together with a clothespin until you finish the project or garment and then return them to the envelope.

◆ Large envelopes are also a great way to organize small items. The contents can be listed on the outside and stored in Perfect boxes or in a drawer. Suggested items to store are small scraps of fabric, ribbons, pipe cleaners, lace, bias tape, elastic, zippers, and stencils.

- Baskets are a fun way to store art and craft materials such as pin cushions and pins, scissors, measuring tape, ribbons, lace, and elastic.

The above items could be put into one basket and given as a gift to a creative craft friend for Christmas.

Another cute idea is to spray-glue one of the Perfect storage boxes and apply a patchwork of fabric pieces. It looks country and creative. It could be used as a gift or a storage box for fabrics.

fifty-four

How to Organize
Your Closet

*Anyone who wants to follow me must put aside his own desires
and conveniences...every day and keep close to me!*

Luke 9:23

Is your closet a disaster that gives you the feeling of stress and confusion? Take heart, here's a sensible, easy way to clean it out and put every inch of space to good use. A well-put-together closet makes you more organized and your life just a little bit easier.

Cleaning the Closet

Step 1: Sort clothes into three piles. Hold each item up and ask yourself three questions. Be honest and take time to evaluate. 1) "Do I love it and wear it?" 2) "Do I feel good in it?" You seldom wear clothes you don't feel good in. You hang on to them because you think you are throwing money away if you get rid of them, or because they remind you of the past or because you *may* wear them in the future. Everyone does this. 3) "Am I willing to recycle this?" These are clothes you never wear.

Step 2: Remove the recycle pile. Here are three ways to do this: 1) take the clothes to a used clothing store and earn some extra money; 2) give the clothes to a charity, thrift store, Salvation Army, etc. (getting a receipt will give you a tax deduction); 3) give the clothes to friends or needy families.

Step 3: Create an ambivalence center. Put the clothes you can't decide about out of the way in storage boxes in an attic, basement, garage, or storage closet. You may decide later to recycle these clothes after all, but for now it may be too emotional.

Step 4: You have now only the "I love to wear" pile to deal with. But why put your clothes back in the same old closet? It may be part of the reason your wardrobe seems to get so disorganized. Let's think about it.

The average closet consists of one long pole beneath one long shelf. The old-fashioned single-pole system wastes usable space. Far more efficient is a system with at least three poles and several shelves. By placing poles at different heights, you increase the number of items you can hang in a given area. In a his-and-hers closet, this technique can quadruple space (see illustrations in Figures 7 and 8, on pages 211-212). By discarding the one pole you free space for more shelves. Use these shelves for foldable clothes (enough shelves can eliminate your need for a dresser). By keeping shoes off the floor, you'll eliminate jumbled dusty shoes. Hats and purses go on shelves to make your closet workable and pleasant.

You may want to add a light if there is none. If you have the option, avoid sliding doors. It's best to be able to see all your clothes at once. The floor may need a new look. Try inexpensive self-stick vinyl tiles or carpet remnants. Pretty up your closet with wallpaper, wallpaper borders, paint, posters, or eyelet lace glued on the edge of your shelves. Your new closet will save you both time and money. You'll know exactly where to find things and better yet where to put them back. It will be easier to mix and match outfits when you know what you have and can see everything clearly. You'll be able to expand your wardrobe using what you already own. Now you will enjoy your organized closet. Here are some additional tips:

- One of the reasons most closets are a mess is because people forget about closet organizers. Buy them in notions departments, hardware or dollar stores, or use your imagination. These ideas will get you started.

- Mug racks. Good for jewelry, scarves, small purses. Hang vertically or horizontally on closet wall or door.

- Shoebags. Not just for shoes! Use for storing scarves, gloves, stockings...anything.

Figure 7

Hats

Her Tops

Their long Clothes

His shirts

Her skirts, pants

His Pants

shoe shelf

shoe shelf

Figure 8

- Hanging baskets. A decorative way to store socks and small, light items.

- Kitchen towel racks. Two to four hung on the back of your closet door are great for scarves. Use the thick rounded racks for pants.

- Colorful ceramic hooks. They fit anywhere—for hats, belts, bags, jewelry.

- Pegboards. Hang belts, hats, jewelry—you name it. They are great all-purpose organizers.

- Men's tie and belt racks. Ideal for leotards or lingerie.

- Overhead shoe chests. Ones with dividers and clear plastic zip fronts are an easy way to organize your handbags.

- Shoe boxes. For shoes! Write a description of each pair on the outside. To make them pretty, cover your shoe boxes with wallpaper.

- Plastic bags. *Beware*—do not use for leather bags, furs, boots, shoes, silks, or down vests. These accessories need to breathe.

fifty-five

How to Manage Your Mail

There is a time for everything, and
a season for every activity under heaven.

Ecclesiastes 3:1 NIV

Many of us can't wait for the mail to come each day. The thought of receiving news from afar is exciting and fresh. At the same time, however, the thought of processing it all can be depressing. Making decisions about what to throw away, what to save, where to put the mail for hubby to read if and when he gets around to it...and then, again, what to throw away!

I've discovered three easy steps that have helped me manage my mountains of mail. I hope they work for you too!

1. Designate one area where you open and process all your mail. It could be a desk, a table by a chair, or the kitchen counter. If you use the kitchen counter, however, be careful not to use it as a catchall. One woman told me she put her mail on top of her refrigerator, but it piled up so high it took her three weeks to go through it.

2. Don't let it pile up! Set a time each day when you process your mail. If you can't get to it when you receive your mail, then plan a time when you can. Do it daily.

3. Make decisions. Don't put it down; put it away, and don't be a mail scooter. It's easy to scoot mail and papers from one area to another, one room to the next, or from one pile to another. Sort out your mail into categories:

- *Throwaway mail*—junk mail, advertisements, etc.

- *Mail you need to read*, but don't have time for now.

- *Mail you need to file away*, such as bills, insurance papers, and receipts.

- *Mail you need to ask someone about*—husband, children, etc.

- *Mail that needs a phone call.* Perhaps you have a question or need a clearer explanation than the letter gave. Many times people ask me questions by letter. If the person is relatively close, I will call rather than write. It is quicker and I can get that letter taken care of faster.

- *Mail to be answered.* Personal letters, forms to be filled out and returned, RSVP's for invitations.

All these categories can be labeled on file folders and put into a file box or metal file cabinet. As soon as the mail comes in, simply slip it into its proper place. Then when your husband comes home you can hand him his folder of mail to read and process.

One woman told me she covered shoe boxes with wallpaper and labeled them, set them in a row on a shelf and processed her mail very quickly. Remember, however, that with file folders or boxes, you still have to beware of pile-ups.

Junk mail is a time waster, so toss it! Don't let yourself say, "I'll probably use this someday," because you very likely will *not*.

On mail that requires other people's input, mark notes or question marks so both of you can discuss it.

There are times when you don't have time to read publications, missionary letters, and magazines. I slip them into a file folder and take the folder along with me in the car. When I have to wait in the doctor's office, for children, or even in a long line, I use that time to catch up on my mail reading. I make notes on it, and then process it according to its category.

Address changes should be made immediately upon receipt, making sure that you dispose of the old address. Also, an RSVP should be answered as soon as you know your plans. This is a common courtesy to your host or hostess; he or she will appreciate your promptness. If you can't give a yes/no answer, then let that be known also.

Mark dates on your calendar as soon as the invitations arrive. Also write down appointments, birthdays, and other significant days. With our busy, busy lives, we can't always depend upon our memories.

fifty-six

What to Do with Those Piles of Papers

A wise man thinks ahead;
a fool doesn't, and even brags about it!

Proverbs 13:16

Every day we make decisions about paper—from personal mail to children's papers, newspapers to magazines to Sunday School papers. We must sort through mountains of paper each week, accumulated from day to day, week to week, and month to month. Some of us find ourselves buried in years of collected, often-forgotten papers.

One woman who attended my seminar shared that she finally had to hire a person to help her organize her papers. A former school teacher, she had acquired volumes of miscellaneous papers.

She and her helper worked three hours a day, five days a week, for three months during summer vacation just organizing paper; a total of 180 hours each!

A lot of time and expense can be avoided if paper is dealt with when it arrives. Rather than stacking it on counters, appliance tops, tables, dressers, or even on the floor until it takes up nearly every empty space in our homes, we need to file and/or dispose of paper as soon as it is received.

Another lady confessed that she couldn't use her dining room table without a major paper transfer before entertaining company. Still another

217

woman shared that her husband threatened, "It's either me or the papers that go." Needless to say, she began a major paper-filing program and quickly got the paper epidemic under control.

Paper disorganization often begins in subtle ways. With only insurance policies, checking account statements, and canceled checks, car registrations, apartment rental agreements, birth certificates, a marriage license, diplomas, and a few other miscellaneous papers, a person often reasons that a full-fledged filing system is not necessary. Thus the file often consists of merely a cardboard shoebox or metal, fireproof box which can easily be stored away on a closet shelf.

As the years go by, however, there are "his" papers, "her" papers, appliance warranties, and instruction booklets on the television, the toaster, and the lawn mower (along with other gadgets too numerous to mention). The result is paper chaos.

Don't despair. Help is on the way. Here are six simple steps to effective paper-management.

1. Schedule set times for sorting through papers.

2. Collect materials you will need to help you get organized.

   ◆ Metal file cabinet or file boxes
   ◆ Plastic trash bags
   ◆ File folders (I prefer bright colored folders, but plain manila will do.)
   ◆ Black felt marking pen

3. Begin.

   ◆ Start with whatever room annoys you the most. Work your way through every pile of paper; go through drawers and closets. Then move on to rooms where other papers have accumulated. Continue at set times until your project is completed.

4. Throw away.

   ◆ Be determined. Make decisions. Throw away the clutter.

   ◆ Perhaps you have lots of articles, recipes, or children's school papers and artwork which you have been saving for that special "someday." In each category, choose five pieces to keep and get rid of the rest! Try not to be too sentimental.

- Keep the saving of papers to a minimum. Put the throwaway papers into bags and carry them out to the trash. Don't wait. It's a good feeling!

- Don't get bogged down rereading old letters, recipes, articles, etc. It's easy to spend too much time reminiscing and get sidetracked from your purpose of streamlining your paper-filing system.

- Keep legal papers a minimum of seven years.

- If you have trouble determining what to throw away, ask a friend to help you make some of those decisions. Friends tend to be more objective and you can return the favor when they discover how "organized" you are.

5. File.

- Keep your filing system as simple as possible. If it is too detailed and complex, you may be easily discouraged.

- Categorize the papers you want to save (e.g., magazine articles, Bible study notes, family information, IRS papers, bank statements/canceled checks, charge accounts, utilities, and investments).

- Label the file folders with a felt pen.

- Within each category, mark a folder or envelope for each separate account. For example, in the utilities folder, water, gasoline, and telephone. In the insurance folder, it is helpful to designate separate envelopes for life, health, car, and house insurance.

- Label a folder for each member of the family. These can be used for keeping health records, report cards, notes, drawings, awards, and other special remembrances.

- Other suggestions for categories: vacation possibilities, Christmas card lists, home improvement ideas, warranties, instruction booklets, photos/negatives, and car/home repair receipts.

- File papers in appropriate folders. *Do it at the time they are received and/or paid.* (Especially take care to file away your check stubs, paid receipts, and other budget records on the day you receive your paycheck.)

- Place files in cabinet or boxes and store.

6. Store.

- ◆ Store files (cabinets or boxes) in a closet, garage, attic, or some other area that is out of sight, yet easily accessible.

- ◆ Be sure to label the file boxes. (I use a 3 x 5 card stapled on the end of the box with the contents written on the card. Then if I empty the box at a later date, I can easily tear off the card and replace it with another card, or use the box for other items.)

Remember, you don't need to buy a home computer to help you get organized. You do, however, need to start right where you are...tackling your own mountains of paper by filing and storing the information you want, and disposing of the clutter that depresses and discourages you.

fifty-seven

Babysitting Survival Guide

Don't copy the behavior and customs of this world,
but be a new and different person with
a fresh newness in all you do and think.

Romans 12:2

Sixteen-year old Lynn arrives at the Merrihew home, eager to take care of Jenny's three adorable children. Jenny and Lynn chat briefly, and then Jenny goes out the door.

About 45 minutes later, two-year old Christine is still crying and screaming, "Mommy!" Lynn remembers that Jenny was going to be at three different places during the evening, but she can't remember what time she was to be where. She's not even sure if she should call her.

Meanwhile Jenny keeps remembering things she wished she had told Lynn and debates as to whether to call home.

Whether your babysitter is 16 or 66, there are certain steps you can take to ensure a smoother and more enjoyable evening for sitter and parents alike. I call these "survival hints."

For Mom and Dad

- Agree on an hourly fee with your sitter when you make the babysitting arrangement.

221

- Ask a first-time sitter to arrive early so you and your children can get acquainted with the sitter. This gives your sitter the chance to become familiar with your home before you leave.

- Explain your home rules about snacking, visitors, television, and the stereo.

- Tell the sitter what time each child is to go to bed and whether your child has any special needs, such as a favorite toy, blanket, or story.

- Show the sitter, if necessary, procedures for feeding, warming a bottle, and changing a diaper.

- Write down the instructions as to time and dosage for any medications your child may be taking. Leave these next to the bottle with a measuring spoon or dropper nearby.

- Let your sitter know at the time of hiring whether he or she will be expected to prepare and serve a meal.

- Make special arrangements at the time you hire your sitter if you want him or her to do any housework. Most parents pay extra for that service.

- Place a flashlight in a handy place in case of power failure.

- Leave a pad and pen by the phone for phone messages and notes of the evening's events.

- Call home periodically if the sitter will not be able to reach you easily.

- Phone your sitter if you will be arriving home later than you had planned. Let him or her know when you expect to arrive.

- Pay your sitter the previously agreed-upon fee when you return home, unless you have worked out another payment arrangement ahead of time. Be aware that checks are sometimes hard for teenagers to cash. Some parents pay extra for hours after midnight. (If you must cancel a sitter at the last minute, it is courteous to pay the sitter for part of the time he or she was planning on working for you.)

For the Babysitter

- Be sure you understand what is expected of you. Don't count on your memory; write instructions down if the list gets too long.

- Be sure you know where parents or other adults such as grandparents or aunts and uncles can be reached at all times.

- Request that the children be present when parents give you instructions so you all understand the rules.

- Don't open the doors for strangers. (Any deliveries can be left outside or delivered later when the parents are home.)

- Keep all outside doors locked at all times.

- Don't tell telephone callers that parents are not at home. Take a message if possible, and tell the caller that they will return the call when they are able to come to the phone.

- Keep your own phone calls brief.

- Clean up your own mess. Any extra effort you make will encourage the parents to call you again.

- Don't snoop in closets or drawers. Even though you are working in the home, you are still a guest.

- Try to stay alert and awake unless it is a long, late evening.

- Inform the parents of any illness or accident, however minor, or any item broken while they were gone. Accidents do happen, and most parents allow for this.

- Tell parents as soon as possible if you have to cancel.

- Take a first-aid course at your local YWCA, Red Cross, or Community Service Department. Some cities have regular classes designed for babysitters. If not, buy a first-aid handbook.

fifty-eight

Garage Sale Organization

Fear not, for I am with you. Do not be dismayed. I am your God.
I will strengthen you; I will help you; I will uphold you.

Isaiah 41:10

As summer comes to an end and you need something to keep your restless children busy, why not plan a garage sale? Tell them that they can keep the money from the sale of their items, and you'll be surprised at how quickly they get motivated to clean their rooms and get rid of clutter.

Not only will a garage sale tidy up your home, it can also be quite profitable. Our children often use their money to buy back-to-school supplies and new clothes. Another good idea is to give the money to a church project or a missionary family. After you help your children decide how they want to use the money they make, put on your grubbies, roll up your sleeves, and start planning.

Set your date. The first step is to set your garage sale date. It is best to plan a one-day sale, either on a Friday or Saturday. Once that is set, call the newspaper or community shopper handout and place an advertisement.

Your ad should be short, to the point, and should *not* include your phone number. You don't need to answer a lot of phone calls and silly questions. Here is a sample ad:

224

Garage Sale—Saturday, Sept. 6, 9 A.M. to 5 P.M. Bookcase—toys—antiques—appliances—clothing—bike—tools and lots of goodies. 6256 Windemere Way, Chicago at Ransom Road.

Make your signs. Use heavy cardboard or brightly colored poster board and bold felt pens in contrasting colors. Keep it simple. Merely write: "GARAGE SALE," the dates, your house address, and street name. Most people don't need too much prompting to drive by a garage sale. My car goes on automatic when it sees a garage sale sign, and stops dead-center in front of the house!

When placing your signs, make sure they are in a prominent location. Use your own stakes. Do not put them on top of a street sign or speed-limit sign. Always go back and remove your signs the day after your sale.

Make your decisions. Now comes the cleaning out and decision-making process. Spend time with each child going over the items they begin to pull out of their rooms. They sometimes get so excited that they want to sell their bed, favorite teddy bear, and even the dog or cat.

You'll have to watch yourself too. I got so excited at one of our garage sales that I sold our refrigerator! People were coming and buying so fast that I got all caught up in it. I didn't like our refrigerator anyway and thought a new one would be great. Besides, it looked like we were selling plenty and bringing in a lot of money. A couple asked me what else I had for sale and I said, "How about the refrigerator?" They bought it.

I was thrilled—until my husband, Bob, came home. I learned a good lesson: Keep your cool and don't lose your head!

Organize. Display items in categories. For example, put all the toys in one place, and glassware and kitchen utensils in another. Place breakable items on tables if possible.

Have an extension cord available from your garden or house outlet so people can check electrical appliances such as a popcorn popper, iron, razor, or clock. If the item does not work, tell the truth. Your interested customer may still buy it. Many garage shoppers are handymen who can fix anything or can use the parts from a nonworking item.

Hospitality gives a garage sale an added touch. Try serving fresh coffee, tea, or iced tea.

Set your price. Pricing takes a lot of time and thought. As a general rule, keep your prices down. Never mark your price directly on the article.

If your husband's shirt doesn't sell, he may go to the office one day with $1.50 inked on his cuff or pocket. It is best to use stick-on labels, round stickers, or masking tape.

If individual family members are going to keep the money from the sale of particular items, be sure to mark them with appropriate initials or a color code (Linda has the blue label, Tom has the green).

I always price everything in increments of 50 cents—$1.50, $2.50, etc. That way you have some bargaining power. People love bargains.

It's a good idea to have separate boxes containing items priced at five cents, ten cents, and 25 cents. This will save you from having to mark each item separately. Children love these boxes because then they can shop while mom and dad look around. You can even have a box marked "FREE."

Have one person, preferably an adult, be the cashier. All purchases must go through that person. Take a large sheet of poster board and list each person who is selling at your sale. As each item is sold, take off the price sticker and place it under his or her name or write the price in the appropriate column. At the end of the day, simply add up each column. It's best to accept only cash from your customers.

Make time count. On the day of the sale, get up early and commit the day to the sale. Eat a good breakfast; you'll need a clear mind for bargain decisions. Since people interested in antiques and valuable items will come by early, it is best to have everything set up the day before. Then all you have to do on the morning of the sale is to move your tables of items outside on the walkway, patio, or driveway.

Pack lunches the night before for you and your children. You won't have time to make lunch with people in your yard all day. Aim toward having a calm, loving spirit, and keep the family involved and available to help. Remember, this is a family project.

By the end of the day, you'll be ready for a hot bath and a chance to relax. Pop some popcorn, sit down with your family, and enjoy discussing the day's activities and the way you'll use your profits.

fifty-nine

You're Moving...Again?

*What is faith? It is the confident assurance
that something we want is going to happen.*

Hebrews 11:1

I have a friend whose husband serves in the U.S. Army. Every time she finally finishes unpacking the last box and begins to feel somewhat acclimated to her new surroundings, her husband comes home from work and says, "Well, it's time to pack up, we're moving next month." In the past 11 years they've moved 11 times.

To most people, the thought of moving does not exactly bring cheers or happy memories. It can, however, be an easy and smooth process if pre-planned and organized.

Before you even begin to organize your move, however, two questions need to be answered clearly: 1) How long do you have to plan your move—one week, one month, or six months? 2) How are you going to move—a "do it yourself" move, a moving company, or a combination of both?

Once you know when and how you are moving, you are ready to begin.

Step 1: Household Check-off List

There are so many details to remember before moving time, and often important things are forgotten until it's too late. Here is a checklist of the essential details that must be taken care of:

227

Transfer of Records
- School records
- Auto registration and driver's license
- Bank—savings and checking accounts
- Medical records from doctors and dentists
- Eyeglass prescription
- Pet immunization records
- Legal documents
- Church and other organizations
- Insurance

Services to Be Discontinued
- Telephone company
- Electric, gas, and water company
- Layaway purchases
- Cleaners—don't move without picking up all your clothes
- Fuel company
- Newspaper delivery
- Cable television
- Pest control
- Water softener or bottled water
- Garbage service
- Diaper service

Change of Address
- Local post office
- Magazines
- Friends and relatives
- Insurance company
- Creditors and charge accounts
- Lawyer
- Church

Step 2: Getting Ready

- Reserve a moving company if needed.

- Prepare to pack by enlisting some volunteers. Neighbors or friends from church are likely candidates and usually very willing to help.

- Collect boxes from local supermarkets and drugstores. Be sure to go to stores early in the day before the boxes are flattened and thrown out. Some moving companies will loan you boxes such as wardrobe boxes.

- Buy felt marking pens to color-code your boxes. (More details on how to do this later.)

- Prepare a work area such as a card table that can be used for wrapping and packing your goods.

- Make a list of items that need special care when being packed, such as your antique lamp or china cup-and-saucer collection.

- Discard flammable materials—empty gas tanks on mowers and chain saw.

- Be sure to leave space open in your driveway or on the street for your truck, trailer, or moving van.

- Keep handy a small box of tools to dismantle furniture.

- Set aside a bucket, rags, and cleaning products to clean your home after it is empty.

Step 3: Packing

Packing your goods properly is the most important part of your move. A little care on your part can assure that none of your things will be damaged.

Use good, sturdy boxes that you can depend on for protection, and be generous in padding your belongings with paper. Packing paper can be purchased at low cost at your local newspaper plant. This unprinted paper is super for wrapping dishes and glassware.

- Begin packing boxes, if possible, two weeks ahead of moving day.

- Either use colored pens or a number system and mark each box to identify its contents and the room where it is to go. For example: yellow—kitchen; green—garden and garage; blue—Brad's bedroom.

  Or number your boxes 1, 2, 3, etc. Then make out 3 x 5 cards and number them Box 1, Box 2, etc. List on each card what is in each box and to which room it belongs. Put your 3 x 5 cards in a small box. On moving day, as each numbered box is carried into the house, direct it to the appropriate room.

  Because you know by your numbered cards what is in each box without opening it, you can unpack the priority boxes first. This is also a great method for organizing the goods you plan to store in your basement or attic.

- Moving is a good time to weed out things you need to get rid of. Although some items should just be thrown out, other things such as old clothing can be given to churches, orphanages, or the Salvation Army.

  Other ways to get rid of excess items are to run an ad in your local paper, or hold a garage sale.

  Remember, when you give away items to nonprofit groups, you can use the net value as a deduction from your income tax. Be sure to get a signed receipt.

- Don't pack fragile and heavy items in the same box.

- Use smaller boxes for heavier items and larger boxes for lightweight, bulky items.

- Fill each box completely and compactly. Don't overfill or underfill.

- When packing glass dishes, put a paper plate between each plate as a protector. Stack plates on end (not flat). They seem to take the pressure better when packed that way.

- Popcorn is another good packing agent for china cups and crystal glasses. Fill the cups and glasses with popcorn and wrap them in your unprinted paper. Foam padding also works well to protect your breakables.

- To protect your mirrors and paintings, cut cardboard to fit around them, bind them with tape and label them "FRAGILE."

- When packing your tables, if possible remove their legs and pack them on edge. If this is not possible, load tables with their surface down and legs up. Take care to protect the finish with blankets or other padding.

    Furniture pads can be wrapped around items and tied together or sewn together temporarily with heavy thread.

- Seal boxes with packing tape, or put the boxes into trash bags and then tape.

- Move your dresser drawers with the clothes inside.

- Be sure bathroom items, medicines, and cleaning agents are packed and sealed immediately so small children cannot get to them.

Loading Your Van, Truck, or Trailer

- Park next to the widest door of your home and leave enough room to extend a ramp if necessary.

- Load your vehicle one quarter at a time, using all the space from floor to ceiling. Try to load weight evenly from side to side to prevent it from shifting.

- Put heaviest items in front.

- Tie off each quarter with rope. This will keep your goods from banging up against each other and getting damaged.

- Use a dolly for the heavy items. (These can be rented from rental equipment or moving companies.) CAUTION: When lifting heavy objects, bend your knees and use your leg muscles. Keep your back as straight as possible.

- Fit bicycles and other odd-shaped items along the walls of the truck or on top of stacked items.

Finish cleaning up your house, lock your door, and you're on your way!

sixty

Corralling the Chaos

She watches carefully all that goes on
throughout her household, and is never lazy.

Proverbs 31:27

One sunday after church service my husband, Bob, and I were visiting with some friends. When one woman asked me about my "More Hours In My Day" ministry, I told her about some of the seminars I had conducted around the country.

All of a sudden, a man who was listening to our conversation grabbed my arm. "Emilie, our family lives in a cesspool," he complained. Thankfully, his wife was not within earshot.

"My wife doesn't work. We have three children; two of them are in school. Yet she says she doesn't have time to clean the house."

Do you think this is an isolated case? It isn't. In today's hectic society, men and women are so busy that often there is no time left to plan and execute the daily routines of life.

For many people, life is lived in a constant panic, trying to stay on top of the house, family, and career. With more women in the work force, there has never been a greater need for basic organizational skills in our homes.

Establishing the Target

If you don't have a goal for organizing your home and life, you can never know if you have hit or missed the target. Much time is wasted because we don't know where we're going.

232

Early in our marriage Bob and I felt it was important to set goals. We dreamed of the type of home and family we wanted. We realized that in order to achieve those dreams we needed a plan. That plan became the "Barnes' Family Life Goals."

We talked often of those goals, and periodically we adjusted them as our lives changed. The biggest change came as we began to mature in our Christian faith. That's when our goals became more Christ-centered.

Goal-setting doesn't just happen. You must take time to think long-range in order to effectively plan for the next few years. And your goals must be important enough to work at making them happen.

Bob and I have set ten-year goals and then we've broken those down into smaller goals. Where do we want to be in five years if we're to fulfill our ten-year goals? What about three years? One year? Six months? Three months? One month? Today?

See the progression? How can we plan today if we don't know where we're headed? Sure, we can fill our time with activities; that's easy. But by goal-setting, everything we do is directed toward a purpose that we've set.

Priorities—What Comes First?

Jean had set her goals and organized her days according to those goals. But she never was able to complete her daily TO DO list.

I asked Jean to show me a typical list of her day's priorities. With 16 activities written on her list, Jean realized she could not possibly do every one of them. She needed to divide these options into three categories:

Yes: I will do this.

Maybe: I will do this if there is time.

No: I will not attempt this today.

Notice the last option? You must learn to say "NO!" Too many women assume that their only options are "yes" and "maybe." If we can't say no to some things, we become overcommitted and wind up carrying heavy loads of guilt because of unfulfilled commitments.

Making Decisions Using Priorities

Just how does a Christian proceed with decisions when the answers are not obvious?

Priority 1: God

According to Matthew 6:33, our first priority is to seek and know God. This is a lifelong pursuit. When God has first place in our lives, deciding among the other alternatives is easier.

When I feel hassled or hurried, it's often because this priority is out of order. Usually I need to adjust my schedule in order to spend time with God. When I allow Him to fill my heart, I can relax and have a clearer perspective on the rest of my activities.

Priority 2: Family

In Proverbs 31 we read about the woman who "watches carefully all that goes on throughout her household, and is never lazy. Her children stand and bless her; so does her husband" (verses 27-28).

How does a woman receive such praise from her family? The answer is by providing a home setting full of warmth, love, and respect.

Priority 3: Church-Related Activities

Hebrews 10:25 tells us to be involved in our church, but that is not at the expense of the first two priorities.

Priority 4: All Other Areas

This includes job, exercise, classes, clubs, and other activities. Some people are amazed that there is time for any of these items. But there is.

God wants you to live a balanced life, and that means you need time for work and time for recreation—time to cut some flowers, drink a cup of tea, or go shopping with a friend. These activities can revitalize you for the responsibilities of home and church.

With these priorities in mind, Jean attacked her list of activities, beginning with the junk mail. "I think I'll just toss the whole pile," she said. By eliminating three more activities and putting four in the "maybe" category, Jean was immediately more relaxed.

I encouraged her to cross off the "yes" activities as she completed each one to give herself the satisfaction of seeing the list shrink during the day. If time permitted, she could do the "maybe" activities, but if she didn't, some of them might become "yes" activities on another day.

Of course, not all decisions can be made swiftly—some require more time and consideration. I've made Paul Little's five-point outline from his booklet *Affirming the Will of God* my criteria when I have trouble establishing my priorities:

1. Pray with an attitude of obedience to the Lord. God's promise to us is, "I will instruct you and teach you in the way you should go; I will counsel you and watch over you" (Psalm 32:8 NIV).

2. What does the Bible say that might guide me in making the decision? "Be diligent to present yourself approved to God as a workman...handling accurately the word of truth" (2 Timothy 2:15 NASB).

3. Obtain information from competent sources in order to gain all the pertinent facts. "A wise man's heart directs him toward the right" (Ecclesiastes 10:2 NASB).

4. Obtain advice from people knowledgeable about the issue. It's best if our counselors are fellow Christians who can pray with and for us. "Iron sharpens iron, so one man sharpens another" (Proverbs 27:17 NASB).

5. Make the decision without second-guessing God. "He who trusts in the Lord will prosper" (Proverbs 28:25 NASB).

The purpose of establishing priorities is to avoid becoming overextended. If you know you are always doing the most important activities first, you can relax even when you cannot complete everything on your TO DO list.

Family Conference Time

Probably the number-one question women ask me when I give a seminar is "How do I get my husband and children involved?" That's a tough question to answer because each family is different.

One mistake many women make is that they assume every family member understands his or her role. They never discuss their expectations with their husband or children. With many mothers working, it is often necessary for other family members to assume some of the responsibilities that are traditionally the woman's. The family needs to understand the concept of *teamwork.*

Mom is not the only player in the family—everyone plays a valuable part. So I first recommend that moms stop carrying the whole team. That only leads to tired, burned-out, frustrated women.

It did not take the Barnes family long to realize that we needed a regular time to discuss important topics. One of our long-range goals was to raise independent and responsible children, and Bob and I felt that one way to achieve this goal was to allow our children to be part of the decision-making process. Yet how could we set aside more time when everyone was already busy with many activities? Our solution also resolved another chronic problem in our home.

Probably the most hectic time for our family was Sunday morning before church. Mom and dad often had a few cross words because we were late. By the time we drove into the church parking lot, we were rarely in a mood for worship.

In order to solve our two problems—stressful Sundays and the need for family meetings—we decided to start going out for breakfast on Sunday mornings before church. Overnight we saw improvement.

Eating breakfast out eliminated the problem of food preparation and cleanup, and it gave us time to discuss various aspects of our family life. We established Sunday breakfasts as part of our regular monthly budget, and all of us looked forward to this time together.

Our family activities and conference times played a valuable part in establishing harmony, respect, and pride within our family. Not every meeting and activity was a success, but we usually gained greater respect for one another.

Family Work Planner

One idea that helped our family better distribute the housework was to establish a "Daily Work Planner." We would write the weekly chores on separate slips of paper, place them in a basket, and every Saturday each of us drew one or more slips to learn our duties for the upcoming week.

As each assignment was drawn, it was recorded on the Daily Work Planner, which was posted in a conspicuous place. Each family member was responsible to complete his assignment. Mom and dad also drew their chores from the basket—this was a team effort.

If your children range widely in their ages, you may want to use two baskets—one for smaller children and one for the rest of the family. In this way, the younger children do not draw jobs that are too difficult for them.

It is also important that mom and dad inspect the work to make sure chores are being done properly. Occasionally, give a special reward for a job well done.

Please note that I am not suggesting that children assume the load in maintaining a house. As parents you must allow your children to participate in their own activities. They need time to get involved in sports, music, homework, and other school and church activities.

You also need to recognize your priorities in relating to your mate. When my children were still at home, I often remembered the saying, "You were a wife to your husband before you were a mother to your children." Our children will grow up and leave home (hopefully). However, we will still have our mate after the nest is empty.

A couple needs to spend quality time with each other without the children. You must not use the excuse that you can't afford to do it. You can't afford *not* to. Bob and I planned times together and reserved those days on our calendar just as we would any other appointment. We protected those times and didn't cancel them unless there was an emergency.

For single parents who are raising children alone, the pressures are even more intense, especially when the children are young. I believe the family conference time and division of responsibilities can help relieve some of the pressure. However, sometimes as a parent—whether married, single, or widowed—you may have to leave some things unfinished rather than continue to tax your spirit.

There are no rules on how a home should be run; each family needs to set its own standards. My family enjoys working together as we set joint goals, but it is a process that takes time.

In his first letter, the apostle Peter wrote that wives could influence their husbands: "Even if any of them are disobedient to the word, they may be won without a word by the behavior of their wives" (1 Peter 3:1 NASB).

Even though the context of this verse deals with salvation, Peter provides an excellent principle. In our society, the mother sets the tone for the family and home. Many times, dad and junior are not as excited about the home as mom is. If you are aware of this truth, you will be disappointed less often because you will not have as many expectations.

We need to remind ourselves that it is not our role to change our husband and children. God will do that in His time. We must be faithful to the Scriptures and love our family even when they may not return that love.

It is important to realize that there are many areas of stress that you can relieve. I have attempted to give some practical helps in many of those areas. Implementing these organizational techniques can help you enjoy more hours in your day and experience more joy in your home.

sixty-one

Keeping Track of Loaned and Borrowed Items

To err is human, to forgive, divine.
Alexander Pope

For many years I loaned items to my friends thinking I would surely remember who had my turkey platter, Tupperware bowls, picnic basket, and the children's sleeping bags. You know what? I forgot after a short period of time. There was no way I could remember, no matter how hard I tried.

It's even more embarrassing to find you have items that don't belong to you and you can't remember who you borrowed them from.

We once had some brick masonry work done on our home and in talking with our contractor he said he had loaned over $500.00 worth of tools to friends but couldn't remember who the friends were. I showed him the form I use and he thought it would be of real value to him (see Figure 9, page 239).

This form will fit very nicely into your 8½ x 5½ organizer notebook for ease in keeping track of all your records.

Remember, to form new habits you must be consistent in using your new organization tools.

One other reminder is to personally identify items you loan with your name and telephone number. This technique will also help get back those missing items.

Make them loaned, not lost!

238

Items Loaned/Borrowed

Month/Year January–February 2003

Date	Item	Who	Returned
1/3	Cake plate	Church	✓
1/4	Screwdriver	Charlie	✓
1/7	Circular saw	Jimmy	✓
1/15	Plastic cups (10)	Brownies	✓
1/22	Lawn mower	George	✓
1/27	Card table	Christine	✓
1/29	Diving mask	Youth group	✓
2/4	Tent	Scout troop	✓
2/5	Posthole digger	Mr. Brown	✓
2/9	Snow White video	daughter	✓
2/12	Pewter pitcher	Georgia	✓

Figure 9

sixty-two

Keeping Track of Those On-Order Products

A good wife watches for bargains.

Proverbs 31:18

Have you forgotten which manufacturer's rebate coupons you have sent in for a refund, or that blouse you have on order from your favorite catalogue? Well, now you can spend a few minutes recording those "on-order" items that need to be tracked until they have been received (see Figure 10, page 242). I even use this form to track refunds from my Visa card and the utility companies.

Add this form to your organizer notebook along with an index tab for easy location and you can keep an easy record.

There are two rules to remember when using an organizer to help you stay on track:

- ◆ You must write it down.
- ◆ You must read it.

It takes 21 days to form a new habit, so continue to write down what's on order. There are many good commercially manufactured organizer notebooks, for which you can pay anywhere from $40.00 to $250.00. Or you can be industrious and make your own organizer. All you need is:

240

- one 8½ x 5½ three-ring binder
- ten 8½ x 5½ index tabs for labeling and dividing your paper by sections
- fifty 8½ x 5½ lined paper
- one 8½ x 5½ month-at-a-glance calendar on two pages
- thirty 8½ x 5½ daily calendar pages to help you through each day

On Order

Date Ordered	Item	Company	Date Due	Received
1/6	white blouse	Lands' End	1/20	✓
1/6	red socks	"	1/20	✓
1/6	plaid slacks	"	1/20	BO
2/3	crib sheets	J.C. Penney	2/17	✓
2/3	crib mattress	"	2/17	✓
2/15	Patio lights	Malibu lights		
	$1.00 rebate			
2/18	Gas rebate	Southern CA	3/1	✓
	$12.00	Gas Co.		
2/22	Credit $17.00	Bank Visa	3/10	✓
2/27	Coupon rebate	Campbell Soup		
	$1.50			
3/2	T-shirts	Sears	3/14	
3/2	white socks	"	3/14	
3/2	Levis	"	3/14	

Figure 10

sixty-three

Setting Up a Desk and Work Area

*The effective prayer of a righteous man
can accomplish much.*

James 5:16 NASB

As I began to get my home in order and to eliminate all the clutter I soon realized that I didn't have an area to handle all the mail and paper that came into our home. We have had several mottos to help us focus in on our home organization.

One was **"Don't put it down, put it away."** Much of our clutter was little piles of materials that needed to be put away, but we just temporarily put it down until we could put it where it belonged. At the end of the day we had piles sitting all around the home. Now we take the material back to where we found it. Amazing how the piles have disappeared.

Another motto was **"Don't pile it, file it."** Somewhere in the corner of the home we had piles of paper that were in no organized fashion. In our new program we have taken manila folders and given them one-word headings such as: insurance, car, home, foods, patio, children, utilities, taxes. Now we file, not pile our papers.

During all this change in our home, we still had no central desk or work area. Yet we had recognized that we needed one in order to function properly and with maximum efficiency.

243

Paper-handling depends upon a good physical setting with a practical location furnished with a comfortable working surface and a good inventory of supplies. Ideally, this office will become a permanent fixture where the business life of your home is done. It should be accessible, with supplies and files, and located where other household operations do not interfere. However, if your desk/work area can't be this ideal, don't let this stop you from getting started. Your work area might have to be portable, but that's okay. The important thing is to *just get started.*

Since a desk or work area is so basic to a well-functioning lifestyle, I'll give you some practical steps in setting up this area in your home.

Choosing the Location

Where your office will be should depend upon how long you plan to spend in your office daily. If you operate a business out of your home you will need to use different criteria in selecting that special site, giving preference to the needs of the business over those of the person who needs a place to open mail, pay bills, and file papers. You want to choose a location that agrees with your spirit. If after a short while you find you aren't using your new space, but rather find yourself working in the room with a big window, you may have selected the wrong location. In order to help you choose that ideal setting, you might ask yourself these questions:

- ◆ Do you need to be in a place where it's quiet, or is it better for you to be near people?
- ◆ Do big windows distract you, or do you like being near windows?
- ◆ Do you prefer a sunny room or a shaded one?
- ◆ Do you prefer to work in the morning or in the afternoon?

These last two questions are related because different rooms receive varying amounts of light at different times of the day.

The answer to these questions helps narrow your alternatives. Walk around your home to see which areas meet the answers to your four questions. After selecting at least two locations, you might ask yourself another set of questions:

- ◆ Are there enough electrical outlets and telephone jacks?
- ◆ Is there enough space for a desk?
- ◆ Is this location out of the way of other household functions? If not, can the activities be shifted so they won't interfere with office hours?
- ◆ Is the area structurally sound?

Again, add the answers to these questions to your previously selected alternatives and narrow your choices to a final selection. Do you feel good about this selection? Live with it a few days before making a final decision. Walk to and through it several times to make sure it feels good. Sit down in the area and read a magazine or book. If it still feels good, then you will probably like your choice.

Don't begin tearing out walls, adding electrical outlets, moving phone jacks, or building bookcases until you are sure it's the right location.

Selection of Desk, Equipment, and Supplies

After you have selected the location for your office, you need to take a sheet of paper and make a diagram of the floor plan with the dimensions listed. You will use this information when you want to make or select furniture for your new work area.

The Desk

In actuality, all one really needs is a writing surface of some type. In some cases a piece of plywood is all you may have or need. Look around. You may already have around your home a suitable desk or table which would fit into the dimensions of the work area.

If you find a table, it should be sturdy, high enough to write comfortably, and large enough to hold various implements on its surface.

If you can't find a desk or table in your home, buy a desk. It is an investment you won't regret. Check your local classified ads to find a good bargain. Another good place to look is in the yellow pages of your phone book under "Office Furniture—Used." You need not pay full price, and many times these stores will deliver to your home free or with a minimum charge.

You should have no trouble finding a desk which has the practical characteristics of office models, but is still attractive in your home. Here are a few specifications to keep in mind.

1. *Writing surface:* Your desk should be sturdy and comfortable to use, with a surface that doesn't wobble.

2. *Place for supplies:* Your desk should have at least one large drawer in which paper and envelopes can be kept in folders. If you find a desk with large drawers on each side, so much the better. There needs to be a shallow drawer with compartments for paper clips, rubber bands, and other supplies. Or you can purchase at your

local stationery store small trays with dividers that can store these small items.

3. *Files and records:* A home office seldom has need for more than one file drawer, or sometimes two. If your desk has at least one drawer big enough to contain letter-size file folders (legal-size accommodation is preferable), all your files will probably fit. If you can't purchase a file cabinet at this time, use Perfect boxes until you are able to purchase a file cabinet. Watch your newspaper for stationery "sale" offerings.

4. *Typing platform:* If you have a computer and plan to use it in your work area, try to get a desk with a built-in platform for it to rest on.

If you don't have enough space for a regular stationery desk in your home, look into portable storage to house your stationery and supplies. Go again to your local office supply store and have them recommend products that will service this need. You will still need a file cabinet or its short-term substitute (the Perfect box) and a sturdy swivel chair just for the office area. The swivel chair permits you to turn from one position to another without getting up.

Other Storage Ideas

- ◆ Wall organizers are helpful for pads, pens, calendars, and other supplies.

- ◆ Paper, pencils, and supplies can be kept in stackable plastic or vinyl storage cubes kept under the desk.

- ◆ Use an extra bookcase shelf for a portable typewriter, a basket of supplies, or some files.

- ◆ Decorative objects such as a ceramic mug look attractive holding pencils and pens.

- ◆ Use stackable plastic bins that can be added to as your needs expand. Use the small style for stationery and papers, and a larger size (a vegetable bin) for magazines and newspapers.

Supplies

For your shopping convenience I have given you a checklist of supplies that you will need to stock your office. Again, try to purchase these items on sale or at an office supply discount store. Watch your local paper for these sales. Or again, let the yellow pages do the walking for you. Look under "Office Supplies." Many times bulk buying is where you will get your best prices.

___ *Address book or Rolodex.* I personally like both; the address book I take with me when I'm traveling or on business, and a Rolodex is permanently housed on my desk. The Rolodex also has more room for adding other information you might want to use when addressing a particular person/business.

___ *Appointment calendar.* Ideally the calendar should be small enough to carry around with your notebook, as well as for use at your desk. If you search around you can find a combination notebook and calendar that isn't too bulky to carry around in your briefcase or handbag. The date squares should be large enough to list appointments comfortably.

___ *Bulletin board.* This is a good place to collect notes and reminders to yourself. Attach notes with push pins.

___ *Business cards.* A must time-saver.

___ *Computer.*

___ *Desk lamp.* A three-way bulb will give you a choice of light.

___ *Dictionary and/or electronic spell-checker.*

___ *File folders.* I use colored "third-cut" folders in which the stick-up tabs are staggered so they don't block my view of other folders. The colors give a more attractive appearance to my file drawer.

___ *Letter opener.*

___ *Liquid paper or correction fluid.*

___ *Marking pens.* It is useful to have on hand a few marking pens in different colors. I do a lot of color-coding on my calendar. I also use a yellow highlighter when I want some information to pop out at me for rereading.

___ *Paper clips.* Regular and large.

___ *Postcards.* Saves money on your mailing.

___ *Pencil sharpener.* If you use a lot of pencils, I recommend a desktop electric model.

__ *Pencils and pens.*

__ *Postage scale.* A small inexpensive type.

__ *Rubber bands.* Mixed sizes.

__ *Rubber stamp and inkpad.* There are all kinds of rubber stamps that you can use in your office. These are much cheaper than printed stationery or labels. If you use a certain one over and over, you might consider having a self-inking stamp made for you. A great time-saver.

__ *Ruler.*

__ *Scissors.*

__ *Scratch paper.* Use lined pads for this. Post-it-Notes are also great.

__ *Scotch tape and dispenser.*

__ *Stamps.* In addition to regular stamps, keep appropriate postage on hand for additional weight and special handling if you have special needs regularly. Postcards will save you money on certain types of correspondence.

__ *Stapler, staples, staple remover.* If you do a lot of stapling you might consider an electric model. Saves time and the palm of your hand.

__ *Stationery and envelopes.* Usually 8½ x 11 plain white paper with matching business-size envelopes is all you need. If you use printed letterhead stationery you will need to get some plain white or matching colored second sheets. I find 9 x 6 and 9 x 12 manila envelopes good for mailing bulk documents, books, or magazines. Sometimes padded envelopes are needed to ship items that need some protection from rough handling in transit.

__ *Telephone.* An extension right at your desk is great. I use my cordless telephone and it works just fine. Not as good as a permanent phone, but a good alternative.

__ *Wastebasket.*

You now have an office space that can function to your maximum. This addition to your lifestyle should certainly make you more efficient in other areas of your life. It will give you a feeling of accomplishment.

Part 8

AUTOMOBILE

sixty-four

A Checklist for Your Car Before Taking a Trip

Stay away from any Christian who spends his days in laziness and does not follow the ideal of hard work.

2 Thessalonians 3:6

As in all phases of life the three most important parts of any project are to PLAN, PLAN, PLAN. Usually things go wrong when we don't spend enough time in our planning phase. Don't be in such a hurry that you forget to plan. Plan to have your car regularly checked by a reliable mechanic and before starting off on that all-important trip. Many times we think of vacations only in the summer months, but depending upon your schedule flexibility you might well take your trip any time of the year.

Having your car checked regularly is the best way to prevent major car problems down the road when you are really counting on your car to perform properly. A combination of getting your car in shape and then paying close attention to the warning signals your car gives to you are key in assuring a car's smooth performance and longevity.

How do you know when your car needs attention? The Car Care Council gives some very practical suggestions.

1. Watch to see if your engine is hard to start, uses too much gas, seems sluggish, smokes, or is excessively noisy.

251

2. Be sure that your cooling and heating systems are in good condition. Be sure to check your hoses, belts, and antifreeze/coolant.

3. How about those tires of yours? Heavy loads at high speeds are hard on tires. Make sure tires have plenty of tread and are properly inflated.

4. How's your oil? Oil is not only a lubricant, it is also a coolant. Clean, well-filtered oil will help your engine survive the heat as well as the cold.

5. Be sure to check your transmission. Does it slip when you shift gears? Is it noisy? Does it shift erratically? If you are towing a trailer, it is especially vital for your transmission to be in the best working order possible.

6. Be sure that the brakes stop evenly and are not making any strange noises.

7. Watch to see that all lights are working and that they are focused correctly. Also check turn signals and windshield wiper blades (for smearing or streaking).

After checking these areas of your car, you can feel more assured of a problem-free trip, barring unforeseen mechanical failure. If you do find yourself in car trouble in an unknown town and don't know of a good, reputable mechanic, you can look in the yellow pages under "Automotive Repairs" for ASE-certified technicians. These technicians have taken the proper courses to be certified by the National Institute for Automotive Service Excellence. This is an organization that is highly respected in the automotive industry, and is an independent, non-profit group which gives voluntary certification exams to technicians.

sixty-five

Pay Me Now or Pay Me Later

*An empty stable stays clean—but there
is no income from an empty stable.*

Proverbs 14:4

As cars become more expensive it is to your advantage to keep a regular maintenance log on each of your cars. If you purchase a new car you will receive an owner's manual that will specify at what intervals you need to service your car and what maintenance is covered by your warranty. However, many people purchase older cars which are no longer covered by the new-car warranty.

As the old saying goes, "Pay me now or pay me later." You can either invest in preventive maintenance or pay more to repair breakdowns due to improper service on your automobile. A well-maintained car will bring greater driving pleasure; it will also be worth more when it is time to sell the older car to buy a newer model.

Place the following form (Figure 11, page 254) in a plastic divider in your glove compartment. Use one column each time the car is serviced. Your mechanic will tell you how often or how many miles you should service your car.

253

Automotive Information and Servicing Schedule

Model _____ Make _____ License Number _____

Serial # _____ Insurance Company _____ Telephone # (___) _____

Use one column each time car is serviced	Date Mileage	Date Mileage	Date Mileage	Date Mileage	Date Mileage	Date Mileage	Date Mileage
Lube, Oil, Filter							
Check Air Conditioning							
Replace Air Filter							
Service Cooling System							
Rotate Tires							
Replace Tires							
Service Brakes							
Check Belts & Hoses							
Engine Tune-up							
Change Trans. Fluid							
Total Cost	$	$	$	$	$	$	$

Figure 11

sixty-six

What to Do When Your Car Won't Start

Jehovah himself is caring for you! He is your defender. He protects you day and night.

Psalm 121:5-6

You're dressed in your finest Sunday clothes waiting for the family to join you in the car for church. You jump in your car, turn the key—and the car plays dead. If you've ever had that happen to you, you know the empty feeling you have.

The children arrive on the scene and of course ask 100 questions, which makes matters worse. What are you to do? Call a friend? A neighbor? A taxi? Or cancel the church service?

The American Automobile Association says failure of cars to start was the most common emergency last year.

Two ways a car can fail to start are 1) the starter motor may turn, but the engine refuses to catch, or 2) the starter motor may be sluggish, perhaps not turning at all.

Let's deal with the second case first.

If you twist the key and you hear only a click, at least you know the ignition switch works. If there was a click and your car has an automatic transmission, move the shift lever into neutral and then back to park and try starting the car again. Sometimes a little switch that prevents you from starting your car while it's in gear, sticks.

255

Still no start? See if the headlights light and the horn honks. If they seem weak, the battery is either dead or has a bad connection.

1. Find where the battery is—usually under the hood.

2. Look closely at the two terminals and the ends of the two cables, positive (+) and negative (−), that attach to them.

3. Are they clean and firmly secured?

4. If not, remove the negative (−) cable (it's usually black) *first*, followed by the positive (+) cable (usually red).

5. Scrape them with a knife or screwdriver and firmly reattach them.

If your car still won't start, you can either push-start it (but only if it has a stick shift) or jump-start it using cables attached to another car's battery. To push-start, you'll need:

1. A couple of strong children or neighbors, *or*

2. An experienced driver who is willing to give you a push from the rear of the car.

3. Get in the car; turn on the ignition.

4. Put your foot on the clutch and put the shift lever in second gear.

5. When the car reaches about 5 mph, let out the clutch and the car should start.

If you are attempting to jump-start your car, be sure to refer to the owner's manual. Great care should be taken when jump-starting your car.

After the car starts, drive to your mechanic's to check out why the battery was low and wouldn't start the engine. You may need a new battery or it may just need to be charged.

The second area to check if your starter turns, but the engine won't start, is the fuel or the ignition system. Be sure to check that you have gas in your tank!

If your car has fuel injection, you will probably want to have the car towed to your mechanic, because these are very hard to service by the average layman. But if it has a carbureted engine:

1. Pump the throttle pedal three times and try to start the car.

2. Still no response? Open the hood.

3. If you smell gas, you have flooded the carburetor.

4. Wait a few minutes.

5. Press the gas pedal all the way to the floor. Hold it there—*don't pump!*

6. The engine should sputter a bit and then start up.

Cold and damp weather present special challenges to a slumbering engine. On a cold day if the starter turns and if you have a carbureted engine:

1. Open the hood and find the air cleaner (usually big and round on top of engine, although sometimes rectangular).

2. Take off the wing nut or retaining clips and lift off the cover of the air cleaner.

3. Spray a little ether starter fluid (available at auto parts stores) down the carburetor throat.

Another useful elixir to carry in your trunk is WD-40; it absorbs moisture. On a damp day, spray some on the coil, some on the spark-plug wires and on the distributor, and some inside the distributor—if you can get the lid off. Then give the starter another turn.

If on a hot day your car refuses to start after it's been running, it may have a "vapor lock." If your car has a mechanical fuel pump (most carbureted engines do), pour cold water on the pump and nearby gas lines, and that should get you on your way.

If you don't have a very difficult problem, you should get to church in time to participate in the services. Try to relax and not get too uptight.

sixty-seven

Car-Care Checklist

O Lord, you are worthy to receive the glory and the honor and the power, for you have created all things.

Revelation 4:11

Without giving it a second thought, we jump into our car, turn the key in the ignition and expect our faithful buggy to start up and take us wherever we want to go.

But a car is an expensive piece of machinery, and, like our bodies, it needs care to run well. Being stuck with car trouble is no fun and can often be avoided.

Here is a checklist to help you keep your car in tiptop shape. It's especially important to give your car a checkup before going on a vacation or an extended trip.

Basic Checklist Before Taking a Trip

Don't be afraid to look over the service attendant's shoulder as he or she checks your car. You'll learn a great deal and can ask questions. Be sure the mechanic checks the following: engine oil level; coolant level (add only if below "add" mark); battery electrolyte level; windshield washer fluid level; and drive belt tension and condition.

Warning!

Do not remove the radiator cap quickly when the engine is hot, especially if the air conditioner has been used. Turn the cap slowly to let the

258

steam escape. Otherwise you will be severely burned by hot water and steam.

Routine Maintenance Checklist

The following items need to be checked, especially before taking a long trip or vacation. Other than taking a trip, check these things twice a year. (The frequency of checkups depends somewhat on the type of climate you live in.)

If you take your car to a service station, don't assume that they automatically check these items. You'll need to ask for some of these services:

- Engine oil changed and filter replaced
- Air filter cleaned or replaced
- Emission control devices checked
- Headlights and brake lights inspected and adjusted
- Differential fluid level checked and changed (if applicable for your car)
- Transmission fluid level checked
- Wheel bearings inspected and repacked (once a year)
- Brakes inspected (once a year)
- Air-conditioning system checked and serviced once a year
- Cooling system hoses checked and coolant/antifreeze replaced once a year
- Power steering fluid level checked
- Shock absorbers tested
- Battery inspected
- Drive belts checked
- Windshield wipers. Even in summer you will need to replace if needed, in case of summer rainstorms.
- Tire tread depth and inflation pressure checked
- Exhaust system inspected for leaks
- Tune-up. Refer to owner's manual for manufacturer's suggestion for how often a tune-up is needed.

Emergency Organization List

These items should be carried in your car at all times in case of emergency:

- Fire extinguisher
- Jumper cables
- First-aid kit (bee-sting kit)
- Towel(s)
- Flashlight with extra batteries
- Ice scraper
- Spare fuses for electrical system
- Can of tire inflater/sealer
- Flares and/or highway triangular warning signs
- Spare drive belts, fan belts, air-conditioner belts, and air pump belts
- An empty approved gasoline container. *Do not carry extra gasoline in the trunk.*
- Container of water
- Warm blanket
- Metal or wire coat hanger
- Distress flag
- Plastic dropcloth for working under car
- Toolbox with the following: Pliers; screwdriver; adjustable wrench; small socket wrenches; hammer; cleanup wipes for hands; clean rag

Winter Tools

Chains, small shovel, can of sand, extra blankets or heavy coat for emergencies, heavy boots, and gloves.

It may seem overwhelming at first to furnish your car with these items, but it's well worth it. Being prepared could save a life or get you out of a dangerous or difficult situation. Besides, being ready for emergencies and keeping your car tuned up will relieve another whole area of stress in your life.

sixty-eight

Automobile Organization—
Travel Smart!

*Love forgets mistakes; nagging about them
parts the best of friends.*

Proverbs 17:9

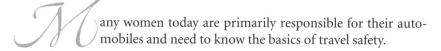

any women today are primarily responsible for their automobiles and need to know the basics of travel safety.

Be Prepared

Here is a helpful checklist of items to take with you in your car so you'll be prepared and ready to prevent minor roadside difficulties from becoming major ones.

Plan Ahead

Glove Compartment

- ◆ Maps
- ◆ Notepad and pen
- ◆ Tire-pressure gauge
- ◆ Cleanup wipes
- ◆ Sunglasses
- ◆ Mirror (best placed above sun visor)

261

- Extra pair of nylon hosiery for that unexpected run.
- Reading material, Bible—you can enjoy prayer and Bible reading during waiting times in the car.
- Can opener
- Plastic fork and spoon, for those yummy stops
- Change for phone calls
- Business cards
- Band-Aids
- Matches
- Stationery—again, waiting can be used constructively to catch up on correspondence.
- Scissors, nail clippers
- Children's books and/or games

Trunk

(See "Emergency Organization List" on page 260 for car-care items that should be carried in case of emergencies.)

Protect Your Ownership

- Hide a key for the times you lock your keys inside the car. Caution: Don't put it under the hood if you have an inside hood-release.

- A good idea to prove ownership of your car is to print your name, address, and phone number on a 3 x 5 file card or use your business card and slide it down your car window-frame on the driver's side. If the car is lost or stolen, it is easier to prove the auto is yours.

- If you live in a potentially snowy area, keep a bag of kitty litter in your trunk. This will help give you traction if you are stuck in the snow.

- Your rubber car mats can be used to keep windshields from freezing. Put them on the outside of windows under your wipers to hold them in place, and presto...clean windows and no scraping either.

- Your car may not start if your battery terminals become corroded. Simply scrub them with a mixture of one cup of baking soda and two cups water. It cleans them right up.

- To remove decals and price lists from windows, simply sponge with plenty of white vinegar. Allow vinegar to soak in and stickers should come off easily. Fingernail polish remover also works well.

- A rechargeable, battery-run, hand vacuum cleaner is very handy to have. It can be used to clean inside the car, carpet, and seats.

Part 9

TIME FOR YOU

sixty-nine

Time for You—
Personal Grooming

Rejoice in the LORD, ye righteous; and give thanks at the remembrance of his holiness.

Psalm 97:12 KJV

The old adage "You only get one time to make a first impression" is certainly true. We live in a time in history that stresses personal grooming. As Christians we need to keep moderation in mind and not be out of balance, but we must also be aware that we often conduct ourselves based on how we feel about our personal grooming. As I go shopping, I realize as I look at people that it takes so little to be above average. God wants us to be groomed properly as we go out into the secular world to be ambassadors for Him. Because how we look can affect our personal witness of who we are, I trust that some of these ideas will be helpful for your improved grooming.

Shampooing Your Hair

Lather hair twice only if very oily or very dirty. Otherwise you'll strip your hair of natural oils.

Don't be surprised if your favorite shampoo seems to leave your hair less bouncy after months of satisfactory performance. No one is exactly sure why but "shampoo fatigue" may be due to a buildup of proteins or other conditioning ingredients. Many people switch brands, only to perceive a drop in performance with the new shampoo within several months. At that point try switching back to the old one.

When you need a dry shampoo, try bran, dry oatmeal, baby powder, or cornstarch. Use a large-holed shaker or an empty baby-powder container to apply. Wash through hair with your fingers and brush out thoroughly.

Conditioning Your Hair

If you have an oily scalp, but dry or damaged hair, condition hair before you shampoo. Wet your hair, towel it dry, and then apply conditioner, starting an inch from your scalp. Work conditioner through your hair, wait five minutes, and rinse. Then shampoo as usual.

To revitalize and give luster to all types of hair: Beat three eggs; add two tablespoons olive or safflower oil and one teaspoon vinegar. Apply mixture to hair and cover with plastic cap. Wait half an hour and then shampoo well.

Here's a hair conditioner that is bound to draw raves! Combine ¾ cup olive oil, ½ cup honey, and the juice of one lemon and set aside. Rinse hair with water and towel dry. Work in a small amount of conditioner (store leftovers in the refrigerator), comb to distribute evenly, and cover with a plastic cap for 30 minutes. Shampoo and rinse thoroughly.

When swimming daily in chlorinated or salt water, alternate hair care, using shampoo one day and conditioner the next.

Skin Products

A patch test for skin-care products: If you suspect you may be allergic to any substance, put a dab of it inside your wrist or elbow, cover it with an adhesive bandage, and leave it on for 24 hours. If no redness or irritation is evident, the product is probably safe. Because you can become allergic to something you have used regularly, repeat this test whenever you haven't used a substance in several weeks and are concerned about a reaction from that product.

Change brands if you are experiencing a rash or lesions, or think you have an allergic reaction.

Cleansing Your Skin

To cleanse your face thoroughly, try the following method: Fill a clean sink with warm water, dip facial soap into the water, and rub the bar over your face. Dip the soap back into the water and make a lather in your hands. Massage this lather over your face. Rinse 15 to 20 times with the soapy water. Finish off with several cold-water rinses. Blot your face dry with a towel.

Excessive stinging or drying are signs that your toner, astringent, or aftershave lotion is too strong. Change brands or add one teaspoon of mineral water to each ounce of the product.

Hot weather tip: Refrigerate your facial toner, freshener, or astringent for a cool skin treat.

Bathing

In winter, your bath or shower water should be tepid—not hot, since hot water inflames the skin and increases moisture loss afterwards. Apply a moisturizing lotion right after bathing while your skin is still damp.

A simple but effective way to relieve dry skin and winter itch is to completely dissolve one cup of salt in a tub of water and bathe as usual. (For a more luxurious bath, try sea salt.) Bathing in salt often works better than using expensive bath oils, but if you really want to use oil, a plain mineral oil will generally fulfill your needs.

Moisturizing Your Skin

Always apply a moisturizer right after cleansing to prevent the surface moisture from evaporating. Moisturizers should last about ten hours. If your face feels tight before that time, freshen it with a toner and reapply your moisturizer. You may need a richer moisturizer.

Don't forget to moisturize your throat area. If this area is especially dry, heat peanut oil until warm and massage upward into your skin.

To avoid that cracked, flaky look on your elbows, make it a habit to pay special attention to them at the same time you lubricate the rest of your body.

If you have begun to get lines around your eyes and want to make them less obvious, rub eye cream between your fingertips to warm it before patting it around the eye area. This makes it easier for the skin to absorb the cream. Do not pull or stretch the skin around the eyes.

Sun Protection

Give your skin time to absorb a sunblock's ingredients before you need them. Apply sunscreen a half-hour before you go outdoors; reapply after you swim or if you perspire heavily.

Take a long lunch hour away from outdoor exposure. The sun is highest in the sky and is most intense between the hours of 10:00 in the morning and 2:00 in the afternoon.

If you're planning on spending some time outdoors, use a moisturizing sunblock or sunscreen along with your regular moisturizer. Choose an SPF (sun protection factor) keyed to your skin's response to the sun. A fair person needs an SPF of 12 to 15.

Makeup Foundation

If you never seem to buy the right shade of foundation, try applying it just under the jawline rather than on the wrist. It should be just slightly lighter than your skin tone.

To transform a heavy, oil-based foundation into one that glides on more smoothly, add a bit of moisturizer or salt-free mineral water to the foundation. Use your palm or a small dish—not the makeup container—to do the mixing.

Blushers and Powders

For those "gray" days, mix a drop of liquid blusher with your foundation. Spread this instant glow all over your skin.

When you're feeling tired and dragged out, use blusher very lightly around the entire outer contour of your face, from the hairline to the chin, blending with a cosmetic sponge.

Under fluorescent lights, which destroy the rosy tones in the skin and give a yellowish look, apply your blusher a little darker and use a little deeper-colored lipstick.

Store loose powder in an old salt or pepper shaker so that you can shake it into your palm. Then dip a makeup brush or puff into the powder and dust it on.

Eye Makeup

Eye makeup is perishable. Bacteria from your eyes can be introduced to the product. Wash applicators frequently or use cotton swabs. Also, label shadows, pencils, and mascaras with their purchase dates. Replace your shadows and pencils every six months, your mascara every three months.

If you use liquid eyeliner, try dotting it on along the lash line. It will look less harsh than a solid line.

To get the sharpest point on your eyebrow, eyeliner, and lip pencils, put them in the freezer for an hour before sharpening.

Tame unruly eyebrows with a little bit of styling gel or mousse applied with an eyebrow brush.

Lip Care

Your lipstick will stay on much longer if you use the following method. Layer on in this order: face powder, lipstick, powder, lipstick. Wipe off excess powder with a damp washcloth or a tissue.

Remove Makeup

Never go to sleep without removing every trace of your makeup—except on your wedding night! Habitually sleeping with a layer of dirt, debris, and dead skin cells stuck to your face will leave your complexion looking muddy and dull.

When you're removing mascara, if it seems to get all over your face, wrap a tissue around your index finger and hold it just under the lower lashes. Remove eye makeup as usual with the other hand.

You are now well on your way of making that first good impression—may it wear well on you!

seventy

Organizing Your Prayer Time

Be anxious for nothing, but in everything by prayer and supplication, with thanksgiving, let your requests be made known to God.

Philippians 4:6 NKJV

During my early years of motherhood, I became frustrated about my personal prayer time. I wanted to spend quality time with my Lord but due to a busy schedule it just never worked out in a practical way.

One day through some trial and error I came up with a prayer organization that worked for me. Here's what I did.

1. *Prayer Noteboook.* I purchased an inexpensive binder (5½ x 8½), one package of tabs, and one package of lined paper. The tabs were labeled "Monday," "Tuesday," "Wednesday," etc. Next I made a list of all things I wanted to pray for—family, finances, church, missionaries, etc. I then delegated these requests into my prayer notebook behind each tab. On Monday I now pray for each member of the family. On Tuesday I pray for our church, the pastor, the staff, etc. On Wednesday, I pray for people who are ill, and so on. The Sunday tab is for sermon notes and outlines. I filter any prayer requests into the weekly tabs so my prayer time does not overwhelm me. I spend time reading my Bible, then I open my prayer

notebook to the tab for that day. I pray for the items behind that tab. The next day I do the same, moving on through the next week.

2. *Prayer Basket.* Try the following steps:

   a. Purchase a medium-size basket with a handle.

   b. Place in your basket your Bible, prayer notebook, a few post-cards, a box of tissue, and a small bunch of silk flowers.

   c. Place your basket in an area you pass daily, perhaps on a table, the kitchen counter, your desk, or in the bathroom, etc.

   d. Schedule a daily time to spend time with your prayer basket in the morning, afternoon, or evening. Plan this time (5 to 50 minutes) to pick up your basket and take it to a quiet place where you will use the ingredients during your prayer time.

      ◆ The Bible—read God's Word daily.

      ◆ Pray for the daily requests.

      ◆ Write a short note to someone who needs encouragement on your postcards. Or you might simply say, "I prayed for you today." Some days I cry through my whole prayer time. My tissue is right there in my basket. The flowers give encouragement and lighten my heart as I look at God's creation.

My prayer basket is so personal and special to me. Some days I walk by my basket and it may be three o'clock in the afternoon. It says to me, "Emilie, you haven't picked me up today." What a reminder and what a challenge to my heart and spirit to pick up my prayer basket, putting it to use every day in spending special time with my Lord.

Proverbs 16:3 says, "Commit your works to the Lord, and your plans will be established" (NASB).

The days I pick up my prayer basket, my day, my life, and my organization as a busy woman go so much smoother. I have strength to meet the schedules and stresses that usually come.

seventy-one

New Year Organization

Oh, give thanks to the Lord, for he is good;
his love and his kindness go on forever.

1 Chronicles 16:34

After finishing a seminar on how to organize your household, I talked to a young mother who said, "I loved all the organizational ideas and tips you gave for the family and the home, but what about me—my personal organization?" Organization really does begin with our own personal lives. Once we have ourselves organized, we can move into the other areas of our lives such as our home or job.

Here are the tools you need to make your own daily planner.

- ◆ A small purse-size binder with paper
- ◆ Blank tabs you can label yourself
- ◆ A calendar

Label your tabs in the following way.

Tab 1: Goals

List long-range and short-range goals including daily, weekly, monthly, and yearly priorities. This will help you get your priorities in order. Include the following: Scriptures to read, prayer requests, priorities to accomplish, and family goals, as well as spiritual, household, work-related, financial, and budget goals.

Tab 2: Calendar

Purchase a small month-at-a-glance calendar at a stationery store and insert it into your binder. As you learn to write activities and commitments down, you will be surprised at how much less complicated your life becomes.

Tab 3: Daily Planner

In this section, list your daily appointments from morning to evening. This is not only useful for the mother who works outside her home but also for the homemaker who wants to get her daily household duties done in a more orderly manner.

Tab 4: To Do, To Buy

Make a note here of all the things you need to do when you have an errand day, such as:

- ◆ Pick up winter coat at the cleaners.
- ◆ Go to the grocery store for birthday candles.
- ◆ Take package to the post office.
- ◆ Buy vitamins at health food store.

Tab 5: Notes

Here is a place to write down notes from:

- ◆ Speakers and sermons
- ◆ Meetings and Bible studies
- ◆ Projects

Tab 6: Miscellaneous

Keep topical lists in this section such as:

- ◆ Emergency phone numbers
- ◆ Dentist/physician
- ◆ Babysitters' phone numbers
- ◆ Favorite restaurant phone numbers
- ◆ Books and music recommended

Tab 7: Expense Account

This section is especially for work-related expense outside the home.

- ◆ Who it was for and the amount and how it was paid for (cash, credit card, or check)

- ◆ What it was for: transportation, parking, food, promotion, or gas

Tab 8: Prayer Requests

Make colored insert tabs for each day of the week, Sunday through Saturday. Then write a comprehensive list of your prayer requests along with those of your friends and family, and divide them into five special lists. Assign each list to one day for one week, Monday through Friday. Leave Saturday as a swing day for immediate prayer requests.

Sunday's section should be left open for the pastor's sermon. That way you have a history of Scripture and content for later reference or study. If someone mentions a prayer request at church, you can assign it to a special day of the week when you get home.

In this way you can cover your prayer needs over a week's time. Date the request when you enter it into your book and then record the date when it is answered. Over a period of time you will have a history of how God has worked in your life. Remember, too, that not all prayers are immediately answered by "yes" or "no." Some are put "on hold" for awhile.

I'll guarantee that by implementing these few helpful ideas into your new year, you'll be on your way to the "organized you."

seventy-two

How to Organize
Your Handbag

*Keep alert and pray. Otherwise temptation
will overpower you. For the spirit indeed
is willing, but how weak the body is!*

Matthew 26:41

Remember the last time you rummaged through your handbag digging through old receipts, papers, tissue, half-used lipsticks, unwrapped Lifesavers, and that unmailed letter you thought was lost months ago? Handbags have a way of becoming catchalls, places where you have everything and can find nothing. You can get your handbag into top shape with just a little effort and organization. If you keep a well-organized handbag, it will be so simple to change bags and do it quickly.

Materials Needed

A nice-size handbag for everyday and three to seven small purses in various colors and sizes. (The small purses can be of quilted fabric, denim, or corduroy prints with zipper or velcro fasteners.)

How to Organize

1. *Wallet*
   Money/checkbook

277

   Change compartment
   Pen
   Credit cards
   Pictures
   Driver's license
   Calendar (current)

2. *Makeup Bag 1*
   Lipstick
   Comb/small brush
   Blush
   Mirror
   Phone change

3. *Makeup Bag 2*
   Nail file
   Small perfume
   Hand cream
   Nail clippers
   Scissors (small)
   Tissues
   Breath mints/gum/cough drops
   Matches

4. *Eyeglass Case*
   For sunglasses

5. *Eyeglass Case*
   For reading/spare glasses

6. *Small Bag 1*
   Business cards—yours & your husband's, hair dresser, insurance
      agent, auto club, doctor, health plan
   Library card
   Seldom-used credit cards
   Small calculator
   Tea bag
   Artificial sweetener
   Aspirin

7. *Small Bag 2*
   Reading material—small Bible, paperback book

Toothbrush
Cleanup wipes
Needle/thread/pins/thimble
Band-Aid
Toothpicks
Tape measure
Feminine protection

By taking some time to set it up, you can organize your purse and avoid last minute frustration and stress.

seventy-three

Planning a Picnic for Happy Memories

Create in me a new, clean heart, O God,
filled with clean thoughts and right desires.

Psalm 51:10

un-filled memories of special family times can happen by taking a picnic meal to the park, lake, mountains, beach, desert, or favorite picnic area.

I was four years old when we took a picnic lunch to the desert under a yucca tree. The setting doesn't sound real exciting but I can still remember the green-and-white checkered tablecloth my mother pulled out and spread on the ground, along with plates, glasses, silver utensils, and delicious food. She took me by the hand and we picked a few wild desert flowers for the table. Later we took a nature walk and collected fun memories.

Picnics are for everyone and loved by everyone, and they can be planned for any time of the year (though as the weather begins to warm up, the creative picnics seem to warm up too). Early American picnics were called "frolics" and consisted of games, music, flirtations, and good food. Keep this in mind as you keep your American picnics filled with the same ingredients.

You can plan themes around your region or other regions of our country or even the world. Some ideas might be:

♦ A Vermont Snow Snack

- A New England Clam Bake
- A Hawaiian Luau
- An Abalone Steak Picnic
- A San Francisco Crab Lunch
- An Indian Summer Brunch
- Mexican Memories
- A Mardi Gras Feast
- A Pumpkin Patch Picnic

These themes are starting points to plan our food selections. Draw the family into this planning and research for what food you are going to take along for this special event. Don't make this just a mom's project—involve the whole family. The Mardi Gras feast might include chicken gumbo, steamed rice, marinated green beans, and New Orleans King Cake.

The pantry is a good source for the basic food selections. If you need to make a market run to purchase special items, do so at a time when the store is less crowded. Try early in the morning or late in the evening. Stay away from peak shopping hours.

Keeping Foods Cold

Once you have purchased and/or prepared your food, you need to plan how to keep your food cold. The length of time in which food can spoil is relative to the temperature outdoors, but it also depends upon the way the food was cooked, chilled, wrapped, and carried. Foods containing mayonnaise, eggs, cream, sour cream, yogurt, or fish are safe unrefrigerated up to two hours if the weather is fairly cool. If it will be more than two hours before you eat, plan to carry along a refrigerated cooler. Cool dishes as quickly as possible after preparing them and leave them in the refrigerator until just before time to leave. *Remember: Never take anything on a picnic that could possibly spoil unless you can provide effective portable refrigeration.*

There are a lot of excellent commercial coolers on the market. Select a size that will be adequate for your family's need. You can chill food in the cooler by using ice cubes, crushed or chipped ice, blocks from ice machines, or blocks frozen in clean milk cartons or other containers. Or you can fill plastic bottles (two-thirds full) with water to allow for expansion and freeze them overnight. These frozen containers eliminate the mess of melted ice.

Packing, Transporting, and Safe-Storing Tips

Prepare all food as close to departure time as comfortably possible for you. Don't cook in advance earlier than the time recommended in the recipe unless the item can be frozen successfully.

Try to pack your hamper or other carryall in reverse order from the way in which you'll use each item at the site. Place your food containers right-side-up to prevent spills and breakage.

Breakable glassware can be wrapped in the tablecloth, napkins, kitchen towels, or newspaper.

Foods such as pies, tarts, cakes, muffins, mousses, molded salads, or home-baked breads that crumble easily can be carried in the pans in which they were prepared. If the supplies do not fill the hamper, fill in with rolled newspaper or paper towels to prevent foods from overturning or bumping together.

Bags

Shopping bags are excellent for holding many items for a simple picnic. Use those fancy, attractive bags for transporting excess items that won't fit into the main picnic hamper. You might also want to carry along a large bag for your unwanted trash. Leave the site clean.

Ground Covers and Tablecloths

Choose a blanket, patchwork quilt, bedspread, sheet, comforter, afghan, or any large piece of fabric for a ground cover and tablecloth. Top it, if you like, with a decorative second cloth that fits the mood of the picnic you've planned.

No-iron cotton or synthetic fabric is easy to keep clean and ready for traveling. Other choices to consider are beach towels, bamboo or reed matting, nylon parachute fabric, flannel shirt material, or lengths of any easy-care fabric stitched at each end.

Purchase one or two plastic painters' drop cloths or carry a canvas tarpaulin to put down before you spread the tablecloth if the ground is damp, dusty, or snow-covered.

Baskets/Hampers

Wicker baskets or hampers are the traditional picnic carryalls. However, anything goes these days. Import shops sell baskets made in many different shapes, sizes, and price ranges.

The important thing is the time spent with your family and friends sharing your love together.

seventy-four

Beating Jet Lag in Travel

*Praise ye the Lord. O give thanks unto the Lord,
for he is good, for his mercy endureth forever.*

Psalm 106:1

We live in a fast-paced world of travel, and many times our body suffers as a result. We find ourselves unable to function as we should even though we have important business and social functions to perform.

As I travel throughout our continent I do certain things that help me minimize the effects of jet lag on my speaking schedule.

Jet lag is caused by rapid air travel over multiple time zones. The sudden change in time upsets synchronized body rhythms, resulting in physical and mental confusion. Research shows that the human body clock, set by stimuli like light and diet, can be "tricked" into adjusting to a new schedule. Here are some facts about jet lag and tips to avoid it.

Effects on the Body Clock

Many of our body cycles are affected by jet lag. We find rapid increases in our heartbeat, breathing, cell division, eye blinking, and swallowing. Our daily cycles of blood pressure, eyesight, mental ability, physical ability, sleep/wake rhythm, digestion, reproduction, temperature, metabolism, and sense of time are also disturbed.

283

Symptoms of Jet Lag

Some of the early signs of jet lag are fatigue, disorientation, reduced physical ability, reduced mental ability, upset appetite, and off-schedule bowel and urinary movements. Later symptoms of constipation or diarrhea, insomnia, acute fatigue, loss of appetite, headaches, lack of sexual interest, and slowed response-time to visual stimulation are also negative side effects.

Fighting Off Jet Lag

◆ *Diet.* Eating certain foods helps adjust the body clock. Foods high in carbohydrates induce sleep; those high in protein produce wakefulness. On a typical seven-hour flight over several time zones, you might try the following schedule to help reduce jet lag.

— *Three days before flight.* Eat a high-protein breakfast and lunch, a high-carbohydrate dinner, and caffeinated drinks (if you use) between 3:00 P.M. and 4:30 P.M. only.

— *Day of flight.* Get up earlier than usual, eat a high protein breakfast and lunch, a high-carbohydrate dinner, and shortly after 6:00 P.M., drink two to three cups of black coffee. Reset watch to destination time.

— *During flight, day of arrival.* Don't oversleep. A half-hour before breakfast (destination time) activate your body and brain, eat a high-protein breakfast and lunch, a high-carbohydrate dinner, drink, no caffeine, avoid napping, and go to sleep at 10:00 P.M. (destination time).

◆ *Consult an aircraft seating chart.* Request bulkhead or emergency exit seats, which have more leg room.

◆ *Don't drink alcohol.* It causes dehydration. Drink water.

◆ *Sleep and eat on your destination time schedule.* Ask the flight attendant to serve your meals at your specified time.

◆ *Avoid big meals.* Air pressure causes gas in the intestines to expand.

◆ *Request a special meal from the airline.* Do this 24 hours in advance if needed.

◆ *Don't wear contact lenses.* On long flights, they dry out.

◆ *Bring a game or book.* This will provide mental stimulation.

◆ *Don't cross your legs.* This interferes with blood circulation.

seventy-five

Tips to Start and Organize a Home Business

She considers a field and buys it;
out of her earnings she plants a vineyard.

Proverbs 31:16 NKJV

Today, more women are feeling the desire to be at-home mothers and career women. That's exciting. We are beginning to see the working woman find balance between work and home, with a new interest in home business (85 percent of new businesses are started by women in their homes). Many women will make a personal choice to be at home, while many will continue jobs outside due to need or desire.

My mother became a single working parent when my father died. I was 11 years old. She opened a small dress shop and we lived in the back in a small, three-room apartment. Home and career were mixed. Mom not only sold clothing but worked late into the night doing alterations. Bookkeeping was also done after hours. We survived because we all helped in a time of need. When our children were small I developed a small business out of our home; the extra money was for extra things. I was able to do that because I felt somewhat organized and in control of our home.

This may very well be the year God will bring into your life the desire to be an at-home woman and develop a from-home business. Yes, to be successful it does take time, creativity, balance, and desire. Our ministry, "More Hours In My Day," began in our home. Books have been written, seminars given, and mail orders sent from our door to many of yours.

A dear and longtime friend, Rose, has a small business called "Tiffany Touch" where she goes into other people's homes in her area and does everything from organizing drawers to hanging pictures. A mother with a new baby designed a slip-over-the-head bib that is sold all over the country out of her home. Still another mom created designer baby bottles.

Connie Lund, out of Olympia, Washington created a small devotional flip chart of inspiration called "Reaching Up to God" and through their sales sent her daughter through college. Most at-home businesses develop family oneness, with everyone working together to help one another.

Direct sales are popular and profitable. Tupperware, Avon, Shaklee, Amway, Mary Kay, Home Interiors, Christmas Around the World, Successful Living Books, Choice Books—from home parties to door-to-door, these are just a few.

One woman I read about shops for working women, buying groceries and gifts, and running errands from picking up dry cleaning to buying stamps at the post office. She even delivered a lunch to a schoolchild who forgot it at home.

Another creative mom started gift wrapping for people (men in offices), which led to food baskets and then homemade wreaths and flower arrangements.

Another mom advertised her famous chili recipe for $1—and sold enough to buy Christmas presents for the whole family. She was very pleased and surprised. Aimee made colorful earrings. Women saw them on her and wanted a pair for themselves. From friends to boutique shops, sales multiplied.

All kinds of arts and crafts have created many added funds for the family income.

I was visiting some friends who received an adorable loaf of bread shaped like a teddy bear, a novelty gift that is now being shipped all over the state.

Nancy is a single parent who quit her computer job and started her own service in her home. She is able to be home with her three children and still run a very successful business.

Nancy and Elizabeth teamed up and are designing and selling Christian greeting cards, business cards, and Christmas cards, and are doing very well.

Some women are working at home as employees—sales reps, technical service reps, claim adjusters, and many others who are unsalaried employees but who spend most of their time in the field. Their employers typically don't provide an office so their files, desk phone, etc. are in their homes. Many other women could do part-time employment in the same way. Naturally you have to ask yourself if you have the space in your home for such types of employment.

I have a friend who represents designer clothing out of her home four times a year. She sends out invitations with days and hours, then books appointments and helps the women coordinate their wardrobes.

Set your desires high and chart out your goals for your future. Where would you like to be next year at this time? What will you need to accomplish to get there?

When can you start? Possibly now. 1) Your desire is to be working from home—by next year. 2) Make calls and talk with friends, family, and business associates. 3) Perhaps you need to take a class on business, sales, design, etc.

Many of you may be happy just working where you are. Others may want to cut hours to be at home a little more. Whatever you want to accomplish this year you can do with a positive attitude, desire, and creativity wrapped with prayer.

My desire is to see the busy woman get back to traditional values and to use her God-given creativity wherever she may be—in or out of the home. Changes will come in the future as they have in the past, but yours can come with a positive outlook and priorities of God, family, and career.

The following are some ideas and tips on how to implement or begin a business at home.

Research

1. Find others who are in your same field of home business and talk with them. They can provide a wealth of information.

2. Will it benefit you to advertise in your local telephone book?

3. What kind of advertising should you use other than word of mouth?

Goals

1. Determine a time schedule to be at home with your business. Example: Within one year.

2. Sign up for a class at your local community college on simple business bookeeping.

Finances

1. Draw up a projected budget for yourself. What will be your credits, your debits? How much money do you need to launch your business?

2. Consider the costs involved in advertising.

3. Set aside some money for start-up expenses and supplies such as a computer, copy machine, furniture, and for small desk-top items, such as stapler, scissors, etc.

4. Start writing down hidden costs. There will always be expenses that you did not count on so the more research you do the less likely you will be to have a lot of surprises.

Home Preparation

1. How much space do you need and what area will you use?

2. Can you use your same phone system?

3. Do you need a desk, work tables, file cabinets, etc.?

4. Will any carpentry work be required?

Legalities

1. Get information on what legal matters need to be considered. Some home businesses will require a business license. Check with your local county records department.

2. Obtain a resale number if needed.

3. What kind of deductions are you eligible for? It is advisable to contact a CPA who is knowledgeable in the field of home business deductions.

Hours

1. Think through how many hours you will reasonably be able to work per day, per week, per month.

2. Will you need to work around children's schedules?

3. Will you have regular business hours?

4. When will you clean your home, cook meals, etc.?

5. Don't forget you—schedule time to do a few things for yourself, such as hair appointments, shopping, church, friends, Bible studies, etc.

Like many situations, there will be a lot of trial and error. You'll learn much as you grow along, and the benefits will be great!

Part 10

MISCELLANEOUS

seventy-six

27 Things to Help You Survive an Earthquake

We are hard-pressed on every side, yet not crushed.

2 Corinthians 4:8 NKJV

In California we are always concerned about the earth moving. Animals often hear the rumble of the earth before their owners sense that something is about to happen. It is truly an experience that a person will never forget—his or her first earthquake and every one thereafter.

If you live in California or some other earthquake-prone area, or are planning to visit such an area for business or pleasure, you may want to become familiar with the following recommendations as suggested by the American Red Cross.

Basics to Do During an Earthquake

1. Stay CALM.

2. *Inside:* Stand in a doorway, or crouch under a desk or table, away from windows or glass dividers.

3. *Outside:* Stand away from buildings, trees, and telephone and electric lines.

4. *On the road:* Drive away from underpasses, overpasses; stop in safe area; stay in vehicle.

293

Basics to Do After an Earthquake

1. Check for injuries—provide first aid.

2. Check for safety—check for gas, water, and sewage breaks; check for downed electric lines and shorts; turn off appropriate utilities; check for building damage and potential safety problems during aftershocks, such as cracks around chimney and foundation.

3. Clean up dangerous spills.

4. Wear shoes.

5. Turn on radio and listen for instructions from public safety agencies.

6. Use the telephone only in emergency situations.

Basic Survival Items to Keep on Hand

1. Portable radio with extra batteries.

2. Flashlight with extra batteries.

3. First-aid kit, including specified medicines needed for members of your household.

4. First-aid book.

5. Fire extinguisher.

6. Adjustable wrench for turning off gas and water.

7. Smoke detectors properly installed.

8. Portable fire escape ladder for homes and apartments with multiple floors.

9. Bottled water sufficient for the number of members in your household for a week.

10. Canned and dried foods sufficient for a week for each member of your household. *Note:* Both water and food should be rotated into normal meals of household so as to keep freshness. Canned goods have a normal shelf-life of one year for maximum freshness.

11. Nonelectrical can opener.

12. Portable stove such as butane or charcoal. *Note:* Use of such stoves should not take place until it is determined that there is no gas leak in the area. Charcoal should be burned only out of doors. Use of charcoal indoors will lead to carbon monoxide poisoning.

13. Several dozen candles. The same caution should be taken as in the above note on portable stoves.

14. Matches.

15. Telephone numbers of police, fire, and doctor.

Basics You Need to Know

1. How to turn off gas, water, and electricity.

2. Basic first aid.

3. Plan for reuniting your family.

As with any emergency program that you have for your family, you must review it every three months to make sure the members of your family know what to do in case of an earthquake. The plan for evacuating the home and the plan for reuniting the family if the various members of the family are away from home should be walked through so the instructions are thoroughly understood by all members of the family.

Remember, *the best survival is a prepared survival!*

seventy-seven

Record-Keeping Made Simple

No one can become my disciple unless he first sits down
and counts his blessings—and then renounces them all for me.

Luke 14:33

his is the year to get our records, bills, and receipts out of shoe-boxes, closets, drawers, and old envelopes. I found that I could clean out my wardrobe closet fairly easily. I could toss an old skirt, stained blouse, or a misfit jacket with little difficulty; however, where and when I should toss old financial records was very difficult. I didn't want to do the wrong thing, so I kept saving—usually too long.

At income-tax time my neck always got stiff because I knew Bob was going to ask for a canceled check or a paid invoice and I wasn't sure if I had it or not. At that point, I made a decision to get my record-keeping in order so that it was a very easy process to keep my records up-to-date.

I sat down and looked at the whole process of record-keeping and began to break it down into logical steps. My first step was to decide to keep my records. Since I like things to be in order with the minimum amount of paperwork, I had a tendency to throw away records that should have been saved. I found that throwing away Bob's salary stubs, last year's tax return, or current receipts for medical or business expenses would only bring problems further down the road.

Our CPA says that throwing away financial records is the biggest mistake that people make. Throwing away records that later turn out to be

296

important causes people a lot of unnecessary work and worry, he cautioned. When you have an IRS audit and you can't prove your deductions by a canceled check, or a paid invoice, you will lose that deduction for that year, and be subject to a fine and interest due as well. Records are very important.

Good financial records help you make decisions very quickly. In just a few moments you can retrieve valuable information so that a decision can be made for budget planning, future purchases, or just anticipated future income.

As I began to develop a plan to establish good record-keeping, I came up with a seven-step program.

Step 1: *Know what to keep*

I discovered that records generally fall into two categories: PERMANENT records (important to keep throughout your life) and TRANSITORY records (dealing with your current circumstances).

Permanent records would include personal documents required in applying for credit, qualifying for a job, or proving entitlement to Social Security and other government programs. Birth and marriage certificates, Social Security cards, property records, college transcripts, diplomas, and licenses all fall into this category.

Deciding how long to retain transitory records can be more difficult because often you don't know how long you'll need them. As a rule of thumb I suggest you keep all employment records until you leave the job. Other transitory records you want to keep include receipts for any major purchases you have made—jewelry, autos, art—stock certificates, tax returns and receipts (for at least six years), health insurance policies, credit union membership and company stock ownership plans. Canceled checks not relating directly to specifics like home improvements should be kept for a minimum of three years in case of a tax audit; however, I will usually keep them five to six years just to make sure I'm not throwing any records away that I might need on a tax audit.

If you own your home, apartment, or mobile home, be sure to retain the receipts for any improvements you make until you sell the property. They become proof that you added to the property's value and will reduce any capital gains you might owe. Don't discard these receipts or tax returns from the year in which you paid for the improvements. I usually make a copy of this kind of receipt and keep a permanent copy in my "Home" folder. I have found that this saves a lot of valuable time when I need to justify each record. In my "Home" folder I also keep a running log with date, improvement made, cost, and receipt for each expenditure. At any given time we know how much money we have invested in our home. This information really helps when you get ready to sell your home and you want to establish a sales price.

Your tax return, wage statements, and other papers supporting your income and deductions should be kept at least six years (that's the IRS statute of limitations for examining your return). However, you will need to keep real estate and investment records longer if you will need to verify purchase prices in the future. I retain our records for six years, because the IRS has the right to audit within six years if they believe you omitted an item accounting for more than 25 percent of your reported income, or indefinitely if they believe you committed fraud.

Step 2: *Know yourself when you set up your system*

Try to keep your system as simple as you can. I have found that the more disorganized you are, the simpler the system should be. It doesn't make sense to set up an elaborate filing system if it is too complicated for you to follow.

I suggest that you consider these points when setting up your system:

- ◆ How much time can you devote to record-keeping? The less time you have, the simpler your system should be.

- ◆ Do you like working with numbers? Are you good at math? If so, your system can be more complex.

- ◆ How familiar are you with tax deductions and financial planning? If you are a beginner, set up a simple system.

- ◆ Will anyone else be contributing records to the system?

This last point is a very important consideration if you are married. Mates may have a different opinion on what type of system you should have. I have found among married couples that it usually works best when you determine who is most gifted in this area and let that person take care of the records. Bob and I get along very well in this area. I write the checks for our home expenses and balance this account's checking statement. Then I forward the material to Bob for record-keeping. In our family he is the most gifted in this area of our life.

We have found that the simplest way to organize receipts for tax purposes is to keep two file folders, one for deduction items and another for questionable items. At tax time all you have to do is total up each category and fill in the blank. Be sure to double-check the other entries for overlooked possibilities.

If your return is more complex, set up a system with individual folders for the various deductions you claim: medical and dental expenses, business, travel, entertainment, property taxes, interest on loans, childcare services. When you pay a bill, drop the receipt into the right folder. At the end of the year, you'll be able to tally the receipts and be set to enter the totals on your tax forms.

Be sure to take your questionable-deduction folder with you when you go to see your CPA. Go over each item to see if it is eligible for a deduction. As you can tell by reading this chapter, I strongly endorse using a professional tax-preparer. Tax returns have become so difficult and the tax laws so complex that good stewardship of your money may require that you go to a professional. Tax-preparers will save you much more than you will spend for their services.

Your checkbook can be your best record-keeper if you check off entries that might count as tax deductions. If you have a personal computer at home, you have a wide selection of software programs to help you keep track of these records.

Step 3: *Set aside a spot for your records*

Generally, home rather than office is the best place for personal documents. A fireproof, waterproof file cabinet or desk drawer is excellent for transitory records. However, I use and have thousands of other ladies all across the United States using our Perfect boxes to store records.

Permanent documents generally should be kept in a safe-deposit box. However, your will and important final instructions should be kept in a different place because in many states, safe-deposit boxes are sealed following the owner's death, even if someone else has a key.

Step 4: *Tell someone where your records are*

As I travel around the country, many of the ladies tell me they don't know where their husbands have anything written down in case of death. None of us like to think about death because it is so far away, but we must share this important information with those people who will need to know.

Each year Bob reviews with me his "data sheet" listing all the information regarding insurance policies, stocks and investments, mortgage locations, banking account information, contents in safe-deposit boxes, etc.

That information is very helpful and reassuring to me in case of any changes in our status.

Even if you're a whiz at keeping financial records, the records are not very useful if no one else knows where any of them are located. As a family, make up a list noting where your records are located and give it to a family member or trusted friend.

Step 5: *Get professional advice on handling records*

As I've shared previously in this chapter, Bob and I recommend that you seek professional advice on how better records can translate into tax savings in the future. The expense is well worth the investment of time and money. You can also go to your local bookstore and purchase any number of good paperback books on this topic. Be a reader and a learner. It will serve you well.

Step 6: *Change your record-keeping system when you make a life change*

Major life shifts—a job move, marriage, death, divorce, separation—signal a time to revamp your records. Starting a home-based business also means it's time to talk to the professional regarding new tax allowances. A life change usually necessitates a change in record-keeping.

The costs of looking for a new job in the same field and a job-related move can mean you're eligible for a new tax deduction, so be sure to file all receipts.

Step 7: *Set aside time for your record-keeping*

Try to set a regular time each month to go over your financial records so that you won't be a wreck come April when you have to file your tax return. The best system in the world won't work if you don't use it or keep it current.

Many people prefer to update records when they pay bills. Others file receipts, update a ledger of expenses, and look over permanent records once a month when reconciling a checking account. Whatever works best for you is what's important. You should update at least once a month. If not, you will create a lot of stress playing catch-up. The goal of simple record-keeping is to reduce stress in our lives, not to increase the stress.

I have found that time is worth money. When I can reduce time, I can increase money because my energy is better spent on constructive efforts rather than always dealing with emergencies and putting out fires.

seventy-eight

Home Fire Safety Survey

*I will bless the Lord and not forget
the glorious things he does for me.*

Psalm 103:2

After speaking at a seminar one evening, a lovely woman shared with me her story of how a simple grease fire in the kitchen burned down her whole house. I had given a hint about using baking soda to put out kitchen fires, and about keeping a coffee can filled with baking soda close at hand by the stove. She said until that night she had never heard of that. I was totally surprised because I grew up knowing to use baking soda in case of household fires. Because of her story, I thought we needed to alert all homemakers to home fire safety. Many city and town fire departments will provide free inspections to help you identify any fire hazards in your home or business. Just give them a call and ask their help. On page 302 is a fire safety survey for you who would like to do it yourself. It very well could save a life or the life of your home.

DO-IT-YOURSELF
HOME FIRE SAFETY SURVEY

Kitchen   YES   NO

- Are stove and vent clean of grease buildup?
- Are curtains or towel racks close to the stove?
- Are flammable liquids (cleaning fluids, etc.) stored near a heat source? Remember, even a pilot light can set vapors on fire.
- Is baking soda close at hand?

Bedrooms

- Are smoke detectors installed and tested monthly?
- Are there two ways out of the room?
- If the bedroom is on the second floor, is there an escape ladder by the window?

Halls and Stairways

- Are smoke detectors installed and tested monthly?

Living and Dining Rooms

- Is there insufficient air space around TV and stereo that could cause them to overheat?
- Are curtains, furniture, or papers near a space heater? (Kerosene heaters are not allowed in living quarters.)
- Is there a spark screen on the fireplace?

Garage

- Are gasoline, paint thinners, and/or other flammable liquids stored in a ventilated area away from open flames? (hot water heater, furnace)
- Are flammable liquids stored in an approved safety container?
- Is the hot water heater clear of any storage within 18 inches?

YES   NO

- Is the furnace clear of any storage within 18 inches and are filters changed on a regular basis?   ___   ___
- Is there a fire extinguisher nearby?   ___   ___
- Are oil-soaked rags stored in a covered metal container?   ___   ___

Outside

- Are house numbers visible from the street?   ___   ___
- Are numbers painted on curb?   ___   ___
- Are front and rear yards clear of debris?   ___   ___
- Are trees well-trimmed?   ___   ___
- Is the chimney spark arrester in place?   ___   ___

General

- Are multiplug adapters used with appliances?   ___   ___
- Are electrical cords in good condition?   ___   ___
- Are there overloaded outlets or extension cords?   ___   ___
- Are any extension cords run under rugs or carpets or looped over nails or other sharp objects that could cause them to fray? (The fire department discourages the use of extension cords. However, if using portable or temporary extension cords, check listing label on both cord and appliance to determine appropriate size and configuration of extension cord needed.)   ___   ___
- Are matches and lighters out of reach of young children?   ___   ___
- Has an emergency exit been planned, developed, and practiced?   ___   ___
- Is clothes dryer free of lint?
- Is firewood or lumber stored no less than ten feet from house?   ___   ___
- Is the 9-1-1 emergency number on or by phone?

These safeguards cannot guarantee you will not have a fire, but they will reduce the chances of a fire starting or spreading.   ___   ___

seventy-nine

House-Hunting Checklist

Lovest thou me more than these?

John 21:15 KJV

Buying or renting a house, apartment, condo (or tent!) can sometimes be a source of stress. By midsummer, the anxiety of being settled before school starts can cause you to make the wrong decisions when house hunting in a hurry.

The checklist (Figure 12, page 305) will be helpful in keeping track of the special features of the homes that you've seen. Use it to compare them and single out that special house you want to make your home.

This organized shopping list can be kept and copies made. It will enable you to look back and compare!

If you have a Polaroid camera, take a picture of each home and attach it to the back of each checklist form.

This type of organization will certainly give you more credibility with the realtor and home-seller. They both will give you the benefit of being a wise buyer.

House Hunt Record

Date

Address of home _____ Age

Best route to take

Owner of home _____ Phone #

Salesperson

House design

House color

No. of square feet _____ Size of lot

Asking price _____ Down payment $

Monthly payment $

Type of utilities _____ Cost per month $

Other costs

Garage? ☐ 1 Car ☐ 2 Car ☐ Larger ☐ Carport

Condition/type of roof

Living room: Size _____ Flooring

Kitchen: Size _____ Flooring

Dining room: Size _____ Flooring

Storage space: Adequate? ☐ Yes ☐ No

Husband's first impression

Bedrooms: Number _____ Sizes

Bathrooms: Number _____ Sizes _____ Colors

Fixtures and tile condition

Water pressure check

Family room: Size _____ Flooring

Foyer: Size _____ Closet space

Game room: Size _____ Flooring

Basement: Size _____ ☐ Finished ☐ Unfinished

Laundry room: Size _____ Flooring

Other

☐ Central air ☐ Fireplace _____ Location(s)

Overall interior condition

☐ Patio ☐ Pool ☐ Pantry

Distance from work: Miles _____ Time

Distance from shopping: Miles _____ Time

Neighborhood rating

Overall rating of home and property

Schools: Quality _____ Distance from home

Comments

Wife's first impression

Figure 12

eighty

Pool Owner's Checklist—Safety First

Happy are thy men, and happy are these thy servants, which stand continually before thee, and hear thy wisdom.

2 Chronicles 9:7 KJV

As more and more homes, apartments, condominiums, and mobile home parks offer swimming facilities of all types—above-ground pools, spas, vinyl lining, and conventional gunite pools—we must become more conscious of safety around water. Since there are so many opportunities to go swimming, we can't let down our alertness when we supervise our youngsters.

Nothing is more tragic than to lose a child to drowning or to a life of brain damage because we became complacent with water and its many dangers.

One scenario of a drowning might go like this: A three-year-old child is at home with one parent. A door to the swimming pool is unlocked. There is a fence around the yard per city code, but there is no interior fence around the pool. An outsider can't get to the pool easily, but the child at home is in trouble because he can get to the pool with no problem.

Mom answers the phone or goes to the bathroom. Supervision is interrupted for a minute or two. The child spots a plastic ball at the pool edge and quickly goes out the unlocked door and falls into the water trying to get the ball.

You may think it can't happen to you and your child, but many fire department personnel can give witness that it only takes one or two unattended moments. Here is a pool safety checklist:

- Never leave a child alone near or in a pool or bathtub. Your quick phone call or trip to another part of the house leaves plenty of time for your unattended child to fall into the pool or tub.

- Give your child swimming lessons. (However, lessons don't replace constant supervision.)

- Call the local Red Cross chapter and enroll in a CPR class.

- Build a four- to five-foot fence around all sides of the pool. Use non-climbable material so the children can't climb over. Be sure to have a self-closing, self-latching gate.

- Doors leading to the pool should always be locked. Locks should be out of a child's reach. Kids can crawl through pet doors too.

- If a child can't swim he or she should not be allowed to dive head first into water, play on floats, play on inner tubes unattached to their bodies, or hold onto other children while in the water.

- Don't rely on flotation devices for protection.

- Consider door or floating pool alarms.

- Consider keeping a vinyl cover on your pool when it's not in use.

- Tell your babysitters or other guardians about drowning precautions. Encourage your babysitters to know CPR.

- Keep toys away from the pool. They are too tempting.

- Have a poolside phone with emergency telephone numbers.

- Have a long pole with a hook on it next to the pool so you could extend it to a child who might need some assistance.

- Do you know how to swim? If not, take lessons so you will personally feel confident around water.

- Spas, bathtubs, ponds, lakes, beaches, and toilets are potential drowning pools too.

Safety around children extends life!

See *Survival for Busy Women,* also published by Harvest House, for many samples of useful charts.

"More Hours In My Day" can provide many of the organizational materials that are recommended in this book and others written by Emilie Barnes. You may obtain a price list and seminar information by sending your request and a stamped, self-addressed business envelope to:

More Hours In My Day
2150 Whitestone Dr.
Riverside, CA 92506

Other Harvest House Books
by Bob & Emilie Barnes

Bob & Emilie Barnes

*101 Ways to Love Your
Grandkids*

*Minute Meditations
for Couples*

*A Little Book of Manners
for Boys*

Abundance of the Heart

*15 Minute Devotions
for Couples*

Emilie Barnes

The 15-Minute Organizer

15 Minutes Alone with God

*15 Minutes of Peace
with God*

101 Ways to Lift Your Spirits

A Tea to Comfort Your Soul

*Emilie's Creative
Home Organizer*

*Everything I Know
I Learned from My Garden*

Fill My Cup, Lord

Help Me Trust You, Lord

If Teacups Could Talk

An Invitation to Tea

Join Me for Tea

A Journey Through Cancer

*Keep It Simple
for Busy Women*

Let's Have a Tea Party!

A Little Book of Manners

*Minute Meditations
for Busy Moms*

*Minute Meditations
for Women*

More Hours in My Day

Safe in the Father's Hands

*Strength for Today,
Bright Hope for Tomorrow*

Survival for Busy Women

*The Twelve Teas®
of Celebration*

*The Twelve Teas®
of Christmas*

*The Twelve Teas®
of Friendship*

Bob Barnes

*15 Minutes Alone with God
for Men*

Minute Meditations for Men

*What Makes a Man
Feel Loved*